Randolph Delehanty's
Ultimate Guide to New Orleans

Randolph Delehanty's Ultimate Guide to New Orleans

RANDOLPH DELEHANTY

•

Drawings by SIMON GUNNING

CHRONICLE BOOKS
SAN FRANCISCO

Coeur Sacré de Jesus
j'ai confiance en Vous

Copyright © 1998 by Randolph Delehanty.
All rights reserved. No part of this book
may be reproduced in any form without
written permission from the publisher.

Printed in the United States of America.

Library of Congress Cataloging-in-Publication Data:
Delehanty, Randolph.
    [Ultimate guide to New Orleans]
    Randolph Delehanty's Ultimate guide to New Orleans / by Randolph Delehanty;
drawings by Simon Gunning.
        p.   cm.
        Includes index.
        ISBN 0-8118-0870-X (pbk.)
        1. New Orleans (La.) — Guidebooks. 2. New Orleans (La.) — Tours.
3. Walking — Louisiana — New Orleans — Guidebooks. I. Title.
        F379N53D45   1998
        917.63'350463 — dc21   97-26742
                                                  CIP

Cover illustration: detail from Simon Gunning's *Pirate's Alley*
Interior illustrations: Simon Gunning
Typesetting: Neal Elkin/On Line Typography
Maps: Ellen McElhinny

Distributed in Canada by Raincoast Books,
8680 Cambie Street, Vancouver, B.C. V6P 6M9

10 9 8 7 6 5 4 3 2

Chronicle Books
85 Second Street
San Francisco, CA 94105

www.chroniclebooks.com

Contents

How to Use This Guide

This is an architectural and cultural history of New Orleans experienced through walking, transit, and car tours. It is built around important, accessible historic and contemporary interiors. It gives suggestions for the best times to explore these places and lists some related restaurants and hotels. Much of the practical information (phone numbers, addresses, hours) appears in sidebars, and bold text alerts you to look there for specifics. Each tour tells a story and explores important aspects, or layers, of New Orleans. The index locates proper names, hotels, restaurants, museums, and other attractions.

The guide is written both for carless travelers and drivers; it includes all the transit lines visitors are most likely to use. *It is not advisable to walk from one section of the city to another through areas unfrequented by visitors, even if the distance on a map is short.*

It is best to read the introduction to each tour, if not the entire tour, before your walk. You may wish to select only some of the sites in each neighborhood. Reading all of the tour introductions in sequence is like a jump cut movie of the history of New Orleans' many different social groups and their unique and continuing shared culture.

The changes and errors that are inevitable in a book such as this should be called to my attention in care of Chronicle Books, 85 Second Street, Sixth Floor, San Francisco, CA 94105. I thank in advance all who help me improve subsequent editions of this guide in order to make it as practical and accurate as possible.

Map 1

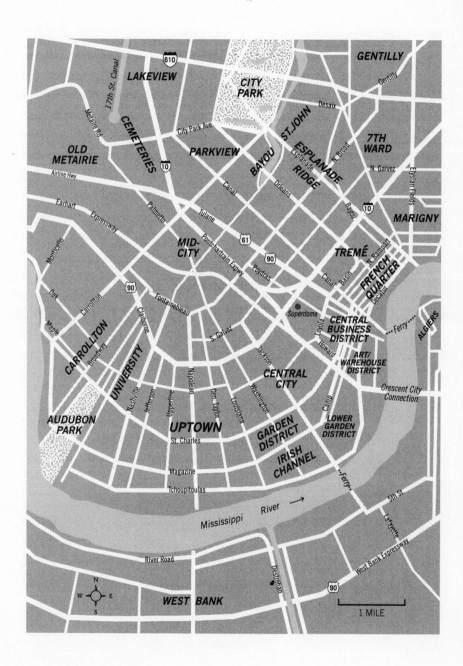

GENTILLY

LAKEVIEW

CITY PARK

17th St. Canal

610

Gentilly

Desaix

ST. JOHN

7TH WARD

Medaria Rd.

CEMETERIES

City Park Ave.

BAYOU

ESPLANADE RIDGE

Esplanade

N. Broad

N. Galvez

Elysian Fields

OLD METAIRIE

PARKVIEW

10

Canal

Orleans

MARIGNY

Airline Hwy.

Earhart

Palmetto

Tulane

61

TREMÉ

10

Bayou

Montecello

Expressway

MID-CITY

Pontchartrain Expwy

90

Poydras

Canal

Basin

N. Rampart

FRENCH QUARTER

Decatur

Oak

90

Fontainebleau

Superdome

Loyola

CENTRAL BUSINESS DISTRICT

Ferry

ALGIERS

Maple

Carrollton

Clairborne

S. Galvez

Howard

Broadway

Jackson

ART/ WAREHOUSE DISTRICT

CARROLLTON

UNIVERSITY

Nashville

Jefferson

Upperline

Gen Taylor

Napoleon

Washington

Louisiana

CENTRAL CITY

Crescent City Connection

AUDUBON PARK

UPTOWN

St. Charles

GARDEN DISTRICT

Camp

LOWER GARDEN DISTRICT

Magazine

IRISH CHANNEL

Ferry

Tchoupitoulas

5th St

Lafayette

Mississippi   River →

River Road

West Bank Expressway

Desrehan

90

N
W   E
S

WEST BANK

1 MILE

New Orleans by the Numbers

New Orleans is losing population but holding on to her soul.

Every month for the past thirty years eight hundred more people have moved out of the City of New Orleans (Orleans Parish) than have moved in. A city built for 630,000 now has some 480,000; New Orleans has shrunk by one-fifth. From its founding in 1718 to about 1960, the city grew and expanded; since then, New Orleans has steadily lost population as her suburbs have exploded. The second key fact about New Orleans is that it is a Populist, antitax, antipolitician "paradise" where 69 percent of all homes pay *no real estate taxes!* Renters, businesses, and high-valued residences *do* pay property taxes. This underfunding plus a self-defeatingly high 9 percent sales tax—higher than that in the suburbs—has to cover the city's expenses. The tax base has fled to politically independent, and predominantly white, suburbs. Within New Orleans, the "two" races have switched places, and New Orleans has shifted from being a white majority to a black majority city. The growing suburban ring now attracts both black and white middle-class families, leaving the city increasingly black, young, and poor at one end of the social spectrum, and white, old, and wealthy at the other. In all these trends New Orleans is typically and distressingly mainstream American, if to a degree. Yet paradoxically, New Orleans' joyous culture—social, musical, visual, and culinary—is alive and still distinctive. And it has drawn you to her.

Preliminaries

Note: *All phone numbers, unless otherwise noted, are for area code 504.*

New Orleans Calendar of Events
This quarterly listing can be obtained by writing to the New Orleans Metropolitan Convention and Visitors Bureau, 1520 Sugar Bowl Drive, N.O., 70112; 566-5011

Arthur Hardy's Mardi Gras Guide
Published each January; for information write to P.O. Box 19500, N.O., 70179; 838-6111, fax 838-0100

BEST SEASONS AND TIMES TO VISIT

Spring, especially April and May, is a temperate, flower-bedecked time in New Orleans. Autumn, beginning in mid-October, is also generally pleasant. The days around Thanksgiving and Christmas, including Twelfth Night (but not New Year's Eve), are also optimal times to visit New Orleans. The weather is fine then, if perhaps a bit cool, and the French Quarter is momentarily quiet and domestic. The off-season here is June to September (or even October), when the intense sun and the oppressive humidity seriously restrict daytime rambles. High summer is when many New Orleanians decamp for the mountains of North Carolina or the coast of Maine. But summer is also the time when conventions are fewest and hotel rates lowest. Mardi Gras and Jazz Fest have the disadvantages of being congested and much more expensive than all other times of the year. Book hotel reservations a year in advance for both festivals and also for major football weekends, when Southerners flock to celebrate the region's established religion at the Superdome. A quarterly **calendar of events** can be obtained from the city's convention and visitors bureau.

MARDI GRAS TIPS

There are almost sixty Carnival organizations (called krewes) that stage annual parades in the city and its suburbs. Within New Orleans itself many parades with floats and marching bands roll during the Carnival season, especially during the *two weekends before* Mardi Gras. The Rex parade on Mardi Gras at midday is the one to see; the other parade worth seeing is Orpheus, the night before Mardi Gras. **Arthur Hardy's Mardi Gras Guide** is the single best listing of parades. Rex climaxes the long cycle of parades and is always a splendid display of traditional Carnival float-building art. The King of Carnival's floats are the real thing: intelligently fanciful, papier-mâché, hand-painted floats rolling on hundred-year-old wooden wagons. They are the rare and tenacious survivors of a locally elaborated and privately sustained artistic tradition that goes back to the 1870s and has continued through an apostolic succession of float designer/artists. Yet many people come to Mardi Gras without seeing the Rex floats, so intensely do they fixate on the throws.

Best Place to See the Parades

St. Charles Avenue uptown, with its overarching oaks looking like dark, frozen dancers, is a good place to see these parades, especially the night parades that are illuminated by cakewalking flambeaux carriers.

Future Dates of Mardi Gras

Because Easter is a movable feast in the Christian calendar and is celebrated on the first Sunday after the full moon that follows the Spring Equinox, and because Mardi Gras is celebrated forty-seven days before Easter, Mardi Gras can occur on any Tuesday from February 3 through March 9.

About Mardi Gras

Just the names of the organizations that participate in Carnival conjure up whole social worlds: The Mistick Krewe of Comus, Twelfth Night Revelers, The School of Design, The Society of St. Anne, The Krewe of Kosmic Debris, The Prophets of Persia, The Mystik Herd of Nutria, The Krewe of Orpheus, The Krewe of Endymion, The Zulu Social Aid and Pleasure Club, The Wild Magnolias, The Krewe of Iris, The Krewe of Bacchus, The Krewe of Petronius, The High Steppers, The Sudan Social Aid and Pleasure Club, The Original Illinois Club, The Aristocrats, Atlanteans. And there are many, many more.

Carnival is not only nor mainly the raucous inebriates on Bourbon Street. It isn't even the crowds lining parade routes snagging throws, though that has become a communal ritual that all New Orleanians now experience from childhood on. (Even greedy throw-catching has developed its distinctively New Orleanian code of etiquette—of crying for, reaching after, catching, disputing, mildly surrendering, or bestowing "treasures.") Carnival is both intensely private and flamboyantly public. There are as

Future Dates of Mardi Gras

1998	February 24
1999	February 16
2000	March 7
2001	February 27
2002	February 12
2003	March 4
2004	February 24
2005	February 8
2006	February 28
2007	February 20
2008	February 5
2009	February 24
2010	February 16

many Carnivals as there are groups of friends and formal clubs in New Orleans. Though the rituals of Carnival are now fused with the debut of young women into high society, the larger Carnival includes everyone who wants to be a part of it, from the poorest to the richest. One would have to be an absolute hermit in New Orleans not to have friends who pull you into *their* Carnival. Whether it's the Wild Magnolias practicing their dance-chants in funky Central City taverns or Uptown debutantes being coached in how to properly wave a scepter (something not generally found in American etiquette manuals), true New Orleanians do not just "observe" Carnival, they act it out as participants. High or low or in-between, New Orleanians go to parties, several parties, and get invitations to more events than the most driven social athlete could endure. There they talk and drink and eat and dance and flirt. Their demand for party music has made New Orleans a fount of happy get-up-and-dance-and-march music. Carnival, at root, is going to parties with your friends, and some of these parties spill out onto the streets as parades. Everything else—all of Carnival's deep secrets, awesome thrones, and arcane dominions—is built on this.

A New Orleanian idea of a *bal masqué* costume is not Mickey, Minnie, or Goofy; it is rather an Old World fantasy of glory and splendor. For one day we are kings and queens, maids and pages, gentlemen of Verona, ladies at court, Venetian eighteenth-century masqueraders, velvet-caped dukes, sheiks of the desert, priests and hierophants, wizards and goddesses, sprites and spirits, punchinellas and punchinellos, jesters and clowns. Everyone appears as someone else. (Some *do* appear as Death; they always have and always will and also belong to Carnival.) Carnival is the city's cementing social ritual and is deeply satisfying in some way to everyone. Not even the "commodification" of Mardi Gras by mass tourism, nor the hordes of callow youths who come to drink too much, have changed its essence. Carnival is a multicolored kaleidoscope of the people and societies of New Orleans.

The parodic, anarchic side of Carnival finds its continuation today in the Krewe du Vieux parade that gathers on

Frenchmen Street and marches up Decatur Street through the Quarter on the third Saturday before Mardi Gras. The Carnival season climaxes in two balls held in adjoining ballrooms at the Fairmont Hotel, one for Rex and one for Comus. The newspaper reports are always formal and ritualized. Like a fairytale, the account always begins: "Rex descended from his summer palace on Mount Olympus for his annual royal ball and imperial reception." To the music of the Rex anthem "If Ever I Cease to Love," the captain, Rex, the Rex president, and the Queen of Carnival arrive in the ballroom for the grand march. After various homages and ceremonies, the peers of the realm and their ladies dance the first dance. Then dancing commences for all. At 9:40 P.M. it is announced that the captain of the Mistick Krewe of Comus has arrived. He hands Rex, his queen, and their court an invitation to join the Comus ball. Rex and his court then leave the Rex reception to attend the Comus ball. The unmasked Rex, selected for his civic contributions, thus pays homage to the mysterious, masked Comus. It is all reminiscent of the Duke of Wellington's commendation of the Order of the Bath.

The New Orleans Visitor Center
529 St. Ann Street, Lower Pontalba Building, facing Jackson Square; 566-5068

Jean Lafitte National Historical Park and Preserve, New Orleans Unit
916 N. Peters Street, off Decatur Street at Dumaine; 589-2636

TOURIST INFORMATION

You can write to almost any public attraction included in this guide, and they will send you information about themselves. There are also several visitor centers and other sources of tourist information.

- **The New Orleans Visitor Center** Open daily from 9 A.M. to 5 P.M. except Christmas and Mardi Gras.

- **Jean Lafitte National Historical Park and Preserve, New Orleans Unit** The visitor center is in the French Market on N. Peters Street, a block and a half from Jackson Square; it's open daily from 9 A.M. to 5 P.M. except Christmas and Mardi Gras. They offer free walking tours with National Park rangers in the French Quarter and the Garden District.

New Orleans Metropolitan Convention and Visitors Bureau
1520 Sugar Bowl Drive, N.O., 70112-1255; 566-5011

Greater New Orleans Black Tourism Network
1520 Sugar Bowl Drive, N.O., 70112; 523-5652, 800-725-5652, fax 522-0785

American Automobile Association (AAA) New Orleans and Vicinity
Available only to AAA members

The Greater New Orleans Tourist & Convention Commission Map
Available at the Visitor Center in the Lower Pontalba Building at 529 St. Ann Street, facing Jackson Square, and at most hotel desks

The New Orleans Street Map & Visitor Guide
Can be obtained by mail at no cost by writing to the Regional Transit Authority, 6700 Plaza Drive, N.O., 70127; 569-2625

Louisiana Official Highway Map
Can be obtained at any Louisiana hospitality center at the state line, or by mail at no cost from the Department of Transportation and Development, P.O. Box 94245 Capitol Station, Baton Rouge, LA 70804-9245

- **New Orleans Metropolitan Convention and Visitors Bureau** Write for brochures by mail. E-mail address: tourism@nawlins.com. Internet site: http://www.nawlins.com.

- **Greater New Orleans Black Tourism Network** Dispenses information for African American and all tourists.

MAPS

New Orleans is surprisingly large and spread out, and thus most full city maps have impossibly small type. Here are some of the most useful maps.

- **American Automobile Association (AAA) New Orleans and Vicinity** The best general map of New Orleans, though the map only shows main streets; the Metropolitan New Orleans map on its reverse has a good map of the French Quarter and Central Business District.

- **The Greater New Orleans Tourist & Convention Commission** They give out an eleven-by-seventeen-inch map; the four public transit lines shown on this map (with stops indicated by a dot) are of use to the visitor.

- **The New Orleans Street Map & Visitor Guide** This shows every street in the city, its close-in suburbs, and the airport; it has a street index and includes transit lines in purple with the number of the route appearing in small circles. The French Quarter/Central Business District inset map has the useful feature of distinguishing all public parking.

- **Louisiana Official Highway Map** A unique feature of this official state map is that it distinguishes the historically French and Roman Catholic parishes (counties) of Acadiana and southern Louisiana from the historically Anglo and Protestant central and northern parts of the state. New Orleans and the delta parishes to the south are not part of Acadiana but were predominantly French and Roman Catholic in the colonial and early United States periods.

- **National Geographic Society's *The Making of America: The Deep South*** Published in August 1983, this is the best map showing the peculiar place that New Orleans has always occupied in the South.

MISCELLANEOUS
VISITOR NEEDS

Post Offices

- **Vieux Carré Post Office** Just inside the French Quarter; closed Saturday and Sunday.
- **Main Post Office** Near the train station; has the longest hours and is the best source for stamp collectors.
- **Postal Emporium** A private mailing service in the lower French Quarter.

Film Developing

- **French Quarter Camera & Video** Photographic supplies and one-hour processing and developing.
- **Photofrequency** One-hour processing.

Pharmacies

- **Rite-Aid Drug Store** Located uptown, its prescription counter is open daily, 8 A.M. to 11 P.M.
- **Walgreen Drug Stores** There are two downtown, and both are on Canal Street. The 3311 Canal Street store has a twenty-four-hour prescription service.

Luggage

- **Rapp's Luggage** A fine selection of excellent luggage as well as ankle wallets and money belts.

CLIMATE AND
CLOTHING

New Orleans has a rainy, subtropical climate; there is no real dry season. Late fall is delightful here and winter is cool rather than cold. Spring in New Orleans is soft, balmy, and flower-filled. Summer seems to last from late March through September with temperatures in the nineties and humidity reaching saturation, though the summer thunderstorms are dramatic, memorable, and usually brief.

National Geographic Society's *The Making of America: The Deep South*
Can be found in used bookstores

Vieux Carré Post Office
1022 Iberville Street, between Burgundy and N. Rampart; 524-0072

Main Post Office
701 Loyola Avenue, near Girod; 589-1143

Postal Emporium
940 Royal Street, at St. Philip; 525-6651

French Quarter Camera & Video
809 Decatur, near St. Ann; 529-2974

Photofrequency
241 N. Peters Street, between Bienville and Iberville; 523-7687

Rite-Aid Drug Store
3401 St. Charles Avenue, at Louisiana; 895-0344

Walgreen Drug Stores
900 Canal Street, at Baronne: information 523-7201, prescriptions 523-3875; 3311 Canal Street, at Jefferson Davis; 822-8073

Rapp's Luggage
604 Canal Street, between St. Charles and Camp; 568-1953

Emergencies
In case of emergency dial 911 to summon police, fire, or ambulance assistance; no coin is needed to dial 911 at pay telephones. The nonemergency police telephone number is 821-2222

French Quarter Police Station
The Eighth District police station in the French Quarter is at 334 Royal Street, at Conti, and is open twenty-four hours a day every day of the year; make reports here; 565-7530

Men will be most comfortable in khaki trousers, soft shoes, a cotton shirt, and a light sport coat. Tuck a tie in your coat pocket and you can dine in all the best restaurants. The idea is to dress comfortably for heat and rain, yet a touch formally (khaki trousers instead of blue jeans). Most tourists wear shorts and a T-shirt, but this is not always the best way to dress. New Orleans is a sophisticated city, not a beach resort, and your clothing will influence how you are treated. However, for safety leave fancy watches and jewelry at home. Many of the noted restaurants in New Orleans have dress codes: no jeans, shorts, or T-shirts; jacket and tie for gentlemen. Phone ahead so as not to be embarrassingly out of costume.

Women will find a simple dress worn with a sweater or jacket thrown over their shoulders, and comfortable walking shoes, an appropriate outfit. New Orleans has its own taste in dresses, especially in ball gowns, and clothes-savvy women might want to buy a party dress here as a flamboyant remembrance of New Orleans style. Women here often like to dress like tropical flowers or iridescent, sequined rainbows.

New Orleans gets almost six feet of rain a year. Because some of this rain will probably fall during your visit, it's best to be suitably equipped. Bring a sturdy umbrella, not a collapsible pseudo-umbrella, and ankle-high rain shoes or boots. The rain does not usually linger and the sun is soon out again. The sun is intense here; a sun hat with a wide brim is very useful, as are sunglasses. Also, use a money belt or ankle wallet. Finally, bring a portable radio and tune it to WWOZ, 90.7 FM, so that your wanderings will be accompanied by southern Louisiana's rich musical heritage.

SAFETY IN THE CITY

New Orleans has the best and the worst: a joyous, living culture, but also aching poverty and a high murder rate. Most crime here occurs in the blighted districts tourists are unlikely to frequent.

Carry your money and credit cards in a money belt (not belly bag) or ankle stash. Also, create a "fake" wallet or purse stuffed with maps, notes, business cards, receipts, expired plastic cards, and twenty singles (it looks like a lot of money in the dark). Then if you are mugged, you have something to give up easily, and if you're pickpocketed, it doesn't matter. Don't dress expensively when out walking—fine glove-leather jackets make you an obvious mark—and leave fancy watches and jewelry at home. Be discreet with your photographic equipment. Wear running shoes when out exploring. If you can, walk about in groups of three or more, especially at night. It's ideal to plan your trip to New Orleans with friends. You will be much safer and more comfortable walking the streets of New Orleans, the best way to experience the Crescent City's intricate architecture and lush plant life. Don't be shy about asking fellow travelers to join you in your walks, for safety as well as for companionship. In the Garden District especially, you will spot singles and couples sightseeing. Who knows? You might click, and next thing you know you'll be having dinner together, sharing your experiences, and making new friends.

EXPENSES

New Orleans can be an inexpensive place to visit, since its attractions and restaurants are not especially pricey, but if you want ideal accommodations on the riverside of the French Quarter in order to most easily enjoy Old New Orleans on foot, you will be staying in expensive lodgings. Spending, of course, varies greatly from traveler to traveler, and hotel rates vary significantly with the season. Summer is bargain time and winter is high season. Rates skyrocket during Mardi Gras and football weekends, when rooms must often be booked for several days. In 1997, the average room rate in New Orleans approached $125, to which an 11 percent sales tax and $1 occupancy tax is added. In 1995, one economical traveler spent $125 per day, including $66 for lodging and $22 for dinner, but it is better to budget more than $150 per night for French Quarter lodgings and up to an equal amount for transportation, shopping, admissions, drinks, dining, and music.

Always tip cabbies 15 percent in whole rounded-up dollars. Baggage handlers should be paid 50¢ per bag; $1 minimum. Waiters and waitresses should be tipped 15 percent for good service and 20 percent for especially attentive service. Bartenders are customarily tipped 10 percent, as are wine stewards. Parking garage attendants should be tipped 50¢ or $1 for retrieving your car.

The banks in the Central Business District (CBD) always offer the best exchange rates. Here are a list of banks offering foreign exchange.

- **Airport foreign exchange service** *Whitney National Bank, lobby level, 838-6492.*
- **Whitney National Bank** *Main office, 228 St. Charles Avenue, at Gravier, 586-3636; French Quarter office, 430 Chartres Street, near St. Louis, 586-7502.*
- **First National Bank of Commerce** *Main office, 210 Baronne Street, at Common, 561-1371.*
- **Hibernia National Bank** *Main office, 313 Carondelet Street, at Gravier, 533-5551.*
- **Thomas Cook Currency Services** *111 St. Charles Street, between Canal and Common, 524-0700.*
- **American Express office** *Atrium of First NBC Center, 201 St. Charles Street, between Common and Gravier, open Monday to Friday from 9 A.M. to 5 P.M., and closed Saturday and Sunday; 586-8201. There is also a twenty-four-hour ATM here.*

INTERNATIONAL VISITORS' TAX-FREE SHOPPING

Louisiana is the only state that will refund its sales taxes on goods bought in certain stores by international visitors. When you make a purchase, ask for a refund voucher (you will be asked for your passport; Canadians can use their driver's license). You will have to pay the sales tax at the time of purchase, but you can have it refunded at the airport. You must show both the sales receipt and the voucher to secure a refund. Refunds under $500 are paid in cash; higher amounts are issued by check and mailed to the visitor's home. A handling fee is deducted from the refund amount.

Louisiana Tax-Free Shopping Refund Center
Moisant International Airport; open seven days a week; 467-0721

Directions and Transportation

Downtown/Uptown/Riverside/ Lakeside, and East Bank/West Bank

It is entirely consistent that the normative compass of north-south, east-west is of little use in New Orleans. To ask if a place is north, south, east, or west confounds the local sense of direction, which is based on the local fundamental spatial orientation of the Mississippi River and Lake Pontchartrain. Canal Street divides downtown from uptown, but though uptown is upriver of downtown (as the current flows), it is also southwest, not north as you might expect. Thus, if someone directs you to the uptown-riverside corner of Canal and Carondelet Streets, he or she means the southwestern corner. There is an uptown-riverside, uptown-lakeside, downtown-riverside, and downtown-lakeside corner at every intersection. There is also a pattern to addresses as shown below. It takes a while to get the hang of it, but it works in a crescent-shaped city where the Mississippi River flows due north past the foot of Canal Street and where many important streets make a great, sweeping, disorienting curve. The one time the compass is employed for street names it only makes things more confusing. Canal Street divides some streets into a north and south. Counterintuitively, N. Rampart is the border of the French Quarter and S. Rampart is in the Central Business District. After a while it seems perfectly natural that the Mississippi's West Bank is south of the city.

New Orleans Moisant International Airport
In Kenner, in Jefferson Parish, Louisiana, about a thirty-minute cab ride from Canal Street;
464-0831

Airport Shuttle
465-9780

Regional Transit Authority Airport Downtown Express
737-9611

Jefferson Transit Airport Downtown Express
737-7433

New Orleans Union Passenger Terminal
1100 Loyola Avenue, at Howard Avenue,
528-1610; *Amtrak reservations,*
800-872-7245

FROM THE AIRPORT TO THE CITY

The New Orleans airport has recently expanded and improved its facilities. In 1996 Richard Thomas and six young assistants painted a mural in the Parabola Lobby depicting *Louis Armstrong and His Heavenly All Star Band.* Jazz musicians past and present create a visual fanfare for the legendary city.

From the **airport,** taxis charge a regulated flat rate of $21 for one or two passengers going into the city. The third and fourth passengers each pay an additional $8. There is no extra charge for luggage. Cabbies also frequently provide memorable vignettes of the city as it once was.

Airport Shuttle operates continuous twenty-four-hour coach service from the airport to the downtown hotels; tickets can be purchased near the baggage claim carousels and are $10 one-way.

The Regional Transit Authority's Airport Downtown Express operates from 6 A.M. to 6:30 P.M. and links a bus stop at the airport's upper level (near Delta Air Lines) with a bus stop at Elks Place and Tulane Avenue (across from the modernistic public library), one block from Canal Street. The fare is $1.50, exact change required; call for information about limited evening service between 6 P.M. and midnight.

The suburban **Jefferson Transit Airport Downtown Express** also stops at the upper level of the airport; $1.10, exact change required. Note: Does not run twenty-four hours. Phone 737-7433 for hours of operation.

ARRIVING BY TRAIN

The train station is across the Central Business District and a vast tundra of parking lots from the French Quarter. There are always taxis waiting when trains arrive to take you the short hop to the Quarter. Transit connections from the train station to the Quarter are awkward.

Inside the **New Orleans Union Passenger Terminal,** a modernistic 1954 train station, is a large waiting room with a notable series of frescos by Conrad A. Albrizio, painted in 1954. They represent four imagined stages in the history of New Orleans: the Age of Exploration, the Age of Colonization, the Age of Struggle, and the Modern Age. The culmination of the vast panorama is a gloriously positive vision of the Atomic Age. These frescos are among the most interesting works of art in New Orleans and are from a period that does not get much attention.

The City of New Orleans

This historic train route is the main line from New Orleans to Chicago, with Memphis halfway up. It was and is a great path of commerce, visitation, and the historic migration of Louisianians. As the useful *City of New Orleans Route Guide* notes, this began as two runs, the daytime City of New Orleans, and the overnight run with the sultry name, the Panama Limited. Train buffs may wish to make a short trip up to McComb, Mississippi, and back in order to experience this memorable route. The tracks laid over the Louisiana cypress swamps seem to pass through virgin territory and are not accompanied by a highway. You will spy many elegant white egrets and a few blue herons stalking this primeval wetland. This was the route toward betterment for black Louisianians seeking jobs in the northern cities. It was the route that the blues took from rural Mississippi to Memphis, St. Louis, Kansas City, Chicago, and the world. This was the route that jazz took when Louis Armstrong moved to Chicago in 1922. This was also the route that spirituals took when Mahalia Jackson moved to the same city. It is one of the central arteries in American culture.

DRIVING AND PARKING TIPS

If you're thinking about renting a car and driving in New Orleans, my simple advice is: Don't. Stay in a costly French Quarter hotel and use taxis and public transit. Some say that every other vehicle in Louisiana has a gun in it, and in New Orleans at least 40 percent of the drivers on the road do not carry insurance. Drivers here are also rather—how shall we put it?—whimsical. Law is not a concept that Louisianians take to with much conviction, and that includes traffic law. And while spontaneity and improvisation make for great jazz, the same qualities make for surreal drivers. Those who drive in Orleans Parish should be ready for a different way of doing, and not doing, things. Drivers accustomed to fellow drivers who use turn signals had better be prepared: turn signals are only infrequently used in New Orleans, and when used might not mean to the signaler what it does to you. At feeder ramps onto I-10, many New Orleanian drivers have the disconcerting tendency of suddenly slowing down. It's hard to know what it is that makes merging onto the elevated interstate so difficult for so many New Orleanians. Perhaps they sense that they are about to merge with Modernity, and they are not entirely convinced that it's such a good idea.

Driving in the French Quarter

There are many one-way streets in New Orleans, including almost all the streets in the French Quarter. Also, there are few traffic lights in the Quarter. Streets going to or from Canal Street generally have the right of way; streets going from the river to the lake have stop signs at almost all intersections. Drive cautiously in the Quarter; automobiles and trucks share these roadbeds with mule-drawn buggies and stray inebriates.

Street Signs

Many of New Orleans' street signs are missing, and many of those that exist are faded or hard to read. Uptown, old white-and-blue tile signs inlaid in the sidewalk are helpful to pedestrians but useless to drivers. Downtown, in neighborhoods such as Marigny and Bywater, street signs are printed on thin vertical metal strips nailed to telephone poles—*very* hard to read. In a peculiarly New Orleanian touch, there are even some street signs on one-way streets that face *away* from the traffic. Marking streets clearly and systematically goes against the grain in New Orleans, a society that loves secrets and complication. Finding building and house numbers can also be an adventure.

Parking

Driving a luxury automobile in New Orleans limits the places you can go inconspicuously or street park. It is better to drive a nondescript rental car that you can park on the street and not have to worry about. If you do have a car, your own or rented, be prepared to park it in paid garages and *attended* paid parking lots. Pay this cost willingly, for you are buying three things: parking, safety, and immunity from the ferociously prompt parking meter readers. (The most efficient city operation is ticketing cars in tourist-frequented areas.) Garage attendants are customarily tipped 50¢ or $1 if they fetch your car; no tipping is necessary at paid lots where you retrieve your own vehicle and pay at an exit booth. Never leave *anything* visible inside your car. Decide before you leave the hotel garage what you will carry with you at your destination and what will stay in the trunk, and then put the items to be stored in the trunk *before* you leave. Do not motor to your destination, park the car, and then put things in the trunk. If you do so, you are announcing to anyone watching that you just put valuables in the trunk and are going away. The free, commercial, single-sheet *New Orleans Street Map & Visitor Guide,* generally available at hotels, has a useful map of the French Quarter and Central Business District (CBD) with all public parking marked. Parking lots without attendants are in general dangerous places; attended garages are the safest places to park. There is metered street parking in the CBD. Have a roll of quarters in the car; the meters eat them up quickly. The vast tundra of parking lots between the CBD and the Superdome should be used only at peak times and in conjunction with Superbowl events.

Parking in the French Quarter and Neighborhoods

In the upper Quarter/Bourbon Street area, the garage on Iberville Street between Dauphine and Bourbon is well located. The two parking lots near the river along N. Peters Street, one near Jax Brewery and the other behind the French Market (entered from Decatur and St. Ann Streets), are convenient. Legal street parking is scarce in the French Quarter and time limits are instantly

Parking Tickets
Information, 525-0088

City Auto Pound
*400 N. Claiborne Avenue,
at Conti; open daily 7:30
A.M. to 10:30 P.M., longer
during Mardi Gras;
565-7450*

United Cabs
*627 Polymnia, off
St. Charles Avenue; this
company is recom-
mended; 522-9771,
524-9606, 800-323-3303*

White Fleet Cabs
948-6605

Checker Yellow Cabs
525-3311

Liberty Bell Cabs
822-5974

Taxi Stands:

Upper French Quarter
*• On St. Louis Street,
between Chartres and
Royal, in front of the
Royal Orleans Hotel
• On Orleans Avenue,
between Royal and
Bourbon, in front of the
Bourbon Orleans Hotel*

Lower French Quarter
*• On Chartres Street,
between Gov. Nicholls
and Barracks, in front of
the Le Richlieu Hotel
• On N. Rampart Street,
between Dumaine and
St. Philip, in front of the
Landmark Hotel*

enforced. Many New Orleans neighborhoods have preferential parking for residents. This means that those without city parking stickers can only park for two hours in unmetered spaces. You will be promptly ticketed in the French Quarter and Marigny for exceeding this limit. Parking uptown along St. Charles Avenue and posh uptown streets is generally easy, but read the parking restrictions posted in each area.

Parking Tickets

Parking tickets are a neon-orange fact of life in New Orleans. As in all tourist magnets, parking fines have become important sources of municipal income.

Towed Vehicles

If your car is towed away for illegal parking (often, parking too close to a corner), phone the **City Auto Pound** to see if it is there. Impounded cars may be retrieved at 400 N. Claiborne Avenue, at Conti. Though near the French Quarter on a map, do not walk there; *take a taxi*. The pound will only accept cash, local personal checks, MasterCard, VISA, or traveler's checks. You will also need your driver's license.

Traffic Violations

California, Michigan, Wisconsin, Oregon, Montana, Hawaii, and Alaska drivers should know that their states are not members of the forty-two-state compact by which states guarantee reciprocal enforcement of each other's traffic laws. A traffic violation by drivers from those states in New Orleans means that you will have to surrender your driver's license until you pay the fine.

TAXIS

New Orleans has some of the best cab drivers in the nation. There's a pride in many New Orleans cabbies that leads them to paint their names in Gothic letters on the front fenders of their cabs. Now and then you will see a name with musical notes after it; a musician-cabbie no doubt.

Approached in a friendly and open way, New Orleans cabbies are fountains of knowledge. There are more than fifteen hundred cabs in New Orleans. The Yellow Pages lists a whole column of **taxi companies;** I've just listed a few here.

It is also helpful to know the locations of **taxi stands;** they are indicated by a T in a circle on the maps in this guide.

The standard cab fare is a $2.10 drop charge (plus 75¢ for each additional passenger) and 20¢ for each one-sixth of a mile *or* every forty seconds. There is also a $3 surcharge for pick up and drop off within the Central Business District during special events.

From the airport there is a regulated flat rate of $21 for one or two passengers going into the city. The third and fourth passengers each pay an additional $8. There is no extra charge for luggage. While negotiations with the driver are permitted for half-day or full-day excursions, the standard chartered cab excursion fare is $22.20 per hour with a two-hour minimum.

PUBLIC TRANSIT

The Regional Transit Authority (**RTA**) is a political subdivision of the State of Louisiana, instituted in 1983. It operates seventy bus lines and two streetcar lines. The lines visitors are most likely to use are the **#3 Vieux Carré jitney bus,** the St. Charles Avenue streetcar, the Riverfront streetcar, the **#11 Magazine Street bus,** and the **#48 Esplanade Avenue bus.** Visitors may want to invest in a one- or three-day, unlimited use **transit pass** (see page 28).

New Orleans' most famous transit line was the Desire streetcar immortalized in Tennessee Williams's 1947 play. That line, begun in 1920, served the bars and nightclubs strung out along Bourbon Street in the French Quarter and the unfashionable, working-class side of town downriver. The last streetcar named Desire rattled and swayed through New Orleans in 1948, a victim of post-war "progress." It has been replaced by a diesel bus.

Garden District
• *At 2100 St. Charles Avenue, at Jackson*
• *At 2031 St. Charles Avenue, in front of the Pontchartrain Hotel*

Canal Street and the Central Business District
• *At 500 Canal Street, at Camp, in front of the Sheraton New Orleans Hotel*
• *In front of the Fairmont Hotel, on University Place, off Canal*
• *At 444 St. Charles Street, off Poydras, in front of the Hotel Inter-Continental New Orleans*

Morial Convention Center
Taxis are usually easy to hail in front of the Morial Convention Center when conventions are in progress

Esplanade Avenue
• *At the small triangular park on Esplanade Avenue one block lakeward of N. Broad Street*

Cemeteries
• *At the gate to St. Patrick's Cemetery on City Park Avenue, near Cypress Grove Cemetery*

Uptown
• *In front of the drug store at St. Charles Avenue and Napoleon*
• *At Carrollton Avenue and S. Claiborne, at the end of the St. Charles Avenue streetcar line*

Public Transit / RTA
Fares: buses and some streetcars $1; Riverfront streetcar $1.25; transfers 10¢; exact change required; route information 569-2700

Visitor Transit Passes
Sold at most hotels, and at Woolworth's on Canal at Bourbon; handy and economical; a one-day pass costs $4, a three-day pass $8; good for buses and streetcars

New Orleans Street Map & Visitor Guide
Write to RTA, 6700 Plaza Drive, N.O., 70127; transit lines indicated in purple; available at hotels and other locations

#3 Vieux Carré Jitney
See Tour 1, page 104

#11 Magazine Bus
See Tour 10, pages 318, 330

#48 Esplanade Bus
See Tour 3, page 163

#15 Freret Bus
See Tour 9, page 314

St. Charles Avenue Streetcar
See Tour 9, page 293

St. Charles Avenue Streetcar

The St. Charles Avenue streetcar runs twenty-four hours a day, with frequent service during the day and hourly trains from midnight to 6 A.M. Each car stop has a number, and in this guide both the street name and stop number of suggested stops are given. The best place to board the cars is not stop number 1 at St. Charles and Common Streets, but at the last stop, number 0 (zero), at Carondelet and Canal Streets, across Canal from Bourbon Street. If it is summer, note the side where the experienced riders sit; it will be the shady side once the car turns to head uptown. Avoid riding about 3 P.M., when the line fills up with voluble schoolchildren. A nighttime ride can be delightful; the cut, plate-glass front doors of the grand houses flash like jewels.

The St. Charles Avenue streetcar may be the most pleasant public conveyance surviving in the United States, and it gives a taste of what public transportation was like at its high point in the mid-1920s before the private automobile tragically altered the patterns of city and suburban development. Today, of New Orleans' original, once-extensive streetcar system, only the St. Charles Avenue line that links Canal Street with fashionable Uptown and Carrollton survives. This 6.6-mile line passes through the Central Business District and then describes a crescent up the median of stately St. Charles Avenue. It skirts the Garden District and passes through a virtual tunnel of live oaks through the posh Uptown District, passing an impressive string of grand houses and key institutions (see Tour 9). Near the levee at Riverbend, the line swings up Carrollton Avenue to terminate at S. Claiborne Avenue (the Carrollton Avenue leg is not as interesting). A one-way trip of the entire route takes about forty-five minutes, and a round-trip excursion about an hour and a half. It takes about thirty minutes to go from Canal Street to Audubon Park and the University Section where the walk in Tour 9 begins.

The St. Charles Avenue streetcar line is the oldest continuously operating streetcar in the world. It opened on September 26, 1835, with steam-powered trains as the New Orleans and Carrollton Rail Road, linking the city with its upriver resort at Carrollton six and a half miles away. The line passed through a string of pie-wedge-shaped former sugar plantations, which were bought by speculators who gave up the right-of-way for the railroad and over time subdivided their land for streets and blocks. As developers bought and subdivided these parcels, independent municipalities were established at Lafayette in 1833 (now the Garden District and Irish Channel) and at Carrollton at the end of the line in 1845. Everyone could see that the city would have to expand in this upriver direction along the natural levee (high ground) and that fortunes would be made as one-time cane fields were sold off as house lots. In 1852 Nyades Street, named after the Greek water sprites who animate rivers and streams, was renamed St. Charles Avenue. (Donald A. Gill's *Stories Behind New Orleans Street Names* says this was done to honor Charles III, the reforming monarch during much of the Spanish rule over Louisiana between 1763 and 1801.) Changing the name did not, however, rid the avenue of the noise and smoke of the steam railroad running down its center. About as attractive as living on the shoulder of an interstate, the railroad deterred development *on* the avenue, but it made access to the Garden District easier for the residents who lived a block away from the trains. In 1867 the New Orleans and Carrollton Rail Road made a great leap backward: under railroad president P. G. T. Beauregard, steam engines were replaced with sturdy mules. Far less expensive, much more quiet, and smokeless, mule power permitted an increase in service from three trains per hour to trains every five minutes. In 1893 the mules were replaced by electric trolleys, the first in New Orleans. In 1895, in order to attract an elite clientele, "palace cars" were put on the line with plush upholstery and elegant fittings. These luxurious cars lasted about a decade before individual automobiles made private transportation more attractive to the rich than horse-drawn carriages with their maintenance-intensive animals and refractory coachmen. In 1922 the power and traction companies in New Orleans were reorganized, and investor-owned New Orleans Public Service, Inc. (NOPSI), took over the operation of the city's streetcars. NOPSI was the final consolidation of what had been thirteen street

Riverfront Streetcar
see Tour 5, page 210

railways and six electric and two gas companies operating in New Orleans. The next year a study of New Orleans ridership found strong late-night and early morning patronage and memorably noted that "the people of New Orleans are 'human bats,' as the street traffic is different in this respect from any other city in the U.S."

The spacious 900-class streetcars still in use today were built by the Perley A. Thomas Car Company in High Point, North Carolina, in 1923–24. Racial segregation of passengers, which had been imposed on the streetcars in 1902, ended in May 1958. The St. Charles Avenue streetcar line was listed on the National Register of Historic Places in 1973. In 1983 the line was taken over by the Regional Transit Authority (RTA), ending 150 years of stockholder ownership. The thirty-five olive drab and brown cars and the track bed were reconditioned between 1988 and 1994 with a federal mass transit grant. This is now the oldest original fleet of electric streetcars in regular service in the country, and it carries twenty thousand commuters and visitors daily. The cars are powered by sixty-five horsepower electric motors and travel at an average speed of nine miles per hour and a maximum speed of twenty-eight miles per hour. The rear trolley pole on the roof of the car conducts the six hundred volts of electrical current from the overhead wire to the two motors. The unusual sound you hear now and then are the air compressors that power the brakes recharging. During the holidays the cars are trimmed with green garlands. Occasionally a car might pass you by loaded with balloons, jazz musicians, and happy revelers. These are cars chartered by New Orleanians for rolling birthday parties and other festivities. At the start of the Carnival season the Phorty Phunny Phellows charter a streetcar and toss favors to the commuters.

Riverfront Streetcar

This 1.9-mile route opened in 1988 along the right-of-way of the old Belt Line Railroad that once served the wharfs. It is the first new streetcar line in the city since 1926. The route is not particularly scenic, since it is bounded on the landward side by the critically important concrete floodwall and on the riverside by buildings. There are ten stops between Esplanade Avenue and the Morial Convention Center; the Toulouse Street stop is the one closest to Jackson Square. Vintage streetcars (never called "trolleys" by New Orleanians) operate on this tourist-oriented line. The three cars with their doors at their ends are Perley A. Thomas cars, built in 1923–24, that once rolled on Canal Street. The two cars with their doors in the middle are W-2 cars from Melbourne, Australia, and were constructed in 1924–25; their wider doors accommodate wheelchairs. This line is convenient for conventioneers wishing to go from the convention center to the French Quarter.

Gray Line of New Orleans
Offers a variety of tours, including the useful Loop Tour, which is $15 for adults and $8 for children; two-day Loop Tour passes also available; 569-1401, 800-535-7786.

BUS TOURS AND AIR TOURS

There are several national and local companies that conduct bus tours of the city and its region. Since large buses are not permitted in most of the French Quarter or in any part of the Garden District, tours that utilize small buses and vans are best. This list is only partial. The Visitor Information Center at 529 St. Ann Street, facing Jackson Square, is the best place to secure the latest tour brochures (open daily 9 A.M. to 5 P.M.). **Gray Line** tours depart from the Toulouse Street Wharf behind the Jax Brewery a block from Jackson Square. The most practical tour they offer is the Loop Tour, which makes twelve stops linking major visitor destinations. You may join this tour at any of its stops with exact fare and also hop on or off of these jitney buses at any of their twelve stops; two-day Loop Tour passes are also available.

In addition to Gray Line, the following companies also offer tours:

- **Le'ob's Tours** *African American Heritage Tours; 288-3478.*
- **New Orleans Tours** *offers a variety of city tours; 592-1991.*
- **A Touch of Class Tours** *offers tours in limousines and mini buses; 522-7565.*
- **Pelican Tours** *482-2010.*
- **Tours by Inez** *offers van tours; 522-1442.*
- **Williams Tours** *945-9019; 800-362-6824.*

John James Audubon
Riverboat
800-233-BOAT or
586-8777

Cajun Queen **Riverboat**
800-445-4109 or
524-0814

Cotton Blossom
Sternwheeler
800-233-BOAT or
586-8777

Creole Queen
Paddlewheeler
800-445-4109 or
529-4567

Natchez **Steamboat**
800-233-BOAT or
586-8777

- **Air Reldan** *offers sightseeing flights; Lakefront Airport; 241-9400.*
- **Southern Seaplane** *offers sightseeing flights; in Belle Chasse across the river; 394-5633.*

MISSISSIPPI RIVER BOAT EXCURSIONS

There are various vessels that make scenic excursions from New Orleans up and down the Mississippi River. You can also experience the river for free by riding the Canal-Algiers Ferry (see page 220).

- *John James Audubon* **Riverboat** Departs from the Aquarium of the Americas dock near the foot of Canal Street and sails upriver to the Audubon Zoo uptown at 10 A.M., noon, 2 and 4 P.M.; it leaves the zoo at 11 A.M., 1, 3 and 5 P.M.
- *Cajun Queen* **Riverboat** This replica of a Mississippi steamboat departs the Aquarium of the Americas dock and sails downriver past the French Quarter, the port, plantations, and Chalmette battlefield; no stops. Departs daily at 10:30 A.M. and 2 P.M., dinner and jazz cruise at 8 P.M.
- *Cotton Blossom* **Sternwheeler** Departs from Jax Brewery dock at noon daily for a three-hour tour; no stops.
- *Creole Queen* **Paddlewheeler** Departs from the Canal Street dock at the Riverwalk Mall at 10:30 A.M. and 2 and 8 P.M. and stops at Chalmette Battlefield downriver (see page 221).
- *Natchez* **Steamboat** Departs daily from the Jax Brewery dock for two-hour excursions that leave at 11:30 A.M., 2:30 P.M., and a dinner and jazz cruise at 7 P.M.; no stops. A late-night dance cruise departs at 10 P.M. on Saturday and returns at midnight.

CARRIAGE RIDES IN THE FRENCH QUARTER

Mule-drawn carriages can be engaged from any French Quarter street when the carriage is empty. They ply the Quarter from early morning to midnight. Tours last half an hour and cost $8 per adult and $5 per child under twelve in the larger carriages, and a minimum of $40 in the smaller one-to-four-person vehicles. The stand for carriages is on Decatur Street at the riverside of Jackson Square. Writer Bethany Bultman has the best suggestion for would-be buggy riders: "Hire a carriage at 5 P.M. when most visitors go back to their hotels and tell the driver not to say a word. Look at the architecture from the level of a carriage. Sometimes the light is so magnificent, it's like a Venetian wash on the buildings."

BICYCLE RENTALS Bicyclists are cautioned that riding a bike in the French Quarter is possible but dangerous. Most New Orleans drivers are not ready for bicyclists. Though the city is flat, this is not Holland.

- **Olympic Bike Rental & Tours** *Two locations and open seven days a week from 8 A.M. to 7 P.M.: in the French Quarter at 315 Decatur Street, near Conti, 522-6797; and in the Garden District at 1618 Prytania Street at Terpsichore, St. Charles Avenue streetcar stop #10, 523-1314. Will deliver to hotels at no charge.*
- **French Quarter Bicycles** *522 Dumaine Street, between Decatur and Chartres; 529-3136.*
- **Bicycle Michael's** *In the Faubourg Marigny, 618 Frenchmen Street, between Royal and Chartres; 945-9505.*

WALKING Walking is a most un-Southern practice. And yet it is the only way to really get to know New Orleans architecture and neighborhoods. The broiling summer sun can make afternoon strolls uncomfortable and exhausting. Sudden afternoon downpours may not faze the amphibians who live here, but they do astound and surprise unacclimated "awaybians," curtailing their sightseeing. Then there is the notorious street crime of New Orleans and the paralyzing fear it can engender. And if the weather and potential for crime don't discourage you, the aggressive habits of New Orleans drivers also make walking hazardous. They must *always* go ahead of mere pedestrians at crosswalks, nor will they warn you with turn signals. But don't give up. Walking has many rewards that can be experienced in no other way, and the tours break up the city into manageable, safe chunks. The best advice is to explore the city with others and to stay on main streets; don't live in immobile terror. Walking and sightseeing in New Orleans consists of hopping from one pedestrian island to another pedestrian island, whether by car, taxi, or public transit. *It is not advisable to walk from one section of the city to another through unfrequented areas.*

Organized walking tours are the safest way to see New Orleans, especially the plush New Orleans behind its most elegant facades. Recommended walks and house and garden tours are conducted by the following:

- **Friends of the Cabildo French Quarter Walking Tours** *Tours on Monday at 1:30 P.M. and Tuesday through Sunday at 10 A.M. and 1:30 P.M.; no tours on state holidays. Walks start at the 1850 House Museum in the Lower Pontalba Building on St. Ann Street facing Jackson Square; no reservation needed; 523-3939. $10 adults; $8 students and seniors; children under 12 free; fee includes admission to two of the four Louisiana State Museums in the French Quarter.*

- **The National Park Service walks** *See Tour 1, page 103, and Tour 8, page 273.*

- **Kenneth Holditch** *This Tennessee Williams expert gives literary walking tours of the French Quarter; 949-9805.*

- **Garden Club and House Tours** *See Tour 8, page 273.*

Lodgings by Location

New Orleans Accommodations Guide
For a free copy, write to the New Orleans Metropolitan Convention and Visitors Bureau, 1520 Sugar Bowl Drive, N.O., LA 70112-1255; 566-5011.

Destination Management
World Trade Center, suite 1415, N.O., 70130; 592-0500, 800-366-8882, fax 592-0529

Room Finders USA
1112 N. Rampart Street, N.O., 70116; 522-9373, 800-473-7829, fax 529-1948

Cultural Homes of New Orleans / Bed & Breakfast, Inc., Reservation Service
1021 Moss Street, P.O. Box 52257, N.O., 70152-2257; 488-4640, 800-729-4640, fax 488-4639

New Orleans Accommodations and Bed and Breakfast Reservation Service
671 Rosa Avenue #201, Metairie, LA 70005; 838-0071, 838-0072, fax 838-0140

Southern Comfort Bed and Breakfast Reservation Service
8300 Sycamore Place, N.O., 70118; 861-0082, 800-749-1928, fax 861-3087

Kathy 'n I Travel
2410 Farragut Street, N.O., 70114; 366-6781

The expense rating code used here is based on that of the New Orleans Metropolitan Convention and Visitors Bureau, which also dispenses a free **New Orleans Accommodations Guide.** It represents the approximate tariff for a *single-occupancy room in season.* In addition there is an 11 percent hotel-motel tax used to subsidize the Superdome and the Convention Center. Room rates vary substantially by season and for special events in New Orleans. It is important to make reservations well in advance of your trip in order to get the place you want. Rates are higher during Mardi Gras, football weekends, and other events, when you must book for several days. Rates are lowest during the steamy summer. Advance deposits may be required; be sure to verify refund policies. Plan ahead; New Orleans can fill up completely. Early spring and Thanksgiving to Christmas (but not New Year's) are the optimal times to visit the Crescent City. Expense ratings:

$	=	$50 or less
$$	=	$50 to $75
$$$	=	$75 to $100
$$$$	=	$100 to $125
$$$$$	=	above $125

CHOOSING WHERE TO STAY

Choosing the right hotel makes a big difference in New Orleans—and the key here is location more than facilities. It is worth the extra expense to stay on the *riverside* of the French Quarter, which is relatively safer for pedestrians and within walking distance of most of what you will want to see. There are also many historic bed-and-breakfast inns, which add the dimension of time travel and local neighborhoods to your stay. The selected lodgings listed here are arranged geographically by district. Most lodgings appear alphabetically by street; in some lists the top few listings are recommended. If you bring or rent a car, always ask about *parking arrangements;* secured on-site parking is best.

Destination Management and Room Finders USA can help you find a room if necessary; **Destination Management** makes free hotel reservations in the city and region, and **Room Finders USA** charges a 15 percent commission for their service.

Bed-and-Breakfast Information and Reservations

* **Cultural Homes of New Orleans / Bed & Breakfast, Inc., Reservation Service** A registry of historic houses in many New Orleans neighborhoods.
* **New Orleans Accommodations and Bed and Breakfast Reservation Service**
* **Southern Comfort Bed and Breakfast Reservation Service**
* **Kathy 'n I Travel**

FRENCH QUARTER / RIVERSIDE

This is *the* part of the Quarter to stay in, even though it tends to be the priciest.

* **The Soniat House** $$$$$ An 1830 town house in the quiet Lower Quarter converted into a fine small hotel; 17 rooms, 7 suites; designated a Historic Hotel by the National Trust for Historic Preservation.
* **Hotel de la Poste** $$$ A fine small hotel with a pool and valet parking; the excellent Ristorante Bacco adjoins the hotel; 87 rooms, 13 suites.
* **Omni Royal Orleans Hotel** $$$$$ A full-service luxury hotel with the perfect location; fitness center; Rib Room restaurant, Esplanade Piano bar, LaRiviera rooftop lounge with a view over the Quarter; taxi stand in front; 330 rooms, 16 suites. See page 124 for the history of this important location.
* **The Monteleone Hotel** $$$$$ A luxurious Edwardian hotel with a great location; restaurants, lounges, parking, fitness center; near the best antique shops; good for taxis; 600 rooms, 35 suites.
* **Hotel Villa Convento in the French Quarter** $$ An 1848 American-style town house adapted into a 25-room hotel; some rooms have balconies; across the street from the Croissant d'Or Patisserie Française for breakfast.

The Soniat House
1133 Chartres Street,
N.O., 70116; 522-0570,
800-544-8808

Hotel de la Poste
316 Chartres Street,
N.O., 70130; 581-1200,
800-448-4927

Omni Royal Orleans Hotel
621 St. Louis Street,
N.O., 70140; 529-5333,
800-843-6664

The Monteleone Hotel
214 Royal Street, N.O.,
70140; 523-3341,
800-535-9595

Hotel Villa Convento in the French Quarter
616 Ursulines Avenue,
N.O., 70116; 522-1793

Le Richelieu in the French Quarter
1234 Chartres Street,
N.O., 70116; 529-2492,
800-535-9653

St. Louis Hotel
730 Bienville Street,
N.O., 70130; 581-7300,
800-535-9706

Hotel Ste. Helene
508 Chartres Street,
N.O., 70116; 522-5014,
800-348-3888

Provincial Hotel
1024 Chartres Street,
N.O., 70116; 581-4995,
800-535-7922

French Quarter Maisonettes
1130 Chartres Street,
N.O., 70116; 524-9918

Hotel Chateau Dupre
131 Decatur Street,
N.O., 70130; 569-0600,
800-285-0620

The Bienville House
320 Decatur Street,
N.O., 70130; 529-2345,
800-535-7836, fax
525-6079

Historic French Market
Inn – A Clarion Carriage
House
501 Decatur Street,
N.O., 70130; 561-5621,
800-548-5148

Bourbon Orleans Hotel
717 Orleans Street,
N.O., 70116; 523-2222,
800-521-5338

Nine-O-Five Royal Hotel
905 Royal Street,
N.O., 70116; 523-0219

Rue Royal Inn
1006 Royal Street,
N.O., 70116; 524-3900,
800-776-3901

Cornstalk Hotel
915 Royal Street,
N.O., 70116; 523-1515

Place d'Armes Hotel
625 St. Ann Street, near
Jackson Square,
N.O., 70116; 524-4531,
800-366-2743

French Quarter Guest
House
623 Ursulines Avenue,
N.O., 70116; 529-5489,
800-529-5489,
fax 524-1902

Ursuline Guest House
708 Ursulines Avenue,
N.O., 70116; 525-8509,
800-654-2351

- **Le Richelieu in the French Quarter** $$$ A completely "French Quartered" former macaroni factory; excellent location; pool, lounge; taxi stand in front; one of the best buys in the Quarter.
- **St. Louis Hotel** $$$$$ 71 rooms, 4 suites.
- **Hotel Ste. Helene** $$$ 15 rooms, 8 suites.
- **Provincial Hotel** $$$–$$$$$ Swimming pools; Honfleur Bar & Restaurant; 97 rooms, 10 suites.
- **French Quarter Maisonettes** $$$ 7 rooms.
- **Hotel Chateau Dupre** $$$$ 17 suites.
- **The Bienville House** $$$ Courtyard, pool, 83 rooms and suites.
- **Historic French Market Inn – A Clarion Carriage House** $$$$ 68 rooms, 6 suites.
- **Bourbon Orleans Hotel** $$$–$$$$$ Lively part of the Bourbon Street strip; 164 rooms, 47 suites.
- **Nine-O-Five Royal Hotel** $$ Kitchen facilities; 10 rooms, 3 suites.
- **Rue Royal Inn** $$–$$$$ An 1830s Creole town house; 16 rooms, 1 suite.
- **Cornstalk Hotel** $$$$ An 1890s Queen Anne house; 14 rooms.
- **Place d'Armes Hotel** $$$ Six historic buildings around a court-yard and pool; valet parking; 74 rooms, 8 suites.
- **French Quarter Guest House** $–$$$$$ Creole cottage with 12 rooms.
- **Ursuline Guest House** $$–$$$ Creole cottage and slave quarter; 13 rooms, 1 suite.

LOWER ESPLANADE AVENUE ADJOINING THE FRENCH QUARTER

- **Lamothe House Hotel** $$$ An opulent Victorian double town house; furnished with antiques; 11 rooms, 9 suites.
- **Quarter Esplanade Guest House** $$$ Greek Revival town house; 5 rooms, 1 suite.
- **Girod House** $$$$ Creole-style double town house with a courtyard; 6 suites.
- **Melrose Mansion** $$$$$ Eclectic Victorian house with an eccentric corner tower and antique furnishings; parking; pool; limo to and from airport; 4 rooms, 4 suites.
- **Hotel de la Monnaie** $$$ Faces the Old Mint; two courtyards; equipped kitchen in each suite; 53 suites.

FRENCH QUARTER / LAKESIDE

This side of the Quarter between Bourbon and Rampart Streets has many good hotels and historic bed-and-breakfast inns, but there is often quite a bit of noise on upper Bourbon Street. The blocks lakeside of Bourbon also have fewer pedestrians at night than those on the riverside of the Quarter. These lodgings are listed alphabetically by street.

- **Royal Barracks** $$ At the residential end of the Lower Quarter; Victorian house with 4 rooms, 1 suite.
- **Royal Sonesta Hotel** $$$$$ Large modern hotel; balconies, courtyard, pool; on the busy part of Bourbon Street; 465 rooms, 35 suites.
- **Best Western / The Inn on Bourbon** $$$$$ Large modern hotel on the site of the French Opera House; balconies; on the busy part of Bourbon Street; 184 rooms, 2 suites.
- **Bourgoyne Guest House** $$ Creole town house with studio apartments and one- and two-bedroom suites; kitchens; quiet part of Bourbon Street.
- **Lafitte Guest House** $$$–$$$$$ Creole town house on the quiet end of Bourbon Street; 13 rooms, 1 suite.

Lamothe House Hotel
621 Esplanade Avenue, N.O., 70116; 947-1161, 800-367-5858

Quarter Esplanade Guest House
719 Esplanade Avenue, N.O., 70116; 948-9328

Girod House
835 Esplanade Avenue, N.O., 70116; 522-5214, 800-544-8808

Melrose Mansion
937 Esplanade Avenue, N.O., 70116; 944-2255, fax 945-1794

Hotel de la Monnaie
405 Esplanade Avenue, N.O., 70116; 942-3700

Royal Barracks
717 Barracks Street, N.O., 70116; 529-7269

Royal Sonesta Hotel
300 Bourbon Street, N.O., 70140-1014; 586-0300, 800-SONESTA, fax 586-0335

Best Western / The Inn on Bourbon
541 Bourbon Street, N.O., 70130; 524-7611, 800-535-7891, fax 568-9427

Bourgoyne Guest House
839 Bourbon Street, N.O., 70116; 524-3621, 525-3983

Lafitte Guest House
1003 Bourbon Street, N.O., 70116; 581-2678, 800-331-7971

Hotel St. Pierre
911 Burgundy Street,
N.O., 70116; 524-4401,
800-225-4040,
fax 524-6800

St. Ann / Marie Antoinette Hotel
717 Conti Street,
N.O., 70130; 525-2300,
800-535-9706,
fax 524-8925

Prince Conti Hotel
830 Conti Street,
N.O., 70112; 529-4172,
800-366-2743,
fax 581-3802

Dauzat House
1000 Conti Street,
N.O., 70112; 524-2075,
800-272-2075

Chateau LeMoyne French Quarter Holiday Inn
301 Dauphine Street,
N.O., 70112; 581-1303,
800-522-6963,
fax 523-5709

Grenoble House
323 Dauphine Street,
N.O., 70112; 522-1331

Dauphine Orleans Hotel
415 Dauphine Street,
N.O., 70112; 586-1800,
800-521-7111,
fax 586-1409

Landmark Hotel French Quarter
920 N. Rampart Street,
N.O., 70116; 524-3333,
800-535-7862,
fax 522-8044

P. J. Holbrook's Olde Victorian Inn
914 N. Rampart Street,
N.O., 70116; 522-2446,
800-725-2446

- **Hotel St. Pierre** $$$ Creole slave quarters; two pools; balconies; 66 rooms, 9 suites.

- **St. Ann / Marie Antoinette Hotel** $$$$ Balconies; courtyard and pool; restaurant; 65 rooms.

- **Prince Conti Hotel** $$$ Valet parking; restaurant; 48 rooms, 2 suites.

- **Dauzat House** $$$ Courtyard and pool; kitchens; 8 suites.

- **Chateau LeMoyne French Quarter Holiday Inn** $$$$–$$$$$ Modern hotel with restaurant, lounge, pool; 159 rooms, 12 suites.

- **Grenoble House** $$$$ A town house with 17 suites.

- **Dauphine Orleans Hotel** $$$$ Modern hotel with courtyards, balconies; pets permitted; 98 rooms, 11 suites.

- **Landmark Hotel French Quarter** $$$$ Modern hotel with courtyard, pool, restaurant, lounge; 98 rooms, 1 suite.

- **P. J. Holbrook's Olde Victorian Inn** $$$$–$$$$$ An 1840s house with 6 rooms.

- **A Creole House** $–$$ An 1850s Creole-style house with 19 rooms; some kitchen facilities.
- **St. Peter House** $–$$ A nineteenth-century building with a courtyard; 17 rooms, 6 suites.
- **Hotel Maison de Ville and the Audubon Cottages** $$$$$ A modern seventeen-room hotel and a row of seven adapted cottages; pool, restaurant.
- **Hotel St. Marie** $$$$ A modern hotel near Bourbon Street; courtyard and pool, balconies, bar and restaurant; 93 rooms, 1 suite.
- **Olivier House Hotel** $$$ An 1836 town house with a courtyard and pool; some kitchen facilities; 28 rooms, 12 suites.
- **Maison Dupuy Hotel** $$$$$ A modern hotel with a courtyard, pool, lounge, restaurant; fitness center; 186 rooms, 11 suites.
- **New Orleans Guest House** $$$ An 1848 Creole cottage; 14 rooms.

A Creole House
1013 St. Ann Street,
N.O., 70116; 524-8076,
800-535-7858

St. Peter House
1005 St. Peter Street,
N.O., 70116; 525-9232,
800-535-7815,
fax 943-6536

Hotel Maison de Ville and the Audubon Cottages
727 Toulouse Street,
N.O., 70130; 561-5858,
800-634-1600,
fax 561-5858

Hotel St. Marie
827 Toulouse Street,
N.O., 70112; 561-8951,
800-366-2743,
fax 581-3802

Olivier House Hotel
828 Toulouse Street,
N.O., 70112; 525-8456

Maison Dupuy Hotel
1001 Toulouse Street,
N.O., 70112; 586-8000,
800-535-9177,
fax 525-5334

New Orleans Guest House
1118 Ursulines Avenue,
N.O., 70116; 566-1177,
800-562-1177

The Pontchartrain Hotel
2031 St. Charles Avenue,
N.O., 70140; 524-0581,
800-777-6193,
fax 529-1165

Avenue Plaza Hotel
2111 St. Charles Avenue,
N.O., 70130; 566-1212,
800-535-9575,
fax 525-6899

The Terrell House
1441 Magazine Street,
N.O., 70130; 524-9859,
800-878-9855

Garden District Bed and Breakfast
2418 Magazine Street,
N.O., 70130; 895-4302

Beau Sejour
1930 Napoleon Avenue,
N.O., 70115; 897-3746

Fairchild House
1518 Prytania Street,
N.O., 70130; 524-0154,
800-256-8096,
fax 568-0063

Prytania Park Hotel
1525 Prytania Street,
N.O., 70130; 524-0427,
800-862-1984,
fax 522-2977

St. Charles Guest House
1748 Prytania Street,
N.O., 70130; 523-6556

Prytania Inns
1415, 2041, and 2127
Prytania Street, N.O.,
70130; 566-1515

Sully Mansion–Garden District
2631 Prytania Street,
N.O., 70130; 891-0457,
fax 891-0457

GARDEN DISTRICT AREA

Most of these lodgings are not inside the posh Garden District but are clustered near its edges along St. Charles Avenue, on Magazine Street, or in the gentrifying Lower Garden District. You should have a car if you stay here, since the French Quarter is not within walking distance. Ask about the parking arrangements; secure on-site parking is to be preferred. Both the St. Charles Avenue streetcar and the #11 Magazine Street bus link these neighborhoods with Canal Street and the French Quarter.

- **The Pontchartrain Hotel** $$$$$ The recently refurbished 1926 grande dame of uptown hotels; on the streetcar line; Caribbean Room restaurant, cafe, bar; valet parking; taxi stand in front; 67 rooms, 35 suites.

- **Avenue Plaza Hotel** $$$ A large modern hotel with a courtyard pool, lounge, restaurant; on the streetcar line; 240 suites, all with kitchens; popular.

- **The Terrell House** $$$ An antique-furnished 1858 house; 6 rooms, 3 suites.

- **Garden District Bed and Breakfast** $$ On the edge of the Garden District; 4 suites with kitchens for two to six people.

- **Beau Sejour** $$–$$$ A circa-1900 house with 4 rooms, 1 suite.

- **Fairchild House** $$ An 1840s Greek Revival house with 6 rooms, 1 suite.

- **Prytania Park Hotel** $$$ A modern hotel with 49 rooms and 6 suites in an 1840s building, some kitchen facilities.

- **St. Charles Guest House** $$ Pool, patio, some kitchen facilities; 24 rooms.

- **Prytania Inns** $$ Three vintage structures with about 50 rooms.

- **Sully Mansion–Garden District** $$$–$$$$$ An 1890 Queen Anne house with 5 rooms, 2 suites.

UPTOWN

- **Park View Guest House** $–$$$ A fine 1884 Queen Anne building across the street from Audubon Park and Tulane University; on the streetcar line; 25 rooms; some shared baths.
- **Columns Hotel** $$–$$$$$ An 1883 Victorian house with a large-columned porch added; 19 rooms with antiques; even if you are not staying here, the front porch is a fine place to have drinks while watching life on the avenue.

CANAL STREET AREA

This was once the city's great, wide commercial street where the uptown and downtown streetcar lines met. It was once lined with department stores, and today only two survive, Maison Blanche and Krauss. After the department stores decamped to suburban malls, national chain hotels moved into New Orleans and built large modern high-rise hotels along the foot of Canal Street. Since Canal Street is one of the borders of the French Quarter, these hotels have the French Quarter at their feet or just across wide Canal Street. These hotels are convenient for visitors both with and without cars.

- **La Salle Hotel** $$ A recommended, budget hotel with 60 rooms; parking.
- **Chateau Sonesta Hotel New Orleans** $$$$$ The historic D. H. Holmes department store has been converted into a modern hotel; see page 248; courtyards, pool, fitness center, lounge; 98 rooms, 11 suites.
- **Holiday Inn French Quarter** $$$$ A high-rise hotel just off Canal Street inside the French Quarter; pool, restaurant, lounge; 224 rooms, 28 suites.
- **Le Meridien New Orleans** $$$$$ High-rise tower with pool, fitness center, business services, restaurant, jazz club; some 500 rooms, 7 suites.
- **New Orleans Marriott** $$$$$ High-rise tower with 1,236 rooms, 54 suites.

Park View Guest House
7004 St. Charles Avenue, N.O., 70118; 861-7564, fax 861-1225

Columns Hotel
3811 St. Charles Avenue, N.O., 70115; 899-9308, 800-445-9308, fax 899-8170

La Salle Hotel
1113 Canal Street, N.O., 70112; 523-5831, 800-521-9450, fax 525-2531

Chateau Sonesta Hotel New Orleans
800 Iberville Street, N.O., 70112; 586-0800, 800-SONESTA, fax 524-1770

Holiday Inn French Quarter
124 Royal Street, N.O., 70130; 529-7211, 800-HOLIDAY, fax 566-1127

Le Meridien New Orleans
614 Canal Street, N.O., 70130; 525-6500, 800-543-4300, fax 586-1543

New Orleans Marriott
555 Canal Street, N.O., 70130; 581-1000, 800-228-9290, fax 581-5749

ITT Sheraton New Orleans Hotel
500 Canal Street, N.O., 70130; 525-2500, fax 525-2500

Doubletree Hotel New Orleans
300 Canal Street,
N.O., 70130; 581-1300,
800-528-0444,
fax 522-4100

Westin Canal Place
100 Iberville Street,
N.O., 70130; 566-7006,
800-228-3000,
fax 553-5120

Fairmont Hotel
123 Baronne Street,
N.O., 70140; 529-7111,
800-527-4727,
fax 522-2303

Lafayette Hotel
600 St. Charles Avenue,
N.O., 70130; 524-4441,
800-733-4754,
fax 523-7327

Hotel Inter-Continental New Orleans
444 St. Charles Avenue,
N.O., 70130-3171;
525-5566, 800-332-4246,
fax 523-7310

Le Pavillon Hotel
833 Poydras Street,
N.O., 70140; 581-3111,
800-535-9095,
fax 522-5542

Hyatt Regency New Orleans
500 Poydras Plaza,
N.O., 70140; 561-1234,
800-233-1234,
fax 587-4141

Courtyard by Marriott
124 St. Charles Avenue,
N.O., 70130;
800-321-2211

- **ITT Sheraton New Orleans Hotel** $$$$–$$$$$ High-rise tower with pool, fitness center, restaurants and lounges; 1,047 rooms, 53 suites.
- **Doubletree Hotel New Orleans** $$$$ Between the French Quarter and the Convention Center; restaurant, lounge, fitness center; 363 rooms, 5 suites.
- **Westin Canal Place** $$$$$ A luxury high-rise hotel adjoining the toniest shopping mall in the region, with 397 rooms, 38 suites.

 CENTRAL BUSINESS DISTRICT AND SUPERDOME

Historically, the social center of old New Orleans was the St. Charles Exchange Hotel in the middle of the business district. Today it might be the Fairmont Hotel, where Carnival's two courts of Comus and Rex meet on Mardi Gras night. In the last few years many smaller, less expensive hotels in converted, pre-1940 office buildings have appeared all over the CBD.

- **Fairmont Hotel** $$$$ This large, famous hotel consists of three buildings, one from 1908, one from 1925, and another built in 1965; stylish old lobby; pool, tennis courts, restaurants, lounges, the classy Sazarac Bar; some kitchen facilities; 600 rooms, 72 suites; see page 246.
- **Lafayette Hotel** $$$$$ Small luxury hotel with 44 rooms, 20 suites; lounge; Mike's on the Avenue restaurant is downstairs; on the St. Charles Avenue streetcar line; see page 262.
- **Hotel Inter-Continental New Orleans** $$$$$ Complete modern hotel with a good contemporary art collection; 480 rooms, 32 suites; some kitchens. Here Rex toasts his Queen on Mardi Gras.
- **Le Pavillon Hotel** $$$–$$$$$ Splashy entrance and lobby; pool, restaurant, lounge; 220 rooms, 7 suites.
- **Hyatt Regency New Orleans** $$$$$ High-rise atrium hotel; pool, fitness center, restaurant, sports bar; near the Superdome; free frequent shuttle to the French Quarter; 1,084 rooms, 100 suites.

- **Courtyard by Marriott** $$$$ Restaurant, lounge, fitness center; in the center of the CBD; 140 rooms.

Budget Hotels

- **Comfort Suites** $$ A converted office building with 102 suites; fitness center, laundry; refrigerators and microwaves.
- **Hampton Inn Downtown New Orleans** $$$ A new hotel in a 1902 building; see page 241; 186 rooms, 2 suites.

CONVENTION CENTER AND RIVERFRONT AREA

The Ernest N. Morial Convention Center is large and expanding and located on former railyards between the docks and the old Warehouse District. Convenient hotels have sprouted across Convention Center Boulevard and up nearby streets to serve conventioneers. The #3 Vieux Carré jitney bus makes an easy link between the Convention Center and the French Quarter.

- **Windsor Court Hotel** $$$$$ New Orleans' most highly acclaimed hotel; pool, fitness center, restaurant, lounge, afternoon tea; 58 rooms, 266 suites.
- **The Pelham Hotel** $$$$$ Small hotel in a historic commercial building; Graham's Restaurant adjoins; 60 rooms.
- **Holiday Inn Crowne Plaza** $$$$–$$$$$ Modern hotel with a pool, fitness center, restaurants, lounge; 439 rooms.
- **New Orleans Hilton Riverside** $$$$$ Two hotels, one in a twenty-nine-story tower and the other a low-rise on the river built over the Riverwalk mall; on the Riverfront streetcar line; pools, restaurants, Kabby's Sports Edition bar, Pete Fountain's Jazz Club, fitness center; 1,200 rooms, 82 suites.
- **Embassy Suites Hotel New Orleans** $$$$$ In the Arts District; near the Riverfront streetcar line; pool, restaurant, lounge; 226 suites.
- **Wyndham Riverfront Hotel** $$$ A new hotel near the Convention Center and Harrah's Casino.
- **Holiday Inn Select** $$$ Near the Convention Center and Hertz car rental office.

Comfort Suites
346 Baronne Street,
N.O., 70112; 524-1140,
800-221-2222,
fax 523-4444

Hampton Inn Downtown New Orleans
226 Carondelet Street,
N.O., 70130; 529-9990,
800-HAMPTON,
fax 529-9996

Windsor Court Hotel
300 Gravier Street,
N.O., 70130; 523-6000,
800-262-2662,
fax 596-4513

The Pelham Hotel
440 Common Street,
N.O., 70130; 522-4444,
800-659-5621,
fax 539-9010

Holiday Inn Crowne Plaza
333 Poydras Street,
N.O., 70130; 525-9444,
800-522-6963,
fax 568-9312

New Orleans Hilton Riverside
2 Poydras Street,
N.O., 70140; 584-3848,
800-HILTONS,
fax 568-1721

Embassy Suites Hotel New Orleans
315 Julia Street,
N.O., 70130; 525-1993,
800-362-2779,
fax 522-3040

Wyndham Riverfront Hotel
701 Convention Center Boulevard, N.O., 70130;
524-8200

Holiday Inn Select
881 Convention Center
Boulevard, N.O., 70130;
524-1881,
800-HOLIDAY

Mentone Bed and
Breakfast
1437 Pauger Street,
N.O., 70116; 943-3019

The Claiborne Mansion
2111 Dauphine Street,
N.O., 70117; 949-7327

La Maison Marigny Bed
and Breakfast
1421 Bourbon Street,
N.O., 70116; 948-3638

Marigny Guest House
615 Kerlerec Street,
N.O., 70116; 944-9700

Casa de Marigny Creole
Guest Cottages
818 Frenchmen Street,
N.O., 70116; 948-3875,
800-725-3875

Sun Oak Inn Bed and
Breakfast / House Museum
2020 Burgundy Street,
N.O., 70116; 945-0322,
fax 945-0322

Chartres Street House
2517 Chartres Street,
N.O., 70117; 945-2339

The House on Bayou Road
2275 Bayou Road,
N.O., 70119; 945-0992,
949-7711, 800-882-2968,
fax 945-0993

MARIGNY AND
ESPLANADE AVENUE

The Faubourg Marigny is just across Esplanade Avenue from the Lower French Quarter and is well located for carless travelers. Those who stay on Esplanade Avenue beyond N. Rampart Street should have a car.

Marigny

These lodgings are all near the Frenchmen Street music clubs; see pages 155 and 205.

* **Mentone Bed and Breakfast** $$$ Cozy second-floor suite in a Victorian camelback; especially comfortable for women.
* **The Claiborne Mansion** $$$$$ This 1859 house faces Washington Square; recently adapted as an inn with 2 rooms and 5 suites; contemporary decor; pool and garden.
* **La Maison Marigny Bed and Breakfast** $$$ This 1890s house has 3 upstairs rooms, some with a gallery.
* **Marigny Guest House** $$$ An 1890s house with 5 rooms with private baths; parking.
* **Casa de Marigny Creole Guest Cottages** $$$ Five early-nineteenth-century cottages; pool; kitchen facilities.
* **Sun Oak Inn Bed and Breakfast / House Museum** $$$ An 1836 house furnished with antiques; parking; two rooms with private baths share a double parlor, kitchen and garden, parking.
* **Chartres Street House** $$–$$$$$ An 1850 town house with a pool and garden; 2 rooms.

Esplanade Avenue

This once-elegant avenue is lined with oaks and fine old houses. See Tour 3, page 165, on its up and down and up again history. Travelers at these locations need an automobile even though the Esplanade Avenue bus runs from Rampart Street at the edge of the French Quarter out to City Park.

* **The House on Bayou Road** $$$$ A beautiful, antique-furnished, circa 1798 Louisiana colonial house set in a large garden; a classic of regional architecture, see page 169; parking; 4 rooms, 1 suite.

- **The Nicholas M. Benachi House** $$$ An 1859 Greek Revival mansion furnished with early Louisiana antiques, see page 169; 4 rooms; parking.
- **Robert Gordy House** $$$ This fine 1870s Italianate house was the home of artist Robert Gordy, and examples of his work hang here.
- **The Edgar Degas House** $$–$$$ Restoration is in progress at this 1852 house, where Edgar Degas probably stayed during his visit to New Orleans in 1872–73; see the Musson House, page 170; 4 rooms, some kitchen facilities.
- **Mechling's Guest House** $$$–$$$$$ An 1860s house with 2 rooms and 1 suite; parking.
- **The Dufour-Baldwin House, Inc.** $$$–$$$$ An important 1859 antebellum mansion designed by Henry Howard, it's in the process of restoration with great cavernous interiors stripped down to the structure; see page 167; 4 rooms in a modernized dependency; parking.
- **Maison Esplanade** $$$$ An 1846 house with 7 rooms, 2 suites; some balconies.
- **Rathbone Inn** $$ An 1850s double-galleried Greek Revival house with 8 rooms and 1 suite, all with kitchenettes.

HOSTELS

- **Hostel on Burgundy** $ In the French Quarter; 3 bedrooms, 1 apartment; equipped kitchen; street parking.
- **International YMCA Hotel** $ On the streetcar line at Lee Circle; 50 rooms; pool, fitness center; shared baths.
- **Marquette House New Orleans International Hostel** $ A century-old house with 80 dormitory beds, community kitchen, laundry, 2 private rooms, 12 suites with private kitchens and baths; one block from the St. Charles streetcar; parking at inn, on-street parking at hostel.

The Nicholas M. Benachi House
2257 Bayou Road, at Tonti, N.O., 70119; 525-7040

Robert Gordy House
2630 Bell Street, at Crete, N.O., 70119; 486-9424

The Edgar Degas House
2306 Esplanade Avenue, N.O., 70119; 821-5009, fax 821-0870

Mechling's Guest House
2023 Esplanade Avenue, N.O., 70116; 943-4131, 800-725-4131

The Dufour-Baldwin House, Inc.
1707 Esplanade Avenue, N.O., 70116; 945-1503, fax 947-6587

Maison Esplanade
1244 Esplanade Avenue, N.O., 70116; 523-8080, 800-290-4BED, fax 527-0040

Rathbone Inn
1227 Esplanade Avenue, N.O., 70116; 947-2100, 800-947-2101, fax 947-7454

Hostel on Burgundy
Office at 1114 Royal Street, N.O., 70116; 581-4607, 895-9087

International YMCA Hotel
920 St. Charles Avenue, N.O., 70130; 568-9622, fax 568-9622 ext 298

Marquette House New Orleans International Hostel
2253 Carondelet Street, N.O., 70130; 523-3014

Jude Travel Park of New Orleans
7400 Chef Menteur Highway, N.O., 70126; 241-0632, 800-523-2196

New Orleans KOA Kampground
11129 Jefferson Highway, River Ridge, LA 70123; 467-1792, fax 464-7204

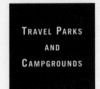

TRAVEL PARKS
AND
CAMPGROUNDS

- **Jude Travel Park of New Orleans** Take I-10 East to the 240B exit (US 90), located eight blocks east on Chef Menteur Highway; 43 sites with full hookups; shuttle bus to the French Quarter; car rental.

- **New Orleans KOA Kampground** $ Campground, recreational vehicle sites; pool; city bus to French Quarter; car rental.

Recommended Restaurants

The Creoles had a proverb: *Çà qui dourmi napas pensé manze* ("When we sleep we don't think about eating"). Today, New Orleanians even dream about eating. The easiest topic of conversation in New Orleans is where you ate last and where you intend to eat next. This alphabetical list seeks out the best varieties of specifically New Orleans cooking. It includes mostly good new restaurants, but also lists places that are famous because they are famous. Most restaurants stop serving at 10 P.M. Phone ahead for hours and reservations. For dinner at the best restaurants, especially during conventions, make reservations well in advance of your visit. I've listed a tour number for many of these places; in some cases, the restaurant or take-out counter is mentioned in the tour preliminaries, while in others, its location is near the tour. "Downtown" in this list means in or near the Central Business District. There is also a list of groceries and places that sell prepared food to go. Expense ratings:

Very Expensive	=	$$$$
Expensive	=	$$$
Moderate	=	$$
Inexpensive	=	$

- **Antoine's** $$$$ (Tour 1) Proprietor Bernard Guste conducts the oldest restaurant in North America and the birthplace of many famous New Orleans dishes; see page 125.
- **Arnaud's** $$$ (Tour 1) A culinary landmark in New Orleans since 1918, in a landmark setting.
- **Ristorante Bacco** $$ (Tour 1) Cindy and Ralph Brennan have created a superb Creole-accented Italian menu; a serene, airy interior.
- **Bayona** $$$ (Tour 1) Chef Susan Spicer's outstanding contemporary Creole restaurant in an elegant reworking of a traditional Creole cottage.

Antoine's
In the French Quarter at 713 St. Louis Street, between Royal and Bourbon; 581-4422

Arnaud's
In the French Quarter at 813 Bienville Street, between Bourbon and Dauphine; 523-5433

Ristorante Bacco
In the French Quarter at 310 Chartres Street, between Conti and Bienville, adjoins Hotel de la Poste; 522-2426

Bayona
In the French Quarter at 430 Dauphine Street, between St. Louis and Conti; 525-4455

Bella Luna
In the French Quarter at 914 N. Peters Street, and in the French Market near the foot of Dumaine Street; 529-1583

Brennan's
In the French Quarter at 417 Royal Street, between St. Louis and Conti; 525-9711

Brigsten's
Uptown at 723 Dante Street, between Maple Street and River Road; 861-7610

Broussard's
In the French Quarter at 819 Conti Street, between Bourbon and Dauphine; 581-3866

Cafe Atchafalaya
Uptown at 901 Louisiana
Avenue, at Laurel Street;
891-5271

Cafe Degas
On Esplanade Ridge at
3127 Esplanade Avenue,
near Grand Route St.
John; 945-5635

Camilla Grill
Uptown at 626 S.
Carrollton Avenue, near
Hampson Street;
866-9573

Casamento's
Uptown at 4330
Magazine Street, near
Napoleon Avenue;
895-9761

Chicory Farm Cafe
Uptown at 723 Hillary
Street, near Maple;
866-2325

Clancy's
Uptown at 6100
Annunciation Street, at
Webster; 895-1111

Coffee Pot Restaurant
In the French Quarter at
714 St. Peter Street, near
Royal; 524-3500

Commander's Palace
Uptown at 1403
Washington Avenue,
between Prytania and
Coliseum; 899-8231

Creole Celebration
1555 Poydras Street;
527-5244

Croissant d'Or Patisserie
In the French Quarter at
617 Ursulines Avenue,
near Chartres; 524-4663

- **Bella Luna** $$$ (Tour 5) Chef Horst Pfeifer's fusion of Italian, contemporary Creole, and Southwestern elements; the airy rooms have views of the Mississippi River and its ships.

- **Brennan's** $$$$ (Tour 1) One of New Orleans' most noted restaurants; housed in the landmark Faurie House of 1795, see page 127.

- **Brigsten's** $$$ (Tour 9) Chef Frank Brigsten prepares superb Louisiana specialties.

- **Broussard's** $$$ (Tour 1) Gunter, Evelyn, and Marc Preuss present Creole cuisine with a light touch.

- **Cafe Atchafalaya** $$ (Tour 9) Iler Pope's sophisticated Southern country cooking.

- **Cafe Degas** $$ (Tour 3) Chef Denemon Britt's welcome oasis of French cooking; its covered wood deck overlooks Esplanade Avenue, see page 163.

- **Camilla Grill** $ (Tour 9) A popular diner with pecan waffles and omelettes; counter service; on the St. Charles Avenue streetcar line; open until 1 A.M. Sunday through Thursday and until 3 A.M. on Friday and Saturday.

- **Casamento's** $ (Tour 10) A New Orleans classic; raw and fried oysters and gumbo served in an immaculate 1940s tiled interior; closed from May to August.

- **Chicory Farm Cafe** $$ (Tour 9) Chef Daniel Abel prepares the best Creole vegetarian cuisine in New Orleans; they grow their own mushrooms and greens at their farm in Mississippi; set in an old house.

- **Clancy's** $$ (Tour 9) Chef Steve Manning prepares a varied menu of Louisiana specialties; a favorite with Uptowners in a New Orleans setting.

- **Coffee Pot Restaurant** $ (Tour 1) Authentic Creole breakfasts including callas (rice cakes with pecans and syrup); open until midnight, Monday through Thursday, until 1 A.M. on Friday and Saturday.

- **Commander's Palace** $$$ (Tour 8) The Brennan family's flagship restaurant; chef Jamie Shannon's Creole menu is consistently fine; set in an 1880 Queen Anne building in the Garden District, see page 285.

- **Creole Celebration** $ (Tour 6) The Baquet family's Creole restaurant serves true New Orleans and Southern food.
- **Croissant d'Or Patisserie** $ (Tour 2) Quaterites favor pastry chef Maurice Delechelle's excellent brioches; set in the old Angelo Brocato tiled ice cream parlor.
- **Dooky Chase** $$ Leah Chase's soulful Creole cuisine served in an interior filled with African America art; open until midnight on Friday and Saturday.
- **Emeril's** $$$ (Tour 7) Chef Emeril Lagasse's contemporary Creole cuisine is outstanding. The sleek interior of hard surfaces can be loud, so dine early.
- **Felix's Restaurant and Oyster Bar** $ (Tour 1) A traditional oyster bar in an anywhere setting.
- **G & E Courtyard Grill** $$ (Tour 2) Chef Michael Uddo serves Sicilian and New Orleans cuisine; indoor and outdoor dining; popular and can get noisy, dine early.
- **Galatoire's** $$$ (Tour 1) As much a New Orleanian institution as a restaurant, Galatoire's survives behind its glass-curtained doors as an island of civility on this raucous strip. Jean Galatoire purchased Victor Bero's cafe in 1905, and it has long been run by the Galatoire and Gooch families. Inside the 1831 building is an Edwardian interior with mirrors lining the parallel walls, so that you can survey the room. Friday is when the local legal fraternity gathers here in conclave to power lunch; Sunday afternoon lunch is when the Old Guard comes to see and be seen. Ask the waiter for recommendations; the fried foods are superb. Reservations for eight or more only; dress code for gentlemen: coats and ties after 5 P.M. and all day Sunday; no jeans or shorts.

Dooky Chase
In Mid-City at 2301 Orleans Avenue, at Miro; 821-0600

Emeril's
In the Arts District at 800 Tchoupitoulas, at Julia; 528-9393

Felix's Restaurant and Oyster Bar
In the French Quarter at 739 Iberville Street, near Bourbon; 522-4440

G & E Courtyard Grill
In the French Quarter at 1113 Decatur Street, between Ursulines and Gov. Nicholls; 528-9376

Galatoire's
In the French Quarter at 209 Bourbon Street, between Iberville and Bienville; 525-2021

Gautreau's
Uptown at 1728 Soniat Street, between Dryades and Danneel; 899-7397

The Grill Room & Bar
Downtown at the Windsor Court Hotel, 300 Gravier Street, at Tchoupitoulas; 522-1992

The Gumbo Shop
In the French Quarter at 630 St. Peter Street, between Chartres and Royal, near Jackson Square; 525-1486

K-Paul's Louisiana Kitchen
In the French Quarter at 416 Chartres Street, near Conti; 524-7394

La Crepe Nanou
Uptown at 1410 Robert Street, between St. Charles Avenue and Prytania Street; 899-2670

Louisiana Pizza Kitchen
In the French Quarter at 95 French Market Place, at N. Peters and Barracks; 522-9500

Mike's on the Avenue
Downtown at 628 St. Charles Avenue, at S. Maestri Place, on Lafayette Square; 523-1709

Mother's
Downtown at 401 Poydras Street, at Tchoupitoulas; 522-9656

Mr. B's Bistro
In the French Quarter at 201 Royal Street, corner of Iberville; 523-2078

Napolean House Bar and Cafe
In the French Quarter at 500 Chartres Street, at St. Louis; 524-9752

NOLA
In the French Quarter at 534 St. Louis Street, between Chartres and Decatur; 522-6652

Olivier's Creole Restaurant
In the French Quarter at 204 Decatur Street, between Iberville and Bienville, across the street from the House of Blues; 525-7734

- **Gautreau's** $$$ (Tour 9) Chef Rob Mitchell serves French and Creole cuisine in a former pharmacy; intimate, reservations recommended.

- **The Grill Room & Bar** $$$$ (Tour 6) Chef Jeff Tunks's outstanding restaurant in a plush setting is a culinary highpoint in New Orleans.

- **The Gumbo Shop** $$ (Tour 1) Traditional New Orleans Creole cooking in a bustling setting; good for families with children; open late; popular, go at off-peak hours; see page 119.

- **K-Paul's Louisiana Kitchen** $$$ (Tour 1) Chef Paul Prudhomme popularized "blackened" Cajun dishes, and his celebrity draws people to wait here in long lines.

- **La Crepe Nanou** $ (Tour 9) A French restaurant with more than crepes; a cozy setting and a favorite with locals.

- **Louisiana Pizza Kitchen** $ (Tour 2) Good pizzas and spinach salads; a simple interior that exhibits local artists; a favorite with Quarterites; open late.

- **Mike's on the Avenue** $$$ (Tour 7) Chef Mike Fennely artfully fuses Creole cuisine with Southwestern, Asian, and Cuban elements; an airy, gracious interior; see page 255.

- **Mother's** $ (Tour 7) A bustling New Orleans cafeteria near the Convention Center, with excellent down-home fare.

- **Mr. B's Bistro** $$$ (Tour 1) Cindy and Ralph Brennan's restaurant serves excellent Creole cuisine in a bistro setting.

- **Napoleon House Bar and Cafe** $$ (Tour 1) Muffulettas and gumbo in an atmospheric landmark; has a courtyard; open until midnight Monday through Thursday, and until 1 A.M. on Friday and Saturday; see page 130.

- **NOLA** $$$ (Tour 1) Chef Emeril Lagasse's second local restaurant serves contemporary New Orleans cuisine in a modern interior; good counter for singles; open until midnight on Friday and Saturday.

- **Olivier's Creole Restaurant** $$ (Tour 1) Soulful Creole cooking.

- **Palace Cafe** $$$ (Tour 6) Cindy and Ralph Brennan's and chef Robert Bruce's excellent contemporary Creole restaurant is in the landmark Werlein Music showroom overlooking Canal Street.

- **Palm Court Jazz Cafe** $$ (Tour 1) The best combination of Creole cuisine and traditional jazz in New Orleans; a comfortable, old-fashioned setting; has a bar; see page 59.
- **Praline Connection** $ (Tour 2) Down-home cooking, if overrated; memorable rum pralines in the candy shop.
- **Red Fish Grill** $$ (Tour 1) Casual New Orleans seafood in a fresh, artistic setting with metal sculptures by Luis Colman; on the first block of Bourbon Street.
- **The Rib Room** $$$ (Tour 1) A fine restaurant in an elegant setting; recommended for lunch.
- **Ruth's Chris Steak House** $$$ Two justly renowned steak houses, one in Mid-City, where politicos flock for Friday lunch, and one in Metairie.
- **Sapphire** $$$ (Tour 6) Kevin Graham's newest fine restaurant has an interior featuring the work of furniture designer Mario Villa.
- **Upperline** $$$ (Tour 9) JoAnn Clevenger and chef Richard Benz serve sophisticated yet unpretentious cuisine.
- **Zachary's Restaurant** $$ (Tour 9) Chef Kevin Nichols serves genuine Creole cooking in a comfortable Victorian cottage.

TAKE-OUT FOOD

Picnics are a good idea when making day trips outside the city.

- **Progress Grocery Company** (Tour 2) An excellent Italian delicatessen with good muffulettas and cold-cut sandwiches with an olive spread.
- **Verti Marte Grocery** (Tour 2) Good for travelers on a budget; open late.
- **Matassa Grocery** (Tour 2) Where Quarterites shop; good take-out foods, including muffulettas.
- **Martin Wine Cellar** (Tour 9) Good selection and prices; also has take-out food counter.

Palace Cafe
Downtown at 605 Canal Street, between Chartres and Exchange Alley; 523-1661

Palm Court Jazz Cafe
In the French Quarter at 1204 Decatur Street, between Gov. Nicholls and Barracks; 525-0200

Praline Connection
In Faubourg Marigny at 542 Frenchmen Street, at Chartres, 943-3934; and in the Arts District at 901 St. Peter Street, at St. Joseph Street, 523-3973

Red Fish Grill
In the French Quarter at 115 Bourbon Street, just off Canal; 598-1200

The Rib Room
In the French Quarter in the Royal Orleans Hotel at 621 St. Louis Street, at Royal; 529-7045

Ruth's Chris Steak House
In Mid-City at 711 N. Broad Street, at Orleans Avenue, 486-0810; also in Metairie at 3633 Veterans Boulevard, at Hessmer Street, 888-3600

Sapphire
Downtown in the Omni Royal Crescent Hotel, 228 Camp Street, at Gravier; 524-0081

Upperline
Uptown at 1413 Upperline Street, between Prytania and St. Charles Avenue; 891-9822

Zachary's Restaurant
Uptown at 8400 Oak
Street, at Cambronne;
865-1559

Progress Grocery Company
In the French Quarter at
915 Decatur, between
Dumaine and St. Philip;
525-6627

Verti Marte Grocery
In the lower French
Quarter at 1201 Royal
Street, corner of Gov.
Nicholls; 525-4767

Matassa Grocery
In the lower French
Quarter at 1001
Dauphine, corner of
St. Philip; 525-9494

Martin Wine Cellar
Uptown at 3827 Baronne
Street, at General Taylor;
899-7411

Langenstein's Supermarket
Uptown at 1330 Arabella,
at Pitt; 899-9283

Chez Nous
Uptown at 5701
Magazine Street, at
Arabella; 899-7303

Dorignac's Food Center
In Metairie at 710
Veterans Memorial
Boulevard; 834-8216

- **Langenstein's Supermarket** (Tour 9) This old-line Uptown grocery store has an excellent prepared foods counter in the back.

- **Chez Nous** (Tour 10) A superb place for prepared foods, especially Creole dishes.

- **Dorignac's Food Center** One of the best food and wine stores in the region.

Performing Arts, Museums, History, and Literature

Arrive ARTScene
111 Veterans Boulevard,
Metairie, LA 70005;
831-3731

Gambit: New Orleans
Weekly
3923 Bienville Street,
N.O., 70119; 486-5900

Lagniappe
Available at newsstands
on Fridays throughout the
city

Louisiana Jazz Federation
Events Hotline
333 St. Charles Avenue,
N.O., 70130; 522-3154

OffBeat
333 St. Charles Avenue,
suite 614, N.O., 70130;
522-5533, fax 522-1159

WWOZ/90.7 FM
Music information
840-4040

New Orleans Jazz and
Heritage Festival
1205 N. Rampart Street,
N.O., 70116; 522-4786;
tickets available through
Ticketmaster: 522-5555
or 800-488-5252

October: Jazz Awareness
Month
Louisiana Jazz
Federation, 333
St. Charles Avenue,
N.O., 70130;
522-3154

PERFORMING ARTS
INFORMATION

- **Arrive ARTScene** This annual booklet lists cultural festivals, theater, concert, and dance events in New Orleans; available in many art galleries.
- **Gambit: New Orleans Weekly** A free newspaper and an excellent guide to the performing arts; advertisers include many interesting shops; subscriptions are available. Published every Monday; available at cafes and some shops.
- **Lagniappe** This is the culture and entertainment guide that appears in the *Times-Picayune* every Friday. It lists performing arts and other cultural events in metropolitan New Orleans.
- **Louisiana Jazz Federation Events Hotline** This hotline covers jazz events all over the city.
- **OffBeat** New Orleans' and Louisiana's free, monthly music and entertainment magazine is a key source of information on New Orleans music and culture; available at many clubs and by mail subscription.
- **WWOZ/90.7 FM** A superb "jazz and heritage station" that is a great source of music information.

JAZZ EVENTS

Jazzfest

Jazzfest—**the New Orleans Jazz and Heritage Festival**—is staged at the racetrack at the New Orleans Fair Grounds off Gentilly Boulevard. This mega-event spreads out over two long weekends in late April and early May; each day lasts from 11 A.M. to 7 P.M. Go when the gates open to avoid the crush; Thursday is usually the least crowded day. Admission in 1996 was $15 for adults and $2 for children under twelve. Music, food, and crafts are spread out over ten large tents and outdoor stages, featuring a wide array of music. Not to be missed is the uplifting Gospel Tent ("My soul is a Holy Ghost witness! Ain't nothin' but a witness!"), one of the most joyous experiences to be had here. The Traditional Jazz Tent is always superb. Mardi Gras Indians appear at the Congo Square stage and are also worth experiencing if you have never seen these gorgeously feathered African American "tribes" dance through the city's poorer neighborhoods. And, oh yes, all that jazz, R&B, rock, zydeco, Afro-Caribbean, and other musics! The music clubs all over town are especially active during Jazzfest nights, so the party continues long after Jazzfest ends each day.

The celebrants at Jazzfest come from all over the country and the world. Some are not celebrants as much as devotees; the intensity of rapt listening can be almost religious. The crowd is much younger than you might expect. It is overwhelmingly white, hip, and well-educated (very few people smoke cigarettes and no drugs are openly taken on the grounds). As in so much of New Orleans culture, spirited blacks are often the entertainers and appreciative whites constitute most of the audience.

Unfortunately, the weather rarely cooperates with the festival. It alternates between baking sun in a place with no trees and torrential downpours in what nature intends to be a swamp. Since enjoying Jazzfest requires adequate preparation, here are a few suggestions: The city fills up for this event (it is second only to Mardi Gras), so reserve your hotel room a year in advance and be prepared to pay premium rates. Do not drive to the Fair Grounds. Parking there is inadequate and costs $10. You will be ticketed or towed if you park in the surrounding neighborhoods. Instead, ask at your hotel about special buses to the grounds, or park in City Park's Marconi Meadows and take the shuttle bus from there. Fleets of buses are continually shuttling between the festival and City Park, the Canal Street side of the French Quarter, and the Superdome. Round-trip bus tickets cost $7 and tickets from City Park include parking. Protect yourself with sunscreen and dress in light, loose, cotton clothing. Long pants and long-sleeve shirts are a good idea, though most college boys appear shirtless wearing khaki shorts and hi-tech sandals. A wide-brim hat that can withstand sun *and* rain is eminently useful. A big umbrella can serve as a parasol or a rain shelter as the fickle May skies dictate. Since the floors of the tents become shallow lagoons when it rains, and running shoes (which most people wear) get soggy and uncomfortable, wear either sandals that let you slosh through the puddles or comfortable, waterproof boots.

Many seasoned Jazzfesters bring folding aluminum lawn chairs so that they can sit just outside the wall-less tents wherever they want.

The food sold on the grounds is superb and is an important part of this southern Louisiana experience; eat at off times when the lines are shortest. Beer, soft drinks, and bottled water are sold on the grounds, but no wine or hard liquor. (You will be cursorily searched at the gate for beverages and video and audio recording equipment; leave all at home.) The contemporary Louisiana crafts are of good quality and make great souvenirs, along with unusual CDs. Last, and sadly, the amplification levels are just this side of the pain threshold for those of us unfortunate enough not to have already lost part of our hearing spectrum. Jazzfest would be twice as enjoyable if the cranked-up sound level was half as loud. Bring ear plugs. The *Times-Picayune* publishes a useful map and schedule of events each day of the festival.

Jazz Awareness Month

Every October (since 1980), the Louisiana Jazz Federation conducts **Jazz Awareness Month,** a month-long program of performances, parades, lectures, tours, and other events; this grassroots endeavor spreads jazz all over the city.

 Devotees make the pilgrimage to New Orleans in search of authentic jazz expecting that here, at last, they will find their musical mecca. But traditional jazz—though forever young—is now a very old kind of music, and true believers must search for it even in its holy city. Other faiths have ensnared the young, and "def" black New Orleanians prefer rap to roots, though even in this there is a local twist: New Orleans has its own kind of rap happily called "bounce," and it is what gets airplay on local black-oriented commercial radio. Traditional jazz is to the new black generation what Gregorian chant is to teenage white rockers. They're exposed to it, if they're lucky, in school. You have to *search* for traditional jazz in the Crescent City, for both the local black market and the waves of white out-of-town tourists have made it an endangered ritual almost as recherché as a Latin mass. The Bourbon Street strip, where waves of to-go-cup-toting tourists think they'll stumble upon real New Orleans music for free, is not the best place to find traditional New Orleans jazz. This listing is for lovers of traditional New Orleans jazz who are also open to contemporary New Orleans' evolving musical styles.

Consistently Best Jazz Venues

The **Palm Court Jazz Café** is a comfortable restaurant/cafe/bar offering fine music and good Creole food; it is where locals go to hear traditional New Orleans jazz. A reasonable surcharge is added to your dinner for the music. There is no cover charge or drink minimum to stand at the bar, from which you can also hear the music. Phone for programs and reservations; there is also a fine Sunday jazz brunch. This is *the* place for those seeking traditional jazz in a civilized setting. Conveniently located in the lower French Quarter near the French Market, the Palm Court Jazz Café also sells rare recordings of traditional New Orleans jazz that you can't find anywhere else. Danny Barker's *Palm Court Strut* is a New Orleans classic. See Jazzology Records under "Best Music Stores" (page 64).

   Maxwell's Toulouse Cabaret offers fine New Orleans jazz seven nights a week; cover charge; serves drinks.

Best-Known Venue

Preservation Hall was opened in 1961 by Philadelphians Allan and Sandra Jaffe. It has become New Orleans' most famous venue for traditional jazz. No food or drinks are served, prices are inexpensive, and children are welcome. Get there early because there is usually a long line waiting to get in. Beginning at 8:30 P.M. and lasting till midnight, various house bands play thirty-minute sets. While the small front room with the decaying, peeling walls is redolent of Old New Orleans, and the often slow-tempo music is authentic, the seating is uncomfortable and the room is almost always overcrowded. Rainy days, when the crowds thin out, are

Palm Court Jazz Café
1204 Decatur Street, between Gov. Nicholls and Barracks; 525-0200

Maxwell's Toulouse Cabaret
615 Toulouse Street; 523-4207

Preservation Hall
726 St. Peter Street, between Bourbon and Royal; daytime 522-2841, *evenings* 523-8939

Pete Fountain Night Club
Hilton Hotel, 2 Poydras Street at the river;
523-4374

Jazz Meridien
614 Canal Street;
525-6500

The House of Blues
225 Decatur Street, between Iberville and Bienville Streets; for advance tickets, call the box office at 529-2583; concert line 529-1421

best. Preservation Hall also sells excellent rare recordings—buy a few and listen in comfort at home.

Major Hotel Venues for Traditional Jazz

Pete Fountain Night Club is a comfortable, modern hotel setting for traditional Dixieland jazz. Shows are at 10 P.M. on Tuesday, Wednesday, Friday, and Saturday. **Jazz Meridien** is at the Hotel Le Meridien; it's a sleek contemporary setting for jazz.

Best New Venue

The House of Blues is New Orleans' most ambitious new venue for live music. It's open seven nights a week, from 8 P.M. until at least 2 A.M.; the Sunday gospel brunch, at 11 A.M. and 2 P.M. (reservations required), is recommended for the music. There are now four House of Blues venues across the country, which were founded by Isaac Tigrett, one of the original partners in the Hard Rock Cafe. An ambitious booking policy showcases contemporary popular music, especially blues, but not much traditional jazz.

The interior design of the Decatur Street location, a converted shoe warehouse, is memorable; it was done by the local architectural firm of Billes/Manning. Much of the interior is painted with decorations and the walls are covered with a collection of works by mostly Southern folk artists. The ceiling of the restaurant consists of a coffered barrel vault with inset plaster bas relief portraits of 108 famous blues musicians, which was executed by Andrew Wood and titled the *Blues Angels Ceiling*. Los Angeles artist Brent Spears painted the ceilings above the restaurant booths with graffitilike designs. The music room is a comfortable small theater seating about a thousand, and it's decorated as a postmodern religious collage. Over the stage is a multicultural confusion of religious symbols and mottos. The African bar upstairs is lined with black-and-white mudcloth and decorated with African masks and instruments. A brilliant yellow feathered Mardi Gras Indian costume bursts from the center of the bar. (Another interior showcasing contemporary Southern folk art is Doug's Restaurant; see page 263.)

Some Outstanding Jazz, Blues, R&B, and Rock Venues Citywide

- **Tipitina's Uptown,** *501 Napoleon Avenue; 897-3943.*
- **Maple Leaf Bar** *Uptown in the Riverbend area, 8316 Oak Street; 866-9359.*
- **Muddy Water's** *Uptown in the Riverbend area, 8301 Oak Street; 866-7174.*
- **The Howlin' Wolf** *In the Warehouse District, 828 S. Peters Street; 523-2551.*
- **Irma Thomas' Lion's Den** *In Mid-City, 2655 Gravier Street; 822-4693.*
- **Mid-City Rock 'n' Bowl** *In Mid-City, 4133 S. Carrollton Avenue; 482-3133.*

BOURBON STREET

Bourbon Street is a relative late-comer to the New Orleans music scene and is by no means its most important venue today. It wasn't until the 1920s, after the closing of Storyville, that jazz cabarets such as the Silver Slipper and the Old Absinthe House began appearing on the strip. Speakeasies also infiltrated the street during Prohibition. Elizabeth Prall Anderson, writer Sherwood Anderson's wife, said of ultra "wet" New Orleanians, "we all seemed to feel that Prohibition was a personal affront and that we had a moral duty to undermine it." In 1925 massive federal raids tried to shut down the "liquor capital of America." The repeal of Prohibition in 1934 led to a rash of saloons on Bourbon. (The street is named for the royal family of France, not the Kentucky county and its famous product.) World War II saw the emergence of strip clubs catering to soldiers and sailors. From the 1940s through the 1960s, more and more R&B and blues clubs appeared here. Some, as is always true of this part of the entertainment industry, were linked to mobsters. In the early 1960s, District Attorney Jim Garrison launched a crusade to "clean up" Bourbon Street and shut down gambling and prostitution. Some think he threw out the baby with the bath water. The seedy Bourbon Street joint will live forever in American literature

Fritzel's
733 Bourbon Street;
561-0432

Old Absinthe House Bar
240 Bourbon Street,
corner of Bienville

Can-Can Cafe
300 Bourbon Street in the
Royal Sonesta Hotel;
553-2372

The Original Old Absinthe
Bar
400 Bourbon Street, at
Conti; 525-8108

544 Club
544 Bourbon Street, at
Toulouse; 566-0529

Pat O'Brien's
718 St. Peters Street, off
Bourbon; 525-4823

as the Night of Joy bar in John Kennedy Toole's *A Confederacy of Dunces.*

The current cold war between club owners and the local American Federation of Musicians has also hurt music on the street. Today the musician's unions have almost no power on this "right to work" strip, and wages are scandalously low. Drummer Kerry Brown said in 1994, "When I was [on Bourbon] ten years ago, they were paying $15 per set, but now it's $8." The way music is marketed on Bourbon also hurts the music: the music is "free" but the beers are $7. The music clubs with serious musicians in other parts of the city impose a cover charge, as they should, and then have reasonable drink and food prices. But it's primarily the nature of today's mass market that has accelerated the decline of music on Bourbon. The college-age crowd that surges down the closed-off street has had little musical education, and they are often people from abroad seeking jazz in New Orleans. Between the "maximizing" landlords, the high-profit T-shirt shops, the high-octane walk-away hurricanes, and karaoke, it's amazing that there's anything left to listen to here at all. Bourbon Street demonstrates a musical Gresham's Law: bad music drives out the good.

- **Fritzel's** A hole-in-the-wall club near the very end of the strip with the best jazz on Bourbon; occasionally, well-known musicians unexpectedly sit in to jam here.
- **Old Absinthe House Bar** Noteworthy as an architectural type, not a music venue, this is a rare entresol town house. Looking like a two-story building, it originally had three floors; the second was lit by the large fanlights and served as a storage area for the commercial ground floor. The third level accommodated the shopkeeper. Bitter absinthe, "the green fairy," was a potent psychoactive drug distilled from wormwood, mixed with alcohol, and drunk with water and sugar; it was banned in 1903.
- **Can-Can Cafe** The fine, traditional Silver Leaf Jazz Band plays Tuesday to Sunday, 9 P.M. to 1 A.M.

- **The Original Old Absinthe Bar** One of the most atmospheric clubs on Bourbon for blues and R&B (not to be confused with the Old Absinthe House at 240 Bourbon Street).
- **544 Club** Funk, soul, R&B, and jazz—it's good but loud.
- **Pat O'Brien's** A landmark saloon with an old courtyard; check out the small bar on the St. Peter Street side; dodge the hurricane and have a mint julep instead.

Other French Quarter Clubs

- **Gazebo Restaurant** *1018 Decatur Street; good for jazz brunch on Saturday and Sunday; 522-0862.*
- **Margaritaville Cafe** *1104 Decatur Street, lower French Quarter; Jimmy Buffett's club for "parrotheads"; 592-2565.*
- **Crescent City Brewhouse** *527 Decatur Street; a microbrewery that attracts a college crowd; 522-0571.*
- **Frenchmen Street Music Clubs** *See Tour 2, page 155.*
- **N. Rampart Street and Tremé Music Clubs** *See Tour 4, page 189.*

| MUSIC STORES, ARCHIVES, AND MORE MUSIC VENUES | There is a lot of great music in New Orleans, and this is an eclectic list of other venues that didn't fit in above. There are several excellent places to buy music as well. |

- **UNO Jazz Program Performances** The University of New Orleans (UNO) has an outstanding music program, with a noted jazz studies component, Jazz Program Performances. For concerts, phone the UNO Box Office or the Music Department.
- **The Steamboat *Natchez*** This steamboat offers a dinner and jazz cruise nightly at 7 P.M.; reservations advised.
- **Michaul's Live Cajun Music Restaurant** If you're looking to see live Zydeco or Cajun music, try either Michaul's or Mulate's.
- **Mulate's Cajun Restaurant**

UNO Jazz Program Performances
Box office, 286-SHOW; Music Department, 286-6381

The Steamboat *Natchez*
Toulouse Street Wharf, behind Jax Brewery; 586-8777

Michaul's Live Cajun Music Restaurant
840 St. Charles Avenue, between Julia and St. Joseph; 522-5517

Mulate's Cajun Restaurant
201 Julia Street, at Convention Center Boulevard; 522-1492

Louisiana Music Factory
210 Decatur Street, one block from Canal Street; 586-1094

Magic Bus
527 Conti Street, between Decatur and Chartres; 522-0530

Record Ron's Stuff
239 Chartres Street, between Iberville and Bienville; 522-2239

Record Ron's Good & Plenty Records
1129 Decatur Street, between Ursulines and Gov. Nicholls; 524-9444

Tower Records / Tower Video
The Marketplace at the Jackson Brewery, 408–410 N. Peters Street; records 529-4411; video 581-2012; mail order 800-648-4844

Jazzology Records / GHB Foundation
61 French Market Place, between Gov. Nicholls and Barracks, second floor; 525-1776

Jim Russell Rare Records
1837 Magazine Street, near St. Mary; 522-2602

Werlein's for Music
*Main store in Metairie, 3750 Veterans Highway; 883-5077
French Quarter branch, 229 Decatur Street, between Iberville and Bienville; 883-5080*

International Vintage Guitars of New Orleans
1011 Magazine Street, near Howard Avenue, two blocks toward the river from Lee Circle, N.O., 70130; 524-4557

That's Trash That's Cool
3117 Magazine Street; 891-2665

William Ransom Hogan Jazz Archive
Tulane University, Howard-Tilton Memorial Library; 7001 Feret Street, N.O., 70118; 865-5688

Best Music Stores

- **Louisiana Music Factory** Specializes in Louisiana recordings both new and used; open daily 10 A.M. to 7 P.M.
- **Magic Bus** Has Louisiana (and other) records and CDs.
- **Record Ron's Stuff** Sells recordings, posters, patches, and more.
- **Record Ron's Good & Plenty Records** Sells jazz, soul, rock, blues, zydeco, R&B, gospel, big bands, sheet music, and lava lamps; good for traditional Mardi Gras music tapes and rare local recordings. Open daily 11 A.M. to 7 P.M.
- **Tower Records / Tower Video** Has the largest selection of recorded music in the city and carries traditional New Orleans and Louisiana music and new local music. Tower also sells and rents videos; if you're looking for a video about Mardi Gras, *Always for Pleasure* is probably the best. Open daily, 9 A.M. to midnight; free forty-five-minute parking with purchase; Ticketmaster outlet.
- **Jazzology Records / GHB Foundation** This self-proclaimed "world's largest and most important catalog of authentic jazz" is a treasurehouse of rare gems. Open Monday to Friday, noon to 6 P.M.; ring buzzer.
- **Jim Russell Rare Records** Open Monday to Saturday 10 A.M. to 7:30 P.M., Sunday 1 to 6 P.M.

Musical Instruments and Sheet Music

- **Werlein's for Music** There are two locations, one in Metairie and one in the French Quarter.
- **International Vintage Guitars of New Orleans** Used and vintage Fender, Gibson, Martin, and Rickenbacher guitars.
- **That's Trash That's Cool** Vintage acoustic and electric guitars and amps.

Jazz Archives

These archives are for serious researchers.

- **William Ransom Hogan Jazz Archive** Open Monday to Friday 8:30 A.M. to 5 P.M., Saturday 9 A.M. to 1 P.M.

- **Historic New Orleans Collection** Houses the William Russell Jazz Collection. Open Tuesday to Saturday 10 A.M. to 4:30 P.M.
- **Louisiana State Museum Jazz Archive** Open by appointment only.

THEATER, DANCE, CHOIRS, AND CONCERTS New Orleans has a very lively performing arts scene; this is just a short list of some of the best and most interesting venues, from the symphony and ballet to African American gospel choirs and several excellent theaters. For jazz venues, see "Traditional Jazz," page 58.

- **Christ Episcopal Cathedral Concerts** Fine occasional musical programs; see page 299.
- **Contemporary Arts Center** A rich and varied program of new theater, film, music, dance, and visual art; see page 265.
- **Gospel Soul Children** Sing at First Emanuel Baptist Church; noted for its programs of sacred music at 8:30 P.M. on the second Sunday of each month.
- **Holy Hill Gospel Singers** This group presents African American sacred music at St. Monica's Roman Catholic Church at the 10:30 A.M. mass on the first, third, and fourth Sunday of each month.
- **Le Petit Théâtre du Vieux Carré** The oldest continuously running community theater in the nation; see page 118.

Historic New Orleans Collection
410 Chartres Street;
598-7171

Louisiana State Museum Jazz Archive
Old Mint, 400 Esplanade Avenue, N.O., 70116;
568-6968

Christ Episcopal Cathedral Concerts
Near the Garden District in Christ Church Episcopal Cathedral, at 2919 St. Charles Avenue;
895-6602

Contemporary Arts Center
In the Arts District at 900 Camp Street, at St. Joseph; box office,
528-3800

Gospel Soul Children
At First Emanuel Baptist Church in Central City at 1829 Carondelet Street, at Felicity; 524-8891

Holy Hill Gospel Singers
At St. Monica's Roman Catholic Church in Mid-City at 2327 S. Galvez Street, at First; 821-9500

Le Petit Théâtre du Vieux Carré
In the French Quarter at 616 St. Peter Street, at Chartres; 522-2081

Louisiana Philharmonic Orchestra
In the Orpheum Theater at 129 University Place, near Canal, in the Central Business District; 305 Baronne Street, suite 600, N.O., 70112; 523-6530

Moses G. Hogan Chorale
P.O. Box 2402, N.O., 70176-2402

New Orleans Ballet
305 Baronne Street, suite 600, N.O., 70112; 522-0996

New Orleans Black Chorale
P.O. Box 51871, N.O., 70151; 899-1811

New Orleans Film and Video Society
108 Royal Street, suite 400, N.O., 70130; 523-3818

New Orleans Gay Men's Chorus
At the UNO Performing Arts Center at the Lakefront campus; P.O. Box 19365, N.O., 70179-9365; 245-8884

New Orleans Musica da Camera
1035 Eleonore Street, N.O., 70115; 897-1624

New Orleans Opera
At the Mahalia Jackson Theater for the Performing Arts in Armstrong Park; 305 Baronne Street, suite 600, N.O., 70112; 529-2278

Saenger Performing Arts Center
143 N. Rampart Street, at Canal; 524-2490

- **Louisiana Philharmonic Orchestra** Professional symphony orchestra founded by musicians and housed in the historic Orpheum Theater; see page 247.

- **Moses G. Hogan Chorale** African American choral music.

- **New Orleans Ballet** Professional classical ballet.

- **New Orleans Black Chorale** Sacred, classical, and spiritual music by African American composers.

- **New Orleans Film and Video Society** Presents an excellent fall film and video festival.

- **New Orleans Gay Men's Chorus** This chorus sings at the UNO Performing Arts Center at the Lakefront campus.

- **New Orleans Musica da Camera** Preclassical music programs.

- **New Orleans Opera** Annual productions at the Mahalia Jackson Theater for the Performing Arts in Armstrong Park.

- **Saenger Performing Arts Center** Stages traveling Broadway shows and other programs in a historic theater; see page 199.

- **St. Alphonsus Art and Culture Center** Occasional musical and other programs in a historic church in the Lower Garden District; see page 329.
- **St. Francis de Sales Roman Catholic Church** In Mid-City; the 9 A.M. Sunday mass incorporates black gospel music; see page 195.
- **St. Joan of Arc Roman Catholic Church** Gospel choir sings at the 9 A.M. Sunday mass.
- **Southern Repertory Theater** Excellent productions in Canal Place mall (third floor).
- **Trinity Artist Series** Fine musical programs most Sundays at 5 P.M.; near the Garden District in historic Trinity Episcopal Church.
- **Tulane University Theater and Dance** Varied programs in Dixon Hall on the Tulane campus uptown.
- **University of New Orleans Department of Music** Jazz and other musical programs at the Performing Arts Center on the Lakefront campus.
- **Zeitgeist** An alternative arts center for many media including film and video.

St. Alphonsus Art and Culture Center
In the Lower Garden District at 2045 Constance Street, N.O., 70130; 524-8116

St. Francis de Sales Roman Catholic Church
In Mid-City at 2203 Second Street, at Loyola; 895-7749

St. Joan of Arc Roman Catholic Church
8321 Burthe Street, at Cambronne; 866-7330

Southern Repertory Theater
In Canal Place mall (third floor) at Canal Street and N. Peters, N.O., 70130; 861-8163

Trinity Artist Series
Near the Garden District in Trinity Episcopal Church, 1329 Jackson Avenue, N.O., 70130; free; 522-0276

Tulane University Theater and Dance
In Dixon Hall on the Tulane campus uptown; box office, 865-5106

University of New Orleans Department of Music
At the Performing Arts Center on the Lakefront campus; 280-6381

Zeitgeist
Uptown at 2010 Magazine Street, N.O., 70130; 524-0064

Louisiana Superdome
*1300 Poydras Street,
mezzanine level, gate A;
open daily for tours from
10 A.M. to 4 P.M., except
during some events;
parking at Poydras Street,
gate A; $6 adults, $5
seniors, $4 children 5 to
10; 587-3810*

**New Orleans Museum of
Art / NOMA**
*In City Park at 1 Collins
Diboll Circle; 488-2631*

**Historic New Orleans
Collection**
*533 Royal Street, between
St. Louis and Toulouse;
523-4662*

**The Presbytere / Louisiana
State Museum**
*On Jackson Square;
568-6968*

K & B Sculpture Plaza
*At Lee Circle on St.
Charles Avenue.*

Amistad Research Center
*Tulane University
campus; 865-5535*

Newcomb Art Gallery
*Tulane University
campus; 865-5327*

Contemporary Arts Center
*900 Camp Street, at St.
Joseph; 523-1216*

**Ogden Museum of
Southern Art / University of
New Orleans**
*615 Howard Avenue, at
Camp; 539-9600*

LOUISIANA SUPERDOME

The gargantuan Louisiana Superdome is advertised as the largest column-free room in the world—large enough to fit the Houston Astrodome inside it. It can seat almost seventy-seven thousand spectators. The hovering dome is 680 feet in diameter, and its center is twenty-seven stories high. Design work on it began in 1967 and construction in 1971. It is the work of Curtis & Davis; Nolan, Norman & Nolan; Edward B. Silverstein & Associates, with Sverdrup & Parcel, engineers. The Dome has complete broadcasting facilities and eighty-five TV monitors for instant replay and close-ups. Under the building is parking for 5,000 cars and 250 buses. It hosts many sports and entertainment events, including the annual Sugar Bowl at New Year's. A remarkable thing about the Superdome is how close it is to the heart of the Central Business District and the French Quarter, even though it is cut off from them by a tundra of parking lots. The Dome sits near what was once the Girod Street Protestant cemetery behind the municipal Charity Hospital. In the age of expressways, the Dome occupies the perfect location: inside the L formed by I-10 and US 90 so that drivers see it continually and first-time visitors can't miss it. It's startling to see this space-age saucer hovering so near the CBD highrises. The huge Dome gives Old New Orleans a monumental brush with Modernity.

MUSEUMS

New Orleans has a rich mix of both major art and history museums and many intimate house museums, especially in the French Quarter. Combined with the active contemporary gallery scene along Julia Street, these treasure-houses offer revelatory glimpses into the city's soul.

Art Museums

- **New Orleans Museum of Art / NOMA** See page 177.
- **Historic New Orleans Collection** See page 123.
- **The Presbytere / Louisiana State Museum** See page 142.
- **K & B Sculpture Plaza** See page 267.

- **Amistad Research Center** See page 312.
- **Newcomb Art Gallery** On Tulane University campus; see page 312.
- **Contemporary Arts Center** In the Arts District; see page 265.
- **Ogden Museum of Southern Art / University of New Orleans** To open in 1999 in the Arts District; see page 266.
- **Walter Anderson Museum of Art** A gem in Ocean Springs, Mississippi, about one hundred miles east of New Orleans.

Historical and House Museums

- **Beauregard-Keyes House and Garden** See page 146.
- **The Cabildo / Louisiana State Museum** See page 116.
- **Confederate Museum / Louisiana Historical Association** In the Arts District; see page 265.
- **1850 House / Louisiana State Museum** See page 143.
- **Gallier House Museum / Women's Christian Exchange** See page 147.
- **Hermann-Grima Historic House / Women's Christian Exchange** See page 126.
- **Historic New Orleans Collection** See page 123.
- **Longue Vue House and Gardens** Near Metairie Cemetery; see page 180.
- **"Madame John's Legacy" / Louisiana State Museum** See page 144.
- **New Orleans Fire Department Museum & Educational Center** On the edge of the Garden District. Free; open Monday to Friday, 9 A.M. to 4 P.M. See page 286.
- **New Orleans Pharmacy Museum**
- **Pitot House Museum / Louisiana Landmarks Society** On Bayou St. John; see page 174.
- **Ursuline Convent / Archbishop Antoine Blanc Memorial** See page 145.
- **Williams Residence Museum / Historic New Orleans Collection** See page 123.

Walter Anderson Museum of Art
510 Washington Avenue, P. O. Box 328, Ocean Springs, MS 39566; 601-872-3164

Beauregard-Keyes House and Garden
1113 Chartres Street, between Ursulines and Gov. Nicholls; 523-7257

The Cabildo / Louisiana State Museum
On Jackson Square; 568-6968

Confederate Museum / Louisiana Historical Association
929 Camp Street, between Howard Avenue and St. Joseph; 523-4522

1850 House / Louisiana State Museum
523 St. Ann Street; 568-6972 or 568-6968

Gallier House Museum / Women's Christian Exchange
1132 Royal Street, between Ursulines and Gov. Nicholls; 523-6722

Hermann-Grima Historic House / Women's Christian Exchange
818-820 St. Louis Street, between Bourbon and Dauphin; 525-5661

Historic New Orleans Collection
533 Royal Street, between St. Louis and Toulouse; 523-4662

Longue Vue House and Gardens
7 Bamboo Road;
488-5488

"Madame John's Legacy" / Louisiana State Museum
623 Dumaine Street, between Chartres and Royal; 568-6968

New Orleans Fire Department Museum & Educational Center
1135 Washington Avenue, near Magazine; 896-4756

New Orleans Pharmacy Museum
514 Chartres Street, near St. Louis; small fee; open Tuesday through Sunday, 10 A.M. to 5 P.M.; 524-9077

Pitot House Museum / Louisiana Landmarks Society
1440 Moss Street; 482-0312

Ursuline Convent / Archbishop Antoine Blanc Memorial
1100 Chartres Street, between Ursulines and Gov. Nicholls; 529-2651

Williams Residence Museum / Historic New Orleans Collection
533 Royal Street, between St. Louis and Toulouse; 523-4662

New Orleans Auction Galleries, Inc.
In the Arts District, 801 Magazine Street, at Julia; 566-1849

AUCTION HOUSES

Auction houses are one of the most interesting experiences in New Orleans by far—they fuse tedium, knowledge, society, business, and personal rivalries in a public theater of competition and savvy. They also make for some fascinating shopping. Auctions are held frequently, usually on Saturday mornings; phone for schedules.

- **New Orleans Auction Galleries, Inc.** Excellent for decorative arts; see page 264.
- **Neal Auction Company** Excellent for suites of furniture and decorative arts; see page 326.
- **New Orleans Auction Arcade** Furniture and decorative arts.

HISTORIC SITES

Jackson Barracks Military Museum

This outstanding museum sits behind a display of weaponry on the left side of St. Claude Avenue and is separate from Jackson Barracks. It was the barracks' power magazine, and it was kept far behind the post, away from any river bombardment. Today this is one of the best military history museums in the region. The 1837 brick magazine is paired with a contemporary building, which spans the colonial period to Operation Desert Storm. There is also a good gift and book shop. The collection of tanks, guns, and fighter planes out front is a beautifully maintained garden of death and a monument to America's military expenditures.

Jackson Barracks

Located on the east bank of the Mississippi River just inside the New Orleans city limits, this post is a tight quadrangle of fourteen 1830s two-story red-brick buildings with white columns and shady galleries. It is one of the finest groups of military buildings of its type in the nation. While the French and Spanish stationed their troops in the heart of the city when they occupied it, the American government, in 1834–35, chose to station its troops farther away from the city's Latin population and corrupting temptations. The American governor, however, did not want the troops to be too far away, in case they needed to quell any slave uprisings. Thus the U.S. Army's New Orleans Barracks were erected at the city's eastern limits. The plans for the 300-by-900-foot walled parallelogram, with a parade ground at its center and four round towers at its corners, were drawn by Lt. Frederick Wilkinson, a West Point graduate. A sally port originally faced the river and led to a wharf that served the downriver defensive forts. Four two-story officers' quarters with stuccoed brick columns and deep verandahs made a defensible citadel for the officers at the heart of the post. The tapered shape of their columns and pilasters is powerfully convincing. Between this complex and the river is the central parade ground, flanked by more colonnaded housing. Barracks for the troops occupied separate structures. A notable feature of the complex is the deep, brick-lined French drainage ditches that surround the buildings. They are a microcosm of the vast and costly system of drainage canals that make this watery fringe of Louisiana habitable.

These barracks opened in time to house troops moving through Louisiana during the 1836 war on the Seminoles in Florida. Uprooted Seminoles passed through the post's grounds on their way to exile on Oklahoma reservations. During the Mexican War, many of the troops in Louisiana planter and Brigadier General Zachary Taylor's Army of Observation stopped here briefly before boarding ships for Texas and Mexico. The barracks were deactivated in 1853 but reactivated two years later as sectional tensions approached the breaking point. During the 1850s,

Neal Auction Company
Uptown, 4038 Magazine Street, at Marengo; 899-5329

New Orleans Auction Arcade
Uptown, 1330 St. Charles Avenue, at Thalia; 586-8733

Jackson Barracks Military Museum
6400 St. Claude Avenue; open Monday to Friday 7:30 A.M. to 4 P.M.; also open on the first weekend of every month from 9 A.M. to 4 P.M.; free; 278-6242

Jackson Barracks
6400 St. Claude Avenue; this post is always open; 271-6262

Chalmette Battlefield National Historical Park and Monument

Off US 46 about six miles from New Orleans on the East Bank. Mailing address: 365 Canal Street, suite 3080, N.O., 70130-1142; open daily 8 A.M. to 5 P.M.; free; 589-4430

several young army officers who were to achieve fame later were stationed here, including Robert E. Lee, Ulysses S. Grant, P. G. T. Beauregard, and George B. McClellan. In 1861 Louisiana Governor Thomas O. Moore seized the barracks from its caretaker, but the post did not play a major role in the rebellion, and federal troops reoccupied it in April 1862. In 1912 the levee broke, and the front portion of the quadrangle, including the commandant's quarters and two of the four round corner towers, was demolished for a new levee built slightly inland. Today the Adjutant General of the Military Department of the State of Louisiana has his headquarters on this post, and these fine buildings provide housing for the officers of the Louisiana National Guard. One of the best contemporary and site-sympathetic buildings in Louisiana is the Headquarters State Area Command Armory facing the running track as you enter or leave the post. This large, three-story, red-brick-and-limestone-faced building with two columns flanking its entrance was completed in 1993, and it houses the National Guard's Emergency Operations Center.

To get there, drive back across St. Claude Avenue and down Avenue E past the now closed Orleans Parish minimum security jail. Cross Dauphine Street and make an immediate left onto Lee Street to enter the post. Motor slowly, making the natural loop of Guerre Circle around the historic buildings and the parade ground. There is visitor parking next to the Post Exchange, Building 51.

Chalmette Battlefield National Historical Park and Monument

The causes of the War of 1812 between the United States and Great Britain have long been a field of contention among historians. Most Americans, if they know anything about this conflict, identify it with the British impressment of American seamen, the bombardment of Baltimore's Fort McHenry and the writing of Francis Scott Key's "Star Spangled Banner," and the British torching of the public buildings in Washington, D.C. It was the United States, spurred on by Henry Clay and the "War Hawks" in Congress, that first declared war on the British Goliath and then invaded Canada, where the Americans burned York, the capital of Upper Canada. After the exile of Napoleon in 1814, the British determined on a punitive campaign against their ex-colonies and dispatched an expeditionary force under Major General Sir Edward Michael Pakenham to capture New Orleans. The campaign lasted a little over three weeks.

The British landed east of the city in St. Bernard Parish on December 23, 1814, and were immediately attacked by the troops and militia assembled under Major General Andrew Jackson (including pirate Jean Lafitte's Baratarians). After this first night skirmish, Jackson fell back about a mile and a half to this sugar plantation on the plains of Chalmette, the narrowest piece of land between the river and the impassable cypress swamp that Jackson could defend, about six miles downriver from New Orleans. A breastwork was thrown up here and batteries placed along it. On the cold, wet morning of January 8, 1815, the red-coats attacked and were decisively defeated. In *Struggle for the Gulf Borderlands* (Frank Lawrence Owsley, Jr., 1981), an unidentified Kentucky militiaman under General Adair described the scene after the battle:

> When the smoke had cleared away and we could obtain a fair view of the field, it looked, at the first glance, like a sea of blood. It was not blood itself which gave it this appearance but the red coats in which the British soldiers were dressed.
>
> . . . [I]ndividuals could be seen in every possible attitude. Some laying quite dead, others mortally wounded, pitching and tumbling about in the agonies of death. . . . [S]ome had their heads shot off, some their legs, some their arms. Some were laughing, some crying, some groaning, and some screaming. There was every variety of sight and sound.

The British casualties exceeded two thousand men; the Americans reported only thirteen killed or wounded. As it turned out, the

Creole Queen
524-0814

bloody contest was fought *after* the British and American governments had already come to terms, but the slow communications in those days prevented the news from reaching distant Louisiana in time. The Battle of New Orleans made Andrew Jackson a war hero, and in 1829, Old Hickory was elected the seventh president of the United States and served in that office until 1837. Under his administration, the Native Americans were forcibly removed from the Deep South and exiled to tribal reservations in what later became Oklahoma.

In 1855 the State of Louisiana began the construction of a 155-foot-tall obelisk here, but work was halted by the Civil War. In 1908, the War Department completed a 110-foot truncated version of the obelisk. The doorways at the base of the monument are in the Egyptian Revival style. The other edifice on the historic battleground is the Malus-Beauregard Villa, built in 1833 or 1834, a beautiful example of Louisiana architecture. Only one room deep, with three rooms on the first floor and another three rooms on the second floor, the country villa was built so that river breezes could sweep right through it. A flyer available at the visitor center describes the changes that this building has undergone. The visitor center bookstore has a fine selection of history books, including some hard-to-find books on the military history of the Gulf Coast.

If you'd like to combine your visit to the Chalmette Battlefield with a leisurely boat ride down the river, take a two-and-a-half-hour cruise on the **Creole Queen**, a replica of a nineteenth-century paddlewheeler. Each cruise passes the busy docks of the Port of New Orleans and includes a walking tour of the battlefield and the Beauregard Villa. The *Creole Queen* departs daily from the Canal Street dock at 10:30 A.M. and 2 and 8 P.M.; boarding begins a half hour before departure at the Poydras Street Wharf. Refreshments are available on the boat but are not included in the cost of the tour; $13 for adults, $6 for children from three to twelve (see also page 32).

Chalmette National Cemetery

Bordering the battlefield downriver, with its own entrance from the highway, is the sliver-shaped Chalmette National Cemetery. It was established in May 1864 for the Union troops who died in Louisiana during the Civil War, and there are some twelve thousand northern soldiers buried here, half of them unknown.

Fort Jackson

Fort Jackson on the West Bank and Fort St. Philip on the East Bank were placed here because sailing ships coming up the Mississippi River must tack to turn Placquemines Bend and are then suddenly sailing against the strong current. The French erected Fort Bourbon, an earth-and-timber breastworks, near this site in 1750. The Spanish built Fort St. Philip across the river on the East Bank in 1792. In 1815, during the War of 1812, American-manned Fort St. Philip, in an unheralded defense, repulsed the British fleet after a nine-day bombardment. This prevented the reinforcement of General Pakenham's land forces gathering to attack New Orleans. The United States began clearing the Fort Bourbon site for a new fortification in 1822 using hired laborers and army convicts. This is the extremity of the alluvial Mississippi Delta, and land and water merge here in a spongy filigree of swampy vegetation alive with insects and snakes. Floods, hurricanes, and almost annual outbreaks of yellow fever slowed construction on this exceedingly difficult site, and it took almost a decade to complete the red-brick fort sunk behind its protective man-made embankment. Today, a moat filled with green water partially surrounds the massive ruin. Trees have sprouted inside the ramparts, creating a screen of tall trees around the heart of the fort where the citadel once stood. The ramparts, cracked bastions, and deep brick tunnels make memorable spaces for children to explore.

The Independent Commonwealth of Louisiana seized the virtually unmanned fort from its army caretakers on January 8, 1861. The Confederate government then brought guns from other forts and from the Norfolk Navy Yard to strengthen the key southern fort's armament. The Union Navy began

Chalmette National Cemetery
Off US 46 about six miles from New Orleans on the East Bank, immediately downriver from the battlefield; open daily 8 A.M. to 5 P.M.; 589-4428

Fort Jackson
Off US 23 about sixty-six miles from New Orleans on the West Bank; look for the gate on the left side of US 23 near the stadium lighting; open Monday to Friday 10 A.M. to 4 P.M., Saturday and Sunday 9 A.M. to 5 P.M.; free; 657-7083

bombarding the fort on April 15, 1862, and Flag Officer David Farragut's invading fleet passed by the two forts early on the morning of April 24. When federal forces occupied New Orleans on April 25, the Confederate soldiers at Fort Jackson mutinied and the fort surrendered on April 28. Changes in military technology mercifully made the fever-ridden forts obsolete, and the power of the U.S. Navy in the Gulf of Mexico made land forts redundant. After 1871 only a caretaker occupied this isolated outpost. Mud filled its casements and underbrush sprang up on its walls. In 1927, photographer H. J. Harvey bought the fort and eventually donated it to Placquemines Parish. Judge Leander H. Perez, the parish's all-powerful boss, developed it as a parish historical park. Perez built a legendary fiefdom in this Deep South backwater, with near-total economic and political control of his barony, and was one of the South's arch-segregationists in the 1950s.

A concrete emplacement with flags flying from it stands near the parking area in front of the fort, and there is a fine view across the river from here. A marker points out the direction to Pointe du Mardi Gras, the oldest European place name in the Mississippi valley. That was where the French, under Pierre Le Moyne, Sieur d'Iberville, first sighted land on Tuesday, March 3, 1699. There is a freshwater lake with an embankment around it adjacent to the fort. On its edge rises the De La Salle Monument, erected by Placquemines Parish in 1967. This monument commemorates the fact that on April 9, 1682, La Salle erected a marker three leagues above the mouth of the Missisippi River and claimed and named the territory for Louis XIV. La Salle was searching for a way that French fur traders could export furs from the Illinois country without having to negotiate the difficult portages to Montreal.

The visitor center has informative photocopied handouts; also, the Placquemines Parish Orange Festival is held here.

BOOKS AND LITERATURE

Lloyd Vogt's *New Orleans Houses: A House-Watcher's Guide* (1989) is a useful primer on local house types. John Chase's *Frenchmen, Desire, Good Children: And Other Streets of New Orleans* (1949) is highly recommended. The multivolume series on *New Orleans Architecture* by the Friends of the Cabildo is exhaustive; these inventories cover much of the historic city, though not the French Quarter. The best French Quarter book is architect Malcolm Heard's *French Quarter Manual* (1977). Charlotte Seidenberg's *New Orleans Gardens* (1995) is excellent. *New Orleans: Elegance and Decadence* (1993), by photographer Richard Sexton and myself, celebrates what is distinctive about New Orleans' interiors and gardens. The best guidebook to the Crescent City's rich environs is Shelley N. C. Holl's *Louisiana Dayride: 52 Short Trips from New Orleans* (1995).

New Orleans attracts writers, and writers in turn have shaped New Orleans' sense of self. The traveler who wishes to acquaint him- or herself with this city's literary psyche should read Tennessee Williams' *A Streetcar Named Desire* (1947). John Kennedy Toole's *A Confederacy of Dunces* (1980) is a comedic masterpiece and presents an unforgettable picture of lower-middle-class New Orleanians. Kate Chopin's *The Awakening* (1899) has been discovered by feminist critics. Today, James Sallis's detective novels feature an African American main character. Anne Rice fans will want Joy Dickson's *Haunted City: An Unauthorized Guide to the Magical, Magnificent New Orleans of Anne Rice* (1995), which is better on Rice than on the city, but that is as it should be.

The (non-New Orleanian) nineteenth-century writer who gave voice to the Old Soul of the Crescent City was Lafcadio Hearn, who lived and wrote here between 1877 and 1887. His letters and occasional pieces are far more insightful than the better-known works of George Washington Cable. (Japanese visitors often have a special interest in the **Hearn archive** at Tulane University's Howard-Tilton Memorial Library.)

Hearn archive
Tulane University campus; 865-5685

The best general book on local music is Al Rose and Edmund Souchon's *New Orleans Jazz: A Family Album* (1984), a copiously illustrated encyclopedia of local music and musicians. Al Rose's *Storyville, New Orleans* (1974) is a good history of the tolerated red-light district that once flourished here. *Bellocq: Photographs from Storyville, the Red-Light District of New Orleans* (1996), with an introduction by Susan Sontag and interviews edited by John Szarkowski, is both joyous and haunting. Glancing insights on the contemporary city can be found in Carol Flake's *New Orleans: Behind the Masks of America's Most Exotic City* (1994), and in S. Frederick Starr's *New Orleans Unmasqued* (1985). The captivating *Uptown/Downtown: Growing Up in New Orleans* (1986) by Elsie Martinez and Margaret LeCorgne is a duet of chapters on everyday life in the city in the 1930s and 1940s as seen from both sides of Canal Street. By far the best contemporary history of *all* the people of the city is *Creole New Orleans: Race and Americanization* (1992), edited by Arnold R. Hirsch and Joseph Logsdon, which covers the full sweep of this city's peculiarly complex society. *White by Definition: Social Classification in Creole Louisiana* (1986) by Virginia R. Dominguez is fascinating, if technical. *Africans in Colonial Louisiana: The Development of Afro-Creole Culture in the Eighteenth Century* (1992) by Gwendolyn Midlo Hall is fundamental.

Cookbooks

The number of New Orleans cookbooks is bewildering. The *Dooky Chase Cookbook* (1990) by Leah Chase is real New Orleans cookery. The Junior League of New Orleans publishes excellent cookbooks, available in good book shops. The *Picayune Creole Cook Book,* a paperback reprint of the 1901 edition, is the great classic of Louisiana French cooking; it includes such gems as *Gâteau de Noces Créole a l'Ancienne*—old-fashioned Creole wedding cake. Lafcadio Hearn's *Creole Cook Book,* a handsome hardbound republication of Hearn's 1885 cookbook with Creole proverbs, is amusing: *Çà qui dourmi napas pensé manze*—"When one sleeps, one doesn't think about eating."

Select Bookstores

In the French Quarter ask for the list of the Antiquarian Bookshops of New Orleans.

FRENCH QUARTER AND FAUBOURG MARIGNY

- **Faulkner House Books** A fine shop specializing in Southern literature, especially Faulkner's works and contemporary novels.
- **Librairie Books** A good used book store.
- **Arcadian Books** The best place for books on French Louisiana and Acadiana.
- **The Centuries Antique Prints and Maps**
- **Bookstar** The best book superstore in the city, also has magazines.
- **Beckham's Bookshop** Two locations; two large general interest bookshops.
- **Crescent City Books** An excellent used book shop for art books and history.
- **Faubourg Marigny Bookstore** Gay, lesbian, and feminist literature and images.

CENTRAL BUSINESS DISTRICT

- **De Ville Books and Prints** An excellent general interest bookshop with local titles; two locations.
- **Afro-American Book Stop** African American books.

Faulkner House Books
624 Pirate's Alley;
524-2940, fax 525-2245

Librairie Books
823 Chartres Street,
between St. Ann and
Dumaine; 525-4837

Arcadian Books
714 Orleans Street,
between Chartres and
Royal; 523-4138

**The Centuries Antique
Prints and Maps**
517 St. Louis Street,
between Chartres and
Decatur; 568-9491

Bookstar
414 N. Peters Street,
between Conti and St.
Louis; 523-6411

Beckham's Bookshop
228 Decatur Street,
between Iberville and
Bienville; 522-9875

Crescent City Books
204 Chartres Street,
between Iberville and
Bienville; 524-4997

**Faubourg Marigny
Bookstore**
600 Frenchmen Street, at
Chartres; 943-9875

De Ville Books and Prints
322 Carondelet Street,
near Poydras, 525-1846;
and on the riverfront at
Riverwalk Mall,
595-8916

Afro-American Book Stop
New Orleans Centre,
second floor near Macy's;
588-1474

Garden District Book Shop
The Rink at 2727 Prytania Street, at Washington Avenue; 895-2266

George Herget Books
3109 Magazine Street, between Eighth and Harmony; 891-5595

Beaucoup Books
5414 Magazine Street, above Jefferson Avenue; 895-2663, 800-543-4114

Tulane University Bookstore
Tulane campus in the University Center; 865-5913

Maple Street Book Shop
7523 Maple Street, between Cherokee and Hilary; 866-4916

Uptown Square Book Shop
200 Broadway, in Uptown Square shopping center; 865-8310

Little Professor Book Center
1000 S. Carrollton Avenue, at Freret; 866-5628 or 866-7646

Community Book Center and Gallery
217 N. Broad Street, between Bienville and Iberville; 822-2665

UPTOWN

- **Garden District Book Shop** Where signed copies of Anne Rice's books are first available; local interest titles.
- **George Herget Books** An excellent used book shop.
- **Beaucoup Books** An excellent bookshop; good for guides, local interest books, and foreign languages.
- **Tulane University Bookstore** Books on New Orleans architecture.
- **Maple Street Book Shop** A shotgun cottage full of fine books; next door is their excellent children's bookshop.
- **Uptown Square Book Shop** Good for local interest books.
- **Little Professor Book Center** Good for regional titles.
- **Community Book Center and Gallery** African American titles.

LITERARY EVENTS

- **Tennessee Williams / New Orleans Literary Festival** *The city's annual literary festival; University of New Orleans Metro College, N.O., 70148; 286-6680.*
- **The Pirate's Alley Faulkner Society, Inc.** *Stages occasional events including the New Orleans Writers Conference; contact 632 Pirate's Alley, N.O., 70116-3254; 277-3835.*

Special Interests

New Orleans Spring Fiesta
*826 St. Ann Street,
N.O., 70116; 581-1367*

**Preservation Resource
Center**
*604 Julia Street, at
Magazine, N.O., 70130;
581-7032*

**New Orleans Garden
Society**
*3914 Prytania Street,
N.O., 70115; 899-1789*

**Patio Planters French
Quarter Tours**
*P.O. Box 72074, N.O.,
70172; 529-1481*

**Longue Vue House and
Garden Tours**
488-5488

**New Orleans Museum of
Art Home and Art Tours**
488-2631, ext. 316

**Junior League Decorator
Showhouse**
*4319 Carondelet Street,
N.O., 70115; 891-5845*

**Barataria Preserve / Jean
Lafitte National Historical
Park and Preserve**
*Off Highway 45 on the
West Bank, near Crown
Point about twenty
minutes west of New
Orleans; Visitor Center
open daily 9 A.M. to 5
P.M.; free; 589-2330;
see map with Tour 12,
page 351*

**GARDEN CLUB
AND
HOUSE TOURS**

Occasional noncommercial house and garden tours are the best way to see the private side of New Orleans. These organizations can tell you if there will be a neighborhood house or garden tour during your visit.

- **New Orleans Spring Fiesta** Spring Fiesta week begins on the Friday after Easter Sunday. Tours are conducted in the French Quarter, Garden District, Uptown, and Audubon Park / University neighborhoods, and at plantation houses along the Mississippi River.

- **Preservation Resource Center** The PRC Holiday Home Tour in mid-December is excellent, see page 263.

- **New Orleans Garden Society**

- **Patio Planters French Quarter Tours** Each fall visitors can experience some of the hidden gardens of the French Quarter.

- **Longue Vue House and Garden Tours** Occasionally Longue Vue hosts tours of private gardens, see page 180.

- **New Orleans Museum of Art Home and Art Tours** Occasionally NOMA sponsors tours of art-filled homes.

- **Junior League Decorator Showhouse** Every three years the Junior League conducts this fundraiser.

**SOME SWAMPS
AND GARDENS**

Here is a short list of some of the best places to experience nature both wild and cultivated in and around New Orleans. South Louisiana's moss-hung cypress swamps with their luxurious semitropical plants, elegant white egrets, and primeval alligators are mystic worlds.

Barataria Preserve / Jean Lafitte National Historical Park and Preserve

Facing Lake Salvador, this twenty-thousand-acre national park preserves a choice slice of freshwater marsh, cypress swamp, and natural levees with hardwood forests. There are eight miles of boardwalk and trails here and over twenty miles of waterways (canoes can be rented just outside the park). A remarkable year-round sight here is the beautiful palmetto forests flourishing under the canopy of taller trees. In mid-April the Louisiana iris blooms here like blue mists in the cypress swamps, an unforgettable sight.

Before the coming of the Europeans, native peoples lived here, and their mounds and shell middens still pepper the marshy land. Early in the eighteenth century, the French opened up these virgin cypress forests for lumbering. A hard country to penetrate—never mind police—this tangle of swamps and bayous attracted fishermen, trappers, and smugglers; the French nicknamed it "Barataria," meaning fraudulence or illegality. The most famous smugglers were Bordeaux-born Jean and Pierre Lafitte, who organized a gang in 1808 and set up their headquarters at Grand Terre. They smuggled slaves as well as goods. The Lafittes volunteered to serve under Andrew Jackson and fought in the Battle of New Orleans in 1815. In 1820, Jean Lafitte set sail from Galveston, Texas, for South America and disappeared from history. The French-speaking Acadians who settled here engaged in marginal rice and sugar cane cultivation. *Isleños,* immigrants from the Canary Islands, settled here in the 1770s. Later, Chinese and Filipino workers came to labor in the shrimp drying industry. Logging lasted here into the twentieth century, as did moss gathering for mattresses and furniture. Shrimping, crabbing, and oyster harvesting continue here today.

Just outside the park is **Restaurant des Familles;** it serves local seafood and Cajun cooking in a setting of live oaks overlooking Bayou des Familles.

Near New Orleans

- **Honey Island Swamp / Pearl River Wildlife Management Area** This is the most interesting swamp to visit; many commercial tours will take you there.
- **The Crosby Arboretum** This superb regional arboretum displays the native flora of the Pearl River drainage basin shared by Louisiana and Mississippi.
- **Zemurray Gardens** Still a private estate, the Zemurray Gardens are opened to the public during the six weeks of spring, which

Restaurant des Familles
Hwy 45 and Hwy 3134, next to Bayou Barn; 689-7834

Honey Island Swamp / Pearl River Wildlife Management Area
Brochures on swamp tours are available at the Visitor Information Center, 529 St. Ann Street, across from Jackson Square; see page 13

The Crosby Arboretum
1986 Ridge Road, Picayune, MS 39466; open Tuesday to Saturday 10 A.M. to 5 P.M., Sunday 2 to 5 P.M.; fee; 601-799-2311

Zemurray Gardens
On Hwy 40, about ten miles north of Hammond; mailing address: Route 1, P.O. Box 201, Loranger, LA 70446; fee; 878-6731

Afton Villa Gardens
On Hwy 61, four miles north of St. Francisville; mailing address: P.O. Box 993, St. Francisville, LA 70775; open March 1 to July 1 and October 1 to December 1; open daily 9 A.M. to 4:30 P.M.; fee; 635-6330

Danneel Park
Uptown on St. Charles Avenue

Longue Vue House and Gardens
7 Bamboo Road; 488-5488

Storyland and Carousel in City Park
At the head of Esplanade Avenue; open Saturday and Sunday 10 A.M. to 4:30 P.M.; $1.50

Louisiana Children's Museum
420 Julia Street, at Constance; open Tuesday to Saturday 9:30 A.M. to 5:30 P.M., Sunday noon to 5:30 P.M.; closed holidays; 523-1357

Audubon Zoological Gardens
6500 Magazine Street; open daily 9:30 A.M. to 5 P.M., until 6 P.M. in the winter; $8 adults, $4 children from two to twelve; $4 seniors; under two free; 581-4629

Audubon Zoo Shuttle Bus
On St. Charles Avenue, at the main entrance to Audubon Park across from Tulane University; operates every fifteen minutes daily 9:30 A.M. to 5 P.M.; free

include the peak of the spring azalea season. The azaleas are at their best in March or April.

- **Afton Villa Gardens** A fire destroyed the Gothic Revival antebellum mansion on this magnificent property. In 1972 its basement ruins were transformed by Genevieve Trimble into a garden with twenty acres of lawns, ponds, and moss-draped live oaks. It is at its peak in the spring with displays of bulbs and azaleas, some of which date from the 1850s.

SUGGESTIONS FOR FAMILIES

New Orleans is essentially an adult destination, though the city has made efforts to provide facilities attractive to families with children and teenagers.

- **Danneel Park** This park is ideal for families with toddlers; see page 306.
- **Longue Vue House and Gardens** Has a new Discovery Garden for children. See page 180.
- **Storyland and Carousel in City Park** This playground makes famous nursery rhymes three-dimensional; the carousel nearby is delightful. See page 179.
- **Louisiana Children's Museum** In the Arts District; see page 265.
- **Audubon Zoological Gardens** The Audubon Zoo has something for everyone and is New Orleans' premier attraction for families with children. Originally the Mertz Memorial Zoo, it opened in 1938 with buildings erected by the WPA. Redesigned in the 1980s, the animals are now displayed by continents in recreated habitats. The Louisiana swamp has alligators and other local fauna; the new butterfly pavilion is delightful. Parts of the handsome grounds are distinguished by ancient live oaks that cast welcome shade. Ponds and fountains and the refreshing sound of gushing water everywhere make the zoo a virtual water garden. A free **Audubon Zoo Shuttle Bus** will take you the one mile from the Audubon Park entrance on St. Charles Avenue to the zoo entrance on Magazine Street. See page 32 for the *John James Audubon* cruise.
- **Aquarium of the Americas** See page 217.

- **Fort Jackson** A car trip down the river to Fort Jackson makes a great trip for active youngsters who want to run around and play; see page 75.

Especially for Teenagers

Tower Records near Jax Brewery and the franchise restaurant-music clubs including **The House of Blues, The Hard Rock Cafe,** and **Planet Hollywood** attract teenagers. Decatur Street from St. Philip to Barracks Streets is the young people's shopping strip for clothing and accessories with which to continue the war between the generations.

Tower Records
408 N. Peters Street, near Conti; 529-4411

The House of Blues
227 Decatur Street, near Iberville; 529-2583, concert line 529-1421

The Hard Rock Cafe
418 N. Peters Street, between Conti and St. Louis; 529-5617

Planet Hollywood
620 Decatur Street, at St. Peter; 522-7826

COOKING
NEW ORLEANS
STYLE

Cooking Demonstrations for Visitors

- **New Orleans School of Cooking** *In the French Quarter in Jax's Brewery, 620 Decatur Street at St. Peter, classes Monday through Saturday, 10 A.M. to 12:30 P.M. ; 525-2665.*
- **Cookin' Cajun Cooking School** *In the Riverwalk mall at the foot of Poydras Street, Store #116; classes daily 11 A.M. to 1 P.M.; 586-8832.*
- **Hermann-Grima House Museum** *820 St. Louis Street, between Bourbon and Dauphine; Creole cooking demonstrations on Thursdays from October through May; closed legal holidays; see page 126; 525-5661*

Condiments

There are many packaged Creole seasoning mixes and hot pepper sauces. Tabasco sauce is a proud Louisiana product, as is Crystal's Louisiana Hot Sauce. Check out the right-hand wall as you enter the French Quarter A&P at 701 Royal Street, corner of St. Peter, open twenty-four hours. Many local cooks use either Zatarain's or Rex spices and condiments, and large racks of both can be found in local supermarkets. Zatarain's red or white bean spice mix and Community brand's New Orleans blend coffee with chicory make flavorful souvenirs or gifts.

AFRICAN AMERICAN NEW ORLEANS

New Orleans was a major port of entry for West African and Caribbean slaves in the French and Spanish colonial periods. After 1808, when the importation of slaves was shut off due to one of the sectional compromises behind the ratification of the Constitution, New Orleans became the largest domestic slave market in the United States. Slaves from soil-exhausted Virginia and South Carolina were moved west to be sold in New Orleans to planters opening up virgin land in Mississippi, Louisiana, and East Texas. Other slaves were "sold down the river" from Kentucky and the Upper South (that is part of the story in *Uncle Tom's Cabin*). Clusters of slave auctioneers and their "pens" existed in the French Quarter, near Esplanade and Chartres, and in the American sector near the St. Charles Hotel and along Magazine and Gravier Streets. New Orleans, like Venice, grew rich from selling human souls.

Before the Civil War and Emancipation, New Orleans evolved a complex and unusual (for the United States) three-caste Caribbean society with the largest and most cultivated population of free men and women of color in North America. A few of these French-speaking free people of color themselves owned slaves; some even hired Irish immigrant assistants. The writers, teachers, lawyers, and journalists among them were consistent voices for equality in nineteenth-century New Orleans. Intellectual leaders such as newspaper publisher Rodolphe Desdunes (active from the 1880s to 1910) never accepted the idea of racial inferiority and political subjugation. After Louisiana abolished slavery in 1864, men of mixed African and white blood emerged as political leaders in the Reconstruction Louisiana of the 1870s.

The enduring pillars of black New Orleans have been her many small churches, her independent schools, and her press. From this network emerged the early leaders of the Civil Rights Movement in the 1950s and 1960s. New Orleans has been a black majority city since 1980, and the city's current and most recent mayors have been African Americans. Today, many African

Americans work in municipal and other public agencies. The greatest community achievement of African American New Orleans is the city's constellation of high-quality Roman Catholic, Protestant, and secular primary and secondary schools, colleges, and universities. St. Augustine High School occupies a special place in black New Orleans. Architecturally, **Dillard University,** with its 1935 Georgian Revival campus, is outstanding, and visitors may wish to make a special trip to see it. Roman Catholic Xavier University in Mid-City is another noted institution, as is public Southern University at New Orleans near the lake, which has a fine collection of African art on view in its library. Especially important is the **Amistad Research Center,** founded in 1966 by the American Missionary Association. This is one of the preeminent archives of African American history and of the Civil Rights Movement. There is a small art gallery with changing exhibits attached to this research library. Inquire about Amistad programs and talks.

Resources

- **Greater New Orleans Black Tourism Network** This organization, part of the Greater New Orleans Tourist & Convention Bureau, promotes African American tourism in New Orleans. Write for information and for their Greater New Orleans Black Tourism Center Official Visitor's Guide. They also publish a Visitor's Guide Map.
- *The Fabric of Our Culture: A Pictorial Directory of Louisiana's African-American Attractions* This is published by the Louisiana Office of Tourism.
- *New Orleans Tribune* A weekly African American newspaper.
- *The Louisiana Weekly* A general interest newspaper and one of the oldest black papers in the nation.
- **WYLD 98.5 FM-AM 940** The radio station with the largest following among black New Orleanians.

Art Galleries

- **Stella Jones Gallery** An excellent new gallery devoted to African American art, see page 240.

Dillard University
In Gentilly at 2600 Gentilly Boulevard;
283-8822

Amistad Research Center
Uptown at 6823 St. Charles Avenue, in Tilton Hall, Tulane University campus; open Monday to Friday 8:30 A.M. to 5 P.M., Saturday 1 to 5 P.M.;
865-5535

Greater New Orleans Black Tourism Network
Official Visitor's Guide available at the Superdome at 1520 Sugar Bowl Drive, N.O., 70112; 523-5652, 800-725-5652, fax 522-0785. Visitor's Guide Map available from 1615 St. Philip Street, N.O., 70116; 595-8631

Our Culture Abounds
P.O. Box 94291, Dept. 5701, Baton Rouge, LA 70804-9291; free

New Orleans Tribune
2335 Esplanade Avenue, N.O., 70119; 945-0772

The Louisiana Weekly
1001 Howard Avenue, N.O., 70113; 524-5563

WYLD 98.5 FM-AM 940
827-6000

Stella Jones Gallery
First NBC Center, 201 St. Charles Street; 568-9050

YA/YA Gallery
628 Baronne Street, near Girod; 529-3306

Visual Jazz Art Gallery
In Faubourg Marigny at 2337 St. Claude Avenue, at Spain; 949-9822

The Neighborhood Gallery
In Mid-City in the Community Book Center at 219 N. Broad Street, at Iberville; 822-2665

Davis Gallery
Uptown at 3964 Magazine Street, at Constantinople; 897-0780

New Zion Baptist Church
In Central City at 2319 Third Street, at Lasalle; Sunday worship at 10:55 A.M.; 891-4283

First United Baptist Church
In Central City at 131 S. Jefferson Davis Parkway, at Cleveland; Sunday worship at 10:45 A.M.; 488-2657

St. Francis de Sales Roman Catholic Church
In Central City at 2203 Second Street, at Loyola; Sunday mass at 7 and 9 A.M.; 895-7749

St. Augustine's Roman Catholic Church
In Tremé at St. Claude Avenue and Gov. Nicholls; Sunday mass at 9 A.M.; 525-5934

- **YA/YA Gallery** Young Artists/Young Aspirations is a nonprofit organization that helps young African American artists learn their art and also the business side of art; whimsically painted recycled furniture is a specialty here.
- **Visual Jazz Art Gallery** Artist Richard C. Thomas's vibrant paintings and prints are available here.
- **The Neighborhood Gallery** A multicultural base for many visual, performance, literary, and other creative activities; phone for programs.
- **Davis Gallery** A fine selection of African tribal art.

Some Historic Black Churches in New Orleans

There are more than ten pages of churches listed in the New Orleans Yellow Pages. For the black community in particular, among both Catholics and Protestants, vibrant churches are the key institutions in the community. This sampling only introduces the vast network of building-block congregations in black New Orleans. All Congregations Together is a multicongregational, multiracial alliance of New Orleans' more active churches.

- **New Zion Baptist Church** This church was pastored for forty-three years by Reverend A. L. Davis, who also became the first black city councillor in this century. This is also the birthplace of the Southern Christian Leadership Conference, which was founded here on February 14, 1956. The first president of the SCLC was Dr. Martin Luther King, Jr.
- **First United Baptist Church** This recent merger of a white and a black Southern Baptist congregation in a declining part of the city is a harbinger of things to come among Southern Baptists. The traditional Baptist services include spirited gospel music.
- **St. Francis de Sales Roman Catholic Church** This congregation was the first to form an African American Catholic Gospel Choir in the United States. White Catholics will find these services warm and alive; see page 195.
- **St. Augustine's Roman Catholic Church** See page 203.

Secular Sunday Morning Gospel Music Programs

Many come here to experience jazz, but only a few seek out New Orleans' even more powerful sacred music. This city is the cradle of both Louis Armstrong *and* Mahalia Jackson. New Orleans has fervent congregations and they love to sing and shout. Unfortunately, many people are uncomfortable in churches, especially in other people's churches. This has resulted in the opening of secular venues that present black gospel music together with brunch on Sunday. Two major venues are the **Palm Court Jazz Cafe** and the **House of Blues** (see page 60); the **Praline Connection #2** also has brunch and gospel music on Sundays. If you can't do church, do brunch!

Museums

The Louisiana State Museum's **Cabildo** on Jackson Square has the best historical overview of African Americans in Louisiana from the colonial period to the late 1870s (see page 116). No museum adequately presents the dramatic story of New Orleans African American history from the 1880s to the present.

JEWISH NEW ORLEANS

Like so much else in New Orleans history, the earliest period of Jewish New Orleans was linked with the Caribbean. In 1757, Isaac Monsanto, a Sephardic Jew, briefly moved his trading business from Dutch Curaçao to Spanish New Orleans. The largest port and most cosmopolitan city in the Old South, New Orleans has had an organized Jewish community since 1828 and the founding of Congregation Gates of Mercy. German-speaking Sephardic Jews from Alsace-Lorraine, the Rhineland, and Bavaria were drawn to the booming city in the 1840s, and their descendants became part of the Reform movement in the late nineteenth century. The Jewish community of New Orleans emerged as the intermediary between New York City merchants and manufacturers and the many Jewish peddlers and shopkeepers sprinkled across the South's agrarian interior. After the Civil War, some Jews achieved new levels of prosperity and

Palm Court Jazz Cafe
1204 Decatur Street;
525-0200

The House of Blues
225 Decatur Street;
529-2583

The Praline Connection #2
In the Arts District at 901
S. Peters Street; 523-3973

Cabildo
701 Chartres Street;
568-6968

Kosher Cajun Deli & Grocery
3520 N. Hulen Street, behind the Lakeside Shopping Center in suburban Metairie; 888-2010, fax 888-2014

Jewish Community Center
5342 St. Charles Avenue, at Jefferson; 897-0143

Jewish Federation of Greater New Orleans
1539 Jackson Avenue, N.O., 70130; 525-0673

The Jewish Voice
1539 Jackson Avenue, suite 323, N.O., 70130; 525-0673

community philanthropy. In the decades bracketing 1900, Eastern European Orthodox Ashkenazic Jews settled in New Orleans centering along old Dryades Street in Central City (see page 196). After World War II, more European Jewish immigrants came to the Crescent City.

In the nineteenth century, Jewish businessmen were especially active in wholesaling dry goods, cigar manufacturing, Canal Street department stores, and shopkeeping. The city's Jewish elite favored upper St. Charles Avenue (see Tour 9). Jews in New Orleans prospered, and today are active in all aspects of the city's professional, academic, business, civic, and cultural life. The old divisions between the different streams of migration have blurred with time, intermarriage, and higher education. A survey conducted in 1990 estimated the Jewish population of metropolitan New Orleans to be about twelve thousand. There are seven different congregations in New Orleans and its suburbs. Reform Jews outnumber Orthodox and Conservative Jews, and this makes the Jewish community here unusual among those in large American cities. Among the best-known Jewish citizens of New Orleans are Judah Touro (see pages 239 and 301), Samuel Hermann of the Hermann-Grima House (see page 126), Judah P. Benjamin (see below), and Edgar and Edith Stern, who built Longue Vue House and Gardens (see page 180).

Resources and Places to Visit

- **Kosher Cajun Deli & Grocery** The only kosher deli restaurant in Louisiana, they will deliver to hotel rooms.
- **Jewish Community Center** Members of other Jewish community centers can use these facilities upon showing their membership card when accompanied by a local member; see page 306. Call for tours and programs.
- **Jewish Federation of Greater New Orleans**
- ***The Jewish Voice*** The only Jewish newspaper in New Orleans comes out twice a month; available at the Jewish Federation offices.

- **Touro Synagogue Reform Congregation** (see page 301) and **Temple Sinai Reform Congregation** (see page 310) These are two of the best-known synagogues.
- **Hebrew Rest Cemetery** Of the several Jewish burial grounds, this is the most interesting; about a twenty-minute cab ride from the French Quarter; see page 342.
- **Judah P. Benjamin House** Judah P. Benjamin was the Jewish New Orleanian who served as the Confederate secretary of state; after the war he became a distinguished barrister in London. Built in 1835, the house is now the Bourbon Burlesque Club.

Gay New Orleans

Free gay publications in New Orleans include *The Weekly Guide, Impact,* and *Ambush.* They are usually available at the Bourbon Pub at St. Ann and Bourbon Streets. For announcements of gay events and theater, and access to what gay New Orleans is reading, visit the **Faubourg Marigny Bookstore.** There are many gay-friendly bed-and-breakfast inns in New Orleans; see *The Weekly Guide* and the *Impact* directory for listings. The following addresses and phone numbers may be helpful:

- **The New Orleans Gay/Lesbian Business & Professional Association** P.O. Box 350, 940 Royal Street, N.O., 70116; 586-9156.
- **New Orleans Gay Men's Chorus** 245-8884.
- **Lesbian & Gay Community Center** 816 N. Rampart Street, near Dumaine, 522-1103.

Annual Events

Along with the general celebration of New Year's Eve, Sugar Bowl weekend, the Superbowl, the Carnival season and Mardi Gras, and Jazzfest, high points in the gay calendar in New Orleans include the following:

- **Early April, French Quarter Festival** 522-5730.
- **Early June, Gay Pride Celebration**
- **Labor Day Weekend, Southern Decadence**

Touro Synagogue Reform Congregation
4238 St. Charles Avenue, at the corner of General Pershing; 895-4843

Temple Sinai Reform Congregation
6227 St. Charles Avenue, at Calhoun; 861-3693

Hebrew Rest Cemetery
Off Gentilly Boulevard, near Elysian Fields Avenue

Judah P. Benjamin House
327 Bourbon Street

The Weekly Guide
P.O. Box 71501, N.O., 70172-1501; 522-4300

Impact
2118 Burgundy Street, N.O., 70116; 944-6722

Ambush
828-A Bourbon Street, N.O., 70116-3137; 522-8049

Faubourg Marigny Bookstore
600 Frenchmen Street, at Chartres, 943-9875

- **Early September, NO/AIDS Walk** *948-9255.*
- **Halloween** *Major costumed fundraiser for NO/AIDS, 945-4000.*

Gay Bourbon Street

St. Ann Street is sometimes referred to as "the lavender line," for it marks the end of the Bourbon Street straight tourist club strip and the frontier of the gay residential lower French Quarter. The gateway gay bars at Bourbon and St. Ann are especially popular rendezvous for young people.

The history of gay New Orleans is only just now being researched. Most of it, of course, will never be known. New Orleans has probably always had the varied sexual tastes characteristic of opulent world ports. We know that lesbians ran a few of the brothels in Storyville and that there was a male brothel on Baronne Street at the turn of the century that staged drag balls. Some say there was a speakeasy in the Lower Pontalba Building in the 1920s that drew lesbians and gay men along with straight patrons. With the repeal of Prohibition in 1934, bars proliferated and specialized. A few became known as places where "deviates" were accepted among their bohemian clientele. The James Beer Parlor at the corner of Royal and Toulouse Streets was the best known. Dixie's Bar of Music was popular in the 1940s (see the mural in the Old Mint, page 206), as was Lafitte's Blacksmith Shop on Bourbon. A part of Pat O'Brien's was gay for a time.

But police and press harassment were common in New Orleans until the early 1980s, so the "out" culture of gay New Orleans is really quite recent. A celebrated local event is the annual Bourbon Street Awards, a costume contest held each Mardi Gras day at noon at the corner of Burgundy and St. Ann Streets. Despite the losses among gay men to AIDS, gay Carnival krewes continue to dazzle New Orleans. The Krewe of Petronius, the Krewe of Amon-Ra, the Krewe of Armeinius, and the Lords of Leather all stage elaborate Carnival balls. The Krewe of Barkus costumes and parades the Quarter's canines. Halloween has become the night when the gay community stages its biggest costumed fundraiser for AIDS causes.

Some Gay Bars

There are more than thirty gay bars in New Orleans—something for almost every taste. All are in the lower French Quarter and Faubourg Marigny. Here are a few of the most popular:

- **Bourbon Pub and Parade Disco** Open twenty-four hours a day, seven days a week. Music videos and a young crowd make this a happening place. Upstairs is the Parade Disco with a gallery overlooking this lively intersection.

- **Oz** This new gay dance bar occupies what was Pete Fountain's old club and attracts a young disco crowd bent on a good time. Galleries on the second floor let you look down on this active corner.

- **Cafe Lafitte in Exile** When the proprietors of Cafe Lafitte lost their lease in 1953, they moved a block up Bourbon and opened this two-story bar with a gallery looking down Bourbon Street. This is the oldest continually operating gay bar in New Orleans and is an institution in the Quarter.

- **Rubyfruit Jungle** A new and popular lesbian and gay bar; occasional entertainment.

- **Charlene's/Over C's** A lesbian bar with occasional live entertainment.

- **Feelings Cafe** A restaurant with a cozy bar redolent of Old New Orleans and welcoming to all.

- **The Mint** A large, roomy piano bar with a small stage and entertainment including drag shows; phone for programs. One of the gay bars that straight visitors enjoy most.

Voodoo is one of the things New Orleans is noted for, and there has long been a cottage industry here that caters to the curious. "Voodoo" walking tours of the French Quarter are widely advertised through handbills and are quite popular. While many visit what is reputed to be Marie Laveau's tomb in St. Louis Cemetery No. 1 (see page 340) and make their connection with New Orleans voodoo there, the best place to reflect on voodoo in New Orleans is the quiet bank of

---

Bourbon Pub and Parade Disco
801 Bourbon Street, corner of St. Ann;
529-2107

Oz
800 Bourbon Street, corner of St. Ann;
593-9491

Cafe Lafitte in Exile
901 Bourbon Street, corner of Dumaine;
522-8397

Rubyfruit Jungle
In Marigny at 640 Frenchmen Street, at Chartres; 947-4000

Charlene's/Over C's
In Marigny at 940 Elysian Fields Avenue, at Burgundy; 945-9328

Feelings Cafe
In Marigny at 2600 Chartres Street, at Franklin; 945-2222

The Mint
504 Esplanade Avenue, at Decatur; 525-2000

Voodoo Spiritual Temple
828 N. Rampart Street, between St. Ann and Dumaine; 522-9627

Ava Kay Jones
866-3969

F & F Botanica and Candle Shop
801 N. Broad Street, near Orleans; 482-9142 or 482-5400

Island of Salvation Botanica
835 Piety Street, near Dauphine

Divine Light
3316 Magazine Street, near Louisiana; 899-6617

The Westgate Museum of the Necromantic Arts
5219 Magazine Street, between Dufossat and Bellcastle; 899-3077

Barrister's Gallery
526 Royal Street, between St. Louis and Toulouse; 525-2767

Marie Laveau's House of Voodoo
739 Bourbon Street, between Orleans and St. Ann; 581-3751

New Orleans Historic Voodoo Museum
724 Dumaine Street, between Royal and Bourbon; 523-7685

Musée Conti Wax Museum of Louisiana
917 Conti Street, between Dauphine and Burgundy; 525-2605

Magic Walking Tours' Vampire & Ghost Hunt Walk
588-9693

Bayou St. John. There, on St. John's Eve at the summer solstice, was where the practitioners of voodoo gathered on their most sacred night. There they danced themselves into visionary trances and exhaustion. Though the bayou is quiet now, once it was the spirit gate for the *loas;* see page 168 and page 172. Below are some businesses, commercial museums, and a walk, all of which at least touch upon voodoo.

- **Voodoo Spiritual Temple** In the French Quarter.
- **Ava Kay Jones** Voodoo and Yoruba priestess.
- **F & F Botanica and Candle Shop** In Mid-City.
- **Island of Salvation Botanica** In Bywater; Sallie Ann Glassman and Shane Norris, voodoo practitioners; no phone.
- **Divine Light** Uptown, this place sells candles, including the St. Expedite candle, herbs, charms, and incense.
- **The Westgate Museum of the Necromantic Arts** Uptown; not voodoo, this art gallery and bookshop specializes in death imagery and the Eros-Thanatos theme.
- **Barrister's Gallery** A shaman's attic; in the French Quarter.
- **Marie Laveau's House of Voodoo** In the French Quarter.
- **New Orleans Historic Voodoo Museum** A commercial voodoo museum; in the French Quarter.
- **Musée Conti Wax Museum of Louisiana** Includes a tableau of voodoo dancers; in the French Quarter.
- **Magic Walking Tours' Vampire & Ghost Hunt Walk** Meets at 8 P.M. in front of Lafitte's Blacksmith Shop Bar at 941 Bourbon Street, at St. Philip.

New Orleans House Design and Sociability: Stoops, Balconies, Galleries, and Porches

Uptown and downtown, in fact all over town, New Orleans was a city of porches. They dominated the scene like a web of cool oases, providing summertime refreshment and almost year-round pleasure. Most houses could boast at least one porch, some houses sprouted them at random and others were completely wreathed by them. But the front porch was the universal favorite.

—Margaret LeCorgne, describing
New Orleans in the 1930s,
in *Uptown/Downtown,* 1986

Southern Louisiana's intensely sunny and incessantly rainy climate—combined with the people-loving proclivities of its Latin-Caribbean culture (here French, West African, and Spanish)—created, over time, an architecture that positively encouraged sociability. The earliest French colonial city houses were sealed like vaults with solid board shutters for security. The Spanish introduced narrow, spare wrought-iron balconies on the second floors of the houses of the rich. (A balcony, in new Orleans usage, is relatively narrow and cantilevered from the side of the building; the more commodious gallery covers the width of the sidewalk and is supported by posts.) New Orleans houses opened out to the sidewalk over time as the city became better policed. Eventually the dwellings of both rich and poor were linked with the public life of the sidewalk through narrow porches and low stoops designed like settees in working-class cottages; airy, sidewalk-wide, cast-iron galleries on middle- and upper-class townhouses; and the comfortable wide porches that graced later houses. Many of these stoops and cast-iron galleries stand on or over the public space of the sidewalk. This space is free and is not taxed by the city. The Pontalba Buildings of 1849–51 framing Jackson Square were the first to reach out into public airspace to provide both a cast-iron balcony between the second and third floors, and a sidewalk-wide gallery at the second floor that shelters the arcade of shops along the sidewalk below.

Stoops, balconies, galleries, and porches saw the sidewalk and the street as linear stages and provided domestic theater seating along its edge and up in "sky boxes." Humble one-story, two-family shotgun houses were often built with a narrow porch raised about four feet all along their front, with two sets of stairs, one at each end, linking it with the sidewalk. These simple, shelflike porches look just like stages because that is what they are, or can be, especially during neighborhood processions. Stoops, galleries, and porches are perfect perches for watching parades, New Orleans' continual and unending communal dance.

Cast-iron (and wooden) galleries on middle-class dwellings permit their residents to walk out of the "box" of their building into the open air and to enjoy a discreet relationship with the sidewalk life below. (People-watching, need I mention, is a rewarding activity in New Orleans; the attentive observer spots a new mutation of urban life every day.) Second- and third-floor balconies and galleries are simultaneously private and public. The resident can observe the outside world but still evade direct public view through judicious chair placement. On the other hand, when you spot a friend or someone you want to talk to, it is easy to have a brief conversation from the gallery down to the sidewalk or to invite them up for a chat. Parts of the French Quarter retain this easy communal style.

Later, in the Victorian and Edwardian periods, up and down Esplanade and St. Charles Avenues and along countless lesser streets, frame houses were wrapped with wide, white-columned porches invitingly furnished with rocking chairs, capacious wicker furniture, and lazy swings. The hospitable Victorian porch was something the South could use all year round and *needed* to use during the long, steamy summer. Sitting on a porch could be an invitation to socialize, talk about the heat and the mosquitoes, and gossip. Neighbors then had a natural, daily way of meeting each other, especially at the end of the working day when people walked home from their streetcar stop and passed their neighbors' porches along the way. Private side, back, and upper-story screened porches garlanded opulent houses and offered different views of their lush garden settings. Now standing under magnificent canopies of live oaks that filter the light, these comfortable, porch-wreathed houses represent the acme of environmentally responsive house building and landscape design in traditional New Orleans. Porches began disappearing from New Orleans house facades with the flat-facade, stucco Italian villas of the 1920s (see Audubon Street, page 314).

Automobiles, air-conditioning, and television have changed completely the way most people live and have made contemporary houses and apartments inward-looking, sealing them off from their surroundings and their neighbors. The sidewalks have become less enjoyable and much more dangerous to walk. It is now harder for neighbors to meet casually. New Orleans officially turned away from its traditional cast-iron galleries in the 1930s when the city ordered their removal in order to modernize Canal Street. Post-1940s houses "conquered" the necessity to work with the climate, and the last two generations have chosen television over observing their immediate world. Much of newer suburbia now doesn't even have sidewalks. In these areas, there is no mixed sociable zone between the harsh public street and the inward-looking private house with its television in the back room. Today most of New Orleans has adopted national lifestyles and lost much of the easy sociability of her past that once shaped her best domestic architecture. Stoop-sitting lives on in older and poorer neighborhoods, and balconies and galleries continue to be enjoyed in the French Quarter, but the beautiful porches of late-nineteenth- and early-twentieth-century houses now have few chairs and are only infrequently enjoyed, even during perfect weather.

From our vantage point almost three hundred years after the foundation of New Orleans we can now see that stoops, balconies, galleries, and porches were only a phase—if the most famous one—in New Orleans house design. The earliest French colonial town dwellings were small, closed-in structures with few windows, solid board shutters, and no balconies, galleries, or porches. The Spanish introduced narrow balconies, and later galleries and porches blossomed during the Victorian American era. But today most new houses do not have front porches, balconies, or second-floor galleries. They have reverted to brick-veneered boxes with small windows in order to increase insulation for air conditioning. Still employing steeply pitched roofs to shed the tropical downpours, the new houses look surprisingly like the earliest French cottages in their self-enclosedness. Lacy cast-iron galleries and welcoming white-columned porches no longer open buildings out to their physical and social environment. Commodious front porches are now "historic" architecture, not a part of modern building. But the memory of the traditional New Orleans gallery remains in the decorative cast iron that is attached to modern facades but that supports no shady, sociable oasis.

*The LaBranche Building on the downtown-riverside corner of
Royal and St. Peter Streets is a symbol of the French Quarter. The useful and ornate cast-
iron galleries were wrapped around a plain 1840s brick building in the opulent 1850s.*

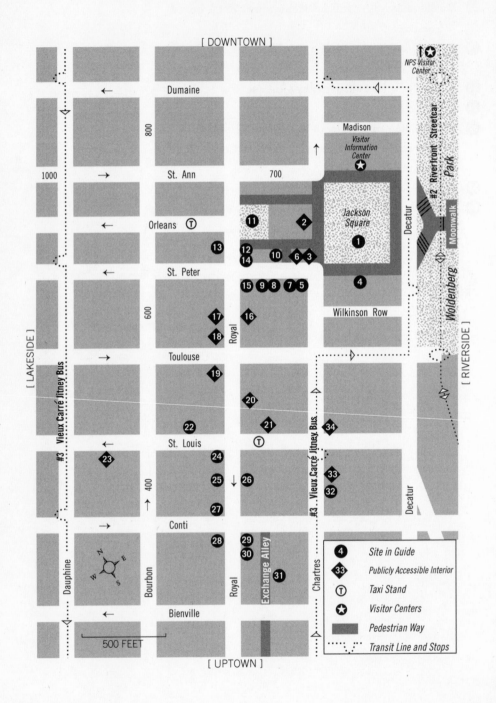

What This Tour Covers

This walk makes a circle around Jackson Square and then proceeds up Royal Street, looping back to end at the atmospheric Napoleon House Bar and Cafe. It includes the cathedral, three fine history and art museums, three important house museums, and several courtyards that let you experience the hidden side of the French Quarter. Choose from among the museums on this walk; the Cabildo and Historic New Orleans Collection are the key history and art museums here and the best windows into New Orleans' rich past.

Preliminaries

Make sure the museums or house museums you wish to see are open when you do this tour. You can end your day with dinner at one of the restaurants listed here, or perhaps dinner and jazz at the **Palm Court Jazz Cafe.**

Visitor Information

You can secure a map, brochures, and transit passes at the **Visitor Information Center.**

Guided Tours

The French Quarter Unit of the far-flung Jean Lafitte National Historical Park offers free, regularly scheduled, **ranger-led walks** seven days a week, rain or shine, except Christmas, New Year's Day, and Mardi Gras. Tours offered include the French Quarter, St. Louis Cemetery No. 1, the Garden District uptown, and a changing "tour du jour." All walks begin at the Folklife and Visitor Center at 916–918 N. Peters Street in the French Market, off Decatur Street, between Dumaine and St. Philip Streets, a block and a half downriver from Jackson Square. Times and lengths of tours vary and some tours require reservations.

Palm Court Jazz Cafe
1204 Decatur Street, between Gov. Nicholls and Barracks; 525-0200

Visitor Information Center
Lower Pontalba Building, 529 St. Ann Street, facing Jackson Square; open daily 9 A.M. to 5 P.M.; 566-5031

Jean Lafitte National Historical Park Walks
Tickets are generally available the day of the tour beginning at 9 A.M.; one ticket per person; 589-2636

ATMs

There is an automatic teller machine inside an alcove catercorner from Jackson Square, at the corner of Chartres and St. Ann Streets. **Whitney National Bank** has a branch and an ATM on Chartres Street. **First NBC's** ATM is on Royal Street at Bienville. **Regions Bank** has a branch and an ATM on Chartres Street, at Toulouse. **Hibernia National Bank** has a branch and an ATM at 137 Royal Street, at Iberville.

Parking

To park near the end of this walk, use the **paid parking lot off N. Peters Street,** at Conti; walk three blocks down Decatur Street to Jackson Square and the beginning of this walk. To park near the beginning of this walk, use the **French Market lot off Decatur Street,** at St. Philip, across from Jackson Square.

Taxi Stands

The best place to catch a cab in the Quarter is in front of the **Omni Royal Orleans Hotel** on St. Louis Street, between Royal and Chartres. There is another taxi stand in front of the **Bourbon Orleans Hotel** on Orleans Street, between Royal and Bourbon.

Public Transit

The **3 Vieux Carré jitney bus** makes a loop through the French Quarter from Washington Square in Faubourg Marigny, through the "back" of the Quarter up Dauphine Street to Canal Street, across the Central Business District on Baronne Street, down Poydras and Magazine Streets through the Arts District, and on to Morial Convention Center. The line then loops back down Convention Center Boulevard to Canal Street, into the French Quarter and across the "front" of the Quarter down Chartres and Decatur Streets.

Antiques

The upper French Quarter has a wealth of shops for visitors, and, of course, they are always changing. The toniest shopping, and the most delightful window shopping at night, are the antique shops on Royal Street from Iberville to Toulouse Streets. **The Royal Street Guild** publishes a **map and guide** available by mail or in guild shops. Junk shop aficionados and hip teenagers will want to check out funky lower Decatur Street, from Dumaine to Barracks Streets. **The Centuries Antique Maps and Prints** is also a fascinating shop.

Royal Street Guild map and guide
828 Royal Street, P.O. Box 522, N.O., 70116; 524-1260, fax 891-1228

The Centuries Antique Maps and Prints
517 St. Louis Street, near Decatur; 568-9491

Introduction:
The Heart of Old New Orleans

> Nothing could be shabbier than the [French Quarter's] streets. . . .
> I liked it all from the first; I lingered long in that [first] morning
> walk, liking it more and more, in spite of its shabbiness, but
> utterly unable to say then or ever since wherein its charm lies. I
> suppose we are all wrongly made up and have a fallen nature; else
> why is it that while the most thrifty and neat and orderly city only
> wins our approval, and perhaps gratifies us intellectually, such a
> thriftless, battered and stained, and lazy old place as the French
> quarter of New Orleans takes our hearts?
>
> —Charles Dudley Warner,
> *Studies in the South and West,* 1885

> [The French Quarter is] the most civilized place I've found in
> America and I have been writing like a man gone mad. . . . I have
> a large room with a fireplace and windows that go from the floor
> to the high ceilings. By stepping out through the windows I come
> upon a balcony, running the entire length of the old house and as
> wide as a city pavement. . . . Below me the life of the street goes
> on. Here I work and look at life. Then I go to write.
>
> —Sherwood Anderson,
> in a letter from 1922
> (*Preservation in Print,* October 1992)

The French Quarter is a living fragment of old Europe, but with its own distinct American evolution. The Quarter is not just a place, it is a state of mind, one marked by freedom and Carnival-season license. Protected as a historic district since 1937, this flavorful "old square" (*vieux carré*) continues to evolve in ways both obvious and subtle, both positive and negative. Before 1788, the Quarter was the entire city of *la Nouvelle Orléans,* and today it is several subdistricts. There is the core of museum and church buildings facing Jackson Square, the predominantly commercial upper Quarter—with elegant antique shops along Royal Street and raucous bars and clubs crowding down Bourbon Street—and the quiet, residential, and visibly gay lower Quarter. There are also two contrasting "sides" to the rectangular Quarter: booming, tourist-oriented Decatur Street near the river and semideserted and dangerous N. Rampart Street on its lakeside frontier. An aerial view of the low-rise French Quarter reveals a complex mosaic of buildings lining all the streets, hidden courtyards, and more small buildings inside the blocks that are completely invisible from the street. (A good place to get a view of this is the top floor of the Omni Royal Orleans Hotel.) As in old Europe, commerce and residence are layered one over the other. Narrow, gated alleyways between buildings lead to secluded courtyards lush with banana trees and potted plants. You should peek through the gates that protect these mini-islands and peer down the alleyways that lead to these enclaves. This walk singles out a few publicly accessible courtyards in order to give you a taste of the hidden Quarter.

Into this complex honeycomb of private spaces has settled an equally complex population. Millionaires in grandly furnished mansions and poor artists living out of laundry bags, priests in seclusion and hustlers on the street, intellectuals and prostitutes, salesclerks and doctors, renters and tourists, straights and gays, occasional old-timers and daily new arrivals: all gravitate to the fabled Quarter. The only thing they have in common is that they are all refugees from mass-culture uniformity. In exchange for "impossible" parking (or no car), no supermarkets, and no front yards, Quarterites live on their own civilized island where they can walk to all that they really need and find mental and social stimulation at their doorstep. There are still Quarterites today (not Creoles any longer) who think of Canal Street as a frontier, their sharp border with fast-food America, which is a place they only go to the way migrant farmworkers trek to alien fields: just for the money, and only in order to get back home. The best thing about this little universe is that it's a club anyone who wants to can join. In this, the Quarter is very different from Uptown, and therein lies all the difference between open downtown and exclusive Uptown.

New Orleans was founded in a cane break in 1718 by Jean-Baptiste Le Moyne, sieur de Bienville. A town plan was designed by Pierre le Blond de la Tour and surveyed in 1722 by Adrien de Pauger. Today, the French Quarter consists of a rectangle of some 120 squares (blocks) set on the inside of a bend of the Mississippi River. The new military outpost was placed on "one of the most beautiful crescents of the river," hence the city's nickname, the Crescent City. It sits on relatively high ground astride a shortcut between the Gulf of Mexico and the river. The French had colonies in both Canada and the Caribbean and wished to link them up into a North American empire via the Mississippi River. In 1699 Choctaw guides showed the French how to reach the great river from the Mississippi Sound and Lake Borgne, through passes called the Rigolets, into shallow Lake Pontchartrain. A stream that feeds into that lake, Bayou St. John, penetrated about four miles south to Gentilly Ridge and the overland portage along Bayou Road. The portage met the river near a Native American gathering place that later became the French Market. The eccentric angle of Bayou Road across the later grid of city streets preserves the route of that ancient Choctaw portage (see page 168).

The settlement was christened *la Ville de la Nouvelle Orléans* after Philippe, duc d'Orléans, a notorious roué and the Regent of France during the minority of Louis XV. Behind the town were dense cypress swamps and a string of earlier royal land grant plantations along the Bayou Road. Pauger sited a battery facing the river and staked out a military parade ground, today Jackson Square. Facing that open space, sites for a church and government buildings were reserved. Around this core of army, state, and church he laid out a rectangular grid four blocks above and below the central square, and six blocks deep back toward the cypress swamps and Lake Pontchartrain. Down the center of his town plan, axial with the centrally placed church, Pauger surveyed a slightly wider street that he named the Rue d'Orléans. The other streets in his orderly grid were only thirty-eight feet wide, giving the French Quarter its intimate scale. These streets were named after the patron saints of persons associated with the French crown. Drainage ditches were dug around each block, giving them the nickname of *islets* (islands). Cypress planks were used to cross these drainage ditches and were called *banquettes,* still the local word for "sidewalk" in New Orleans. Space was reserved around the frontier town for fortifications, but they were not commenced until 1760 after French Canada fell to the English. In 1812, nine years after New Orleans became part of the United States, these common spaces were surveyed and subdivided for Canal Street, N. Rampart Street, and Esplanade Avenue, and the prestigious lots facing them were auctioned off. Except for the street plan, the street names, and the old Ursuline Convent, little survives from the French era. Most of what the visitor sees today is due to the virtually complete rebuildings under Spanish rule (1763 to 1803), which took place after the two great fires of 1788 and 1794, and then to the continuous changes that took place under American rule, which began with the Louisiana Purchase of 1803 and climaxed in a great wave of denser rebuilding in the Quarter between 1830 and 1860.

The earliest French buildings were one-story houses built with a heavy wooden framework set directly on the ground called *poteaux-en-terre.* Given the climate here, frame buildings set directly on the wet ground soon rotted. Brick construction was recognized as superior, but the bricks made from local clay were soft and easily crushed. The solution was to use strong cypress timbers for the framework of buildings and to use brick as infill between the cypress beams. This was called *briquete entre poteaux,* and modern exposed examples of it survive today, such as Lafitte's Blacksmith Shop and Bar (see page 156). As a rule, to protect the brick from the rain, walls were coated with stucco and then painted pastel colors, such as yellow, apricot, light green, or pale blue. Few early buildings were more than one story high. Space was precious, and many buildings combined shops facing the street with living quarters behind them. The interior plan of these Creole houses was distinctive: four rooms were symmetrically arranged like a square with a cross drawn inside it. There were no interior hallways; French doors connected the two front rooms to each other and also to the two back rooms. Houses were raised only a step or two above the ground and their front French doors opened right onto the sidewalk. The front edge of the roof was extended three or four feet out over the sidewalk to shade the house and to protect it from rain. Separate, brick outbuildings were generally built in the backyards for the kitchen and slave quarters. Placing the kitchen outside the house kept the house cooler and minimized the danger of fires. The standard Creole cottage floor plan with its four similar rooms did not assign set functions to each room unless the front rooms were used for commerce. Instead, any room might be used for sleeping, dining, or receiving guests. The Creoles furnished their rooms sparingly with portable chairs and tables. Clothes and linens were kept in tall armoires.

These one-story cottages, and the larger, multi-story Creole town houses that followed them, differed sharply from the houses with internal hallways and rooms dedicated to specific uses that English-speaking Americans introduced to New

Orleans after 1803. The difference between public, Latin culture and privacy-craving Anglo culture can be read in the city's old house plans. Occasionally, as you walk through the French Quarter, you will glimpse a Creole cottage with its French doors open, and you will see just how blatantly public life in the old city was. For this reason many contemporary owners of Creole cottages keep their solid front shutters perpetually closed, use the side alley as the principal entrance, and make their house "face" the small private garden at the back of the lot.

When French West Indian Creoles migrated to Louisiana, they brought with them a more environmentally suitable way of building in this climate. Following Spanish Caribbean house types, raised cottages with galleries (porches) were built. This lifted the building off the flood-prone soil, while the gallery roofs shielded the walls from the baking sun and the torrential rains. Raising the building even slightly also caught whatever cooling breezes there might be. The ground floor under the principal floor, called the *rez-de-chausee,* was used as a storage area or work space. The sheltered galleries supported by light wooden colonnettes provided shady places to live and work, and even to sleep on hot nights behind temporary curtains. Eventually Louisiana carpenters introduced a French door in every other bay of the house facade, making windows and doors one. Pronounced dormers on the roof let hot air rise up through the building. In the country, where there was space, the Louisiana plantation house became a raised building under a double-pitched roof that spread out over all four sides of the building like a great sun-and-rain-shedding parasol/umbrella. A rare surviving example of a raised house with a gallery in the lower French Quarter is "Madame John's Legacy" at 632 Dumaine Street, built in 1788 (see page 144). Destrehan on the River Road is a grand survivor of French Creole plantation architecture (see page 356).

No Spanish architects are known to have worked in *la Nueva Orleans* during the thirty-five years of Spanish rule. Spanish-era building continued French traditions with certain improvements. One important Spanish-inspired innovation were the louvered jalousies (shutters) covering the French doors that allowed privacy, security, *and* ventilation. Previously, the French had used solid wood shutters over their doors, which sealed the building in completely. The Spanish also introduced the use of light, elegant wrought-iron balconies (not to be confused with the heavier cast iron of the 1840s and later). Large Creole town houses began to appear along prestigious residential streets such as Royal and Bourbon. A few of these multistory town houses reached the scale of mansions. Slave quarters were built behind these houses, set like the long part of an L to the wider, street-facing main house. Slave quarters always had windows on only one wall, the one facing the courtyard, so that the master and mistress could watch. This prevented slaves from communicating with one another from neighbor-facing windows. Common staircases were placed between the master's house and its slave dependency. The open space behind the house became a utilitarian courtyard where food was prepared and laundry and other chores were done. Grand houses had a narrow passageway, *à porte cochère,* that gave access to stables at the rear of the lot. Less costly town houses had a long interior passageway along one side of the ground floor that led to the back of the house and the stairs. The Spanish imported oleander from Havana, along with bananas and other showy tropical plants, to cultivate in their back courtyards. Old, yellow-glazed, clay olive-oil containers, *jars de Provence,* were reused for exotic potted plants such as Spanish daggers.

After the United States' purchase of Louisiana in 1803, and for about twenty years thereafter during the early Federal Period, several important buildings appeared in the Quarter in a new architectural style marked by strong geometrical forms. Landmarks of this new refined taste include English-trained Benjamin H. Latrobe's Louisiana State Bank of 1820 at 403 Royal Street (now Manheim's Galleries), Jacques Tanesse's much-added-onto French Market of 1813–23, Arsene Lacarriere Latour and Henry S. Latrobe's Thierry House of 1814 at 721 Governor Nicholls Street, the Banque de la Louisiane of 1795 at 417 Royal Street (now Brennan's Restaurant), the Girod House of 1814 at 500 Chartres Street (now the Napoleon House), and the Absinthe House of about 1806 at 238 Bourbon Street. All appear in this guide.

During the antebellum era, from about 1825 to 1860, American New Orleans boomed. A new American city sprouted across Canal Street from the old Creole Quarter. The French Quarter also experienced a transforming building boom that hit its peak between 1830 and 1860. Much of the physical fabric of today's Quarter is, in fact, American. Many multistory, red brick town houses were built, some of them in speculator rows of as many as fifteen houses. With their stylistic roots in Georgian building, these buildings acquired more and more Greek Revival details as the boom continued. All continued the colonial pattern of connected slave quarters. A fine example is the Hermann-Grima House of 1832 built by architect-builder William Brand (now a house museum, see page 126). The most famous row houses of the period are the Upper and Lower Pontalba Buildings flanking Jackson Square with shops downstairs and residences above. Built between 1849 and 1851, they introduced cast-iron galleries built out over the public sidewalk to New Orleans, the most distinctive of New Orleanian amenities.

The most important innovation in the decades just before the Civil War was the widespread adoption of cast iron. The new industrial technologies of the 1840s and 1850s made cast-iron building elements increasingly affordable. Cast-iron columns, railings, brackets, fences, and ornaments were imported from New York City, Philadelphia, Baltimore, and as far away as Germany. Irish, German, and English ironmasters also established foundries in New Orleans. The new material resisted rot (very important here!) and could be cast into almost any form: geometric, Gothic, Neoclassical, or romantic. A carnival of fantastic patterns appeared. Naturalistic motifs were especially popular, including roses, fuchsias, morning glories, oak leaves and acorns, trailing vines, and even cornstalks (see page 284 for the cornstalk fence). New buildings were designed with iron galleries, and plain old buildings had them added. The French Quarter's stern masonry blocks were overlaid with a filigree of fanciful iron galleries that completely transformed the appearance of the city. A good example of this is the originally stern Greek Revival LaBranche buildings at Royal and St. Peter

Streets, built in 1840 but with elaborate cast-iron galleries added after 1850 (see page 121). These broad, upper-story galleries made the French Quarter much more livable. Residents of upper stories now had cool places to sit, house facades were shielded from the broiling sun, and pedestrians were protected from both constant sun and sudden showers. Aesthetes languidly contemplating the passing of the hours while smoking their cigars could now watch the shifting, patterned shadows cast by the lacy ironwork against patinated walls. A fine example of a house built with cast-iron galleries is the one that architect James Gallier, Jr., built for himself in 1857 (today a house museum, see page 147). Cast-iron galleries gave mid-nineteenth-century New Orleans the distinctive architectural look now universally associated with the Crescent City.

Over time, the roomy French Quarter mansions and middle-class town houses became absentee-owned rental properties profitably subdivided for commerce and working-class tenants. Among the businesses that clustered along Royal and Bourbon Streets in the 1870s were gambling parlors. When gambling was outlawed in the 1890s, gaming simply retreated to illegal, but tolerated, second-floor rooms. In 1909, Baedeker's *Guide to the United States* noted that "of late years many negroes and Italians have crowded into" the French Quarter. This important phase, from the 1880s to the 1920s, is the ignored period in French Quarter history. Little was written about it at the time except for melancholy forays by elite New Orleanians who left disappointed accounts of the decline of the formerly genteel Creole Quarter. At the same time, wharves and industry expanded along the riverfront. In 1879 the city leased the land between Jackson Square and the river for the construction of a freight depot that cut the French Quarter off from the river for a hundred years. Massive Jackson Brewery invaded Jackson Square in 1891. In the 1900s, Canal Street businesses expanded one block back onto Iberville Street, turning it into a service alley for department stores. The French Market also expanded, bringing more traffic into the Quarter. Many Italians and Sicilians worked on the docks and in the fruit and vegetable businesses at the old market. From there they branched out into restaurants and food processing, including bakeries and macaroni factories. Poverty, and the high rents that congested slums traditionally generated, preserved most of the old Quarter. Italian Americans invested in real estate since they mistrusted and did not have access to most banks. As landlords they tended to be conservative and did not significantly alter their buildings.

St. Joseph's Day on March 19, called Mi-Careme or mid-Lent, became an important holiday in the Quarter at the turn of the century. As the WPA's *New Orleans City Guide* reported in 1938:

In Italian homes, many of which are in the Vieux Carré, elaborate altars are erected and statues of saints or holy pictures are placed here amidst a profusion of flowers, shrubs, and lighted candles. The larger shrines are built in tiers, but large or small, they are always decked with all manner of foodstuffs. In the background of each are small disks of bread and toasted [fava] beans which are distributed to visitors, it being said that preservation of these will ward off poverty. Tables covered with food stand about the room. Visitors stroll from house to house making wishes and leaving silver coins to hasten their fulfilment.

In the early years of the twentieth century the French Quarter began to lose important parts of its architectural past. In 1903 the city demolished an entire block of historic buildings for the erection of a new court building. Especially tragic was the loss by fire of the old French Opera House on Bourbon Street in 1919. It had been the heart of Creole high culture and the scene of many early Carnival balls. But just as public and municipal indifference were at their height, a handful of prescient New Orleanians began to appreciate the historic value of the Quarter. While artists generally get the credit for "discovering" the old Quarter, other more establishment New Orleanians actually made the critical investments that rescued the decaying district. Key among them was businessman William Ratcliffe Irby. In 1918 he bought and restored the Seignouret House of 1816 at 520 Royal Street and made it his home (see page 124). He purchased other key landmarks in the Quarter, including the Lower Pontalba Building, the Jackson House at St. Peter Street and Cabildo Alley, the Creole House next to it on Pirate's Alley, and the Banque de la Louisiane of 1795 (now Brennan's Restaurant).

During the "Roaring Twenties," prosperity encouraged the opening of art galleries, bookshops, restaurants, clubs, and because this was the era of Prohibition, speakeasies. In the French Quarter, tearooms and art galleries sprouted that attracted both artists and socialites. Royal, Charters, St. Peter, and St. Ann Streets became the focus of this new activity. About 1921 French Quarter preservationist Martha Gasquet Westfeldt opened the Green Shutter tearoom and bookshop at 633 Royal Street, which became an artists' hangout. In 1922 Le Petit Théâtre du Vieux Carré purchased the Orue-Pontalba House at 616 St. Peter Street and built a small theater there. About 1920 the Quartier Club was established as a woman's organization to host talks by artists and writers. By 1924 it had become Le Petit Salon, and the next year the club purchased the Greek Revival Victor David town house of 1838 at 620 St. Peter Street, which it restored as its clubhouse. In 1922, the Arts and Crafts Club opened its gallery and classrooms in William Ratcliffe Irby's Seignouret House. It became an important venue for the teaching, display, and sale of art. The Arts and Crafts Club's annual *Bal Masqué des Artistes* helped revive the mystique of the French Quarter. In January 1922, Sherwood Anderson, one of the best-known American writers of the day, came to visit New Orleans. He announced that the Crescent City should be "the winter home of every American artist." In 1924 he returned with his wife, Elizabeth Prall, and their home became the center of the city's nascent literary scene until his huffy departure in 1926. Anderson's 1925 novel *Dark Laughter* is partially set in New Orleans. In 1925 William Faulkner came down from Mississippi to meet Anderson. While in the city he wrote *Soldier's Pay* and *Mosquitoes*. Other writers who were briefly in New Orleans in the 1920s included F. Scott Fitzgerald, Edmund Wilson, Anita Loos, and Ernest Hemingway.

The depressed 1930s were a turning point in the preservation of the French Quarter. All at once, the Stock Market Crash of 1929 stopped intrusive new building and the preservation of the French Quarter achieved political popularity. Le Petit Salon and the local chapter of the American Institute of Architects requested that Mayor Martin Behrman propose a plan to preserve the French Quarter. The mayor urged the city council to support the idea, and in 1932 a city ordinance was passed to protect the historic district from "the encroachment of modern business," but the original ordinance did not prohibit demolition in the Quarter. In 1936, with the support of preservationists and the Chamber of Commerce, a state constitutional amendment authorized the creation of a commission with the power to preserve the *tout ensemble* of the Quarter, and the next year the city created the Vieux Carré Commission. (The French Quarter was the only landmark district in the city until the rebirth of preservation in the mid-1970s.) Popular books made the public aware of the Quarter. In 1936 Stanley Clisby Arthur wrote *Old New Orleans: A History of the Vieux Carré, Its Ancient and Historical Buildings*. It painted this gloomy picture in the mid-1930s:

Many doors are shut and clamped and grayed with cobwebs. Many windows are nailed fast. Half the balconies are begrimed and the iron railings rust-eaten, and humid arches and alleys which characterize the older Franco-Spanish piles of stuccoed brick betray a fatalistic squalor. Yet . . . beauty and the picturesque still linger here, which the blare of radios and smart reconditioning of crumbling facades seem only to emphasize by contrast. . . . [Occasionally] through a chink between some pair of heavy batten window-shutters opened with a reptile wariness, your eye catches a glimpse of lace and brocade upholstry, silver and bronze, and similar rich antiquity.

The New Deal employment programs greatly benefited the French Quarter. In 1936 there was a major rebuilding of the French Market and the Pontalba Buildings under the WPA. The new Historic American Buildings Survey engaged unemployed writers, architects, draftsmen, and photographers and began the scientific study of the Quarter's landmarks. The WPA's Federal Writers' Project produced the fine *New Orleans City Guide* (1938) and *Gumbo Ya-Ya* (1945), a rich collection of old Louisiana folk tales and superstitions. In 1938 General and Mrs. L. Kemper Williams bought and restored the historic Merieult House and adjoining properties on Toulouse Street. Their building at 718 Toulouse Street became the WPA art school and gallery. The Williamses engaged artist Boyd Cruise to be the curator of their private collection of books, maps, paintings, and papers documenting Louisiana history. In 1966 that collection became the seed of the important Historic New Orleans Collection (see page 123).

The wartime 1940s saw the beginning of mass tourism as strip joints proliferated along Bourbon Street catering to soldiers and sailors passing through this port of embarcation. In 1946 New York City planner Robert Moses proposed building an elevated expressway between the French Quarter and the river. This touched off what has been called "the Second Battle of New Orleans" as preservationists rallied to stop the misconceived expressway. Not until 1971 was this invasive "improvement" definitively stopped. The first motel in the Quarter opened in 1959. The next year the large Omni Royal Orleans Hotel opened on the site of the lost St. Louis Hotel. The French Quarter was about to consume itself to accommodate the visitors who came to see it. In 1970 a moratorium on new hotels was imposed on the district to preserve what was left of its residential character.

By the 1960s the popularity of the French Quarter was assured. Bourbon Street became an outdoor barroom and Royal Street a pricy row of antique shops. A quiet migration of gay men, many associated with the antiques and decorator trades, began buying, restoring, and decorating buildings in the French Quarter. Movies and television also discovered the old French Quarter. As Bernard Lemann, a professor of architecture at Tulane University, noted in 1966 in his *The Vieux Carré: A General Statement,* a self-conscious "Vieux Carré style" emerged:

> There was the inevitable gaslight street lamp, the bit of misunderstood iron-work pattern, a few exposed beams, some rugged brickwork, or a wine cask, or crossed swords hanging on the wall. The next step, naturally, soon followed. The renovations of Vieux Carré nightclubs or apartments were influenced by television scenery based on simplified versions of the "Vieux Carré style," which in turn was intended to imitate the mid-nineteenth century American adaptation to earlier modes of building in Creole New Orleans! . . . A scenic style, the copy of the television copy, has become so prevalent and is moving apace so steadily, it is already a recognizable phase in the French Quarter's sequence of styles.

Not just the looks of the Quarter have changed; more fundamentally, its population has and is changing as tourism begins to overwhelm what was always a district characterized by an attractive mixture of transients, residents, and commerce. Between 1940 and 1990 the population of the Quarter dropped from over ten thousand to just under four thousand. Both median incomes and property values have increased greatly, and lower income African Americans have been squeezed out by rising rents. Household size has gone down dramatically as singles have replaced families. A hot issue in the neighborhood is the illegal, unpoliced use of rental units as more profitable bed-and-breakfast accommodations. Left unchallenged, this trend will drive *all* the residents out of the Quarter. In 1940 only about 10 percent of the Quarter's shops catered to tourists. Today just under half the shops are strictly for tourists, including some 120 T-shirt shops. The controversy over permitting fast-food outlets in the Quarter is another hot issue. Franchise outlets lacking in local ambiance could completely overwhelm the character of the Quarter, turning the area into a mall-like food court. In 1995 the National Trust for Historic Preservation put the French Quarter on its short list of most endangered places. How can the ambiance that draws free-spirited residents and some nine million visitors a year be conserved and yet be allowed to evolve? The Quarter is in danger of becoming the victim of its own success.

①   Jackson Square / *Place d'armes*, *1721; 1851; 1969*

Enter the park and find a shady corner to sit and admire hand-somely gated and beautifully landscaped Jackson Square, which remains the historical heart of the City of New Orleans. It was reserved as a drill field, or *Place d'armes,* for the French militia by military engineer Adrien de Pauger in 1721, following the town plan of Pierre le Blond de la Tour, Engineer-in-Chief of Louisiana. It was placed here to be next to what became the French Market, the head of the Bayou St. John portage. Because of the many twists and turns that the Mississippi River makes, the river here is flowing due *north* before turning to the southeast. The square faces toward the southeast, meaning that the sun rises *across* the river from the city even though the settlement lies on the east bank. This peculiar siting, along with the fact that principal later streets such as St. Charles Avenue follow the curve of the river, is the reason why New Orleanians rarely refer to the compass when giving directions.

The French *Place d'armes* was a rude affair, a dirt parade ground where troops and citizen militias assembled when threats of slave insurrections or foreign invasions loomed. This is where official proclamations were read and also where crim-inals and rebellious slaves were executed. The square was not elab-orately landscaped until 1851, when the handsome cast-iron fences designed by Louis H. Pilie were erected. The square was then renamed Jackson Square in honor of the Tennessee-born hero of the 1815 Battle of New Orleans and the seventh president of the United States. The bronze equestrian statue by Clark Mills was unveiled in 1856 and is a replica of the statues in Washington, D.C., and Nashville, Tennessee. The declarative inscription cut into its granite base, "The Union Must and Shall Be Preserved," is a slightly garbled quote of Jackson's during the nullification controversy of 1832. It was carved at the order of Union general Benjamin F. Butler when federal troops occupied the briefly Confeder-ate city in 1862. The square was elegantly relandscaped in 1969 to designs by Stewart Farnet. The city's Parkway and Park Commission and the private **Friends of Jackson Square** are jointly responsible for this beautifully maintained garden with its tropical plantings. The statues in its corners represent the four seasons. In 1975, three of the streets around the square were closed to traffic to create a three-block pedestrian mall. Sketch artists, jugglers, palm and tarot card readers, and street musicians entertain the passing crowds in front of the cathedral as in a medieval city.

Jackson Square / *Place d'armes*
Bounded by Chartres, Decatur, St. Peter, and St. Ann Streets; open from 7 A.M. to 6 P.M.

Friends of Jackson Square
c/o Parkway Partners, 2829 Gentilly Boulevard, N.O., 70122; 286-2100

Cathedral of St. Louis, King of France
Chartres Street facing Jackson Square; Mass: Sunday at 7:30, 8:45, 10, and 11:15 A.M., 12:30 and 6 P.M.; holy days at 8 and 10 A.M., noon and 6 P.M.; weekdays at 7:30 A.M. and 6 P.M.; novena to Our Lady of Prompt Succor every Wednesday at the daily mass; gift shop with religious articles; 525-9585

②   Cathedral of St. Louis, King of France, *1849–51, J. N. B. de Pouilly*

Three needle-sharp, slate-clad steeples crown this, the third church on this key site. The first church was built in 1724–27 by Adrien de Pauger and destroyed in the Good Friday fire of 1788. The second church, a gift of Don Andres Almonester y Roxas, was designed by Gilberto Guillemard, begun in 1789, and dedicated as a cathedral on

Cathedral Restoration Fund
615 Père Antoine Alley,
N.O., 70116

Christmas Eve, 1794. The present church was designed by J. N. B. de Pouilly and built in 1849–51. Though it has a dry, neoclassical interior with little warmth or emotion, it is nonetheless central in the history of New Orleans. While under construction, the central tower of the cathedral fell and de Pouilly was dismissed; architect-builder Alexander H. Sampson supervised the completion of the building. The cathedral was redecorated in 1872, and at that time Erasmus Humbrecht painted the (since repainted) ceiling and the mural above the main altar of St. Louis, King of France, announcing the seventh crusade. The large bell that tolls the hours here is named "Victoire" and was cast in Paris in 1819; two smaller bells cling-clang every quarter hour. The cathedral is served by the Oblates of Mary Immaculate. (There is a **Cathedral Restoration Fund** for those who wish to help preserve this landmark.)

The baroque altar screen was carved in 1852 in Ghent, Belgium, and designed by Louis Gille. It is crowned with statues of Faith (center), Hope (left), and Charity (right). A Sacred Heart of Jesus burns in the triangular pediment. The high point here is the tabernacle: two almost life-size angels in attitudes of adoration and a host of cherubs surround the tabernacle door emblazoned with a chalice and consecrated host. It is all splendidly theatrical and calls to mind Protestant William Faulkner's description of alien, opulent, Roman Catholic New Orleans in *Absolom, Absolom!*: "a place whose denizens had created their All-Powerful and His supporting hierarchy-chorus of beautiful saints and handsome angels in the image of their houses and personal adornments and voluptuous lives." To the left of the main altar is the altar of reservation for the Blessed Sacrament with a statue of Our Lady of Prompt Succor, the patronness of New Orleans and of Louisiana. Each Wednesday prayers are recited to her begging that she "Hasten then to our help, as you once saved our beloved city from destruction by fire and invasion by an alien foe." To the right of the main altar is the chapel of St. Joseph. The most beautiful object here is the elegant carved marble baptismal font. The marble slab set into the floor marks the tomb of Don Andres Almonester y Roxas and lists in Spanish his many benefactions to his adopted city. Born in Andalucia, Spain, in 1725, he came to Louisiana in 1769 as an officer in the Spanish colonial government. Once here he acquired a fortune, including much of the originally state-owned property flanking the *Place d'armes*. After the Good Friday fire of 1788, he financed the construction of a new cathedral, the Cabildo, and began the Presbytere. There is a full-length portrait of him next door in the Presbytere. His daughter, Micaela, built the red brick Pontalba Buildings that symmetrically frame her father's benefactions.

3   **The Cabildo / Louisiana State Museum,** *1795–99, Gilberto Guillemard; 1847, Henri Gobet and Victor Amiel, builders; restoration, 1994, Robert Cangelosi of Koch and Wilson*

Flanking the cathedral are two important heirlooms from Spanish New Orleans: the Cabildo of 1795–99 and the Presbytere, begun in 1791 but not completed until 1813. Both are imposing arcaded masonry structures with Tuscan columns. Their counterparts can be found in many Spanish colonial government seats. Today both are part of the Louisiana State Museum and are well worth visiting. (For descriptions of the Presbytere and the Lower Pontalba Building with the 1850 Town House Museum, see page 142.)

In French colonial days a *corps de garde* stood here along with a court and prison. The first cabildo was erected by Spanish Governor Don Alexandro O'Reilly in 1769, and it burned in 1788. ("The Very Illustrious Cabildo" was the legislative assembly of the Spanish colonial government; the Spanish themselves called this building the *Casa Capitular,* or capitol house.) The present building, designed by Gilberto Guillemard, was begun in 1795 and completed in 1799. Guillemard was born in France but served in the Spanish army. It was in the *sala capitular* on the second floor of this building on December 20, 1803, that the documents were signed that transferred the Louisiana Territory's 828,000 square miles from Napoleon's France to the United States, doubling the size of the republic. The Cabildo then became the city hall of New Orleans until the construction of Gallier Hall in 1853 (see page 261). The Louisiana territorial legislature met here, and the first Protestant service in New Orleans was also conducted here. In 1847 the mansard roof and cupola were added by Henri Gobet and Victor Amiel. From 1853 to 1910 the building housed the Supreme Court of Louisiana. The case of *Plessy v. Ferguson,* which established the doctrine of "separate but equal" public accommodations for African Americans, was first argued here in 1892 before being appealed to the U.S. Supreme Court.

Since 1911 the Cabildo has been part of the Louisiana State Museum (the private **Friends of the Cabildo** also helps maintain it). This is the best place to introduce yourself to Louisiana's complex history, from its French colonial foundation to the end of Reconstruction in 1877. The contributions of Native Americans, French colonists, African slaves, free people of color, and later immigrant groups such as the Anglo-Americans, Germans, Irish, and Italians are included. Carefully examine the rare paintings as you ascend the grand staircase. On the second floor is a death mask of Napoleon and the historic *sala capitular.* Other rooms here cover the territorial and early statehood period, the Battle of New Orleans, Zachary Taylor, and antebellum Louisiana. The third floor has fascinating exhibits on plantation life, slavery, urban life, the Civil War, and the tumultuous Reconstruction period of the 1870s. What is thought to be a slave auction block is on display here.

Note on Louisiana State Museum Admissions:
The Louisiana State Museum operates five important museums in the French Quarter: the Cabildo and Arsenal, the Presbytere, the Old Mint, "Madame John's Legacy," and the 1850 House. All are open Tuesday to Sunday 9 A.M. to 5 P.M. Single building tickets are $4 for adults, $3 for seniors, students, and military; and free for children twelve and under. Combination tickets, good for all five buildings for three days, are recommended and cost $10 for adults and $7.50 for seniors, students, and military; 568-6968

The Cabildo
701 Chartres Street, at St. Peter; open Tuesday to Sunday 10 A.M. to 5 P.M.; closed legal holidays; shop on third floor; see note on admission fees; 568-6968

Friends of the Cabildo
701 Chartres Street, N.O., 70116-3290; 523-3939

Upper Pontalba Building
502–46 St. Peter Street

Le Petit Théâtre du Vieux Carré
616 St. Peter Street, at Chartres; box office, 522-2081

The Arsenal / Louisiana State Museum
615 St. Peter Street; enter from the Cabildo

④ Upper Pontalba Building, *1849–50, James Gallier, Sr., Henry Howard*

Walk along the St. Peter Street mall past the Upper Pontalba Building. Madame Pontalba (see page 143) briefly lived in one of the apartments in this building. This landmark is owned by the City of New Orleans and was restored in 1997.

⑤ Le Petit Théâtre du Vieux Carré, *1789–95, Hilaire Boutté, builder; reconstructed 1962–63, Richard Koch and Samuel Wilson, Jr.*

On the uptown-lakeside corner of St. Peter and Chartres Streets is the severe Orue-Pontalba House, 616 St. Peter Street, with its delicate wrought-iron balcony made by Canary Island native Marcelino Hernandez. This house was begun in 1789 by builder Hilaire Boutté for a Spanish government official, but it was damaged in the fire of 1794. The next year it was bought by Joseph Xavier Pontalba, who completed it for his aunt Celeste Macarty. It was reconstructed in 1963 by architects Richard Koch and Samuel Wilson, Jr., for Le Petit Théâtre du Vieux Carré. This community theater group was organized in 1919 just as the old Quarter was becoming attractive to the artistic set and is the oldest community theater in continuous operation in the nation.

⑥ The Arsenal / Louisiana State Museum, *1839, James Harrison Dakin*

The white-painted building across the street is the Arsenal, built in 1839. It was designed by James Harrison Dakin, who trained in the New York office of Town and Davis before coming to New Orleans, where he worked until he moved to Baton Rouge to complete the old Gothic Revival state capitol (recently restored as a museum of Louisiana's gothic politics). The Arsenal was built on the site of an old Spanish prison and became the headquarters of the elite Louisiana Legion, a militia company with both Creole and Anglo-American members. Dakin created a powerfully expressive facade in this constricted space, with four severe pilasters framing deeply inset, grilled openings with strap-iron grilles in a diagonal pattern. It is an outstanding example of Greek Revival design. From here the Orleans Artillery set off for the war with Mexico under Louisianian Zachary Taylor in 1846. The Anglo-dominated nativist American Party (the "Know-Nothings") occupied the arsenal during their insurrection against the Creole-dominated Democratic municipal government, which they toppled in 1855. During the Civil War, both Confederate and Union troops successively stored arms here. In 1915 the landmark was turned over to the Louisiana State Museum to become the state's "Battle Abbey," a hall for war relics. Today it is part of the restored Cabildo complex and houses changing exhibits.

7   Le Petit Salon / Victor David House, *1838, Greek Revival town house, architect unknown*
Up from Le Petit Théâtre is this four-story, 1838 Greek Revival town house, which has settled into the soft ground. It was built for Victor David, a wealthy merchant, and his family lived here until 1867. Its three galleries each have a different ironwork, including an elegant design of crossed arrows. The house was purchased in 1925 and restored by Le Petit Salon, a woman's club that seeks "to promote enjoyment, harmony, refinement of manners and intellectual improvements" and that hosts weekly meetings, inviting speakers to talk about literature, history, or the arts. Among its founding members were author Grace King and columnist Dorothy Dix. This club helped make the French Quarter chic again.

Le Petit Salon / Victor David House
620 St. Peter Street

Gumbo Shop Restaurant / Commagere-Mercier House
630 St. Peter Street; inexpensive; no reservations so go at off-peak hours; open late; good for families with children; 525-1486

Avart-Peretti House
632 St. Peter Street

Pirate's Alley

Faulkner House Books
624 Pirate's Alley; 524-2940

8   Gumbo Shop Restaurant / Commagere-Mercier House, *circa 1795*
This old house dates from about 1795. Since 1945, the Roberts family's Gumbo Shop has been here, serving moderately priced Creole dishes. The dining room murals of Old New Orleans painted on burlap by Marc Anthony in 1925 date from when this was a tearoom. The courtyard shelters a banana tree.

9   Avart-Peretti House / Birthplace of *A Streetcar Named Desire*, *1842, J. N. B. de Pouilly*
Next to the Gumbo Shop is this brick town house with a T-shirt shop on its ground floor. Upstairs was once the home of painter Achille Peretti. From October 1946 through March 1947, St. Louis–born Tennessee Williams lived here in a two-story apartment with his lover, Pancho Rodriguez, while writing *A Streetcar Named Desire*. Williams's writing room was under a skylight on the third floor. "I know of no city where it is better to have a skylight than New Orleans," he reminisced. "You know, New Orleans is slightly below sea level and maybe that's why the clouds and sky seem so close" (from *Preservation in Print*, August 1993). Much later Williams bought an 1830s Greek Revival town house at 1014 Dumaine Street, though he lived mostly in Key West, Florida, and in a restless succession of hotel rooms.
           Cross the street and turn left down the narrow alley facing Le Petit Salon and walk toward the side of the cathedral.

10   Pirate's Alley / Faulkner House Books
The half-block-long Cabildo Alley makes a T with Pirate's Alley. There were never any pirates here; the name is a twentieth-century concoction. The view up the alley toward Royal Street has long been a favorite with local painters and photographers. At 624 Pirate's Alley is cozy **Faulkner House Books**. It occupies the ground floor of an 1840

Cathedral Garden
*Royal Street, between
Pirate's Alley and Père
Antoine Alley*

town house built by Melasie Trepagnier LaBranche, and is one of eleven buildings she had built here and on Royal and St. Peter Streets. The two LaBranche buildings on Pirate's Alley retain their original, simple wrought-iron balconies (the houses facing Royal Street, as we shall see, were later remodeled with much fancier cast iron). In 1925 William Faulkner rented a room here in silversmith and Tulane teacher William Spratling's apartment. Here he wrote his first novel, *Soldier's Pay*, and *Mosquitoes*, a satire on the local art colony. In 1988 this fine bookshop specializing in Southern literature and rare books opened in what had been Faulkner's ground-floor room. It is an oasis of civilization and an appropriate place to recall Faulkner's evocative characterization of elegantly decadent Old New Orleans, written for the *Times-Picayune* in 1925:

> A courtesan, not old and yet no longer young, who shuns the sunlight that the illusion of her former glory be preserved. The mirrors in her house are dim and the frames tarnished, all her house is dim and beautiful with age. She reclines gracefully upon a dull brocade chaise-longue, there is the scent of incense about her, and her draperies are arranged in formal folds. She lives in an atmosphere of a bygone and more gracious age. And those whom she receives are few in number, and they come to her through an eternal twilight.

⓫   Cathedral Garden / Père Antoine's Garden / Old Dueling Ground

The gated park here with its magnolia and sycamore trees and flourishing palmettos is the Cathedral Garden, known as Père Antoine's Garden in memory of Père Antoine de Sedella, a Capuchin monk who first came to Louisiana in 1788 as chief of the Spanish Inquisition. Spanish Governor Miro immediately sent him back to Spain, but he returned in 1795 to become rector of St. Louis Cathedral, where he served as a contentious, much-loved pastor until his death in 1829. In the eighteenth century, this stub end of Orleans Street was a favorite place for duels. In 1831 the city surveyed Ruelle d'Orleans Sud and Ruelle d'Orleans Nord, creating this small park. The wardens of the cathedral fenced it in; near its center, buried under flat granite slabs, are past rectors of the cathedral. The white marble statue of the Sacred Heart of Jesus, with his arms outstretched toward Bourbon Street, is illuminated at night and casts a looming shadow across the back of the cathedral. Statues of the Sacred Heart are powerful guardians all over New Orleans. This devotion has its origin in a vision experienced by Saint Margaret Mary Alacoque in a convent chapel in Paray-le-Monial, France, in 1673. Jesus' heart was aflame with love for humankind and he asked for Sister Margaret's heart, which he put inside his own and then gave back to her "like a burning flame in the shape of a heart." The slim marble obelisk capped by an urn facing Royal Street dates from 1859 and commemorates the officers and men of the French ship of war *Tonnerre,* who died of yellow fever in the Gulf of Mexico.

⑫   Fleur de Paris / Site of the Arts and Crafts Club, *1823*

At the corner of Pirate's Alley and Royal Street is the large window of Fleur de Paris, one of the finest shops for ladies' apparel and millinery in New Orleans. It occupies the ground floor of a house built in 1823 for Dr. Pierre Frederic Thomas. From 1933 to 1951, this building housed the New Orleans Arts and Crafts Club.

Fleur de Paris
712 Royal Street;
525-1899

711 Royal Street

Royal Cafe
706 Royal Street, at
Toulouse; 528-9086

⑬   Site of Truman Capote's Apartment, *before 1831; 1831, second floor added, James Longprea*

At **711 Royal Street** is a two-story galleried building. Truman Capote, born in 1925 in New Orleans at Touro Infirmary uptown, rented a room here in early 1945 after returning from New York City. He described it as "a small hot bedroom almost entirely occupied by a brass bed, and it was as noisy as a steel mill. Streetcars racketed under the window, and the carousings of sight seers touring the Quarter, the boisterous whiskey brawlings of soldiers and sailors made for continuous pandemonium" (from *Preservation in Print,* April 1993). Here he enjoyed the freest time of his life and wrote his first book, *Other Voices, Other Rooms.*

At Royal and Toulouse Streets, with its one polished red granite column at the corner, is the Quarter's busy A&P grocery store, open twenty-four hours a day (except Mardi Gras) and a good place to buy refreshments and culinary souvenirs. Check the shelves to the right as you enter for local products. Zatarain's red bean seasoning mix is a flavorful and compact souvenir (remove the flat packet from the bulky box for traveling). Community brand New Orleans blend coffee with chicory makes another flavorful reminder of your visit.

⑭   Royal Cafe / LaBranche Building, *1840, Greek Revival town houses; cast-iron galleries added after 1850*

On the uptown-lakeside corner of Royal and Toulouse Streets (best seen from near the A&P across the street) is one of the much-photographed LaBranche buildings. They were built as plain brick Greek Revival town houses in 1840 by Melasie Trepagnier LaBranche, widow of Jean Baptiste LaBranche, a wealthy sugar planter from St. Charles Parish. After 1850 the lacy cast-iron galleries were draped around the building, greatly enhancing its livability and creating this quintessential New Orleans building, the architectural trademark of the French Quarter. An elaborate oak leaf and acorn design embellishes the lush cast-iron tracery. Jean Baptiste LaBranche's ancestors came to Louisiana from Metz, Germany, where the family name was Zweig ("twig"); in Louisiana the name was translated into French, becoming LaBranche. Writer Sherwood Anderson lived here briefly in 1922.

Pedesclaux-LeMonnier Mansion
636–40 Royal Street, at Toulouse

Le Monde Créole
624 Royal Street; call 568-1801 for walk times

⑮   Pedesclaux-LeMonnier Mansion / 'Sieur George's Apartment, *after 1794; completed in 1811, Arsene Lacarriere Latour and Hyacinthe Laclotte*

On the uptown-riverside corner, facing the LaBranche Building, is the sober "Skyscraper Building" with its beveled corner. This four-story masonry building was probably begun shortly after the fire of 1794, perhaps to the designs of French architect Barthelemy Lafon. It was completed as a three-story house by Arsene Lacarriere Latour and Hyacinthe Laclotte in 1811. Dr. Yves LeMonnier occupied the two middle floors, and his YLM monogram embellishes the wrought-iron balconies. Originally there was a terrace garden on the roof. After 1876 a new owner, Bertrand Saloy, added the fourth floor and broke the house up into apartments. George Washington Cable set his 1873 story *'Sieur George* here and said of the building, "with its gray stucco peeling off in broad patches, it has a solemn look of gentility in rags, and stands, or, as it were, hangs, about the corner of two ancient streets like a faded fop who pretends to be looking for employment." In a second-floor apartment, Jon and Louise Webb printed the first issue of *The Outsider* on a hand press in 1961. This avant garde journal published works by Kerouac, Ginsberg, Burroughs, Corso, McClure, Olson, Creely, Patchen, Ferlinghetti, Snyder, LeRoi Jones, Diane DiPrima, and Bukowski.

⑯   Le Monde Créole / Labatut-Puig Courtyard, *1831, Creole-style town house*

This was once one of the best blocks of luxury shops and elite residences in old New Orleans. Walk through the tunnel-like porte cochere to the secluded courtyard with its benches. As in European cities, commercial uses have always existed on the ground floor here. At the end of the porte cochere you can look through the glass doors at the staircase that originally gave access to the house upstairs, now divided into apartments. There were originally only two rooms on the second and third floors, and they opened into each other Creole style without benefit of hallways. The rear wing visible from the courtyard with its lower ceiling heights was originally the kitchen with slave quarters above. It is also accessed from the one staircase via narrow galleries. At the back of the flagstone-paved court was a two-story stable with horse stalls on the ground floor and the coachman's quarters upstairs. Master and slave lived together on the same city lot in separate but connected buildings. **Le Monde Créole** is a shop of *objets curieux;* Creole-themed walks begin here daily.

On December 8, 1794, a fire broke out here when children accidently set fire to a warehouse full of hay. That conflagration destroyed the entire upper French Quarter as far as what is now Canal Street. In 1831 Dr. Isidor Labatut bought two lots here, demolished the old Spanish buildings that stood on them, and built this three-story, Creole-style house for his clinic and home. He built 616–18 next door as income property. He and his descendants lived here until 1953. U.S. Supreme Court Chief Justice Edward Douglass White read law in a law office here. When Richard Roth bought the landmark after Miss Ysabel Puig's death, he donated the old Creole Rococo Revival furniture to the Louisiana State Museum's 1850 House (see page 143). Across Royal Street are two other courtyards you can check out.

⑰   Old Town Praline & Gift Shop / Spanish House, *Spanish-style house and shops, circa 1789*

This plain, two-story, brick-and-stucco house was built about 1789 with a narrow gallery across its facade and a simple railing. There is a central passageway between two shops that leads to stairs and the back of the lot. You can walk through the praline shop here and see the utilitarian back of the house with its sheltered work areas. Beyond is a brick paved court and a simple garden. Opera singer Adelina Patti lived here in 1860–61.

⑱   Royal Blend Coffee & Tea House / Labatut House, *begun about 1795; 1821, addition by Pinson and Pizetta*

Next door is the cool tunnel of the porte cochere of 623–25 Royal Street. Here are the welcome shade and outdoor tables of the Royal Blend Coffee & Tea House. This is an ideal place to secure refreshments and to listen to the trickle of water in the soothing fountain. Quiet, brick-walled gardens tucked behind almost every French Quarter building are part of the essence of living in the Quarter (galleries overlooking the streets are another essential French Quarter architectural experience). This brick, three-story Creole town house was begun about 1795 for General Jean Labatut, who also built its twin next door at 619–21 Royal Street. It was originally a one-story building, but a second story was added in 1821 by the builders Pinson and Pizetta. This continued to be valuable property rewarding more intense development, and in the late nineteenth century a third story was added. Cross Toulouse Street to the square, gray granite pillars of the Historic New Orleans Collection.

⑲   The Historic New Orleans Collection / Merieult House Museum / Williams House Museum / Lafon House

The outstanding Historic New Orleans Collection owns a complex of five historic buildings at Royal and Toulouse Streets, connected by a flagstone-paved courtyard at their center. The Jean François Merieult House faces Royal Street and was built in 1792 on the site of the barracks and workshops of the Company of the Indies. It is one of the very few buildings to have escaped the fire of 1794. Remodeled in 1832 by Manuel J. de Lizardi, its ground floor had ten monolithic granite pillars inserted in it. The delicate balcony railing on its second floor is cast iron, though it looks like wrought iron. The landmark was bought by General and Mrs. L. Kemper Williams in 1938, and architect Richard Koch was engaged to restore it. The free Williams Gallery here has informative changing exhibits and a fine gift shop. Upstairs in the Merieult House is a series of handsome galleries filled with rare treasures. Various rooms display art and artifacts from the French and Spanish colonial periods, the Louisiana Purchase of 1803, the Battle of New Orleans of 1815, the American Empire and Victorian periods,

Old Town Praline & Gift Shop
627 Royal Street; 525-1413

Royal Blend Coffee & Tea House
623–25 Royal Street

The Historic New Orleans Collection
527-529-533 Royal Street; 718 and 726–28 Toulouse Street; open Tuesday to Saturday, tours at 10 and 11 A.M. and 1 and 2 P.M., small fee; free changing exhibits gallery and gift shop open Tuesday to Saturday 10 A.M. to 5 P.M.; 523-4662

**Seignouret-Brulatour-Irby
House**
520 Royal Street

Omni Royal Orleans Hotel
*621 St. Louis Street,
corner of Royal;
529-5333, 800-843-6664*

The Rib Room
529-7045

Louisiana plantations, and the River Gallery. Among such rarities i
is hard to pick out the most interesting ones; certainly John
Antrobus's dramatic 1860 painting of *A Plantation Burial* is impor
tant to Southerners, as is Mauritz F. H. de Haas's 1866 marine
painting of *Farragut's Fleet Passing the Forts Below New Orleans*
An elegant room on the ground floor of the Counting House dis
plays a fine group of New Orleans portraits.

The Williamses lived around the corner at 718 Toulouse Street
They decorated it in the 1940s and 1950s, and it has been preserved
as it was, giving a good idea of the opulence of restored French
Quarter homes in the mid-twentieth century. You can also see the restored exterior o
the Creole double cottage at 726–28 Toulouse Street, built about 1830 and a charac
teristic early French Quarter dwelling. From 1876 to 1883 this was the home of Thom
Lafon, a Creole of color landlord and philanthropist who willed his home to the Soci
ety of the Holy Family, an order of African American nuns who cared for orphans and
continue today to educate girls.

20   **Seignouret-Brulatour-Irby House,** *1816, attributed to Henry S. Latrobe; 1822
Robert Brand*

Cross the street and walk through the central carriage tunnel of 520 Royal Street int
the large, flagstone-paved courtyard with its welcome splashing fountain. Potted plant
and benches invite you to sit and rest. The Seignouret House is attributed to Henry .
Latrobe and was built in 1816 for Francois Seignouret, a famous maker and importe
of furniture. He conducted his business in one of the ground-floor shops and live
upstairs. Architect-builder Robert Brand added a rear wing in 1822. Wine importe
Pierre Brulatour bought the house in 1870 for his business and residence and lived her
until 1887. After that the building began to decay until it was bought and restored b
businessman and banker William Ratcliffe Irby in 1918 for his residence. In 1922 Irb
invited the Arts and Crafts Club to open its gallery and classrooms here to help reviv
the Quarter. The large arched openings facing the courtyard, the green-painted woode
gallery with its turned wood columns, and the twisting staircase in a back corner mak
this a classic French Quarter oasis much depicted by early-twentieth-century artists an
photographers. From 1949 to 1996, WDSU-TV, the first television station in Nev
Orleans, had its offices and studios here. As you leave the building look back at th
facade and note the fierce, emasculating, wrought-iron *garde de frise* at the left-han
end of the third-floor gallery.

21   **Omni Royal Orleans Hotel / Site of the St. Louis Hotel,** *1960, Curtis and Davi
plan and interior, Koch and Wilson, facade*

Tall iron columns on the corner announce the Omni Royal Orleans Hotel, the fir
large contemporary hotel built in the French Quarter. **The Rib Room** restaurant's win
dows look out onto Royal Street. Koch and Wilson were engaged to model an exterio
reminiscent of the lost St. Louis Exchange Hotel of 1838, which was draped over

taller modern building designed by Curtis and Davis. The original St. Louis Hotel was designed by J. N. B. and J. I. de Pouilly using the buildings of Paris' Rue de Rivoli as its model. It became a center of high Francophone Creole society (while the St. Charles Exchange Hotel across Canal Street was the epicenter for Anglo-American high society). The St. Louis Hotel originally had a great central rotunda where sugar planters bought slaves and other valuables at auction. As Creole society waned, so did its favorite hostelry. The former hotel served as the state capitol of Louisiana from 1874 to 1882. In 1876, the chaotic scenes that signaled the end of Reconstruction in Louisiana were acted out here when two legislatures, one Republican and racially integrated and one Democratic and white supremacist, vied for control of the state. Two governors also simultaneously contested the governorship. Federal troops were able to prevent violence but not the eventual political takeover by the white "Redeemers." Democratic governor Francis T. Nicholls and a Democratic "Bourbon" legislature emerged victorious and began the changes that resulted in *de juré* racial segregation.

Antoine's Restaurant
713 St. Louis Street; very expensive; jackets for gentlemen; reservations required; 581-4422

Eventually, in 1898, the building was left empty, and the hurricane of 1915 ripped off its roof. The historic ruin was demolished in 1916 for a parking lot. Up the marble stairs in the lobby is a fine painting by Boyd Cruise imagining the lost St. Louis Hotel in all its glory. The Omni Royal Orleans Hotel incorporates a fragment of the old granite arcade of the St. Louis Hotel along its Chartres Street side (visible from the Napoleon House at the end of this walk). At this point you should turn off Royal Street and walk a block and a half up St. Louis Street, past Antoine's Restaurant, to number 820 St. Louis Street, the Hermann-Grima House.

㉒   Antoine's Restaurant, *1825; additions in the late nineteenth century*

This is New Orleans' oldest, and probably most famous, restaurant. It began as a French Quarter boarding house opened by Marseilles-born Antoine Alciatore in 1840. It is the oldest restaurant in the country in continuous ownership by a single family, and the current proprietor, Bernard Guste, is Antoine Alciatore's great-great-grandson. In 1868 the restaurant moved to this building, a former residence built in 1825 for James Ramsey; the cast-iron galleries and mansard roof are later additions. Today the restaurant occupies the adjoining buildings as well. The front ground-floor dining room behind the frosted glass windows is the restaurant's most elegant room. As Baedeker's guide noted in 1909, Antoine's has "excellent French cuisine, high charges." Neither has changed. The encyclopedic menu is in French; Oysters Rockefeller was invented here, as was *pompano en papillote*. The souffléed potatoes and *filet mignon marchand de vin* are notable. Antoine's serves New Orleans-French cuisine and boasts an extensive wine list; many, however, consider the service impersonal. Cross festive, tawdry Bourbon Street; up ahead on the left-hand side of St. Louis Street is the Hermann-Grima House.

Hermann-Grima House Museum
820 St. Louis Street; open Monday to Saturday 10 A.M. to 3:30 P.M.; tours every half hour; cooking demonstrations on Thursday from October through May; closed legal holidays; small fee; 525-5661

James H. Cohen Antique Weapons and Coins
437 Royal Street; 522-3305

23   Hermann-Grima House Museum / The Christian Woman's Exchange, *1832, William Brand*

This house fuses Creole and American floor plans. It has an American-style central hall, unlike the older hall-less Creole floor plans, but the rear of the house has a loggia and two *cabinets,* traditional Creole design elements. This fine Federal-style mansion was built for Samuel Hermann, a wealthy German-born commission merchant, and designed by Scotland-born William Brand in 1831–32. The elegant, symmetrical brick facade is painted red with white penciled mortar joints in the American manner. The facade has two elegant openings, one the fanlighted front door and the other on the second floor opening onto the gallery that runs the width of the building. Alongside the mansion is a courtyard with the last private stable in the French Quarter. There is also a working kitchen where traditional Creole foods are prepared. Judge Felix Grima bought the house in 1844, and five generations of his descendants lived here until 1921. In 1924 the Christian Woman's Exchange took title to the old house. The purpose of this originally Protestant organization was "the encouragement, improvement and reclamation of our own sex." In addition to a dormitory and lunch room, the Exchange operated a salesroom where women could sell what they made, from jelly to needlework. In 1971 the Exchange restored the house and opened it to the public; many of the items in its gift shop are on consignment from local women artists. Many of the fine furnishings were provided by the Colonial Dames of America. The interpretive focus here is the social history of the French Quarter from 1830 to 1860. The courtyard is a good example of early French Quarter courtyard gardens. Walk back to Royal Street and turn right; one building down is James H. Cohen Antique Weapons and Coins.

24   James H. Cohen Antique Weapons and Coins / Site of Peychaud's Apothecary and Birthplace of the Cocktail, *1800*

Antoine Amedee Peychaud was a Creole refugee from Haiti who came to New Orleans in 1795 and opened the Pharmacie Peychaud. Here he dispensed drugs and his own tonic bitters. He created a concoction consisting of cognac laced with a dash of bitters, using a double-ended egg cup as his measure. French-speaking New Orleanians called these *coquetiers,* and the English-speaking patrons took to calling Peychaud's drinks "cocktails." Peychaud's Aromatic Cocktail Bitters are still made in New Orleans by L. E. Jung and Wolff Company and sold in bottles with old-fashioned labels that boast that they are used *dans tons les meilleurs cafes,* a lingering vestige of bilingual New Orleans. Cross the street to the white court house.

25   **Old New Orleans Court Building,** *1910, Frederick W. Brown, A. Ten Eyck Brown, and P. Thornton Marya; 1994, restoration, Lyons and Hudson*

Old New Orleans Court Building
400 Royal Street

Brennan's Restaurant
417 Royal Street; expensive; dress code at dinner; reservations advised; breakfast begins at 8 A.M.; 525-9711

This monumental white marble and terra cotta Beaux Arts building framed by dark green magnolia trees was originally the New Orleans Court Building. Built in 1910 and designed by Frederick W. Brown, A. Ten Eyck Brown, and P. Thornton Marya, this massive building required the demolition of an entire square block of historic French Quarter buildings. At the time the French Quarter was considered an expendable slum. When the municipal courts relocated to the city's International-style complex off Loyola Avenue in the 1950s, this grand building became the Louisiana Wildlife and Fisheries Museum and eventually fell into extreme dilapidation. The return of the courts promises the restoration of this now-prized -twentieth-century intruder with its grand interiors. It is slated to house the Louisiana Supreme Court (which sits in New Orleans, not Baton Rouge), the Fourth Circuit Court of Appeals, the Louisiana Supreme Court Library, and a small Louisiana Supreme Court Museum.

Here it is appropriate to make a brief *excursus* on law in the sovereign Commonwealth of Louisiana. Napoleon ruled Louisiana for only one month in 1803 before selling the vast territory to the United States. In 1808, the territorial legislature of Orleans adopted a *Digest of Civil Laws* modeled after the Napoleonic Code. This confirmed Louisiana's status as an exotic island of Roman civil law in an English common law sea. Needless to say, this has been good for local lawyers if bad for Louisiana. National corporations doing business here have long had to retain local counsel to deal with this expensive anomaly. A. Oakley Hall, a self-proclaimed *Manhattaner in New Orleans,* noted in his very fine guide of 1851:

> The legal profession has been, and ought always to be, a lucrative one as pursued in New Orleans. Merchants who have traded and leased and speculated under the laws of Massachusetts or New York or Ohio, will very naturally, in the conceit of human knowledge, proceed to contract, while resident in New Orleans, in the same manner as before; and thus proceeding will run upon some snag in the undercurrents of Louisiana law and only be saved from total wreck by paying 'your humble servant of the bar' a very nice fee by way of salvage.

Visible from here is a handsome row of historic buildings across Royal Street.

26   **Brennan's Restaurant / Banque de la Louisiane,** *1795*

This end of Royal Street was the preferred location for Louisiana's early banks, each of which bought or built a grand edifice here. The pink stucco building across from the Supreme Court was erected in 1795 for Jose Faurie as a combination commercial building and residence. In 1805 it became the home of the Banque de la Louisiane

Manheim's Galleries
*403 Royal Street, at
Conti; 568-1901*

Waldhorn & Adler
*343 Royal Street, at
Conti; 581-6379*

under its first president, Julien Poydras; it was the first bank in Louisiana. At that time the cast-iron shields with the LB monogram and the two horns with coins spilling out of them were added to the building's balconies. In 1820 Martin Gordon bought the building from the liquidators of the defunct bank. In 1841 Alonzo Morphy bought the building at auction, and his family lived here until 1891.

Chess prodigy and failed lawyer Paul Morphy died here at age forty-seven in 1884. Businessman-preservationist William Ratcliffe Irby bought the landmark and gave it to Tulane University in 1920. The chic Café Royal bustled here from the 1920s into the 1940s. The historic mansion has housed Brennan's Restaurant since 1956. Brennan's was founded in 1946 by Owen E. Brennan, Sr., and this is now one of a Brennan family dynasty of outstanding New Orleans restaurants. Brennan's has twelve dining rooms on two floors, including tables in a banana-planted courtyard. The best indoor seats enjoy views of the courtyard and its fountain.

㉗   Manheim's Galleries / Louisiana State Bank, *1820, Benjamin Henry Latrobe*
The intersection of Royal and Conti Streets was once the center of banking in New Orleans and boasted banks on three of its corners. This yellow building on the downtown-lakeside corner was English-born Benjamin Henry Latrobe's last work before his death from yellow fever in 1820. (Latrobe also designed the original Capitol in Washington and the Roman Catholic Cathedral in Baltimore.) Latrobe did not approve of the American introduction of red-brick buildings in the old French section, and he employed light-colored stucco for this exterior in the traditional Creole manner. The bank was on the ground floor, and the cashier's apartment was upstairs. Originally it had a flat terraced roof; the hipped roof and dormers are later additions. Inside the high-ceilinged ground floor are a series of impressive masonry vaults supporting a shallow dome. Today it is occupied by Manheim's Galleries, established in 1919 and one of the city's toniest antique shops. You are now approaching the heart of the antique district.

㉘   Waldhorn & Adler / Rillieux House / Bank of the United States, *circa 1800, attributed to Barthelemy Lafon; 1972, Freret and Wolfe*
The two-story, dusty rose, corner building across Conti Street from Manheim's is a fine but quiet example of Spanish colonial architecture in New Orleans. The wrought-iron balconies may have come from Seville. From 1811 to 1820, it housed La Banque des Habitantes, the Planters Bank; from 1820 to 1836, the Bank of the United States of Philadelphia; and from 1836 to 1838, the New Orleans Gas Light and Banking Company, the delightfully named Banque du Gaz. The catastrophic panic of 1837 wiped out virtually all the banks in New Orleans, ending the "flush times" in the Deep South. Long the home of Waldhorn Antiques, this landmark became Waldhorn & Adler in 1997.

㉙   Eighth District Police Station / Vieux Carré Commission / Bank of Louisiana, 1826, *Bickle, Hamblet, and Fox; 1840, additions by James Gallier, Jr.*

On the uptown-riverside corner of Royal and Conti Streets is the former Bank of Louisiana, with its giant Ionic orders and a front garden with magnolia trees. It was erected in 1826 and designed by Bickle, Hamblet, and Fox; the fine iron fence was made in New York City in 1827. The portico was a later addition by James Gallier, Jr., erected after a fire in 1840. This building was the state capitol of Louisiana for one year, from 1868 to 1869. In 1874 the Reconstruction city government bought the building, and for many years it housed the Mortgage and Conveyance Office. The landmark was restored in 1971, and today it houses the New Orleans Eighth District Police Station. There is a small exhibit of police memorabilia in two glass cases here, including old star-and-crescent badges. Upstairs is the office of the City's Vieux Carré Commission, which is charged with the preservation of the French Quarter.

㉚   A Gallery for Fine Photography / Antique Row

Almost next door to the police station is A Gallery for Fine Photography, a must-see for connoisseurs of photography. This is one of the most extensive shops of its kind, with both historical and contemporary photographic prints and photography books on two floors. The gallery also represents some of the best photographers working in New Orleans today. Across Royal Street is a splendid row of fine antique shops, veritable treasure-houses of fine furniture and high decorative art. Visible two blocks up Royal Street is Canal Street. The high-rise across Canal is First NBC Center, erected in 1985 on the site of the historic St. Charles Exchange Hotel, the gathering place for the antebellum Anglo-American elite (see page 240). At Royal and Bienville turn left; continue only half a block down Bienville and turn left again to enter narrow Exchange Alley.

㉛   Exchange Alley, 1837, *J. N. B. de Pouilly*

This picturesque alley was cut through from Canal Street to the St. Louis Hotel on St. Louis Street by the New Orleans Improvement Company in 1837. The company bought the long "key" lots that had been surveyed through the center of each block by Adrien de Pauger. A uniform, three-story, arcaded facade designed by J. N. B. de Pouilly was to be imposed on all the buildings along the prestigious pedestrian connector, but this was never completed. Numbers 618 and 620 Conti Street, the "bookends" at the far end of the alley, show what was intended. When Fashion drifted on to other locations, the city's fencing masters opened their schools here. **The Hall-Barnett Gallery and Annex** specializes in emerging New Orleans artists, displaying the fertile artistic work of the Crescent City in the 1990s. (Those more interested in antiques may wish to walk

Eighth District Police Station
334 Royal Street, at Conti; NOPD: Emergency dial 911; nonemergency 821-2222

A Gallery for Fine Photography
322 Royal Street; open Monday to Saturday 10 A.M. to 6 P.M., Sunday 11 A.M. to 5 P.M.; 568-1313

Exchange Alley

Hall-Barnett Gallery and Annex
320 Exchange Alley; open Monday to Saturday 10 A.M. to 5 P.M.; 525-5656

503 Shop
503 Chartres Street; 525-0327

Williams Research Center of the Historic New Orleans Collection
410 Chartres Street; 598-7100

K-Paul's Louisiana Kitchen
416 Chartres Street; lunch is best; now takes reservations for upstairs dining room; validated parking at Omni Royal Orleans garage; 524-7394

Whitney National Bank
430 Chartres Street; 586-7502

Napoleon House Bar and Cafe
500 Chartres Street, at St. Louis; open late; 524-9752

down Bienville half a block farther to the corner of Chartres. To the left, at 503 Chartres, is the **503 Shop,** an old-fashioned antique store crammed with dusty treasures.) Turn right at Conti and left on Chartres.

32   Williams Research Center of the Historic New Orleans Collection / Old Second City Criminal Court and Third District Police Station, *1915, Edgar Angelo Christy, City Architect; 1996, restoration and adaption, Davis Jahncke*
Immediately behind the monumental court building is this former city court building and police station, a handsome piece of municipal architecture from the City Beautiful era when public buildings were elegant additions to the cityscape. It was designed by City Architect Edgar Angelo Christy and completed in 1915. The Historic New Orleans Collection acquired the Beaux Arts building in 1993 and restored and adapted it for its Williams Research Center. Next door is **K-Paul's Louisiana Kitchen,** named for Cajun chef Paul Prudhomme and his wife, Kay. This is a phenomenally popular new restaurant that often sports a long line. The ample Mr. Prudhomme is celebrated for making Cajun (which is not Creole) "blackened" cooking nationally famous.

33   Whitney National Bank, Morgan State Branch, *1966, Koch and Wilson*
This horizontal, two-story bank is a modern building designed to suavely blend with the historic French Quarter. The long row of square granite pillars is 1830s in appearance; several of them were recycled from the building that once stood on this site. Behind this traditional granite arcade is a cool, white interior with marble columns. Designed in 1966 by Koch and Wilson, this refined banking hall has a Jeffersonian quality, with its fluted Doric colonnade and gently bowed ceiling. A window at the back of the room looks out into a shallow courtyard. This building is a sophisticated homage to New Orleans commercial architecture from the hand of a great regional architect and historian.

34   Napoleon House Bar and Cafe / Girod House, *1814, probably by Hyacinthe Laclotte*
At the downtown-riverside corner of Chartres and St. Louis Streets is one of the most atmospheric buildings in the French Quarter, the picturesque Napoleon House Bar and Cafe. It is the perfect place to end this walk through the past and present of the Vieux Carré, relaxing and reflecting while eating muffulettas (a local cold cut and cheese sandwich on round bread with an olive salad relish) or smoky gumbo, drinking champagne by the glass, and listening to classical music in a cool, cavelike setting. There is also a pleasant courtyard. The Impastato family's Napoleon House has achieved the

impossible: remained a local institution frequented by Quarterites while welcoming visitors, something you will have noticed much of the upper Quarter has not managed to do. The fact-lazy buggy drivers announce to tourists that this building was built in 1797. It wasn't; only the two-story wing facing St. Louis Street was erected then for Claude François Girod, Nicholas's brother. The three-story corner building with the practical sidewalk covering, hipped roof, and cupola was built in 1814 for Mayor Nicholas Girod. It is one of very few buildings left in the Quarter with an old-fashioned tile roof. Girod was mayor from 1812 to 1815, and it is a much-repeated local legend that he offered his house as a place of refuge to the exiled emperor of the French.

*Hidden gardens are the essence of the residents' French Quarter.
The old-fashioned walled garden added to the Beauregard-Keyes House in 1955 is a quiet
oasis with a trickling cast-iron pelican fountain.*

Tour 2

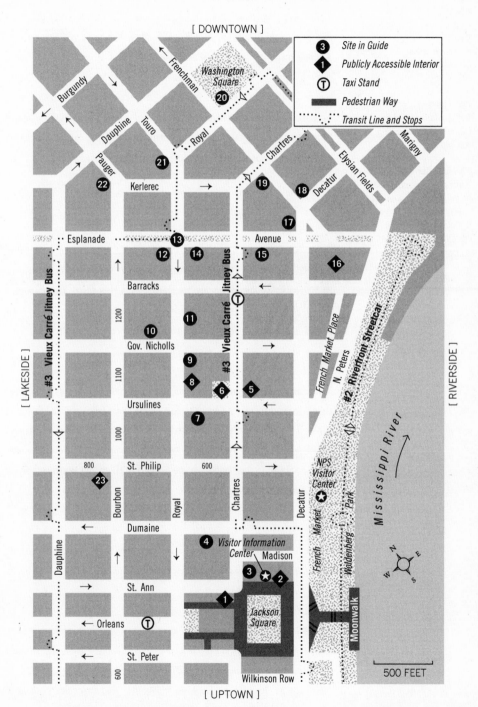

[DOWNTOWN]

Site in Guide ③

Publicly Accessible Interior ◆1

Taxi Stand ⓣ

Pedestrian Way

Transit Line and Stops

Washington Square

20

Burgundy

Frenchman

Dauphine

Touro

Royal

Pauger

21

22

Kerlerec

Chartres

Marigny

19

Decatur

Elysian Fields

18

17

Esplanade

13

Avenue

12   14   15

16

Barracks

1200

11

10

Gov. Nicholls

#3 Vieux Carré Jitney Bus

#3 Vieux Carré Jitney Bus

9

1100

8

6   5

Ursulines

7

French Market Place

N. Peters

#2 Riverfront Streetcar

St. Philip

1000

800   600

NPS Visitor Center ★

Mississippi River

23

Bourbon

Royal

Chartres

Decatur

Dumaine

French Market

Waldenberg Park

[LAKESIDE]

[RIVERSIDE]

Dauphine

4 Visitor Information Center

Madison

3 ★ 2

1 ◆

Jackson Square

St. Ann

Orleans ⓣ

Moonwalk

N
W   E
S

St. Peter

600

Wilkinson Row

500 FEET

[UPTOWN]

Parking
• *Behind the Gallier House at 1132 Royal Street*
• *Lots between the French Market and the river; enter from Barracks Street*

Taxi Stand
Le Richlieu Hotel on Chartres Street, near Barracks

#3 Vieux Carré Jitney Bus
Runs from about 5 A.M. to 5:30 P.M. on weekdays, and from about 8 A.M. to 6 P.M. on weekends; fares are $1, transfers 10¢

What This Tour Covers

This walk begins at Jackson Square and heads downriver through the residential side of the French Quarter to leafy Esplanade Avenue and across it into Faubourg Marigny. It includes the (now open to public!) only surviving Louisiana French colonial–style house in the Quarter, three other important house museums, a "secret" garden, the interior of the old French colonial Ursuline Convent, and the Old Mint's Jazz and Mardi Gras exhibits. It ends at Frenchmen Street's happening musical venues.

Preliminaries

BEST TIMES TO DO THIS TOUR

The days and times when the house museums, the old Ursuline convent, and the Old Mint are open are the best to do this tour. You can end your day with dinner on Decatur Street and music later on nearby Frenchmen Street.

Parking

You need a residential parking sticker or visitor's parking pass to park in the lower Quarter for more than two hours. There is limited parking **behind the Gallier House** at 1132 Royal Street, between Ursulines and Governor Nicholls Streets. There is longer term parking in lots **between the French Market and the river;** enter from Barracks Street.

Taxi Stand

There is a taxi stand in front of **Le Richlieu Hotel** on Chartres Street, near Barracks, a few blocks from the end of this walk.

Transportation

The **#3 Vieux Carré jitney bus** terminus is at Washington Square near the end of this walk. It can bring you back into the French Quarter via Dauphine Street. The Riverfront streetcar line has its terminus at the foot of Esplanade Avenue and can take you back to Jackson Square or farther up to Canal Street or the convention center.

Music Venues

This side of the Quarter and Faubourg Marigny have some of the best music venues in the city, the places where locals go to hear live music. See the Frenchmen Street venues (see page 155).

Shopping

This residential district has very little shopping. Decatur Street, from about St. Philip to Barracks Streets, has a cluster of funky antique/junk shops where you can rummage through old, sequin-encrusted Mardi Gras costumes. There are also a couple of trendy post-punk clothing shops on Decatur that are popular with teenagers.

You can also take a taxi to **Inferno Glass Studio;** this former industrial building now houses various artists and lets you sometimes glimpse glassmaking. Telephone ahead to be sure they are open. An off-the-beaten-track restaurant favored by locals is **Feelings Cafe and Patio Lounge** located deep in Faubourg Marigny with an atmospheric courtyard bar. **Adolfo's** upstairs at 611 Frenchmen Street near the music clubs serves pasta, chicken, and seafood.

Inferno Glass Studio
3000 Royal Street, at Montague Street, in Bywater; 945-1878

Feelings Cafe and Patio Lounge
In Faubourg Marigny at 2600 Chartres Street, at Franklin; 945-2222

Adolfo's
In Faubourg Marigny at 611 Frenchmen Street, near Chartres; dinner only; 948-3800

Introduction:
The Residents' Vieux Carré

> They told me to catch a streetcar named Desire and then transfer
> to one called Cemeteries.
>
> —Blanche Dubois in Tennessee Williams's
> *A Streetcar Named Desire*, 1947

Blanche was going from working-class downtown to then-posh Canal Street uptown.
Blanche's neighborhood (Marigny) has changed and not changed. The lower French
Quarter, once-grand Esplanade Avenue, and funky Faubourg Marigny remain vital
residential neighborhoods. They are home to open, interesting people committed to
living in the cultural heart of the old city. Though there are many apartments in the
upper Quarter over the almost continuous strip of businesses that line the ground
floors of its tall brick buildings, it is only downriver of Jackson Square that residences
predominate over businesses and that the French Quarter begins to feel like a neighborhood. And a strong, feisty community it is, dedicated to keeping the Quarter an
island of civilization against all odds. The lower Quarter also preserves the intimate,
now almost obsolete "walker's city" of pre-automotive days.

True Quarterites are a rare amalgam of promiscuity and privacy.
They live here not only for the quaint streets and picturesque architecture, though those
qualities certainly distinguish this neighborhood, but also because they treasure the
individual in people. Quarterites are among the very last of the true city people, those
who crave variety, difference, and mental stimulation. They buy both antiques at
auctions and contemporary art from living artists. In their houses and apartments a
kind of happy chaos reigns. There are big art books in small rooms, modern novels that
have actually been read, CDs of old jazz, classical music, and modern rock, paintings,
artistic photographs, lived-with furniture, and jumbles of personal mementos clutter-
ing the mantles. What makes the Quarter work as a culture is a communal agreement
on what matters most in life: that life be varied in its human relations. You can't
frighten the mules here. This is why Europeans and visitors from large cities "take" to
New Orleans' French Quarter. And yet, here there is a gentle softness, a sensuousness,
most unlike New York City or Los Angeles or Chicago. Quarterites cultivate a taste for
fantasy, for private worlds, for individual dreams.

Physically what distinguishes the lower Quarter from the upper
Quarter is the generally smaller size of its buildings and their lack of pretention. The
historically more prestigious upper Quarter was densely rebuilt over time with three-
and four-story brick buildings. The lower Quarter has always been more humble. The
buildings here tend to be one or two stories, and many are built of wood. There is some
cast iron here, but not all that much. Old one-story Creole cottages survive here and
there. There are also quite a few Victorian shotgun houses from the 1890s, with the
fancy brackets at their eaves their only decoration, and a sprinkling of early twentieth-
century bungalows. Private, walled-in gardens flourish. Monumental buildings are

rare, and commerce is limited to corner groceries and bars and shops that serve residents. As you walk down Bourbon Street at night through the good-time crowds along the bar strip and come to Dumaine Street, all of a sudden it's darker and quieter, residential instead of commercial. Here and there Quarterites sit on wooden stoops (hospitably designed like sidewalk settees) watching the passersby, perhaps with the television still on in the sidewalk-facing front room behind them. This is the real Quarter to those who live here.

Once you pass out of the lower French Quarter and reach wide, leafy Esplanade (rhymes with grenade) Avenue, the houses are suddenly bigger, grander, and built of brick. Esplanade took its name from the parade ground at its foot reserved by City Surveyor Jacques Tanesse in 1810. This strip of the former town commons, originally reserved for fortifications, was subdivided into building lots in 1812. Wider than any street in the old French Quarter, and with a tree-lined median, Esplanade became the elite residential avenue for the city's successful French Creoles, their downtown St. Charles Avenue. The grand houses here date from the 1830s to about 1860 and are mostly intact, though usually subdivided into smaller apartments. Esplanade Avenue leads out of the Quarter to Esplanade Ridge, Bayou St. John, and City Park (see Tour 3). The lower Quarter's most monumental edifice sits at the foot of Esplanade, the Old United States Mint built on the site of Spanish fort San Carlos.

Just across Esplanade things change abruptly again; here is Faubourg Marigny. Among the earliest owners of this land was Claude Joseph Villars Dubreuil, who emigrated from Dijon, France, to Louisiana in 1719. He became the contractor for all the Crown's buildings in the new colonial city. In 1743 he bought this tract from the widow of Pierre Dreux and established a sawmill and a sugar plantation. In 1798 Pierre Philippe de Marigny acquired the plantation, and upon his death in 1800, his son Bernard Xavier Philippe de Marigny de Mandeville inherited it. Bernard Marigny was one of Louisiana's richest Creoles, and he cultivated extravagant tastes. Two Anglo-American developers, James Caldwell and Samuel J. Peters, approached Marigny about buying his land for a suburban extension of the city, but Marigny rebuffed them, and the two entrepreneurs later went on to create the Garden District uptown. Marigny decided to develop his land himself, and in 1805 he engaged architect and surveyor Barthélémy Lafon to lay out blocks and lots to create Faubourg Marigny. Its streets were aligned with the existing north-south sawmill canal that ran down the center of what became Elysian Fields Avenue. Faubourg Marigny's small lots were put on the market in 1809, just before the great flood of refugees escaping the revolution in Haiti arrived. (This sudden influx can best be likened to the exodus of middle-class Cubans who flooded into Miami after the Cuban Revolution.) There were French whites, African slaves, and free people of color in this great migration, and it transformed New Orleans. Some of these Francophone newcomers bought lots and built small Creole cottages in the new downriver suburb. So identified with people of mixed race did this neighborhood become that the adjective "marigny" came to mean a light-skinned African American. Malcolm X described himself as "marigny" because of his reddish bronze skin and reddish hair.

Faubourg Marigny has an eccentric (for New Orleans) grid oriented to the same compass that the rest of the world uses: the streets here run north-south and east-west, so people easily get lost. The modern one-way streets baffle even cab-drivers. In a city noted for imaginative street names, Faubourg Marigny originally had some of the best. There was a *Rue des Grandes Hommes, Rue de Craps, Rue d'Amour, Rue des Bon Enfants, Rue de Bagatelle, Rue de Poets,* and *Rue de Musique.* Alas, they were renamed Dauphine, Burgundy, N. Rampart, St. Claude, Pauger, and St. Roch in 1850; only Music Street kept its beautiful name, if in a harsher tongue. *Rue de Craps* was named by Marigny for the dice game which he is said to have introduced to the United States. An inveterate gambler, Marigny lived to be ninety-three, more than long enough to squander his fortune through high living and rolling the bones. When he died in 1868, a minor functionary in the city government, his creditors took over his estate.

Along with Faubourg Tremé across Rampart Street (see page 202), Faubourg Marigny was one of the places where white lovers ensconced their mulatto mistresses in their own houses under a French Creole custom known as *plaçage.* The custom probably came from Saint Domingue (Haiti) or the West Indies, where there was also a dearth of marriageable white women. In the antebellum period, some wealthy white men in their twenties established permanent liaisons with free women of color. The children born of these unions generally took their father's last name and were supported by him. These children were not considered black but rather free people of color. They were Francophone, Roman Catholic, and evolved their own distinct, enduring society. When these white men married white women to raise their legitimate family, they often set up their former mistresses in their own small houses. Marigny's *Rue d'Amour* and *Rue des Bon Enfants,* today N. Rampart Street and St. Claude Avenue, are said to have been favored locations for such domiciles. Mulatto mistresses often later became boardinghouse keepers, hairdressers, seamstresses, shopkeepers, or landladies. Mixed-race women accounted for the majority of free people of color in antebellum New Orleans, and they were the overwhelming majority of those free people of color who owned property in the city. Some free people of color owned slaves and a few hired Irish assistants. White fathers sometimes paid for the education of their mixed-race children, a fabled few of whom even studied in Paris. A few white men continued to support two families all their lives long: their legitimate white family and their legally unrecognized mixed-race family. Thus some old New Orleanian French last names today denote two very different family networks.

New Orleans' complex three-caste society was sharply different from the two-caste plantation society in the interior of the Old South, where the children of white slaveowners and African American slave women inherited the slave status of their mothers, and where no intermediate society of free people of color emerged. The free people of color lost their distinctive legal status with emancipation after the Civil War. But the descendants of New Orleans' free people of color have never lost their identity, and they flourish today. They are identifiable by their French surnames and sometimes first names, Roman Catholicism, and strong commitment to educating their children in parochial schools. Contemporary city politics has emerged as the avenue of mobility for the educated descendants of this mediating group in New Orleans' now-long-gone, three-caste Caribbean society.

Later, waves of German immigrants favored this neighborhood, and Marigny got the nickname Little Saxony. Still later, in the early twentieth century, many Latin Americans, especially Hondurans, lived here. In the twentieth century, when industry and warehousing invaded the faded neighborhood, industrial structures were erected here and there. After the explosion in house prices in the French Quarter in the late 1970s, some gays and lesbians began buying and restoring the small houses in Marigny. Today, along with the lower French Quarter, Marigny is one of New Orleans' two gay neighborhoods. A 1990 demographic snapshot of Marigny Triangle, the area bounded by Esplanade and Elysian Fields Avenues and Dauphine Street, revealed a neighborhood chiefly composed of renters (83.3 percent), predominantly white (93.4 percent), and chiefly between the ages of twenty and forty-nine. There are many singles and very few children here; only 4.8 percent of the residents were nineteen or younger.

Marigny's one short commercial street, *Rue des François,* now Frenchmen Street, is the heart of New Orleans' present-day bohemia. Hip music venues with a predominantly local following of young people and artists make this the "scene" that is missing on Bourbon Street. One-block-square Washington Square lies between Frenchmen Street and Elysian Fields Avenue. This avenue, with its elevated name and shabby reality, is where Tennessee Williams set *A Streetcar Named Desire.* While that streetcar is long since gone, there is now a Desire bus line. Below Elysian Fields are modest neighborhoods of one-story frame houses originally owned or rented by German, Irish, and later, Italian immigrants; very few Anglo-Americans lived here. Along the riverfront were the cotton presses (giant machines that squeezed cotton bales into smaller dimensions for shipping) that gave wide Press Street, with its railroad tracks, its name. Downriver from Franklin Avenue to the Orleans Parish line was the locally famous white Catholic, working-class Ninth Ward, which developed its own Brooklyn-like accent that New Orleanians call "Yat" (from the ritual greeting: "Where y'at?").

Since the 1970s these neighborhoods have suffered from widespread white flight and have gotten much poorer. Modest but historically and architecturally important houses here are undergoing what New Orleanians call "demolition by neglect." This is the city of dilapidated houses and Third World poverty for which no guidebooks are written. Its bleak future seems to be more and more empty lots, for once buildings here are abandoned and then burn down or are demolished, nothing is built in their place. Amid this unraveling of the working-class city, the low warehouse rents and house prices in Marigny and Bywater have lured many artists. It is an almost invisible bohemia, so close yet so far from the bustling French Quarter.

Note on Louisiana State Museum Admissions:
The Louisiana State Museum operates five important museums in the French Quarter: the Cabildo and Arsenal, the Presbytere, the Old Mint, "Madame John's Legacy," and the 1850 House. All are open Tuesday to Sunday 9 A.M. to 5 P.M. Single building tickets are $4 for adults; $3 for seniors, students, and military; and free for children twelve and under. Combination tickets, good for all five buildings for three days, are recommended and cost $10 for adults and $7.50 for seniors, students, and military; 568-6968

The Presbytere / Louisiana State Museum
751 Chartres Street, at St. Ann; open Tuesday to Sunday 10 A.M. to 5 P.M.; closed legal holidays; see above for admission fees; 568-6968

①   The Presbytere / Louisiana State Museum, *1791, Gilberto Guillemard; 1813, Claude Gurlie and Joseph Guillot; 1847, Henri Gobet and Victor Amiel, builders*

Downriver of the cathedral, making a pair with the Cabildo, is the arcaded Presbytere. It takes its name from its intended use as a residence for the Capuchin monks who served the cathedral, though this imposing edifice was never used as such. (The cathedral's priests live behind the Presbytere on Père Antoine Alley.) The Presbytere was begun in 1791 after the disasterous conflagration of 1788 to designs by Gilberto Guillemard and was financed by Don Andrés Almonester y Roxas. When Almonester died in 1798, construction stopped, leaving a one-story building that the cathedral wardens then rented for shops. The church sued Almonester's estate for the money to complete the building but lost its suit in Madrid. In 1813 the cathedral wardens completed the building's second story to designs by Claude Gurlie and Joseph Guillot, and in 1834 the entire building was rented to the city for a courthouse. It was expanded to the rear in 1840, and in 1847 the third, mansard-roofed floor and a lost cupola was added by Henri Gobet and Victor Amiel, builders. The city purchased the building in 1853 and continued using it as a courthouse until 1911, when the white, monumental Beaux Arts courts building at 400 Royal Street (see page 127) was completed. The landmark was then transferred to the Louisiana State Museum. Under the arcade is a primitive iron vessel discovered sunk in Lake Pontchartrain in 1878 and long misidentified as the Confederate submarine *Pioneer*. While it is true that in 1861 J. H. McClintock built a primitive, manually propelled submarine at his machine shop on Levee (now Decatur) Street, this is not that experimental warship.

The Presbytere houses a collection of Louisiana portraits, marine paintings, and artifacts, including early furniture made in New Orleans. This is the finest historical portrait collection in the state and is an evocative way to make visual connections with (mostly the elite of) old Louisiana. Outstanding is Jean Joseph Vaudechamp's splendid portrait of Antoine Jacques Philippe de Marigny de Mandeville in his scarlet, gold braid–bedecked uniform of the Orleans Lancers of the Louisiana Militia, painted in 1833 by Jacques Amans. A large full-length portrait of Don Andrés Almonester y Roxas, executed in 1796 by José de Salazar, preserves the likeness of the rich Spanish landlord and philanthropist. There is also a small tempera on ivory portrait (circa 1830) of Madame Pontalba, Almonester's daughter who built the Pontalba Buildings.

②   Lower Pontalba Building / 1850 Town House Museum / Louisiana State Museum, *1850–51, James Gallier, Sr., Henry Howard*

Lower Pontalba Building / 1850 Town House Museum / Louisiana State Museum
523 St. Ann Street; open Tuesday to Sunday 10 A.M. to 5 P.M.; optional tours on the hour until 3 P.M.; see page 142 for admission fees; 568-6968

The monumental, red-brick Pontalba Buildings were erected between 1849 and 1851 to designs by architect James Gallier, Sr., and completed by architect Henry Howard; Samuel Stewart was their competent builder. Madame Pontalba's relationships with Gallier, Howard, and Stewart were all conflicted. The Pontalba Buildings consist of two facing rows of sixteen four-story town houses with shops on the ground floor of each dwelling. Stanley Clisby Arthur described them in his *Old New Orleans* of 1936 as "like two companies of red-uniformed soldiers drawn up stiffly on parade." They were built of fine pressed red brick from Baltimore; granite from New England; timber from Louisiana; plate glass, slates, and roofing tiles from England; New Jersey window glass; and cast iron from New York City. The Pontalba Buildings introduced cast-iron galleries over New Orleans *banquettes* (sidewalks), an extremely practical and influential innovation. This custom-made iron work sports cartouches in the railings with the monogram "AP" for the ill-matched Almonester and Pontalba families. As originally built, each house was linked to the gas company's main line and had a water hydrant in its back courtyard. Water closets inside the dwellings emptied into a privy vault under the service court.

Unfortunately, the elegant Pontalba town houses were built just as the focus of the city was shifting away from the old French Quarter to the new American city across Canal Street. The spacious houses soon lost their cachet, and by 1900 they were cut up into tenements. Philanthropist William Ratcliffe Irby willed the Lower Pontalba Building to the Louisiana State Museum in 1926; the City of New Orleans bought the Upper Pontalba Building in 1930. Both were reconditioned by the WPA in 1936. They were long popular among the city's bohemians and artists; in the 1930s writer Katherine Anne Porter lived for a while in the Lower Pontalba Building, as did surrealist photographer Clarence John Laughlin.

In 1955 the Louisiana State Museum furnished one town house in this row as an upper middle-class home and opened it to the public. All the objects in the recreated interiors of the **1850 Town House Museum** were made or available in mid-nineteenth-century New Orleans. There is a parlor furnished with Rococo Revival furniture and a dining room with an extensive set of old Paris porcelain of the type still popular in New Orleans. The master bedroom has a complete suite of Rococo Revival–style furniture made in New Orleans in the 1850s by an unknown cabinet-maker for the Puig House on Royal Street. The gentleman's bedroom is furnished with Gothic Revival and American Empire pieces. The nursery also has Gothic Revival and American Empire pieces, along with Victorian toys. The back rooms have been furnished as a gentleman's study, and a spare bedroom and bathing room with an unusual bathtub. The museum has installed a gift shop in the shopfront on the ground floor with souvenirs and books of local interest. For the Café du Monde, French Market, Moonwalk along the Mississippi River, and Jax Brewery, see Tour 5.

Chartres and Madison Streets

"Madame John's Legacy" / Manuel Lanzos House / Louisiana State Museum
623 Dumaine Street;
568-6968

3   Chartres and Madison Streets / Memories of the Quadroon Balls

From Jackson Square walk half a block down Chartres Street to its intersection with one-block-long Madison Street, cut through in 1826. From here there is a picturesque view of the colonnaded French Market with its 1813 building designed by Gurlie and Gillot and much expanded since. This stretch of Chartres Street from Jackson Square to Esplanade Avenue was called Conde Street until 1865. In this block was the Conde Street Ballroom, where in antebellum days white gentlemen met quadroon women (those with one-quarter black ancestry) for dancing and assignations. Another such rendezvous was the Salle Washington on St. Philip Street, between Royal and Bourbon. In his *Journal*, John H. B. Latrobe left a good description of a *bal paree et masqué* (a full-dress masked ball) there in 1834:

> There were about forty women present of all shades, from the very dark mulatto to the light quadroon whose person bore no mark of her descent, and whose degredation was a matter of tradition only. Nearly all had masks— white masks. Those who had not were young girls as yet destitute of a keeper, and who it seemed to me shewed their faces as a merchant shews samples of his wares to entice purchasers. Some of the women but not very many had fine forms, and a few were graceful and elegant dancers. . . . There were no white women present; and none of the quadroons wore costume. No other disguise to the person than a domino [a long, hooded cape], and to the face than a mask was used.

Walk down Chartres Street to Dumaine and turn left; half a block up on the left-hand side is the only surviving French colonial–style house in the Quarter.

4   "Madame John's Legacy" / Manuel Lanzos House / Louisiana State Museum,
1788, Robert Jones, builder; restoration, 1973, F. Monroe Labouisse, Jr.
This white and light olive color house with the wooden-columned gallery at 632 Dumaine Street is one of the oldest houses in New Orleans and the only one in the French Quarter that displays the traditional French colonial Louisiana house style. It is best seen from across the street. It fits Francis Baily's description of New Orleans houses in 1797 (quoted in *Cities of the Mississippi* by John W. Reps, 1994):

> The houses are generally framed buildings, and are raised about seven or eight feet from the ground, in order to make room for the cellars, which are on a level with the ground, as no building can be carried on below its surface on account of the height of the surrounding water. The upper part is sometimes furnished with an open gallery, which surrounds the whole building. . . . It affords an

agreeable retreat in the cool of the evening in this warm climate, and is much more refreshing than within doors.

Old Ursuline Convent
1100 Chartres Street, at Ursulines; open with tours Tuesday to Friday, 10 and 11 A.M., and 1, 2, and 3 P.M.; Saturday and Sunday, 11:15 A.M., 1, and 2 P.M.; admission fee; 529-3040

This house was built immediately after the great fire of 1788 for Don Manuel Lanzos, the captain of a Spanish regiment. Its builder was Robert Jones, an Anglo-American. It is raised up off the damp earth on brick piers whose exteriors have been covered with stucco. This ground floor was used for storage and also as a cool work space. Raising the house protected it from floods and also maximized ventilation. When its aligned doors and windows are opened, breezes pass right through the building. The house itself has a cypress-beam framework with bricks as in-fill, a technique termed *briquete-entre-poteaux*. Over that are wide beaded boards placed horizontally to protect the soft brick from the rains. The wide second-level gallery has turned wood colonnettes with a typical French colonial profile. The house has a loggia (an open gallery) to its rear framed by two small *cabinet* rooms. Out in the country, where there was more space and houses sat by themselves, galleries sometimes wrapped around all four sides of the house. The gallery was adapted from Caribbean house types perfected by the Spanish. They provided shaded, breezy, protected areas where the inhabitants could sit or work. Deep galleries also meant that the windows could be kept open during the frequent rains. The roof is a typical West Indies double-pitched roof that extends over the gallery. Two tall dormers poke through the roof and allow hot air to rise through the building. All the openings of the house, including the two French doors opening onto the gallery, have solid vertical-board shutters with strap hinges. These secured the house from thieves and hurricanes. There is a two-story brick dependency with a ground-floor kitchen behind the house and a narrow paved court between the two buildings.

In 1813 the house was bought by Dominique Seghers, a wealthy Belgian lawyer. It then passed through many hands. In 1925, Mrs. I. I. Lemann bought the old landmark to preserve it and rented it out for artists' studios. In 1947, this generous lady gave the relic to the Louisiana State Museum. The house is opening in 1998 with an exhibit on early Louisiana architecture on its ground floor and a Louisiana folk art collection upstairs. The house gets its nickname from *Tite Poulette,* a story by George Washington Cable written in 1879. In that story, Madame John, the quadroon mistress of a French Creole, inherits the house. She then sells the house, but the bank where she invests her money collapses, leaving her destitute with a daughter to raise. Return to Chartres Street and walk two and a half blocks down to the white stucco wall and gate lodge of the Ursuline Convent.

5   **Old Ursuline Convent,** *1745, Ignace François Broutin*
The Old Ursuline Convent and the adjoining St. Mary's Church are included in a one-hour tour. This handsome convent, school, and orphanage was designed in 1745 by Ignace François Broutin, engineer-in-chief of Louisiana, and is considered the oldest

St. Mary's Roman Catholic Church
1112 Chartres Street; open only for tours and masses; masses Sunday at 10:30 A.M., Saturday at 4:30 P.M., Monday, Wednesday, and Friday at 8:30 A.M., and Tuesday and Thursday at noon

Beauregard-Keyes House and Garden
1113 Chartres Street; open with tours Monday to Saturday 10 A.M. to 3 P.M.; admission fee; 523-7257

European building in the Mississippi valley. It is New Orleans' only landmark from French colonial times.

The Sisters of St. Ursula came to New Orleans from France in 1727 and established the first convent and school to educate young girls and to care for the colony's orphans. The spacious garden around the convent and a bucket brigade prevented its destruction in the fire of 1788. In 1824 the city insisted on cutting Chartres Street through the convent grounds to allow the city to expand. The nuns then built a new convent and school about two miles downriver (today the site of the Industrial Canal). The former convent became the residence of the archbishop and the chancery office from 1824 to 1899. The entrance portico was added in the 1890s. From 1831 to 1834, the Louisiana Legislature met here. In 1941 landscape architect Edward Woolbright designed the formal garden in front of the convent based on an old plan of the city botanical garden, which was once located across Ursulines Avenue. The complex was restored in 1973–78 for the archdiocesan archives and also houses a modernistic National Shrine of the Order of St. Lazarus of Jerusalem.

• **St. Mary's Roman Catholic Church,** *1845, J. N. B. de Pouilly*
This church, with a simple exterior and a decorated interior, was built in 1845 as the archiepiscopal chapel of archbishop Antoine Blanc. It has served French, Spanish, Creole, Irish, German, Slavonian, and Italian congregations, as well as the African American Sisters of the Holy Family. The church has had many names, including Holy Trinity, Our Lady of Victory, and St. Mary's National Italian church. This church was once the soul of the Italian American community, and various Italian American societies paraded from here to the Italian Hall at 1020 Esplanade Avenue. Today, of course, the Italian American community is assimilated and dispersed. In 1994 the name St. Mary's was revived to honor the Italian American community that was important in the French Quarter for so long. Today it is a chapel of ease and no longer a parish church. Across Chartres Street from the convent and church is the Beauregard-Keyes House and Garden.

6 **Beauregard-Keyes House and Garden,** *1826, François Correjolles; 1955, garden design by James F. Fondren*
This elegant center hall house at 1113 Chartres Street was designed by François Correjolles and built by James Lambert in 1826 for Joseph Le Carpentier, a wealthy auctioneer. It stands on land sold by the Ursuline nuns when they moved their convent farther downriver. It is a fine town house raised up on a full-story basement. Twin curved stairs lead up to a handsome Tuscan portico facing Chartres Street. Inside, a wide hall leads to a rectangular dining room that in turn opens onto a back porch. Flanking the hall are a parlor and large ballroom to the right and a library and two bedrooms to the left. Two *cabinet* rooms open into the back dining room. Behind the

house is a flagstone-paved courtyard with a fountain and a two-story dependency that originally housed the kitchen and slave quarters.

The house was rented by former Confederate general Pierre Gustave Toutant (P. G. T.) Beauregard from 1866 to 1868 while he was the president of the New Orleans, Jackson, and Great Northern Railroad. Many other tenants followed as the neighborhood went into decline. In 1904, Corrado Giacona bought the house and lived upstairs while operating a wholesale liquor business downstairs. In 1945 the prolific novelist Francis Parkinson Keyes (rhymes with "eyes") leased the house and converted the rear dependency into her writing studio. Today the interior is elegantly furnished and gives a good idea of elite Creole interiors of the mid-nineteenth century. A shirt factory that had been built next door on the site of the old corner garden was demolished in 1955, and in its place a brick-walled formal garden with a beautiful cast-iron fountain and boxwood hedges was planted using an 1865 plan of the lost garden. Maintained by the Garden Study Club of New Orleans, it is one of the best-kept secrets in the French Quarter. Walk up Ursulines Avenue, passing (or stopping in at) the Croissant d'Or Patisserie Française at 617 Ursulines Avenue. Near the uptown-riverside corner of Ursulines Avenue and Royal Street is the elegant Magnon-Ingram-Stone House.

Magnon-Ingram-Stone House
620 Ursulines Avenue, above Royal

Gallier House Museum / Christian Woman's Exchange
1132 Royal Street; open with tours Monday to Saturday 10 A.M. to 4 P.M.; tours every half hour; last tour at 3:45 P.M.; also open some Sundays; there is parking behind the house; gift shop; admission fee; 523-6722

7   **Magnon-Ingram-Stone House,** *1819, Gurlie and Guillot, architect-builders; private residence*
This light tan-colored mansion was built for Arnaud Magnon, a shipbuilder. When the city bought his shipyard at the foot of Ursulines Avenue, he used the money to build this house. It was originally two stories high and was designed by architect-builders Claude Gurlie and Joseph Guillot as a Creole-style building. In 1840 a half story and cupola were added to the building, and it was completely remodeled in the then-reigning Greek Revival style. The result is a severe but elegant and imposing city mansion. The cast-iron grilles in the vents along the top of the house are especially beautiful examples of Greek Revival iron work. Koch and Wilson restored the house in 1968 for owner Frederick Ingram. A movie theater that stood on the corner of Royal Street was demolished to give the house a walled side garden. A formal garden was built behind the house with a guest cottage and swimming pool. Turn right on Royal Street and walk only a few steps down to Gallier House.

8   **Gallier House Museum / Christian Woman's Exchange,** *1857, James Gallier, Jr.*
A Paris green, rose-patterned, cast-iron gallery and unique cast-iron front-door gate distinguish the facade of the Gallier House. This house was designed and built by James Gallier, Jr., a noted New Orleans architect and the designer of the now-lost French Opera House. (His father, Ireland-born James Gallier, Sr., designed the old Second

1100 Block of Royal Street   Municipality City Hall, now called Gallier Hall, see page 261.) Its brick-and-stucco facade is scored and painted to look like granite blocks. This Creole-style town house is richly furnished to the 1857–68 decade with some six thousand period artifacts. The interpretive focus here is the social history of the French Quarter from 1860 to 1880. The ground floor has double parlors separated by Corinthian columns and ringed with a florid plaster cornice. There is a rear gallery that connects to the rear wing with the dining room, pantry, and kitchen. On the second floor are four family bedrooms around a skylit central hall, which also served as Gallier's library. The second floor of the rear wing has three slave quarters. Gallier died at forty-one, and the detailed inventory of his estate guided the restoration and refurnishing of the house. The house was restored by the Ella West Freeman Foundation and is now a museum property of the **Christian Woman's Exchange,** which also owns the Hermann-Grima House (page 126). Henry W. Krotzer, Jr., of Koch and Wilson was the restoration architect and Samuel Dornsife designed the interiors. Today part of the property also serves the University of New Orleans' historic preservation, urban archaeology, and neighborhood planning programs.

The tour includes the kitchen, with its early cast-iron range, and an early bathroom with a copper bathtub served by indoor plumbing. During the summer the house is returned to its original "summer dress": the upholstered furniture is protected by white slipcovers; sea-grass matting replaces the woolen rugs; chandeliers are wrapped in gauze; and the silk drapes are removed, leaving the windows covered by lace curtains. This seasonal "undecorating" preserved the fragile fabrics from insects and perspiration and also made the house look and feel cooler.

• 1100 Block of Royal Street

Facing Gallier House is one of the most picturesque block fronts in the Quarter, a great place to study the fanciful patterns of Victorian cast iron. This row of brick-and-stucco houses are part of a cluster of fifteen houses designed by Alexander T. Wood in 1832 for La Compagne des Architectes. As originally built, these houses had semicircular transoms on their first floors and a narrow gallery with a simple iron railing, like the one that survives on the house at 1133 Royal Street. Probably in the 1850s, their facades were remodeled with square-headed Greek key doorways. Wider galleries with oak leaf and acorn designs were also added that reach across the full width of the sidewalk. The three-story building at 1103 Royal Street was also built in 1832, but sometime between 1876 and 1896 a third floor was added to it along with cast-iron galleries.

❾ LaLaurie-Albright House / "The Haunted House," *1831; rebuilt 1837–38, Pierre Edouard Trastour; private residence*

On the uptown-riverside corner of Royal and Governor Nicholls Streets is the stately, three-story LaLaurie House, popularly known as the Haunted House. It was begun in 1831 as a two-story house probably similar to the Hermann-Grima House. It became the home of Dr. Louis and Delphine Macarty de Lopez Blanque LaLaurie, who entertained here on a lavish scale. But on April 10, 1834, so local legend says, an old cook set fire to the house while the LaLauries were away. When the neighbors rushed in to put out the fire they discovered to their horror that the household slaves were chained in the attic. *The Bee* published a sensational account of the alleged abuse, and on April 15 an indignant mob attacked the house. The LaLauries fled to exile in Paris, never to return, or so the story goes. In 1934, journalist Meigs Frost claimed that the LaLauries were the victims of slander by *The Bee*'s reporter, a disgruntled heir to the Macarty fortune who held a grudge against Madame LaLaurie. The revisionist view has never been as popular as the original story. The "haunted" house remained empty until it was bought by architect Pierre Edouard Trastour, who completely remodeled it, adding a third floor and making it one of the stateliest houses in the French Quarter. The elaborate front door in its deep vestibule is especially impressive and depicts Phoebus in his griffin-drawn chariot in the lower oblong panel. The big house later served a variety of institutional uses. During the Reconstruction period it housed the Lower Girls' School, where whites and blacks sat in the same classrooms. The White League ended this "dangerous" novelty by marching on the school in 1874. A conservatory of music occupied the mansion in the 1880s. William J. Warrington established a home for indigent men here in the early twentieth century. In 1969, Dr. Russell Albright bought the mansion, and between 1976 and 1980 Koch and Wilson oversaw its restoration and modernization. This is a private residence and should be left undisturbed. Half a block to the left up Governor Nicholls Street, behind an iron gate and a low, pierced brick wall, you can glimpse the Thierry-Reagan House.

LaLaurie-Albright House / "The Haunted House"
1140 Royal Street, at Governor Nicholls

Thierry-Reagan House
721 Governor Nicholls Street

⑩ Thierry-Reagan House, *1814, Latour and Latrobe; private residence*
This unusually set-back, one-story house was built in 1814 and is considered the oldest Greek Revival house in New Orleans. It was built for Jean Baptiste Thierry, the Creole editor of *Le Courrier de la Louisiane.* This small house was a collaboration between Henry Latrobe and French-born Arsene Lacarriere Latour and was described when it was built as an "elegant and convenient brick house, . . . consisting of five rooms, two *cabinets* and two cellars; with a kitchen likewise built of bricks, both terrace roofed and affording ample lodging for servants; an extensive yard, and a flower garden in front of the house" (*Le Courrier de la Louisiane,* January 4, 1819). At some point in the house's long history its distinctive Doric portico was bricked in, only to be uncovered during the 1940 restoration by Koch and Wilson.

       Governor Nicholls Street is one of the loveliest in the lower French Quarter and is mostly lined with one- and two-story houses. This was originally known as Hospital Street, but its name was changed in 1909 to honor General Francis Tillou Nicholls, a wounded Confederate hero who later served two terms as Louisiana's governor from 1876 to 1879 and 1888 to 1892. Under his first administration the biracial experiment of political Reconstruction was ended and the white "Redeemers" emerged triumphant in post–Civil War Louisiana. Governor Nicholls Street becomes Bayou

Governor Nicholls Street

Victorian Gingerbread Double House
1224–26 Royal Street

John Gauche Mansion
704 Esplanade Avenue, at Royal

Esplanade Avenue

Road beyond Rampart Street, the ancient Choctaw portage to Bayou St. John and the oldest path of travel in New Orleans. Return to Royal Street and walk one block toward Esplanade Avenue.

⑪   Victorian Gingerbread Double House, *probably 1880s, architect unknown*

Tucked in the middle of the riverside of the 1200 block of Royal Street, between Governor Nicholls and Barracks Streets, is this delightful Victorian confection. Looking as frilly as the lavish gingerbread on a Mississippi steamboat, this two-family house was built in the 1880s. Its fanciful woodwork is a testament to the newly perfected woodworking machinery of the Victorian period. Partitions with curved tops divide the two galleries of the separate dwellings.

⑫   700 Block of Esplanade Avenue

•   **John Gauche Mansion,** *1856, architect unknown; private residence*
The Greek Revival Gauche Mansion along with its dependencies and neighboring buildings are all painted the same beautiful coral color and stretch down the length of the 1300 block of Royal Street. This is the second house on this site, and it was built in 1856 for John Gauche, a wealthy crockery merchant. (As fashions changed, his widow removed to St. Charles Avenue uptown by 1877.) In 1882 Patrick R. O'Brian, the owner of a cotton press, bought the mansion. Peter Spicuzza owned the house from 1911 to 1936. In 1937 Matilda Geddings Gray bought the house and restored it. Richard Koch was the architect for the restoration and used his trademark "Richard Koch pink." A second careful restoration that included extensive historic research was undertaken in 1969. A two-story dependency extends from the back of the house embracing a courtyard with a fountain. This fine brick-and-stucco house has a center hall plan, which is announced by a monolithic granite portico framing the front entrance. Such all-stone porticos are rare in New Orleans. But it is the cast-iron work made in Saarbruken, Germany, that catches the eye. The plain walls of the square house are the perfect foil for the fine fence, elaborate gallery railing at the second floor, and the brackets and decorated cast-iron overhang. The second-floor gallery railing has a repeated design of a cherub dancing inside a circle, a heavenly chorus line! Such a light-hearted touch on such a serious house is quintessentially New Orleanian.

⑬   Esplanade Avenue: Elite Creole Boulevard
Walk down the center of the tree-lined median of Esplanade Avenue. This became the prestige address for wealthy Creole families who began moving out of the congested French Quarter. On its corner lots in particular, large brick houses were erected, and most survive today as apartment houses. There is gratifyingly little commerce on the fine avenue and it remains residential. For a time a streetcar track ran down its narrow

neutral ground. (For upper Esplanade Avenue to Bayou St. John, see Tour 3.)

14 600 *Block of Esplanade Avenue*

• **638–40 Esplanade Avenue,** *circa 1822*
On the corner across Royal Street facing the grand Gauche Mansion, at 638–40 Esplanade Avenue, is a small, coral-colored, one-story, hip-roofed Creole cottage that dates from at least 1822, perhaps earlier. The small projecting bay window facing Esplanade, now always shuttered, could have been added when J. D. Junius operated a tailor shop here from 1914 to the 1960s.

• **634 and 632 Esplanade Avenue,** *1885, Middlemiss and Murray; 1886, G. A. Thiesen*
Next down from the one-story corner Creole cottage is a pair of tall, frame, French Second Empire houses with American side-hall plans. Number 634 was built in 1885 by Middlemiss and Murray for Mary Zaeringer, and 632 Esplanade Avenue next door was built in 1886 by G. A. Thiesen for Mrs. Ellen Bugue. Their slate-covered mansard roofs with their projecting dormers bring a hidden hint of Paris to the avenue. The Second Empire style was popular among the elite Creoles of Esplanade Avenue, but not many houses in this style have survived later waves of demolition.

• **628 Esplanade Avenue,** *1868, Eugène Surgi*
This two-story, tan stucco house was built in 1868. Its white-painted recessed entrance is handsomely framed. A cast-iron gallery extends out over the sidewalk. A year after its construction it was bought by Pierre Maspero, who before the Civil War had operated a slave auction at Chartres and St. Louis Streets.

• **622 Esplanade Avenue,** *circa 1892*
This is a late Victorian version of the traditional New Orleans side-hall plan house; it was built about 1892 for liquor dealer Angel Xiques. A wooden balustraded second-floor gallery wraps around the breezy river side of the house.

• **616 Esplanade Avenue,** *circa 1895, shotgun cottage*
This is a late example of the one-story, frame, Italianate shotgun cottage so popular in working-class New Orleans neighborhoods. Four ornamented brackets uphold its projecting roof, and louvered jalousies protect its tall floor-to-ceiling windows. Number 614 Esplanade Avenue is a bastardized two-story building with little to recommend it.

606 Esplanade Avenue

Vatinel-Ninas House
604 Esplanade Avenue

600 Esplanade Avenue

Former Chiesa del Redentore
601 Esplanade Avenue

• **606 Esplanade Avenue,** *1834, architect unknown; 1859, remodeled*
Built as part of a group of three common-wall town houses in 1834 for attorney and real estate developer Henry Raphael Dennis, this house was sold to Felix de Armas. It was remodeled inside and out in 1859 in the lavish Greek Revival taste. A rear wing, large side bay, and frilly cast-iron galleries were added at that time.

• **604 Esplanade Avenue / Vatinel-Ninas House,** *1834, architect unknown; 1850s, remodeled*
The central house in a group of three town houses built in 1834, this house, like the two that flank it, originally had an entresol with Gothic arches between its first and second floors. This explains the unusually tall first floor of the remodeled buildings. The house has a narrow second-floor gallery with a simple Gothic Revival iron railing. In 1860 Madame Egerie Vatinel opened a private school for young children here, and it became a favorite institution for the proper Creole families on the avenue. The school was continued by her daughter Clorinde and lasted until 1925. In 1937 painter Paul Ninas bought the house and installed his studio on the sunlit third floor.

• **600 Esplanade Avenue,** *1834, architect unknown; 1850s remodeled*
At the uptown-lakeside corner of Esplanade Avenue and Chartres Street is this three-story, yellow-painted brick house built in 1834 for real estate developer Henry Raphael Dennis as his own dwelling. The lacy, two-level, wraparound cast-iron gallery was added later, perhaps in the late 1850s. As you cross Chartres Street there is a fine view of the steeples of St. Louis Cathedral and the One Shell Square (left) and First NBC Center (right) high-rises (see page 240).

• **601 Esplanade Avenue / Former Chiesa del Redentore,** *1914, architect unknown*
A Mission Revival former church with a belfry and red tile roof stands on the downtown-lakeside corner of Esplanade Avenue and Chartres Street. It was built in 1914 for the Methodist Episcopal Chiesa del Redentore. California-style buildings popped up all over New Orleans in the teens and twenties as Hollywood-propagated styles swept away two hundred years of regional design. The chapel has been converted into several living units.

15   *500 Block of Esplanade Avenue*

• **544 Esplanade Avenue,** *circa 1860, architect unknown; 1930s remodeled*
This corner house was constructed about 1860 as four two-story brick houses for Claude Tiblier. Its current grand appearance is the result of a 1930s remodel executed for Leon Arnaud Cazenave, the owner of Arnaud's Restaurant. Mrs. Germaine

Cazenave Wells inherited the house in 1954 and is fondly remembered for her festive carriage-borne Easter parades in the Quarter, which she started as a merry widow in 1956 and continued until her death in 1983. Look back to 600 Esplanade Avenue for a classic view of New Orleans' famous cast-iron galleries.

544 Esplanade Avenue, *at Chartres*

Weysham-Ronstrom House *524 Esplanade Avenue*

520 Esplanade Avenue

500–504 Esplanade Avenue

• **524 Esplanade Avenue / Weysham-Ronstrom House,** *circa 1845*

In the middle of the uptown side of the block is a raised-basement brick house built about 1845. Its stucco is scored to look like stone. It is distinguished by a projecting portico with four round columns and a pediment. Twin stairs rise to an entrance marked by a finely detailed Greek key doorway. Two rooms open from either side of its forty-foot-long central hall. In 1893 Gaspar Cusachs, a bibliophile and president of the Louisiana Historical Society, bought the imposing house and lived here until his death in 1929. Dr. and Mrs. George Nelson Ronstrom bought the house in 1939 and installed plumbing and electricity.

• **520 Esplanade Avenue,** *circa 1901*

Next door is a raised cottage slightly set back from the sidewalk that was built about 1901. Its classical design harmonizes with the elegant avenue. Its front gallery has been glassed in. Facing it, on the opposite side of the street, the two-story modern building at 511 Esplanade does absolutely everything wrong. Cross Decatur Street and look back to the uptown-lakeside corner of Esplanade and Decatur.

• **500–504 Esplanade Avenue / 1327–31 Decatur Street,** *circa 1840, E. W. Sewell*

These two red-painted buildings are part of an original group of three three-story houses that face Decatur Street. They were built about 1840 and designed by E. W. Sewell for the Citizen's Bank. These American-style town houses all had arched ground-floor openings with barred transoms, side passageways leading to rear slave quarters, and galleries at their second floors. Dormers appear in their attics. The service wing on the corner building facing Esplanade Avenue was altered in the late nineteenth century. The corner storefront housed George A. Nami's jewelry store from 1891 to 1967. Its final advertisement noted that it would sell "all diamonds, watches, rings, charms and bracelets, fountain pens, rosaries, pearls, necklaces and pendants, opera glasses, crucifixes, cutlery, etc." This is now the wonderfully funky end of Decatur Street. There is a good view from here of the plant- and flag-festooned galleries over the covered sidewalk of Decatur Street.

**Old United States Mint /
Louisiana State Museum /
New Orleans Jazz Museum
and Mardi Gras Exhibit**
*400 Esplanade Avenue, at
Decatur; open Tuesday to
Sunday 10 A.M. to 5 P.M.;
admission fee; 568-6968*

Faubourg Marigny

Check Point Charlie's
*501 Esplanade Avenue;
947-0979*

1407–11 Decatur Street

**16   Old United States Mint / Louisiana State Museum / New
Orleans Jazz Museum and Mardi Gras Exhibit,** *1835, William
Strickland; restoration, 1979, E. Eean McNaughton Architects,
Biery and Toups Architects*

The imposing Old United States Mint at the foot of Esplanade
Avenue stands on the site of the Spanish fort of San Carlos, erected
in 1792 by the Baron de Carondelet. Major General Andrew Jackson reviewed his troops here before the Battle of New Orleans in
1815. That fortification was cleared away in 1821, and in 1835 this
sober Greek Revival mint was constructed to the designs of William
Strickland. Strickland's design sank unevenly into the soft ground.
Captain P. G. T. Beauregard, a West Point trained engineer, stabilized the massive building in the 1850s. Union forces retook the
mint when the city fell in 1862, and the city was shocked into sub-
mission when a defiant Confederate was hanged for hauling down
the Stars and Stripes. It continued operating as a mint until 1909. It
became a federal prison in 1932, and was also occupied by the Coast Guard until 1965.
The monumental landmark was transferred to the State of Louisiana and renovated in
1978–80 for the Louisiana State Museum, which houses its New Orleans Jazz Museum
and Mardi Gras Exhibit here; see page 205 for a description of these collections.

17 · Faubourg Marigny, *1805, Barthélémy Lafon, surveyor*
Cross Esplanade Avenue to the one-story, contemporary Engine No. 9 fire station built
on a small traffic island in 1971. On the downtown-lakeside corner across Decatur
Street is 501 Esplanade, an impressive two-story corner building with a mansard roof
and projecting dormers. It was built for Julien Adolphe Lacroix, a free man of color,
between 1846 and 1867. His widow operated the Louisiana Ball Room here and probably added the dormer windows on the roof in the 1880s. Today **Check Point Charlie's,**
a bar, grill and laundromat, occupies the first floor and features live music for a young
crowd.

18   1407–11 Decatur Street, *late 1830s; 1850s, expanded and remodeled*
This two-and-a-half-story, brick-and-stucco, angled corner building with a gallery-
covered sidewalk was also built for Julien Adolphe Lacroix. He operated a grocery
store in the corner space and lived upstairs. He probably built a brick building on this
corner in the late 1830s, then expanded and remodeled the building in the 1850s with
a wraparound gallery supported by cast-iron columns. Lacroix's widow operated the
store until 1891. More recently the building was owned by art collector William A.
Groves. Today the NO/AIDS Task Force occupies the ground floor and often has art
and photographic displays in its windows. The Lambda Center is across the street at
421 Frenchmen Street.

- **501 Frenchmen Street,** *1830s*

This three-story, corner brick building with two levels of galleries at Frenchmen and Decatur is a fine 1830s Creole town house with a commercial space on the ground floor. The first floor was intended for a shop and is distinguished by fine Quincy granite piers between casement windows. It has a three-story slave quarters attached on the Frenchman Street side; the narrow courtyard between the main house and the dependency has been built over. The galleries here have delicate wrought-iron, not cast-iron, railings. Creole historian Charles A. E. Gayarré, or free black investor Julien Adolphe Lacroix, may have built this elegant building. As a Creole-plan town house, the building is hall-less, has large front rooms, smaller *cabinets* in the rear corners, and a circular stairway giving access to its upper floors. Today it is well restored and houses medical offices.

19 *Frenchmen Street Music Club Strip*

During the long years when this neighborhood was in decline, unsightly intrusions eroded the historic fabric of this street. The Frenchman Orleans Motel at 519 Frenchmen Street is a shoddy parody of New Orleans architecture fit for Airline Highway. The disruptive frontyard parking, the cheesy design, the nailed-to-the-wall shutters that never would fit over their windows, and the fake mansard with its ungainly dormers serve as a compendium of *faux* New Orleans design. Only the valiant banana trees soften the general ugliness. Such disruptive designs would not be permitted today in this historic district.

The **Dream Palace Music Bar,** a new music club, is housed in an old commercial building with a traditional covered sidewalk. The **Faubourg Center** presents punk and ska and modern noize. The **Praline Connection Restaurant and Candy Shop** is one of New Orleans' best known Creole or soul food restaurants. The candy shop sells pralines, a confection made of sugar, pecans, vanilla, and a pinch of salt. This corner building was originally a bank; its exterior is minimally Spanish Mission Revival with a fringe of red tiles along its parapet. The **Cafe Brazil Music Club** is in a vividly painted blue, green, and yellow one-story corner building with iron brackets that support a metal sidewalk awning. The large, airy space inside is the venue for many kinds of contemporary music from New Orleans, the Caribbean, and Africa. Chairs out on the sidewalk let you enjoy the passing scene.

- **Neighborhood Archeology,** *Rain Webb, 1986*

On the side of the building on the downtown-lakeside corner of Frenchmen and Chartres Streets is a mural painted by Rain Webb in 1986. It incorporates pottery shards in its design. If you look to the left of the archeologist examining his find, you

501 Frenchmen Street, *at Decatur*

Dream Palace Music Bar
534 Frenchmen Street;
945-2040

Faubourg Center
508 Frenchmen Street;
949-0369

Praline Connection Restaurant and Candy Shop
542 Frenchmen Street;
943-3934

Cafe Brazil Music Club
2100 Chartres Street, at Frenchmen; 947-9386

Neighborhood Archeology
Corner of Frenchmen and Chartres Streets

Faubourg Marigny Bookstore
600 Frenchmen Street; 943-9875

Adolfo's
611 Frenchmen Street; 948-3800

Theater Marigny
616 Frenchmen Street; box office 944-2653

Snug Harbor Jazz Bistro
626 Frenchmen Street; 949-0696

PJ's Coffee & Tea Cafe
634 Frenchmen Street; 949-2292

Washington Square

Cafe Marigny
1913 Royal Street, at Touro; 945-4472

Lafitte's Blacksmith Shop and Bar
941 Bourbon Street, at St. Philip; 523-0066

will see the old fan-shaped city with sailing ships lining its wharve in the excavated pit. The white clam shells that pave this corne parking lot were the traditional paving material in old New Orlean

Across the intersection is the **Faubourg Marigny Bookstore,** New Orleans' gay and lesbian bookstore, housed in a two-story, corne commercial and residential building. Up the block is **Theate Marigny,** one of New Orleans' experimental little theaters. **Snu Harbor Jazz Bistro** is one of the best, most popular jazz venues i New Orleans; it's a musical treasure-house. **PJ's Coffee & Tea Ca** is a pleasant haven. **Adolfo's** is recommended.

20   Washington Square, *1808*
This gated park was reserved in 1808 and is one of the few neigh borhood parks in the underparked city. Where the unsightly, yello brick Christopher's Inn Apartments looms today on the riverside c the park was Howard and Diettel's imposing Third Presbyteria Church of 1858, lost in Hurricane Betsy in 1965. Walk up Roy Street back toward Esplanade Avenue.

21   Cafe Marigny
This eccentrically angled corner building with a wide gallery is pleasant neighborhood cafe and a good place to rest before headin back into the Quarter. The #3 Vieux Carré jitney bus stops at Roy and Touro in front of the laundromat here and can take you bac into the Quarter via Dauphine Street.

Continuation:

22   Lafitte's Blacksmith Shop and Bar
On your way back into the Quarter you can pass the picturesque Lafitte's Blacksmit Shop and Bar at 941 Bourbon Street. This funky, historic bar is deep in the quie residential lower French Quarter, far past the noisy section of Bourbon Street. Th circa 1781 brick-between-posts Creole cottage in a theatrically decrepit state was n Jean Lafitte's blacksmith shop, but the myth has stuck and proved popular. Jean an Pierre Lafitte were not really pirates; they are more accurately described as fences fo stolen goods and smugglers, especially smugglers of slaves (see page 83). This bar exterior is a favorite subject for amateur photographers. In the late 1940s this was on of the city's earliest bars to attract a gay following, but today it serves a non-gay neighborhood clientele. This dimly lit dive is an atmospheric place to sit and drink i the reassuring presence of the eternally flickering tube.

*Fantastic creatures guard the roof of the
original section of the New Orleans Museum of Art, which was built in 1911
in vast, oak-studded City Park.*

Continued on page 160

Tour 3a

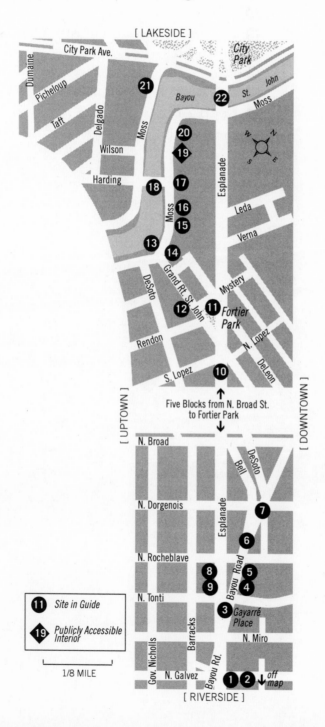

[LAKESIDE]

City Park Ave.

Dumaine
Picheloup
Taft
Delgado
Moss

Wilson

Harding

City Park

Bayou

St. John
Moss

Esplanade

Leda

Verna

Moss

DeSoto
Grand Rt. St. John

Mystery

Fortier Park

N. Lopez

DeLeon

Rendon

S. Lopez

[UPTOWN]

[DOWNTOWN]

Five Blocks from N. Broad St.
to Fortier Park

N. Broad

N. Dorgenois

N. Rocheblave

N. Tonti

Esplanade

Bell

DeSoto

Bayou Road

Gayarré
Place

N. Miro

Gov. Nicholls

N. Galvez

Barracks

Bayou Rd.

11 Site in Guide

19 Publicly Accessible
Interior

1/8 MILE

[RIVERSIDE]

off
map

Tour 3b

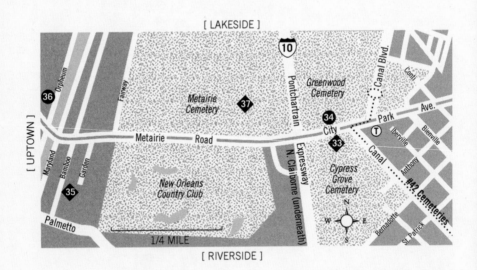

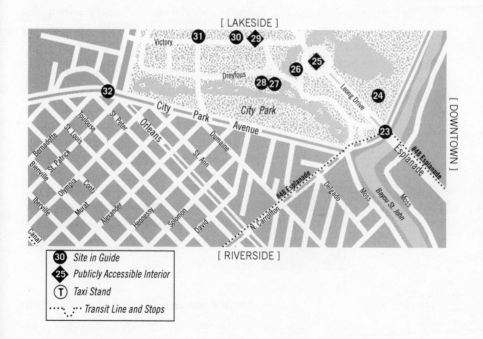

Annual House Tour
Esplanade Ridge Civic
Association; 947-1343

What This Tour Covers

This tour traverses upper Esplanade Avenue, once the fashionable French Creole boulevard. It focuses on two short walks, one at Gayarré Place, where the avenue crosses the ancient Bayou Road, and another up Grand Route St. John to Moss Street and historic Bayou St. John. (Bring something to sit on if you want to enjoy the breezy bayou and its view; there are no benches on this grassy embankment.) The Pitot House Museum here, an eighteenth-century West Indies–style plantation house, is the best window into elite colonial Louisiana in the city. Along Metairie Ridge (the other high ground here) is City Park with the New Orleans Museum of Art and the Botanical Gardens. Continuations farther afield include historic Cypress Grove Cemetery, magnificent and immaculate Metairie Cemetery, and Longue Vue House and Gardens, the finest twentieth-century New Orleans estate open to the public.

Few visitors will want to walk the stretch from the French Quarter to Gayarré Place; make hops by bus. A slow car tour here is architecturally rewarding. Pedestrians will feel safest above N. Broad Street all the way to Bayou St. John and City Park.

Preliminaries

BEST TIMES TO DO THIS TOUR The Pitot House Museum is closed from Sunday through Tuesday, so the best times to do this walk are Wednesday through Saturday. At the New Orleans Museum of Art in City Park you can phone for a taxi to take you to Longue Vue House and Gardens.

Annual House Tours are conducted by the Esplanade Ridge Civic Association, usually in early December.

Car Tour

This tour is easily done by car. Park first on Esplanade near Gayarré Place (do not park on side streets). Drive up Esplanade Avenue and turn left onto Grand Route St. John to Moss Street and the cooling bayou. Parking is permitted on Moss Street.

Esplanade Avenue Bus 48

This bus makes frequent stops along Esplanade Avenue from Esplanade and Rampart (the bus stop is next to the empty corner lot) up to Bayou St. John at Wisner Boulevard, near the entrance to City Park. To do these two walks, alight first at Esplanade and N. Miro to see the Gayarré Place cluster, reboard at Esplanade at N. Miro and get out again at Esplanade and Grand Route St. John, near the K Store and just before Alcée Fortier Park, for a short walk to the bayou.

Gray Line Loop Tour Bus

If you take the **Gray Line Loop Tour,** do this tour in inverse order. Longue Vue House and Gardens is stop #8. The City Park Casino near the Botanical Garden is stop #9. The New Orleans Museum of Art, also in the park, is stop #10. The restaurant cluster at Esplanade and Mystery is stop #11. You can get out here and walk to the Pitot House Museum. The Old U.S. Mint/Louisiana State Museum at the foot of Esplanade Avenue with its Jazz Museum and Mardi Gras Exhibit is stop #12 (see Tour 4). If you do not wish to do stops #1 through #7, take a taxi to Longue Vue and join the Loop Tour bus there. For the Loop Tour bus, see page 31.

Restaurants, Food Markets, and Cafés

Esplanade Avenue near Mystery Street, across from Alcée Fortier Park, is an oasis of good dining and organic food buying. Lunch or dinner at **Cafe Degas** is recommended; this congenial restaurant serves French cuisine on a covered wooden deck looking out at the avenue. Most conveniently, a limited menu is offered all afternoon between lunch and dinner. For Cajun-based cuisine, there is the **Gabrielle Restaurant,** which offers dinner only.

Gray Line Loop Tours
569-1401

Cafe Degas
3127 Esplanade Avenue;
945-5635

Gabrielle Restaurant
3201 Esplanade Avenue;
948-6233

Whole Foods Market
3135 Esplanade Avenue;
943-1626

True Brew Coffee
3133 Ponce de Leon
Street; 947-3948

On Esplanade Avenue is **Whole Foods Market,** one of the best organic markets in the city. Whole Foods sells excellent prepared foods, which you can eat at the outdoor tables here, and there is a good wine selection. Near Whole Foods Market is **True Brew Coffee,** a smoke-free coffeehouse.

Introduction:
Cultural High Ground

Everything is relative. Esplanade Ridge is only about four feet above sea level, but this, in a city that is an average of five feet *below* sea level, makes it high ground—the last place to flood. Animal trails and Native American pathways sought out this higher land, as did the earliest French plantations which predate the founding of New Orleans. Later, it was to this high ground that the French and Spanish Creoles removed as the French Quarter became congested and too commercial.

The word *Creole* has a complex history that continues to change in common usage. Today the *Times-Picayune* uses the word to denote the mulatto descendants of the city's French-speaking free people of color, but this is a relatively recent development. The word comes from the Portuguese *crioulo,* meaning a slave of African descent born in the New World (Brazil). The word was later extended to describe white Europeans born in the Americas, who were barred from the highest offices in the Spanish empire (governor or bishop). Early colonial Louisiana, where white women were scarce, was a racially mixed society, and there were white Creoles, mixed-race Creoles, and black Creoles. Creole also refers to the dialect and folk culture that evolved in southern Louisiana, where French, African, and later Spanish influences mixed and mingled. (Today Creole can also mean "of Louisiana," as in Creole tomatoes.) As racial attitudes hardened in the mid-nineteenth century, "white" Louisianians chose to simplify their early complex racial history and redefined Creole to mean exclusively white French and/or white Spanish ancestry. When Anglo-Americans began to migrate to Louisiana in the early 1800s, Creole came to mean culturally and linguistically French as opposed to English-speaking. Later the phrase "Creoles of color" emerged to describe the many French- or Creole-speaking people of mixed racial descent in southern Louisiana. All we can be certain of is that the word Creole will continue to mean different things to different people at different times.

(Creole is not the same as *Cajun,* an abbreviation of Acadian. Cajuns were French-speaking farmers and trappers who settled along the bayous west of New Orleans after being expelled by the English from Nova Scotia after 1713 as Canada was made English. Cajuns are Roman Catholic and highly family-minded. Cajun music, including its black derivation, zydeco, enlivens a culture that loves to gather all ages together to dance. Their cooking has achieved national recognition through chef Paul Prudhomme [see pages 52 and 130]. St. Martinville, about 125 miles west of New Orleans, may be the most attractive Acadian town.)

The Creoles who moved out of the crowded, profitable, and decaying French Quarter to build grand houses along Esplanade Avenue were, of course, wealthy. Most were "pure" white and spoke French in their homes. They tended to marry among themselves, often to cousins, and they increasingly disdained Anglo-American culture as the energetic English speakers began to dominate the economy and politics of the bicultural city. As *Norman's New Orleans* noted in 1845, "They are remarkably exclusive in their intercourse with others, and, with strangers, enter into business arrangements with extreme caution." French Creole culture was Roman Catholic in its religion but tended to be more ritualistic than moralistic. A double standard existed between men and women. French Creole culture became more inward-looking as time went on. Since it was a society in good measure defined by its language, as succeeding generations adopted English, Creole culture faded away. Historian Joseph Tregle wrote in 1952 in the *Journal of Southern History:*

> Provincial in outlook, style, and taste, the typical Latin Creole was complaisant, unlettered, unskilled, content to occupy his days with the affairs of his estate or the demands of his job. He lived in sensation rather than reflection, enjoying the balls and dances, betting heavily at table, or perhaps at the cockpit, endlessly smoking his inevitable cigar, whiling away the hours over his beloved dominoes, busying himself with the many demands of his close-knit family life.

Nostalgia casts a rosy glow on this lost provincial Creole culture, and it lives in the city's memory. Creole culture is important because it was the first shaper of what has become our own distinctive New Orleanian culture. Creole attitudes and prejudices continue to shape New Orleans. A certain Creole temperament suffuses New Orleanians; work, for example, is not the chief concern of life here.

As nineteenth-century New Orleans grew, the French Quarter lost its desirability as a place for the upper class. Its old buildings were subdivided for commercial use or to profitably house poor immigrants. Esplanade Avenue became the Creoles' St. Charles Avenue. As sociologist H. W. Gilmore noted in the *American Sociological Review* in 1944:

> If the Americans had their fate sealed as to where they might move [to Uptown], so did the Creoles. To move East meant crossing the national boundary line of Esplanade Avenue and invading the [German and Irish] immigrant truck gardening section [of Faubourg Marigny and Bywater] and this would violate their pride and honor. To the west was Canal Street, the central business section and the unthinkable American section. Their only recourse was to move out Esplanade Ridge to Bayou St. John, and here today New Orleans has lovely old homes which are a product of this period.

Esplanade Avenue from N. Rampart Street to Gayarré Place

❶   Esplanade Avenue, *1812, Jacques Tanesse, surveyor*

As Esplanade Avenue adjoining the lower French Quarter built up, development began to move up the extended avenue, which the municipality cut through expropriated land in the 1820s. (For Esplanade Avenue in the lower French Quarter, see page 150.) Brick buildings predominate along the French Quarter end of Esplanade, and large frame houses are characteristic of Esplanade Avenue beyond N. Rampart Street. Especially popular were two-story, double-galleried frame houses with side halls. This archetypical New Orleans house appears all along this stretch of the avenue (see also Tour 8, page 279). Served by a streetcar line that ran down the median, Esplanade became a most desirable place to live. The farther up the avenue you go, the later the house types get, and not only Creoles built them. By 1920 or so the neighborhood stagnated as newer developments in other parts of the city attracted wealthy house buyers. When heirs inherited them, the big old houses here became absentee-owned rooming houses, and later were broken up into small apartments. Serious decline set in during the Depression, and uncontrolled subdivision took off during the wartime housing squeeze of the early 1940s. The construction of elevated I-10 in the 1960s tore out the oak trees along N. Claiborne Avenue, displaced many black-owned businesses, and cut Esplanade Avenue in two. Blight followed the interstate. Vintage buildings were abandoned and stripped of their architectural features. The effects of suburban flight and poor city planning seriously eroded the stretch of the avenue from N. Rampart Street to N. Broad Street. A revival began in the mid-1990s when the Preservation Resource Center targeted the historic avenue for restoration, and a revived Esplanade Ridge Civic Association pressed for better sanitation and police protection. The result is that the former avenue of the Creoles is slowly coming back, most often due to nonnative New Orleanians who can envision a better future for the architecturally distinguished avenue.

Dufour-Baldwin House Historic Museum and Gardens
1707 Esplanade Avenue, at Derbigny; tours by appointment; also a bed-and-breakfast inn; 945-1503

2   Dufour-Baldwin House Historic Museum and Gardens, *Greek Revival-Italianate mansion, Henry Howard and Albert Diettel, 1859*
The original splendor, deep decline, and contemporary heroic rescue-in-progress of the monumental Dufour-Baldwin House is a metaphor for the fate of Esplanade Avenue itself. Designed by noted architects Henry Howard and Albert Diettel, this double-galleried Greek Revival-Italianate mansion with its paired columns was erected during the Old South's most opulent decade. It was built for Cyprien Dufour, a Creole lawyer, state senator, and one-time Orleans Parish district attorney. Dufour's son later recalled the house in its glory days (from *New Orleans Architecture, Vol. V: Esplanade Ridge* by Mary Louise Christovich *et al.*, 1977): "Lofty ceilings, spacious, well-ventilated rooms, beautiful chandeliers, Italian carved mantles, stained glass windows, beveled mirrors, rich carpets, costly fabrics, exquisite centerpieces and cornices" were a few of the features of the house. Attached to this beautiful mansion was one of the most extensive and highly cultivated gardens in New Orleans. "There nature and art were exhuberant, and the whole inexpressibly lovely." In 1869 the property was bought by Albert Baldwin and his wife, Arthemise Bouligny. Massachusetts-born Baldwin made a fortune as a hardware merchant and banker and married into an old Creole family. The Baldwins had thirteen children, and his heirs sold the house in 1912. By the early

1920s the house was sadly faded, and it was eventually chopped up into a rabbit-warren of apartments. By the late 1980s the once grand house stood empty and vandalized. In 1989, attorneys Elizabeth Williams and Rick Normand bought the near-ruin for their home and restored the large dependency wing in the rear for a bed-and-breakfast inn. They are now engaged in an on-going restoration of heroic proportions. The now-stripped interior and the unusual circular rear double gallery convey the romantic feeling of an ancient ruin.

3 Gayarré Place / Esplanade Avenue Crosses Bayou Road

Alight from the #48 Esplanade bus at N. Miro Street, next to the monument. This monument is the best example of cast terra cotta in New Orleans and was originally erected in Audubon Park as part of the World's Industrial and Cotton Centennial Exposition of 1884–85. The elaborate red terra-cotta base is well worth examining, though the cement 1930s statue that caps it is woefully anticlimactic. This small triangular park, formed where Esplanade Avenue cuts across the older Bayou Road, is named for Charles Etienne Gayarré, the noted French Creole historian and author of *The History of Louisiana*. Gayarré was one of the intellectual leaders of French Creole society from the 1850s to the 1880s and penned a lasting picture of Creole culture.

Down the old Bayou Road back toward the city is historic but sadly decayed Faubourg Tremé. It was the largest neighborhood built by free people of color in the United States, and in 1860 it had nearly nineteen thousand residents (see page 202). Most original residents were French-speaking Roman Catholics, and many were engaged in the building trades. Bayou Road is the oldest street in New Orleans and predates the city itself. It follows a Native American trail and portage along the high ground from Bayou St. John to the Mississippi River. At its French Quarter end it becomes Governor Nicholls Street and terminates at the French Market on the riverbank. In the other direction, beyond Broad Avenue, one path becomes the Grand Route St. John and heads directly to the bayou, and another path branches off to become Gentilly Boulevard, the old Spanish Trail to Florida, following the natural high ground along Bayou Sauvage. In the French colonial period the Bayou Road was lined with small plantations and cottages. When Esplanade Avenue was extended straight toward Bayou St. John in the 1820s, it cut across the natural diagonal of the older Bayou Road.

From the 1820s to the 1860s, the famous Haitian-born voodoo practitioner John Montenet, known as Dr. John, lived near here. As Henry C. Castellanos recounted in his 1895 memoirs, *New Orleans As It Was*:

> [Dr. John] was a negro of the purest African type. His ebony face was horribly tattooed, in conformity with the usages of the Congo tribe. He was glib of tongue, neat in his apparel, always wore a frilled shirt front and claimed miraculous powers for the cure of diseases. His room or office was packed with all sorts of herbs, lizards, toads and phials of strange compounds. Thousands visited him. As an Indian doctor, he was a great success.

4   **Benachi-Torre House,** *1859*

This short stretch of Bayou Road is still paved with red bricks. An exclamatory Gothic Revival cast-iron gate crowned with crockets and finials announces this stately house, built in 1859. Set behind a spacious, old-fashioned garden, this monumental, two-story Greek Revival house boasts four sets of double box-columns across its facade. The gallery's cast-iron railings sport an ivy pattern. The ceilings of the galleries are painted the traditional sky blue. This was believed to keep mud-daubers (wasps) from building nests there. A cross-cultural feature of this very American Greek Revival house is the incorporation of French windows (like paired doors) rather than the guillotine sash windows more typically found in Greek Revival houses. Behind the house to the left is a separate two-story dependency with a double gallery, built about 1930. Standing on the lawn are extravagant, oversized, cast-iron urns typical of old New Orleans garden ornaments. This house was built for Nicholas M. Benachi, a native of Greece who became wealthy as the owner of a steamship line. The mansion later became the home of the Rendevous des Chasseurs, a club for wealthy French and Creole New Orleanians. It was restored as a private home in 1982 with covenants requiring its preservation.

Benachi-Torre House
2257 Bayou Road

The House on Bayou Road Bed & Breakfast
2275 Bayou Road;
945-0992

Oasis
2285 Bayou Road;
944-2000

5   **The House on Bayou Road Bed & Breakfast / Fleitas House,** *circa 1802; moved in 1836; 1901 Victorian additions*

This delightful early Louisiana plantation house was probably built about 1802 for Domingo Fleitas on a site across Bayou Road. It sits on a raised basement, has a gallery with slender colonnettes, and is surmounted by a characteristic and graceful double-pitched roof. Pronounced dormers cap the house, providing efficient ventilation. When Esplanade Avenue was projected through the house's original site, it was moved to this location by Fleitas's son in 1836 and added onto with a rear kitchen wing. Joseph Chaufee bought the house in 1901 and added a wing to the left with two bedrooms, and he also enlarged the rear right corner with a bay to accommodate a master bedroom. Recently and tastefully restored by Cynthia Reeves, the landmark is painted a Creole beige and sports light Paris green shutters. Its traditional garden is a secluded oasis. The house now serves as an historic bed-and-breakfast inn. Next door is a converted corner store.

In the days when people walked, corner grocery stores were sprinkled all over old New Orleans neighborhoods. Most closed as automobiles changed shopping patterns. This corner building has been converted into **Oasis**, a reggae and "world beat" nightclub.

6   *Shotgun Temple* **Sculpture,** *Robert Tannen, 1980–88*
Visible up the kink in the road is a gray sheet-metal sculpture, *Shotgun Temple,* by New Orleans artist Robert Tannen. It makes a wry postmodern comment on the Greek Revival architecture so beloved in old New Orleans. At this point it is best to turn back to Esplanade Avenue via the short half block of N. Rocheblave Street, cross Esplanade Avenue, turn left, and see the 2300 block of Esplanade.

7   **View of the Site of the Native American Market**
The intersection of Bayou Road and Dorgenois Street a block lakeward is at the edge of what was the Native American market just outside the colonial town. Visible from here is the red brick Tudor Revival tower of Ste. Rose de Lima Roman Catholic Church, erected in 1914. A city market was eventually built near the site of the Native American market, and the open space was named **Place Bretonne.** The irregular crossroads here is its indelible trace. Today this is a sleepy, unnoticed backwater off the beaten track; the old municipal market building at 2500 Bayou Road is now shuttered and mute. A few small corner stores and beauty parlors survive here. This is one of the few places associated with the aboriginal people who once lived here. Over time, those Native Americans who did not flee seem to have been absorbed into the black community.

8   **2326 Esplanade Avenue and Tannen Sculpture Garden,** *circa 1900*
Concrete block sculptures mark the yard of the Tannen-Nathan residence. This elegant Georgian Revival house with an emphatic front portico supported by paired columns was probably built about 1900. Today it is the home of artist, architect, planner, sculptor, and wit Robert Tannen, who has filled its front yard with his block and gray sheet-metal sculptures. He calls these works "archisculptures," simplified models designed to draw attention to the purely visual aspects of buildings. Tannen often parks unusual over-blown automobiles in front of his house, treating them as found sculptures. The two large-scale, Victorian cast-iron gate posts that frame the entrance path are gutsy examples of the New Orleanian fascination with exuberant decoration.

9   **Musson House / Edgar Degas in New Orleans,** *1854, William Belly*
Built in 1854, this double-galleried frame house was originally a large center-hall house with a detached two-story kitchen and a stable and carriage house all set in a spacious walled garden. At some point, the left-hand side of the building was demolished, turning it into the side-hall plan house seen today. It was built by William Belly for real estate developer Benjamin Rodriguez. In the 1870s the house was rented by Rene Musson, Edgar Degas's brother. Between October 1872 and March 1873, when the Impressionist master visited New Orleans, he is presumed to have stayed here. While

in New Orleans, Degas painted his famous pictures of the interior of his uncle Michel Musson's cotton brokerage on Factors Row (that building survives at Perdido and Carondelet Streets in the CBD). Degas also painted a superb portrait of his sister-in-law and cousin, Estelle Musson deGas, now in the New Orleans Museum of Art. Planted between the sidewalk and the street are flourishing "cast-iron" plants, an old New Orleans garden favorite named for their hardiness. At N. Tonti Street, cross Esplanade to the bus stop in front of the monument at Gayarré Place. Take the #48 Esplanade bus up the avenue and alight at Grande Route St. John, just before the small triangle of Alcée Fortier Park, to do the second part of this walk.

Upper Esplanade Avenue

Alcée Fortier Park

Grand Route St. John

⑩   Upper Esplanade Avenue

As you progress up the avenue toward the bayou, the houses become more modern, with many 1890s Neoclassical or Colonial Revival houses, 1900s Mediterranean or Mission-style houses, and elaborate 1910s bungalows. Fine new house construction seems to have stopped here about 1920 as modern drainage opened up other parts of the city. Elsie Martinez described growing up here in the 1930s in her evocative joint memoir written with Margaret LeCorgne, *Uptown/Downtown* (1986):

> During my childhood my neighborhood was almost a microcosm of the city itself, with a rich variety of peoples and cultures. We had a small enclave of Creole families that had moved from the French Quarter and Esplanade Avenue, a few immigrant Italian families, a cross-section of middle-class New Orleanians of many national origins, and even a family just arrived from France. A couple of blocks from home, just around the corner from the Fair Grounds, lived several mulatto and quadroon families, some of whom were said to "pass for white" when they were in other parts of the city.

⑪   Alcée Fortier Park

This small, triangular park at Esplanade Avenue, Grande Route St. John, and Mystery Street is named for Alcée Fortier, a historian, folklorist, and teacher. Born in St. James Parish in 1856, he studied at the University of Virginia and became a professor of Romance Languages at the University of Louisiana, today Tulane University. He published a four-volume *History of Louisiana* in 1904 and was the president of l'Athenee Louisianais and of the American Folklore Society. This noted Creole scholar died in 1914. You are now near the restaurant cluster. Walk up slanting Grand Route St. John, once the main path to the bayou.

⑫   Grand Route St. John, *1809, Faubourg Pontchartrain; 1809, Faubourg St. Jean*

As you walk down Grand Route St. John with its mixture of modest and large houses, all well kept, you see just how pleasant New Orleans neighborhoods can be. Faubourg St. John is sought-after property in the 1990s as families rediscover the intimacy and

Bayou St. John   livability of these historic houses set in comfortable old gardens.

The blocks to the right (lakeside) were originally subdivided as Faubourg Pontchartrain in 1809, a narrow strip of land that reached to the Gentilly Road. To the left of Grande Route St. John was Faubourg St. Jean, laid out by Barthélémy Lafon in 1809 for Ireland-born land developer Daniel Clark. Walk to the grassy embankment along the bayou and admire the view.

⑬ Bayou St. John / Voodoo Spirit Gate

This placid, impounded bayou edged with well-manicured lawns (but no benches) is the result of the beautification programs of the Orleans Levee Board. This powerful, autonomous board is an independent agency of the State of Louisiana, and it has its own taxing powers separate from those of the city. It maintains some 121 miles of levees that ring the low-lying city, and it fields its own police force. Until the 1920s, Bayou St. John was a busy commercial waterway crowded by barges, which brought building supplies and produce into the city. At its head the bayou was continued by the Carondelet Canal, begun in 1794 and improved under American rule. This canal ended at a turning basin just outside the back of the French Quarter, where Basin Street and the Municipal Auditorium uptown parking lot are today. As railroads superseded the canal, the bayou became filled with a picturesque, if unsanitary, clutter of houseboats and pleasure craft. After the canal was filled in between 1927 and 1938, the bayou came under the jurisdiction of the City Park Board, and in the 1930s the WPA created the grassy embankments we enjoy today.

Bayou St. John is the gateway to New Orleans history. The first French outpost on the Gulf of Mexico was at Mobile, Alabama. Sailing west along the Gulf Coast, the French sought a shortcut so as to avoid navigating the treacherous and bewildering Mississippi delta. In 1699 Choctaw guides showed them how to reach the great river from the Mississippi Sound and Lake Borgne, through passes called the Rigolets, into Lake Pontchartrain. On the south shore of that broad lake was a small stream, later called Bayou St. John, which penetrated about four miles south toward the Mississippi River. From the Bayou St. John headwater it was but a two-mile portage to the river itself, the great highway into the North American interior. Up that great river were more rivers and the Great Lakes, links in a watery chain that connected French Louisiana with long-established French Canada. So the French decided to move their capital from Mobile Bay to where the French Quarter stands today.

A string of plantations with narrow frontages along the bayou, but that cut back deep into the swamps, were parcelled out by the French crown. A series of different crops were experimented with before settling on sugar cane. Colonial Louisiana imported West African slaves, some of whom came via Saint-Domingue (Haiti). They brought their beliefs with them, including the West African snake oracle. A syncretic religion evolved in the Caribbean slave cultures that blended the beliefs of the Mande, Fon, and Yoruba peoples. The word "voodoo" means spirit. It was a cult that believed in ecstacy, sorcery, charms, and fetishes. Enslaved within the dominant Roman Catholic culture, the practitioners of outlawed African beliefs adopted

Catholic saints and identified them with African spirits. The high point of the voodoo year was St. John's eve, June 24, the summer solstice. On that night devotees gathered along Bayou St. John to sing, dance themselves into trances, and invoke the *loas*, or spirits. Louisiana voodoo, unlike that in Haiti, was dominated by women. Its most famous practitioner was Marie Laveau (see page 94). Today, the African American search for spiritual exaltation continues in the city's Spiritualist churches with their singing, ecstatic, Christian congregations.

"Old Spanish Custom House," *circa 1807, Robert Alexander*
A peek through the iron gate at 1300 Moss Street on the corner reveals a traditional New Orleans walled garden with ginger plants, trees hung with giant lemons, and other fruit trees. This plot was part of the concession on the bend of Bayou St. John granted to Antoine Rivard de la Vigne in 1708, a decade before the founding of the city of New Orleans. This French colonial plantation house with its slender colonnettes and great parasol-like roof was probably erected about 1807 for Captain Emile Beauregard by builder Robert Alexander. It is said that Alexander recycled materials from the old Spanish Custom House that stood on Canal Street where the massive granite United States Custom House stands today, hence the house's popular name.

View of the Dome of Our Lady of the Rosary, *1924, Rathbone De Buys*
As you walk up Moss Street you will pass a parking lot and the rear of Cabrini High School and spy the green copper dome of Our Lady of the Rosary Roman Catholic Church at 3400 Esplanade Avenue. This Roman Baroque Revival church was designed by Rathbone De Buys and built in 1924. The church is generally only open during and after mass.

Our Lady of the Rosary Rectory / Blanc Mansion, *circa 1834*
Behind a fence of stucco piers and cast iron is this imposing early plantation house built about 1834 for Evariste Blanc, a real estate developer. It fuses the Louisiana plantation house with its double galleries with elements of the Federal style. Slender colonnettes support the second-floor gallery facing the bayou. The central doors at the first and second levels are handsomely framed by Ionic columns and capped by fanlights. A slate roof with four dormers and a "widow's walk" cap the mansion. In 1905 Sylvanie Blanc Denegre, a descendant of the builder, donated the house to establish Our Lady of the Rosary parish, and the building served as a chapel until the construction of a temporary church in 1907. It then became the parish rectory, which it continues to be today.

"Old Spanish Custom House"
1300 Moss Street

View of the Dome of Our Lady of the Rosary

Our Lady of the Rosary Rectory
1342 Moss Street; masses Sunday 8, 10, and 11:30 A.M.; weekdays 7 A.M., 5:30 P.M.; 488-2659

Cabrini High School
1400 Moss Street;
482-1193

Iron Pedestrian Bridge

Pitot House Museum
1440 Moss Street, N.O.,
70119; open Wednesday
through Saturday, 10 A.M.
to 3 P.M.; admission fee;
482-0312

17   **Cabrini High School,** *1964, Simoni, Heck & Associates*
This white building with slitlike windows is an unfortunate design for such a picturesque and historic location. On the other side of this extensive property, facing Esplanade Avenue, is the old Cabrini High School and Convent, originally the Sacred Heart Orphan Asylum. That monumental, oak-shaded building was erected to designs by Robert Palestrina. St. Frances Xavier Cabrini was born in St. Angelo, Lodigiano, Italy, in 1850; she was educated as a school teacher, became a missionary, and died in 1917. Mother Cabrini founded a new order of Italian nuns, the Institute of the Missionary Sisters of the Sacred Heart, and migrated to New York City in 1889. In 1892 she moved to New Orleans, a port with heavy Italian immigration, and established schools and an orphanage in the French Quarter. (In 1946 Frances Xavier Cabrini was the first United States citizen declared a saint by the Roman Catholic church.) There is still a Cabrini Day Home at 817 St. Philip Street in the heart of today's French Quarter. Needing expansion room outside the dense Italian slum, the nuns bought two old plantation houses here. They were near the loop end of the Esplanade Avenue streetcar, the line that shot straight out of the French Quarter. The sisters built the imposing Sacred Heart Orphan Asylum in 1905 and used the bayou-facing Pitot and Tissot Houses behind it as their convents. In 1959 the orphanage closed, and the old building became the Cabrini High School for girls, with a convent for the nuns on the top floor. In the 1960s the school decided to build a new building facing the bayou on the sites of the Pitot and Tissot Houses. One historic treasure, the Tissot House, was pulverized; the other, the Pitot House, was saved and moved. Alas that this great educational heritage resulted in this design.

18   **Iron Pedestrian Bridge**
Spanning the placid bayou is this delicate, powder blue, iron-truss bridge, which is now restricted to pedestrians and bicyclists. Its turntable is no longer operable.

19   **Pitot House Museum / Louisiana Landmarks Society,** *eighteenth-century West Indies plantation house museum*
Behind a low, weathered board fence is this house museum, the best window into elite French colonial Louisiana that survives in New Orleans. It originally stood where Cabrini High School is today and was moved to this site in 1964 when the nuns threatened to demolish it. The land was provided by the city, which carved out a piece of Desmare Playground to accommodate the relic. The restored and refurnished house opened in 1973 after a long and pioneering campaign by the Louisiana Landmarks Society. Bartholome Bosque began the construction of this West Indies–style plantation house in 1799, and it was continued the next year by Joseph Reynes. It was perhaps completed by builder Hilaire Boutté for the widow of Vincent Rillieux. In 1810 it was bought by James Pitot, the first mayor of the newly incorporated City of New Orleans. Pitot was born in Normandy, France, in 1761. He was a sugar merchant in Saint-

Domingue (Haiti) in the 1780s until the slave uprising there in 1792. He returned to France and then migrated to the United States and became an American citizen in Philadelphia. In 1796 he came to New Orleans to engage in the import-export business. Among his activities here was the presidency of the Orleans Navigation Company, which projected an unbuilt canal from the Carondelet Canal to the Mississippi River; this project gave Canal Street its name. He had an elegant town house at 630 Royal Street (since demolished) and bought this house as a country retreat. The house was owned successively by the Michel, Ducayet, and Tissot families. Felix Ducayet operated a thriving farm here during the 1850s, selling Suffolk hogs, Oxfordshire and Merino sheep, and fancy poultry. In 1904 Mother Cabrini bought the property for her convent.

1454 Moss Street

1451 Moss Street

1455 Moss Street

1459 Moss Street

1463 Moss Street

1467 Moss Street

20   1454 Moss Street, *1850s, Greek Revival*

Behind a white picket fence is this classic center-hall Greek Revival mansion on a raised basement, probably built in the 1850s. It is a handsome and characteristic work of Anglo-American architecture and is what many plantation houses in the American South were like. Continue around the bend in Moss Street toward Esplanade Avenue and the bridge over the bayou.

21   *Moss Street Views Across the Bayou*

Visible from the bend in the road, on the opposite bank of the bayou, is the massive and ancient Indian Trading Oak thought to be the site of a Native American trading place. The giant tree stands in front of **1451 Moss Street,** a Craftsman bungalow. To the right of the oak is a cluster of comfortable early-twentieth-century bungalows. From right to left they are: **1455 Moss Street** with a red tile roof; **1459 Moss Street,** also with a red tile roof; **1463 Moss Street,** a Craftsman-style house with an unusual attic room that pops up above the roof to catch the breeze and the view; and **1467 Moss Street,** a textbook Craftsman bungalow with great sheltering roof planes. The trend toward informality in early-twentieth-century American house design is epitomized in this outstanding group.

22   *Esplanade Avenue Bridge Views*

Before you cross the bridge there is a glimpse of the white marble angels atop the tombs of St. Louis Cemetery No. 3. This cemetery was laid out in 1854 on the site of the old Bayou Cemetery of 1835. The priests of the archdiocese are buried here, as is architect James Gallier, Sr., and Thomy Lafon, the Creole of color philanthropist. While well kept, it is not as interesting or picturesque as St. Louis Cemetery No. 1, or the romantically decayed and dangerous St. Louis Cemetery No. 2 just outside the French Quarter (see Tour 11, pages 339 and 340). Facing the bayou are the execrable Park

**Equestrian Statue of
P. G. T. Beauregard and
Lelong Avenue**

City Park
*1 Palm Drive, N.O.,
70124; main entrance at
the head of Esplanade
Avenue; open daily from
dawn to dusk; free;*
482-4888

Esplanade Apartments, built in 1974 and designed by Ervin Kohler, whose chief architectural ornaments are the air conditioning units crowning its roof.

㉓   Equestrian Statue of P. G. T. Beauregard and Lelong Avenue, *1915, Alexander Doyle, sculptor*
This circle—with its bronze equestrian statue, the monumental stone piers of the 1913 Monteleone Gate to City Park beyond, and tree-lined Lelong Avenue that culminates in the templelike New Orleans Museum of Art—is New Orleans' most impressive example of City Beautiful planning and Beaux Arts architecture.

㉔   City Park, *1931–33, Bennett, Parsons, and Frost*
City Park is the fifth-largest urban park in the nation and comprises some fifteen hundred acres. It is notable for its ancient live oaks and many cultural and recreational facilities. This guide includes only those highlights of the park of most interest to out-of-town visitors. The walk along oak- and magnolia-lined Lelong Avenue from the bus stop to the museum is one of the stateliest in New Orleans. To the left, across a lawn, are oaks and palms and a remnant of old Bayou Metairie. To the right is one of the park's four golf courses and a placid pond. The templelike facade of the New Orleans Museum of Art is a fitting conclusion to the city's most ambitious City Beautiful design.
        The site of City Park was explored by Bienville and granted to François Hery about 1718. While seemingly natural, this picturesque parkscape has been shaped by human hands. Much of it was originally scrub grass with willows and cottonwoods and was impassable, what Louisianians used to call "trembling prairie." The higher, oak-studded land along the bayou eventually became the Allard plantation, a dairy farm. Merchant John McDonogh bought the tract at a public auction. He left his estate to the cities of Baltimore and New Orleans, and in 1858 the City of New Orleans accepted title to this land in lieu of property taxes. (The rest of New Orleans' share of the munificent legacy was used to build public schools across the city named after McDonogh.) But it was to be a long time before the park was developed, and for a generation it lay fallow. Finally, in 1891, the City Park Improvement Association was organized with residents of Esplanade Avenue among its key members, and using private donations and some city funds they began improving the tract. The subsequent pattern of development was tortuous and too complex to relate here. City Beautiful improvements in the park included the Peristyle in 1907, the Isaac Delgado Museum of Art in 1911, the Casino in 1912, and the Popp Bandstand in 1917. In the prosperous 1920s the park doubled in extent. A new park plan was completed in 1933 by the Chicago firm of Bennett, Parsons, and Frost. For six years during the Great Depression, $13 million worth of WPA projects filled out the plan and created a great park here with winding roads, artistic bridges, a rose garden, a stadium, golf courses, tennis courts, fine park buildings, and modern statuary. It was the largest WPA project in Louisiana and gave work to twenty thousand workers. City Park was integrated in

1958. Though the park is a State of Louisiana agency, in 1987 both the state and the city stopped contributing to its operation. Since then the park has had to be self-sustaining; entrance fees for attractions in the park plus fund-raising events cover its $9 million budget.

㉕ New Orleans Museum of Art / NOMA, *1911, Lebenbaum and Marx; 1970, Arthur Feitel and August Perez; 1995, Eskew Filson Architects and Billes/Manning*

The New Orleans Museum of Art was founded in 1910 and recently underwent a major expansion, designed by Eskew Filson Architects and Billes/Manning, that opened in 1993. Its collection is noted for its French, American, Japanese, African, and Latin American art. It is also strong in photography, has a large silver and glass collection, and has some representative nineteenth- and twentieth-century Louisiana art. Highlights of the collection include dramatic Peruvian School of Cuzco paintings, Degas's masterful *Portrait of Estelle Musson deGas,* and Giovani Martinelli's mid-seventeenth-century canvas, *Death Comes to the Dinner Table.* This elegant Beaux Arts temple with its Ionic portico opened in 1911 and was designed by Lebenbaum and Marx of Chicago. Originally known as the Isaac Delgado Museum of Art, it was founded with a gift from that merchant, financier, and philanthropist. A family story claims that Delgado established the museum to please his French mistress, who complained about the lack of culture in New Orleans. Delgado was born in Jamaica in 1839, the son of a sugar planter. He came to New Orleans at age fourteen to work for his uncle, a sugar and molasses merchant. Delgado became a founder of the Louisiana Sugar Exchange and a noted philanthropist. In addition to this museum, he gave a modern wing to Charity Hospital. At his death in 1912 he left a bequest to found a trade school for boys, today Delgado Community College near the park.

New Orleans Museum of Art / NOMA
1 Collins Diboll Circle, City Park; P.O. Box 19123, N.O., 70179-0123; open Tuesday to Sunday 10 A.M. to 5 P.M.; cafe open from 10:30 A.M. to 4 P.M.; museum shop; closed all legal holidays; $6 for adults, $5 for seniors, $3 for children; 488-2631

Dueling Oak

City Park Oaks
For a fine guide to the ancient live oaks send a stamped, self-addressed, business-size envelope to Friends of City Park, 1 Dreyfous Avenue, N.O., 70124; 483-9376; Thanksgiving through early January the Celebration in the Oaks light display is staged from 5:30 to 10:30 P.M. nightly; $5 per car

㉖ Dueling Oak

Just beyond and to the left of the art museum is the famous Dueling Oak, more than sixteen feet in circumference with a crown spread of ninety-nine feet. Here Creole gentlemen settled their *affaires d'honneur* with swords or pistols. The empty crypt near the tree is reputed to have been the tomb of Louis Allard, Jr., who died in 1847.

All of the **great oaks** in the park, some of which are estimated to be as much as six hundred years old, are named, and many have legends attached to them. They are called "live" oaks because they are evergreen—"uttering joyous leaves of dark green" as Walt Whitman put it. They are known to botanists as *Quercus virginiana.*

Casino
*1 Dreyfous Avenue; open
daily; hours seasonal;
488-2896*

**Popp Music Stand /
The Peristyle**

Many very old trees have a branch spread that is twice the height of the tree. These majestic trees are made even more picturesque by their festoons of gray Spanish moss, *Tillandsia usneoides,* a member of the bromeliad family. The moss is an epiphyte, a plant that derives its sustenance from the atmosphere and does not harm the tree. When you examine the oaks closely you will also see that they are often covered with resurrection ferns, *Polypodium polypodioides,* so called because they spring to life and turn green after every rain but look brown and dead during dry spells. The greatest trees in City Park are all members of the Louisiana Garden Club Federation's Live Oak Society. The members of the society are the trees themselves; humans merely administer it. The preamble to the society's constitution is inspired:

> Whereas the Live Oak is one of God's Creatures that has been keeping quiet for a long time, just standing there contemplating the situation without having very much to say, but only increasing in size, beauty, strength and firmness, day by day, without getting the attention and appreciation that it merits from its anthropomorphic fellow-mortals . . . an universal association of Live Oaks is hereby ordained and established.

27   Casino, *1912, Nolan and Torre*
The arcaded, red-tile-roofed Casino houses refreshment stands and park offices; information can be obtained here. Built in 1912 and designed by Nolan and Torre, it is an outstanding example of the Spanish Mission Revival architecture so popular in New Orleans in the early twentieth century. Visible across the bayou is the Allard Oak. Behind it is the McDonogh Oak, the largest and oldest oak, whose trunk has a circumference of 25 feet and whose crown spreads out 150 feet. It is thought to be six hundred years old.

28   Popp Music Stand / The Peristyle, *1917, Emile Weil; 1907, Andry and Bendernagel*
Near the Casino is the Neoclassical, dome-capped, columned rotunda of the Popp Music Stand, built in 1917 and designed by Emile Weil. The tradition of public concerts died out in the 1960s. Just up Dreyfous Avenue is the Neoclassical Peristyle, built in 1907 and designed by Andry and Bendernagel. Ringed by Ionic columns, it was built as a sheltered dancing platform and was initially conceived of as a peristyleum, the entrance to a grand building that was never built.

29   **New Orleans Botanical Garden,** *Richard Koch and William S. Wiedorn, 1936; Jon Emerson & Associates, 1992*
This lush, gated botanical garden was created by the WPA in the 1930s as the City Park Rose Garden. Today it shelters about two thousand varieties of plants native to Louisiana and the Gulf South. The formal flower beds are shaded by ancient oaks, crape myrtles, sweet olives, and magnolias. The graceful Moderne Schriever Fountain of a woman bearing a vase flanked by bas reliefs of reclining nudes was carved by Enrique Alferez in 1932. He also designed many other sculptural grace notes throughout the park. Richard Koch designed the Moderne concrete benches in the park. In 1995, the elegant Pavilion of the Two Sisters, an education and reception hall designed by Trapolin Architects to be reminiscent of an orangerie, opened in the revived garden.

New Orleans Botanical Garden
1 Palm Drive, N.O., 70124-4608; open Tuesday to Sunday 10 A.M. to 4:30 P.M.; $3 adults, $1 children five to twelve, children under five free; twenty-minute guided tours by appointment, $3.50; 482-4888

30   **Storyland and City Park Railroad,** *1950*
This large playground is filled with fanciful structures for children to climb on; it opened in 1950. There are also live storytelling and puppet shows daily. Two miniature railroads wind through the park following a two-and-a-half-mile track.

Storyland and City Park Railroad
Victory Avenue, across from tennis courts, open year round with seasonal schedules; storytelling and puppet shows; fee; 483-9382

31   **William A. Hines Carousel Gardens and Miniature Railroad,** *1907, Mike Illions*
The 1890s Lupin Foundation Carousel Building houses the restored 1907 carousel of wooden horses carved by Mike Illions. It is a great favorite with children and nostalgic adults.

William A. Hines Carousel Gardens and Miniature Railroad
Between Victory and Stadium Drives, next to Storyland; open Wednesday through Sunday; seasonal schedules; fee; 483-9385

City Park Avenue Along Metairie Ridge

32   **City Park Avenue Along Metairie Ridge**
In eons past, as Bayou Metairie overflowed during each spring's floods it built up a natural levee, or high ground, along its banks. This became known as Metairie Ridge, the first (and only) high ground encountered upon leaving the swampy city. The French word *metairie* means small farm. This ridge became the site of the Chauvin brothers' farm and later an important cluster of cemeteries. Metairie Road inside Orleans Parish was renamed City Park Avenue in 1902. It resumes its original name on the other side of I-10.

Greenwood Cemetery
5242 Canal Boulevard;
open daily 8 A.M. to
4 P.M.; 486-6591

Cypress Grove Cemetery
120 City Park Avenue;
open daily from 8 A.M. to
4 P.M.; 482-1555

Longue Vue House and
Gardens
7 Bamboo Road, N.O.,
70124-1065; open
Monday to Saturday
10 A.M. to 4:30 P.M., last
house tour at 3:45 P.M.;
Sunday 1 to 5 P.M., last
house tour at 4:15 P.M.;
adults $5, students and
children $3; fine garden
and gift shop; 488-5488

Old Metairie

33 **Greenwood Cemetery,** *1852*
34 **Cypress Grove Cemetery,** *1840*

At City Park Avenue and Canal Street is a cluster of historic cemeteries. Behind the white Egyptian Revival entrance gates to the left is Cypress Grove Cemetery, designed in 1840. Across City Park Avenue is Greenwood Cemetery of 1852. Both are described in Tour 11.

35 **Longue Vue House and Gardens,** *1939–42, William and Geoffrey Platt*

Built for Edgar Bloom Stern, a cotton broker and philanthropist, and Edith Rosenwald Stern, daughter of a founder of Sears, Roebuck, and Company, this is the finest twentieth-century estate open to the public in Louisiana. The elegant house fuses a sense of Regency refinement with (disguised) modern materials such as concrete walls and steel roof trusses. One facade recalls the Beauregard-Keyes House (see page 146), another the National Trust's Shadows-on-the-Teche in New Iberia, Louisiana. Both the Classical Revival house and its furnishings are sophisticated, light, and hospitable. The baths and dressing rooms have Moderne touches, and quite surprisingly, there is a modern art gallery filled with 1960s "op" art and works by Victor Vasarely, among others. This house replaces an earlier one that was moved from the site so as to be able to utilize the already-begun gardens. The new house was designed so that views of the various gardens could be enjoyed from its rooms. The eight acres of gardens have distinct themes and are principally the work of Ellen Biddle Shipman. They include a wild garden, a walled garden, a Portuguese canal garden, the Spanish court inspired by the gardens of the Alhambra, a yellow garden, a portico garden, and an intimate Pan garden. Beyond the flower-filled gardens are views of the oak-dotted New Orleans Country Club. Magnolias, pink crepe myrtles, sweet olives, azaleas, and camellias are among the many Southern favorites that bloom here. The gardens are at their peak in the spring. A new Discovery Garden has been planted here for children.

36 **Old Metairie**

Metairie Road continues across the 17th Street drainage canal into Jefferson Parish and Metairie. In 1915 an electric streetcar line began operating along Metairie Road, and in the 1920s it became the city's first automotive suburb. The tree-lined streets between the canal and the Metairie Country Club are known as Old Metairie. The public landscaping and private gardens here make this a horticultural paradise.

③⑦ **Metairie Cemetery,** *1872, Benjamin Morgan Harrod, engineer*
See Tour 11 (page 346) for a description of Metairie Cemetery.

Metairie Cemetery
5100 Pontchartrain Boulevard; open daily 8 A.M. to 3 P.M.; taped tours available; 486-6331

*Bass player Richard Payne is a regular at the Palm Court Cafe on Decatur Street
in the French Quarter. The Palm Court is the perfect blend of traditional jazz and Creole
cuisine in an agreeable turn-of-the-century bar and restaurant.*

What This Tour Covers

Preliminaries

Introduction: The Soul of New Orleans

Continued on page 186

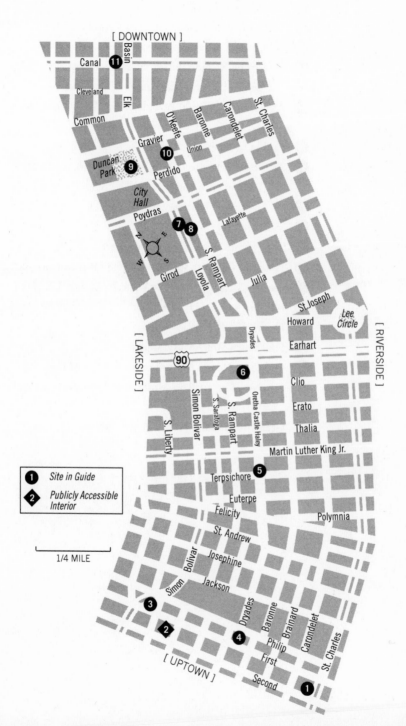

Tour 4a

[DOWNTOWN]

Canal

Basin

Elk

Cleveland

Common

O'Keefe

Baronne

Carondelet

St. Charles

Gravier

Union

Duncan Park

Perdido

City Hall

Poydras

Lafayette

N E W S

S. Rampart

Loyola

Girod

Julia

St. Joseph

Howard

Lee Circle

[LAKESIDE]

Dryades

Earhart

90

Clio

Simon Bolivar

S. Saratoga

S. Rampart

Oretha Castle Haley

Erato

Thalia

[RIVERSIDE]

S. Liberty

Martin Luther King Jr.

Terpsichore

Euterpe

Felicity

Polymnia

St. Andrew

Josephine

Simon

Bolivar

Jackson

Dryades

Baronne

Brainard

Carondelet

St. Charles

Philip

First

Second

[UPTOWN]

1 Site in Guide

2 Publicly Accessible Interior

1/4 MILE

Tour 4b

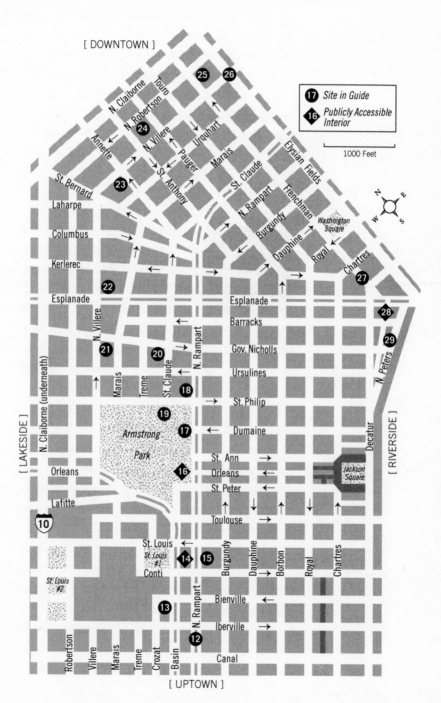

[DOWNTOWN]

17 Site in Guide

16 Publicly Accessible Interior

1000 Feet

N. Claiborne
Touro
N. Robertson
Annette
N. Villere
Urquhart
Pauger
Marais
St. Anthony
St. Claude
Elysian Fields
St. Bernard
N. Rampart
Frenchman
Laharpe
Burgundy
Columbus
Dauphine
Washington Square
Kerlerec
Royal
Chartres
Esplanade
Esplanade
Barracks
N. Villere
Gov. Nicholls
N. Peters
N. Claiborne (underneath)
N. Rampart
Ursulines
Marais
Treme
St. Claude
St. Philip
Dumaine
Armstrong Park
St. Ann
Orleans
Orleans
Jackson Square
St. Peter
Lafitte
Toulouse
Decatur
St. Louis
St. Louis #1
Conti
Burgundy
Dauphine
Borbon
Royal
Chartres
St. Louis #2
Bienville
Robertson
Villere
Marais
Treme
Crozat
Basin
N. Rampart
Iberville
Canal

[LAKESIDE]

[RIVERSIDE]

[UPTOWN]

What This Tour Covers

This car tour is for the intrepid, but cautious, explorer. It makes an arc from downtown to uptown through some poor African American neighborhoods and lets you glimpse the side of the city tourists rarely see. The National Park Service submitted a report to Congress on New Orleans jazz in 1993 as part of the process for establishing a future New Orleans Jazz National Historical Park; that study is the principal source for this exploration.

Preliminaries

BEST TIME FOR THIS CAR TOUR

It cannot be emphasized too much that the safest time to do this tour is *early Sunday morning*. Start with the 7 or 9 A.M. mass at St. Francis de Sales Roman Catholic Church, with its vibrant Africanized liturgy, and end at the Jazz Museum and Mardi Gras Exhibit at the Old Mint, which opens at 10 A.M. To get to St. Francis de Sales, drive up St. Charles Avenue, turn right at Second Street, and continue seven blocks toward the lake. Go to mass early and allow time to find a parking place close to the church. Sunday mornings during services there is good police protection near Central City's many active churches. After mass, make a slow drive all the way to N. Rampart Street, making a loop around the 400 block of S. Rampart. Continue across Canal Street to N. Rampart and park between St. Peter and St. Ann Streets; cross the street to see Congo Square. Return to your car and drive the rest of this tour through the old Creole wards, ending at the Old Mint's Jazz Museum and Mardi Gras Exhibit. If you wish to visit the Black Music Hall of Fame in Armstrong Park, or the African American art museum at Villa Meilleur, phone ahead to be sure they are open.

Since this can be a dangerous neighborhood, be cautious how you drive and stay on the prescribed route. Be both streetwise and respectful—don't drive an expensive car or take photographs if it might seem intrusive. Stay on main streets; there are many confusing, one-way back streets here.

Taxi Stands

There is a United Cab stand at the lakeside of the Quarter at the **Landmark Hotel** at 920 N. Rampart Street, between Dumaine and St. Philip; and in front of **Le Richlieu Motor Hotel** at 1234 Chartres Street, at Barracks.

Music Clubs

There are several music clubs on N. Rampart Street and in Faubourg Tremé. **Donna's Bar & Grill** has great local brass bands; **Funky Butt at Congo Square** features late-night jazz.

Taxi Stands
• *Landmark Hotel at 920 N. Rampart Street, between Dumaine and St. Philip*
• *Le Richlieu Motor Hotel at 1234 Chartres Street, at Barracks*

Donna's Bar & Grill
800 N. Rampart Street, at St. Ann; 596-6914

Funky Butt at Congo Square
714 N. Rampart Street, near Orleans; upstairs; 558-0872

Introduction:
The Soul of New Orleans

By turns witty, joyful, sexual, sorrowful, and spiritual, the musical culture of New Orleans is its greatest achievement. As historian Gwendolyn Midlo Hall wrote in *Creole New Orleans: Race and Americanization* (1992), New Orleanians "tore down the barriers of language and culture among peoples throughout the world and continue to sing to them of joy and the triumph of the human spirit through the sounds of jazz." Ragtime and jazz have a complex early history, and like so many aspects of New Orleanian culture, they have black and white, and downtown and uptown, ingredients. Much of their early history went unrecorded, since jazz was not considered high culture. In fact, in its infancy it was associated with an underworld of shady cabaret proprietors, madams, and gamblers. There is controversy over even the source of the word itself. Some claim it came from black American slang for sexual intercourse; others say it came from the French Creole *jaser,* meaning to chatter. This etymological uncertainty underscores the bicultural and biracial complexity of New Orleans' most important communal artistic creation.

Colonial New Orleans was born with a passion for private dancing and public parading, and for this it needed music. As one early traveler put it, "in the winter they dance to keep warm, and in the summer they dance to keep cool" (from *The Past as Prelude: New Orleans 1718–1968,* 1968). French gavottes and quadrilles came with the first colonists. Dances and masked balls created a steady demand for musicians. Other forms of music and dancing were also evident early on. Grand opera appeared in the city in 1796, and for many years New Orleans had America's only resident opera company. In 1822 the first regular ballet troupe performed in the city. Parades were another local mania: militias, volunteer fire companies, fraternal lodges, and later the very important social aid and pleasure clubs, all had their marching bands for street parades. In 1819 architect Benjamin Henry Latrobe commented that burial parades with music were "peculiar to New Orleans alone among American cities."

Although the French colonists brought European music with them, the essential ingredient in New Orleans music turned out to be West African. As early as 1721 enslaved West Africans were about a third of the settlement's population. Many came via the Caribbean and brought with them Afro-Caribbean rhythms. Forbidden so many other forms of self-expression, such as reading and writing, African Americans found music to be a powerful, improvisational outlet for individual and communal expression. Even without instruments, when working in gangs, African slaves fell to call-and-response chanting. In 1817, even under the repressive Anglo-American municipal government, African slaves were allowed to gather to conduct a market and to dance and make music at the circus grounds across Rampart Street from the old city. Soon dubbed Congo Square, Afro-Caribbean music and dance flourished there every Sunday afternoon until sundown. On a Sunday afternoon in 1819, Benjamin Henry Latrobe wrote, "[A] crowd of 5 or 600 persons assembled in an open space or public square." They "were formed into circular groups in the midst of which was a ring . . . ten feet in diameter." In one ring two women were dancing: "They held each a coarse handkerchief, extented by the corners, in their hands. . . . The music consisted of two drums and a stringed instrument. . . . A man sung a song . . . to the dancing which I suppose was in some African language, for it was not French" (from *Impressions Respecting New Orleans: Diary and Sketches, 1818–1820,* 1951).

Early on, New Orleans also developed a substantial and literate population of free people of color, most of them Francophone. With secure economic bases in crafts and the building trades, and shaped by French culture, these Creoles of color centered their social life around invited dances and were an avid audience for music. Many of them lived in the downtown faubourgs of Tremé and Marigny, and later the Seventh Ward. Some of their children became musicians and composers. Creoles of color formed a Philharmonic Society in the late 1830s with more than one hundred members.

African American musicians adopted European fifes, fiddles, triangles, and tambourines. Influences as varied as French dances, Spanish songs, Caribbean rhythms, Anglo-Saxon Protestant hymns, and West African call-and-response chants all became part of New Orleans' polyglot musical DNA. After the Civil War, emancipated African Americans were able to express their musical tastes more freely. Black musicians composed everything from songs to symphonies in late-nineteenth-century New Orleans. Brass bands were popular all over the United States in the post–Civil War period, nowhere more than in the Crescent City. In the 1890s "spasm bands" formed by young African American boys began to appear on the city streets. (Today the very young black tap dancers on Bourbon Street continue something of their spirit.) The proliferation of fraternal organizations and mutual aid associations that owned their own halls and conducted frequent dances and occasional parades created a steady demand for musicians, and a desire to dance to the latest tunes. Jelly Roll Morton recalled some of the redolent names of these parading clubs: the Broadway Swells, the High Arts, the Tramps, the Iroquois, the Allegroes. Commercial dance halls and cabarets also flourished all over the city and out at the resorts on the shore of Lake Pontchartrain. Dance bands and orchestras softened the brass band sound with violins, guitars, and string bass. String dance bands were popular among the genteel Creoles of color downtown. The fusion of African rhythms, European instruments, and local social functions produced a great musical flowering at the end of the nineteenth and the dawn of the twentieth century.

By 1899 a new syncopated musical style among piano players, known as ragtime, reached its peak. Ferdinand Joseph Le Menthe, "Jelly Roll Morton," a Creole of color, and Tony Jackson, a gay black man, were among its greatest exponents. Ragtime music became the first nationally accepted African American cultural expression. In the late 1890s, uptown cornet player Charles "Buddy" Bolden put the new ragtime piano rhythms in the context of a dance band and increased the tempo of familiar dance tunes. Bolden is credited by many with being the first musician to perfect the new "ratty" uptown jazz style. The standard front line of a New Orleans jazz band became a cornet, clarinet, and trombone. The new jazz had the amalgamating effect of bringing uptown blacks and downtown Creoles of color together to make music for, usually, white audiences. As Warren "Baby" Dodds recalled in *The Baby Dodds Story,* 1959:

> [Big Eye Louis Nelson] lived downtown, and I lived uptown. He was on the north side of town, and I was living on the south side. In other words, he was a Creole [of color] and lived in the French part of town. Canal Street was the dividing line and the people from the different sections didn't mix. The musicians mixed only if you were good enough. But at one time the Creole fellows thought uptown musicians weren't good enough to play with them, because most of the uptown musicians didn't read music. Everybody in the French part of town read music.

Creole musician Paul Dominguez, Sr., a string bass player with John Robichaux's orchestra in the early 1900s, remembered that, "See, us Downtown people . . . we didn't think so much of this rough Uptown jazz until we couldn't make a living otherwise" (from *Storyville, New Orleans* by Al Rose, 1974). Jazz as it evolved melded the uptown improvisational style with the more disciplined downtown Creole approach. One of the key places where downtown and uptown musicians played together was Storyville, the red-light district behind Canal Street and above N. Rampart Street, across from the old French Quarter. The expansion of prostitution along Customhouse Street (today Iberville Street one block into the French Quarter parallel to Canal Street), and rising concern over the invasion of respectable blocks by the sex trade, led to the passage of alderman Sidney Story's antibrothel ordinance in 1897. Strictly speaking, it did not legalize prostitution; what it did was exclude the sex business from all *other* areas in the city. To New Orleanians these approximately thirteen blocks from Basin Street to N. Claiborne Avenue, and from St. Louis to Iberville Streets bracketed by the St. Louis No. 1 and St. Louis No. 2 cemeteries (and now the site of a brick public housing project), were euphemistically referred to as "the District." The press dubbed it "Storyville," much to alderman Story's chagrin. Elaborate "fancy houses" and rude "cribs" flourished here from 1897 to 1917. The "mayor" of Storyville was Tom Anderson, who sat in the state legislature on the committee that oversaw the City of New Orleans. Jazz was not born in the District, but the fancier brothels hired piano "professors" to amuse their clients. As Jelly Roll Morton reminisced about one high-class bordello (from *Mister Jelly Roll* by Alan Lomax, 1950):

> Walk into Gypsy Schaeffer's and, right away, the bell would ring upstairs and all the girls would walk into the parlor, dressed in their fine evening gowns and ask the customer if he would care to drink wine. They would call for the "professor" and while champagne was being served all around, Tony [Jackson] would play a couple of numbers. If a naked dance was desired, Tony would dig up one of his fast speed tunes and one of the girls would dance on a little

narrow stage, completely nude. Yes, they danced absolutely stripped, but in New Orleans the naked dance was a real art.

District saloons and restaurants employed jazz musicians as well. One memorably named hot spot called itself the Fewclothes Cabaret! A famous diversion in the District was the oyster dance, whereby a nude dancer made a shucked oyster slither hesitatingly down her torso. Storyville was one of the few places where uptown blacks and downtown Creoles of color made music together for white audiences. Drug stores here sold cocaine over the counter, and newsboys peddled marijuana cigarettes on the streets. Almost all of the derelict District was wiped away in 1938 by the Federal Housing Authority for the construction of the Iberville public housing project. "The bricks" were originally built for whites, but today it is all black, and it suffers from the crime that persistent poverty always engenders.

The District's brothels could be fancy indeed, as this description of Madame Lulu White from the famous District guide, the *Blue Book,* makes clear:

Nowhere in this country will you find a more popular personage than Madame White, who is noted as being the handsomest octoroon in America, and aside from her beauty, she has the distinction of possessing the largest collection of diamonds, pearls, and other rare gems in this part of the country. To see her at night, is like witnessing the late electrical display on the Cascade, at the late St. Louis Exposition [of 1904]. Aside from her handsome women, her mansion possesses some of the most costly oil paintings in the Southern country. Her mirror-parlor is also a dream. There's always something new at Lulu White's that will interest you. "Good time" is her motto. There are always ten entertainers who are paid to do nothing but sing and dance.

Another common ground was the so-called Tango Belt, the six blocks of the French Quarter across N. Rampart from Storyville. Pops Foster remembered that about 1900 there were three types of bands playing in the Crescent City (in *Pops Foster,* 1971):

You had bands that played ragtime, ones that played sweet music, and ones that played nothin' but the blues. A band like [Creole of color] John Robichaux's played nothin' but sweet music and played the dicty [genteel] affairs. On a Saturday night Frankie Duson's Eagle Band would play the Masonic Hall because he played a whole lot of blues. A band like the Magnolia Band would play ragtime and work the District [Storyville]. . . . All the bands around New Orleans would play quadrilles starting about midnight. When you did that nice people would know it was time to go home because things got rough after that.

In the early 1900s hot jazz emerged in New Orleans' dance halls. Joseph "King" Oliver moved to the city about that time and began to play piano in the

Storyville brothels. In 1909 the Zulu Social Aid and Pleasure Club began its tradition of King Zulu and black Mardi Gras parody parades. The next year Edward "Kid" Ory moved to the Crescent City, where he developed his quintessential New Orleans-style trombone playing. In 1914 thirteen-year-old Louis Armstrong was released from the Home for Colored Waifs; he had learned to play the cornet in the home's band. In 1915 Jelly Roll Morton's *Jelly Roll Blues,* composed about ten years earlier, was published. And in 1917 Nick La Rocca, son of a Sicilian New Orleanian shoemaker, made the first jazz recordings in New York City with his Original Dixieland Jazz Band.

In the second decade of the twentieth century, jazz began its national and then international diffusion. As early as 1907 Jelly Roll Morton was playing his innovative ragtime piano compositions far from New Orleans. The Original Creole Orchestra featuring Freddie Keppard moved to Los Angeles in 1912, and then toured the Orpheum Theater circuit nationally. In 1915 Tom Brown's Band from Dixieland left for Chicago; Nick La Rocca moved to the Windy City in 1916. Jazz was on its way to conquering the world. By 1919 the Original Dixieland Jazz Band was performing in England, and Sidney Bechet was playing in Paris. In 1922 King Oliver formed the trend-setting Creole Jazz Band in Chicago, and in that year he called young Louis Armstrong to join him up north. Armstrong led a revolution in jazz, replacing the polyphonic ensemble style of New Orleans playing with his soloist's art. Improved phonograph records in the mid- and late 1920s made Armstrong's Hot Five and Hot Seven internationally famous.

In 1917 the United States entered World War I, and the secretary of the navy, Josephus Daniels, ordered Mayor Martin Behrman to close all the brothels in New Orleans. Behrman went to Washington to protest the extralegal demand, but he could not get a hearing. On September 24, 1917, Secretary Daniels threatened that if the city did not close down Storyville, the armed forces would. (The legality of all this was doubtful, but war hysteria prevailed.) Under protest, the city council passed an ordinance closing the District at midnight, November 12, 1917. Prostitution did not evaporate—today it clusters at the Asian "spas" and "massage parlors" along Chef Menteur Highway in eastern New Orleans—but jobs for jazz musicians did. The innovative, bright, brassy, happy musical flowering of New Orleans was over. Many of her best musicians moved on to larger markets in St. Louis, Kansas City, Chicago, Los Angeles, and New York City. New Orleans music did not disappear, of course, but the glory days were over. Jazz continued to evolve, but now in places outside the South and far from the city that gave it birth.

In the 1930s jazz fell out of favor, but in the late 1940s its revival began. Turk Murphy's Yerba Buena Jazz Band in San Francisco was among the early revivalists. Jazz scholar Alan Lomax and the Library of Congress began seeking out and recording surviving jazz musicians. Allan Jaffe opened Preservation Hall in New Orleans in 1961. Today traditional jazz is recognized as one of the greatest American arts, but it faces an uncertain future. Today's generation of New Orleans musicians is following other musical paths, like rap and bounce and world beat.

1 *Second Street Toward Central City*

**St. Francis de Sales
Roman Catholic Church**
*2203 Second Street, at
Loyola; Sunday mass at
7 and 9* A.M.*; 895-7749*

2309–11 First Street

As you drive up Second Street, you are imperceptibly leaving the high ground of the natural levee between the river and St. Charles Avenue into what were originally cypress swamps. Low-lying and flood prone, Central City emerged from these swamps in the early 1830s to house the Irish American immigrants who dug the New Basin Canal. That canal (now approximately the alignment of the Pontchartrain Expressway) gave access to the back of the American city from Lake Pontchartrain and competed with the Creoles' older Carondelet Canal, which terminated at Basin Street. Always an area with working-class rental housing, Central City became home to successive waves of immigrants: Irish, German, Italian, Jewish, and today, black. Many of the buildings here are one- or two-story, frame, double-shotgun houses placed close to the sidewalk. Some are camelbacks and have a second story at the rear of the building. Each cottage has a backyard, and many have a bit of Victorian gingerbread and ornamental brackets. This was the cradle of "rough Uptown jazz." Among the great musicians to come from these now mean streets were Buddy Bolden, Joe King Oliver, Kid Ory, Papa Celestin, Pops Foster, the Dodds and Shields brothers, and Tom Zimmerman. The many social halls, dance clubs, and social aid and pleasure clubs that pepper the neighborhood were fertile seedbeds for early jazz. Still today, despite the poverty of the area, Central City and Tremé continue the long and rich tradition of neighborhood marching clubs and spontaneous street parading, especially during Carnival season. Many Mardi Gras Indian organizations thrive here and practice in local bars and clubs. Strangers are welcome to "second line"—march along with the paraders—during Carnival.

2 **St. Francis de Sales Roman Catholic Church,** *1870, architect unknown*

Seven blocks up Second Street is a simple frame church with a square tower built in 1870 by Irish and German immigrants. As the neighborhood changed, so did the congregation. In the 1960s, this was one of the first Roman Catholic churches to adopt a "black liturgy," with spirituals and gospel music and other black cultural expressions incorporated into the mass. All are welcome here; you will feel more comfortable in slacks and shirts than shorts and T-shirts.

3 **Simon Bolivar Boulevard and First Street / Buddy Bolden House,** *1871*

Continue up Second Street to curving Simon Bolivar Boulevard and turn right. Immediately up ahead and to the right is an empty lot with a one-story cottage visible from the side. It is **2309–11 First Street,** a typical working-class, double-shotgun house built in 1871. From 1887 to 1904, it was the home of cornetist Buddy Bolden, who lived here with his mother and sister during his most creative years. His band is considered the first real jazz band. The modest house is now a city landmark. Two blocks up, at the traffic light, past the large Allie Mae Williams Center (a social services center),

Old New Orleans Public Library
1924 Philip Street, between Dryades and Danneel

St. John the Baptist Roman Catholic Church
1101 Dryades Street; Sunday mass at 11 A.M., 4, and 9 P.M.; 525-1726

Cancer Survivors Park

make a right turn onto wide Jackson Avenue. Three blocks down Jackson turn left onto Dryades Street.

4   Old New Orleans Public Library, *1915, William R. Burk*
The recently restored, red-brick, former Dryades Street branch of the New Orleans Public Library, where Dryades makes a slight jog, was a gift from philanthropist Andrew Carnegie, who stipulated that it was to serve the black population of New Orleans. Designed by William R. Burk and opened in 1915, it was the only public library open to African Americans for many years, and it became a center of community life.

5   *Oretha Castle Haley Boulevard / Old Dryades Street*
In Greek mythology, the Dryads were the nymphs of the trees; this is the French spelling. The Dryades-Carondelet area was New Orleans' Orthodox Jewish neighborhood from the turn of the century until the 1950s. Many Polish and Russian Jews settled here and opened businesses along Dryades. They catered to working-class whites and to African Americans, whom the segregated Canal Street stores refused to serve. Dryades became the city's most important black shopping street. In the post–World War II era, Jews began moving to the Lakefront and the suburbs. The end of segregation signaled the end of once-thriving Dryades, and today the street is semiderelict and haunted with the ghostly ruins of Handelman's department store. In 1989 a part of Dryades Street was rechristened Oretha Castle Haley Boulevard in honor of this civil rights activist.

6   View of St. John the Baptist Roman Catholic Church, *1869–72, Albert Diettel*
The stately baroque brick church in the distance with the gold onion dome was designed by Albert Diettel and built between 1869 and 1872. It is one of the finest monuments of the bricklayer's art in New Orleans. Continue along Dryades, pass under elevated I-10, make a left at Howard Avenue and a right onto Loyola Avenue.

7   Cancer Survivors Park, *1995, Miloslav Cekic*
In the median of Loyola Avenue, between Poydras and Girod Streets, rises this strange double row of fanciful columns. Designed in 1995 by Miloslav Cekic of Austin, Texas, each of the fourteen columns represents a different culture. The eight bronze sculptures are by Mexican artist Victor Salomones. This unusual monument was the gift of Richard Bloch.

8   *Clarinet* Mural / Holiday Inn Downtown Superdome, *1995,*
Robert Dafford

Clarinet Mural / Holiday
Inn Downtown Superdome

City Hall / Duncan Plaza

On the south wall of the high-rise Holiday Inn is a 150-foot-tall mural of an Albert System clarinet, painted by Robert Dafford in 1995. It is one of the most effective and appropriate pieces of public art in the city, and it certainly improves the building and the surroundings.

9   City Hall / Duncan Plaza / Site of Back o' Town and the Battlefield

Green Duncan Plaza, facing Loyola Avenue between the 1950 green glass City Hall and the state Supreme Court, was once the poor black Back o' Town. The African House Pavilion that stands in the center of the park has four concrete columns and a steep shingle roof and was erected in 1987 to the designs of Arthur Q. Davis. Mixed in with working-class housing in the old Back o' Town were gambling parlors, cribs, saloons, social halls, dance halls, and dives where "rough Uptown jazz" emerged. This was where Louis Armstrong was born on August 4, 1901 (though he later chose July 4, 1900, as his "birthday"). In 1954, he described the Battlefield in his memoirs:

> James Alley—not Jane Alley as some people call it—lies in the very heart of what is called The Battlefield because the toughest characters in town used to live there, and would shoot and fight so much. In that one block between Gravier and Perdido Streets more people were crowded than you ever saw in your life. There were churchpeople, gamblers, hustlers, cheap pimps, thieves, prostitutes and lots of children. There were bars, honky-tonks and saloons, and lots of women walking the streets for tricks to take back to their "pads," as they called their rooms.

Young Louis grew up with his mother, Mayann, his stepfather, Gabe, and his grandmother. At a young age he helped his stepfather deliver coal in Storyville downtown across Canal Street. As he instantly noted:

> Music, food, and everything else was good there. . . . What I appreciated most about being able to go into Storyville without being bothered by the cops, was Pete Lala's cabaret where Joe Oliver had his band and where he was blowing up a storm on his cornet. Nobody could touch him.

Soon Armstrong was frequenting the District as part of a quartet singing for change on the sidewalk. When he was twelve, Louis was sent to the Home for Colored Waifs for firing a pistol in Storyville on New Year's Day. He spent two years there and was taught the elements of music by Peter Davis. He played the cornet in the home's brass band. When he was released he formed a sextet with Joe Lindsey. By this time, red-light Storyville had been shut down and many of the great early jazzmen had left New Orleans, but not Louis's idol, Joe Oliver. "Papa Joe" took Louis under his wing. Louis's first real gig was playing at Henry Matranga's cabaret. Armstrong left New Orleans in 1922.

Odd Fellows Hall
1100 Perdido Street

Iroquois Theater
413 S. Rampart Street

427–31 S. Rampart Street

Frank Douroux's Saloon
449 S. Rampart Street

Loyola Avenue was bulldozed through here in the late 1940s, clearing away the Battlefield and New Orleans' small Chinatown, which bordered it.

 **10** *A Loop Around the 400 Block of S. Rampart Street*

Cross wide Poydras Street, turn right at Gravier Street, and then make an immediate right onto S. Rampart Street. S. Rampart Street was the principal African American entertainment strip during the long era when segregation kept blacks from the shops and theaters on Canal Street. Today it is part of the vast tundra of parking lots that serve the Superdome and the CBD. Here were clustered vaudeville theaters along with saloons, social halls, and dance clubs; early jazz flowered here. A few original jazz spots (the buildings, that is) survive in this wasteland and have recently received much attention from jazz historians.

• **Old Eagle Loan and Pledge Company / Eagle Saloon / Odd Fellows Hall,** *1850, architect unknown*
This three-story, brick-and-stucco commercial building was built in 1850 and housed a pawn shop and saloon on its ground floor. In 1897 the Masonic and Odd Fellows Association leased the top floor for a meeting room and dance hall. There Buddy Bolden and Louis Armstrong played their immortal jazz.

• **Site of the Iroquois Theater**
This now-dilapidated, two-story brick theater catered to black audiences and featured music between its vaudeville shows; Jelly Roll Morton and Louis Armstrong may have played here. The theater's manager was Papa Stringbean, a vaudevillian famous for his "Elgin watch movement dance."

• **427–31 S. Rampart Street**
This is the site of the first record shop in the city as well as of the tailor shop that employed Louis Armstrong.

• **Site of Frank Douroux's Saloon**
This now-derelict building was once a dance hall where early jazz was played. Later it was a Chinese restaurant on the edge of the Chinatown that was cleared away in the 1940s. Turn right at Poydras, and then right again onto Loyola. Past Tulane Avenue, Loyola becomes Elks Place. Across Canal Street, Elks Place becomes famous Basin Street.

⑪   Canal and Basin Streets / Edge of the Theater District / Saenger Theater, *1927, Emile Weil*

Saenger Theater
143 N. Rampart Street;
box office, 524-2490

239 Basin Street

Canal and Basin, where major streetcar lines crossed, was once the center of the city's entertainment district. Theaters near here once included the Crescent, Lyric, Strand, No Name, Alamo, Plaza, and Trianon. They staged minstrel shows, vaudeville, ragtime music, and eventually jazz. Important music publishing companies, such as Piron-Williams Publishing, the Hackenjos Music Company, and L. Grunwald and Company, also clustered here and disseminated sheet music of the new New Orleans musical styles. Today the legitimate Saenger Theater at Canal and N. Rampart Streets is a splendid survivor. Built in 1927 and designed by Emile Weil, this scenic theater's biggest surprise is its interior. The lobby seems to bring the street into the building, while the atmospheric auditorium is ringed by a Renaissance palace "exterior" capped by statues and urns under a blue-black night sky. An inscription above the terra-cotta arch over the N. Rampart Street entrance reads: "A monument devoted to the best in music, photoplay & the theatrical arts."

⑫   *Basin Street*

Everyone has heard of Basin Street, so perhaps it is all too appropriate in America that there is almost nothing to see on these bleak, redeveloped blocks, though the sounds once generated here have never stopped reverberating. Once there was a turning basin at Basin Street and N. Rampart Street at the head of the Carondelet Canal. That canal opened in 1794, and it both drained the swampy city and served as a transportation artery for flat-bottomed scows from Lake Pontchartrain which delivered lumber, bricks, firewood, fish, and oysters to the back of the old French city. Later the Southern Railroad paralled the canal and erected its terminal at Basin and Canal Streets in 1904. (In 1927 the old canal was filled in; Lafitte Street follows its filled-in bed.) At the turn of the century, busy Basin Street became a transient zone and attracted bars, no-tell hotels, and prostitution.

⑬   *Remnants of Lost Storyville*

Two relics of lost Storyville survive on its Basin Street edge along the 1200 block of Bienville Street; you can see them by pulling over to the downtown-riverside corner of Basin and Bienville. The truncated, brick corner building at **239 Basin Street,** at the uptown-lakeside corner of Bienville, was the annex to the demolished Mahogany Hall bordello, where Lulu White specialized in octaroons. On the second floor of this building, Tom Anderson's right-hand man, Billy Struve, wrote the famous *Blue Books,* the guidebooks to the District now prized by collectors. Visible behind it is the roof of Joudeh's Food Market, a corner grocery store across from the Iberville housing project. Once it was Frank Early's My Place Saloon, and it was probably there that Tony Jackson, the great Storyville piano "professor" who was black and gay, wrote *Pretty Baby* for a boyfriend. The Iberville housing project was built in 1939–41.

14   Our Lady of Guadalupe Roman Catholic Church

At Basin and Conti Streets, turn right and then make an immediate left onto N. Rampart Street. At the corner of Conti and N. Rampart is Our Lady of Guadalupe Roman Catholic Church. Visible over the protective wall is the top of a statue of St. Jude with a flame dancing atop its head, see page 338.

15   *N. Rampart Street and the Old Tango Belt*

Today N. Rampart Street is the depopulated frontier between the white and middle-class French Quarter and the black and poor Tremé, and it is one of the sharpest racial borders in the contemporary city. But once this was a street where different social worlds intermingled and sweet jazz soared.

N. Rampart Street, as its name memorializes, was once the line of the old French city's fortifications. In 1807, after the American purchase, Congress granted title to the fortifications and the common land around them to the city, and Canal Street, N. Rampart Street, and Esplanade Avenue were surveyed and the lots lining them sold. All became important boulevards lined with impressive houses. N. Rampart Street later became a traffic corridor and attracted entertainment venues, among other businesses. The block where you are standing was the edge of the old Tango Belt, the six blocks bounded by N. Rampart and Dauphine, and from Iberville to St. Louis Streets. This area in the northwest (uptown-lakeside) corner of the French Quarter once had one of the highest concentrations of jazz venues in the city, including the Oasis Cabaret, the Elite, and the Black Orchid. As the new music changed at the turn of the century, so did dancing. The one-step emerged along with ragtime, and about 1910 the turkey trot—a fast, bobbing one-step where the arms flapped about like a turkey—became the craze. Soon there was a rage for "animalistic" dances. The *Daily Item* noted that "every little freak step that wriggles its way into life masquerades under the name . . . of some barnyard or menagerie relative" (quoted in *HNOC Quarterly*, fall 1992). There was the grizzly bear, chicken scratch, bunny hug, crab step, kangaroo dip, possum trot, camel walk, and the lame duck. In 1913 the Argentine tango became an international craze. The tango emerged from the Buenos Aires slums in the 1880s and fused the spirited Spanish tango with the sexual, low-life Argentine Milonga. New Orleans embraced the new dance with a passion. Tight tango skirts with deep slits became the fashion in the cabarets. This corner of the French Quarter was dubbed the "Tango Belt" in the local press. The forces of propriety, of course, disapproved. In 1914 New Orleans police superintendent James W. Reynolds announced that light had to be visible between the dancers. "The tango," he fulminated, "has been carried to extremes by unprincipled people. . . . Vulgar forms of the tango, bunny hug, grizzly bear, and turkey trot would not be permitted" (*Daily Item*, January 14, 1914).

At 222 N. Rampart Street, next to a parking structure, stands the handsome home of the New Orleans Athletic Club, founded in 1872. This Beaux Arts clubhouse with marble interiors was erected in 1929 just before the stock market crash.

Demolition along Rampart Street in the 1920s, when this was the city's auto row, has scarred the street.

Armstrong Memorial Park, St. Peter Street Gate
N. Rampart and St. Peter Street; open 9 A.M. to 10 P.M.; avoid this park after dark

⓰   Armstrong Memorial Park, St. Peter Street Gate / Congo Square / Beauregard Square

You may wish to park along N. Rampart Street, between St. Peter and Orleans, cross N. Rampart Street and enter Armstrong Park through the St. Peter Street (corner) gate to see historic Congo Square. Now paved with stones and ringed by live oaks, this was originally the location of Fort St. Ferdinand. It was cleared away by American Governor Claiborne in 1804, and the site became a public market and circus grounds. From about 1806 to the 1850s, slaves gathered here every Sunday in what was an open field just outside the city limits. In 1817 a city ordinance decreed that "the assemblies of slaves for the purpose of dancing or other merriment, shall take place only on Sundays, . . . and no such assembly shall continue later than sunset." Circus Place was designated for these gatherings. Here African Americans sold goods and food, drummed, danced, and played music till sundown. No alcohol could be sold, though a kind of Creole ginger ale made from fermented apples was drunk. White New Orleanians and visitors came here to watch African Americans dance the bamboola and other dances. The music here, of course, predated jazz. Composer Louis Moreau Gottschalk's family lived close by on N. Rampart Street. Years later, while living in Paris, Gottschalk composed *Bamboula* and other music based on the rhythms he remembered from Congo Square. In 1851, however, the city council designated this open space as the place where the militia would drill on Sundays once the old *Place d'armes* was fenced and turned into landscaped Jackson Square. In his *New Orleans as It Was* (1895), Creole Judge Henry C. Castellanos penned this memory of the Congo Square of his youth:

> Attired in their picturesque and holiday dresses, [Creole African slaves] would gather by thousands in the afternoon under the shade of the old sycamores, and romp in African revelries to the accompaniment of the tam-tam and jaw-bones. Nothing could be more interesting than to see their wild and grotesque antics, their mimicry of courtly dames in the act of making an obeisance, and the dances peculiar to their country. In the midst of the ludicrous contortions and gyrations of the Bamboula, not unlike those performed in the equally famous Voudou dance, they would sing with a pleasing though somewhat monotonous rhythm the Creole songs, the burden of one of which, I remember was: *"Danse Calinda, bou doum, bou doum."* To these festivities *negres 'Mericains* were not invited. There was no affinity between them. . . . As soon as the shadows of approaching night began to deepen, the crowd would slowly disperse, singing in chorus: *"Bonsoir dance, soleil couche."*

In 1893 this ring of oaks was planted and the square was renamed Beauregard Square to honor the recently deceased Creole Confederate general P. G. T.

Beauregard. The large building behind the square is the Municipal Auditorium, which opened in 1930 and was long the scene of Carnival balls. Festivals are often held in Congo Square, and those are the liveliest times here.

17   Armstrong Memorial Park, Dumaine Street Gate / View of French Quarter Galleries

From the French Quarter side of N. Rampart Street, at the uptown-riverside corner of Dumaine Street, there is a fine view of French Quarter cast-iron galleries stepping out into the distance.

18   Faubourg Tremé

Tremé is a neighborhood in steep decline. The best time to pass through it is early Sunday morning, and photography is often not welcome. Drive carefully, as many young children play here. Tremé was one of the earliest extensions of the old French city across Rampart Street, and it was partially the site of Claude Tremé's plantation, which the municipality bought and subdivided in 1810. It was home to a French-speaking Creole of color community; many of the breadwinners here were prosperous free men of color engaged in the building trades. In 1834 lawyer John H. B. Latrobe made an evening ramble through what was probably Tremé and left this description (*Southern Travels,* 1986):

> [O]ff we went for that part of the City where the American spirit of improvement has made the fewest alterations in the mode of building of the old Spanish times. I found entire Squares [blocks] where there has been no innovation, without a single two story building but composed of rows of one storied dwellings with sheds projecting from the eves over the pavements. The windows were of the French fashion, opening like doors, and were very frequently placed on the inside of the wall so as to put the window seat in the street. . . . The [roof] sheds just mentioned besides giving a singular and highly picturesque appearance to the street, answer many useful purposes. They shade the house from the sun and shield it from the rain, and perform the same office to the foot passenger, whom they further benefit in the unpaved street by keeping in some measure the ground dry under his feet. The doors as I passed along were generally occupied by the female part of the inmates, and these were in most cases quadroons, or the French of the inferior classes.

Musicians associated with Tremé include George Lewis, Chris Kelly, Jimmie Noone, and Henry Ragas. Today Tremé is a neighborhood with a problematic future. Gentrification and its displacement is actively resisted, while the historic Creole buildings suffer demolition by neglect. This old part of town has one of the highest concentrations of brass bands and parading in the city today, especially during Carnival. They are like flowers blooming in the ruins. The parades of the various social aid and pleasure clubs in the pre-Carnival season are the happiest moments in the neighborhood, and strangers are most welcome then.

Armstrong Memorial Park, St. Claude Avenue Gate

① Armstrong Memorial Park, St. Claude Avenue Gate

WWOZ / 90.7 FM
Concert information, 840-4040

You can drive through the gate here into the edge of Armstrong Park. Here stands a loose scattering of historic buildings divorced from their original settings and converted to other uses, including a fire station and an almost invisible NOPD back office. This strange compromise is the result of a disasterous 1961 urban renewal scheme that demolished a vast swath of historic Creole houses in Tremé in order to expand Armstrong Memorial Park for a grandiose, five-building cultural center. Only one building was built, the banal 1973 Mahalia Jackson Theater of the Performing Arts. The anti–urban park plan with the high berms—which hide the park users from the street—stagnant pond, and clunky bridges was designed by Laurence Halprin and Associates and could hardly be more inappropriate in New Orleans. The two-story former slave quarters with the second-floor gallery houses **WWOZ (90.7 FM)**, a listener-supported station that broadcasts all the varieties of Louisiana music at different times of the day. Their concert information line is one of the best sources for current New Orleans music, though not necessarily for traditional jazz.

Old Perseverence Lodge No. 4
901 St. Claude Avenue, inside Armstrong Park

St. Augustine's Roman Catholic Church
St. Claude Avenue at Gov. Nicholls; open only during mass at 10 A.M.; donations for the upkeep of St. Augustine's: 1210 Gov. Nicholls Street, N.O., 70116; 525-5934

• **Perseverence Lodge No. 4,** *1830, François Correjolles and Jean Chaigneau*
The two-story, yellow-and-white former Masonic hall beyond WWOZ is severe but handsome. Chartered by the Grand Lodge of Pennsylvania in 1810, principally for free-thinking free Creoles of color who were refugees from Cuba and Haiti, this is probably the oldest Masonic lodge in the Mississippi valley. It moved to this site in 1819; this hall was built in 1830 by François Correjolles and Jean Chaigneau. Early jazz dances were held here for elite Creoles of color. The building was restored in 1979, and in 1996 the city announced that it would become the Black Music Hall of Fame.

② St. Augustine's Roman Catholic Church, *1842, J. N. B. de Pouilly*
Originally a Creole Catholic neighborhood, Tremé is mostly Baptist or evangelical today. This large complex of towered church, rectory, school, and playground has lost many of its parishioners and stands faded and ghostlike along the 1200 block of Governor Nicholls Street. As the neighborhood has become poorer and more violent, the church has had to wall itself in, until today it seems reminicent of a fortified Moorish mosque. An elegant bell tower with a beautifully shaped green copper dome capped by a fine cast-iron cross rises from the corner. (This tower is visible from inside the French Quarter when looking up Gov. Nicholls Street.) The church was designed by J. N. B. de Pouilly and completed in 1842. In 1926 the red brick church was stuccoed over. As

Villa Meilleur
1418 Governor Nicholls Street; open only for special events; phone 826-1624 or 565-7494

The Seventh Ward

Holy Aid Comfort Spiritual Church / Perseverance Hall
1644 N. Villere Street, between St. Bernard Avenue and Annette

Genesis Missionary Baptist Church / Francs Amis Hall
1820 N. Robertson Street, between Pauger and St. Anthony

Roulhac Toledano and Mary Louise Christovich's *New Orleans Architecture, vol. VI: Faubourg Tremé and the Bayou Road* (1980) notes: "At the time of its construction, half of St. Augustine's congregation consisted of Creoles of French and Spanish ancestry and recent French immigrants; the other half was composed of free people of color, with a few pews reserved for slaves."

㉑   Villa Meilleur, *1828; 1996, Williams & Associates*
Surrounded by a stout fence and set behind raised planting beds with bananas and other lush vegetation, the corner Villa Meilleur was built in 1828 and restored in 1996. This delightful villa once stood on a large plot that fronted on Bayou Road. Bookseller William Franklin Goldthwaite was a later owner. In 1996 the restored house was opened by the city with an exhibit of the work of African American New Orleans artists, and it was announced that the villa would become a museum of African American art. It is currently open only for special events.

㉒   The Seventh Ward / The Creole Ward
The Seventh Ward, roughly the triangle of residential blocks lodged between Esplanade Avenue and Elysian Fields Avenue, was the stronghold of the Creole and Creole of color communities. The great musicians associated with this neighborhood include Jelly Roll Morton, Paul Barbarin, Barney Bigard, Lizzie Miles, Manuel Perez, Buddy Petit, Omer Simeon, and Lorenzo Tio, Jr.

㉓   Holy Aid Comfort Spiritual Church / Perseverance Hall
This plain, clapboard, one-story, camelback building was the second-oldest Masonic hall in the Mississippi valley and was built by the Benevolent Mutual Aid Association, an African American fraternal organization founded in 1853. Important early jazz musicians who played here included Buddy Bolden, Freddie Keppard, Chris Kelly, Kid Rena, Buddy Petit, and Sam Morgan.

㉔   Genesis Missionary Baptist Church / Francs Amis Hall
This two-story building with a modern brick veneer was built as a Masonic hall and was described by guitarist Johnny St. Cyr as "a place of dignity" for downtown Creole of color society. The sweet music of the John Robichaux Orchestra, the Superior Orchestra, and the Olympia Orchestra graced "dicty" affairs here. You can see bits of the original Victorian millwork popping through the modern brick that encases it. The windows have been painted to look like stained glass for this evangelical church.

25   Birthplace of Jelly Roll Morton

This corner house is the birthplace of Jelly Roll Morton. Born in 1885 to a middle-class Creole family, Ferdinand Joseph Le Menthe was of mixed racial descent. He began his career playing piano in the bordellos of Storyville and was a seminal figure in jazz. He was the first jazzman to write his arrangements in musical notation and was the creator of a great many compositions that became staples in the repertory, including *Jelly Roll Blues, King Porter Stomp, New Orleans Blues, Wolverine Blues, The Pearls,* and *Kansas City Stomp*. He took New Orleans music to Memphis, California, Chicago, and New York City. He was also a pool hustler, card-sharp, sometime pimp, and master monologist. In 1938 he related his version of the creation of jazz to Alan Lomax and made fifty-two recordings for the Library of Congress. He died alone and broke in Los Angeles in 1941, convinced he was under a voodoo curse.

26   Elysian Fields Avenue

Wide Elysian Fields Avenue is the border between the 7th Ward uptown and the 8th Ward downriver. Named by Bernard Marigny after the Champs Elysées in Paris, this has always been a zone of modest one-story cottages and houses. For many years the Pontchartrain Railroad, the first railroad in the South, ran out the median here from the river to Milneburg on Lake Pontchartrain. There, a cluster of democratic restaurants and dance halls attracted daytrippers. Many early jazzmen found work out at the lake.

27   *Frenchmen Street Music Clubs*

This is one of the most congenial clusters of good music clubs in the city. The old buildings with their galleries or canopys over the sidewalks have a western look. This is a good block to come back to in the evening when the music is happening. See Tour 2 for a list of several popular clubs.

28   Old United States Mint / Louisiana State Museum

See page 154 for the architectural history of this landmark. Enter the red-painted Old Mint from its principal entrance facing Esplanade Avenue. To either side as you enter are two shops; one sells coins struck in this building between 1838 and 1909, among other things, and the other shop carries CDs, tapes, books, and magazines on New Orleans jazz.

•   United States Mint Museum / Ground Floor

The Mint was essentially a factory that converted gold and silver bullion into coins; it operated here from 1838 until 1909. The ground level of this massive stone, brick, and

Birthplace of Jelly Roll Morton
1443 Frenchmen Street

Elysian Fields Avenue

Old United States Mint / Louisiana State Museum / New Orleans Jazz Museum and Mardi Gras Exhibit
400 Esplanade Avenue, at Decatur; open Tuesday to Sunday 10 A.M. to 5 P.M.; admission fee; 568-6968; the Coin Vault at the Mint sells coins struck in this building between 1838 and 1909, among other things, 523-6468; The Louisiana Music Factory carries CDs, tapes, books, and magazines on New Orleans jazz, 524-5507

GHB Jazz Foundation /
Jazzology Records
61 French Market Place,
near Gov. Nicholls;
525-1776
iron building has an exhibit on William Strickland, its architect, and P. G. T. Beauregard, the Army engineer who stabilized the sinking building in the 1850s. In 1861–62 the mint briefly struck Confederate gold coins. Architectural plans are hung among the exposed brick supports that once supported the steam engine. A substantial Egyptian Revival smokestack stood behind the building until the 1920s.

• New Orleans Jazz Museum / Second Floor, River End

This shrine exhibits treasures from the Louisiana State Museum's jazz collection, much of which was gathered by the New Orleans Jazz Club and given to the museum in 1978. Jazz plays softly in the background. The galleries here trace the development of jazz in New Orleans and its continuing manifestations in the present. Researchers can make appointments with the museum's Curator of Jazz to study the recordings and documents preserved here.

• Mardi Gras Exhibit / Second Floor, Lake End

Happy New Orleans Mardi Gras music plays in the background of the rhinestone heaven of this Carnival exhibit. Costumes of many kinds, crowns, tiaras, scepters, collars, and all sorts of treasures and trinkets fill this exhibit. The eye-catching items here include the feathered Mardi Gras Indian costumes, the painted, papier-mâché Krewe of Proteus *Neptune* float, and the feather and sequin Zulu Carnival ball Cleopatra costumes. Certain panels should not be missed. The one labeled *The Flowering of Krewes, 1870–1920* has a short chronology of key Carnival organizations. The panel titled *Mardi Gras Invitations* displays treasures of colorful lithography from the Gilded Age. Wildly inventive and opulent, they represent an art perfected here between the 1880s and World War I. The panel on *Float Design* features watercolors by Miss Jennie Wilde from the 1890s to early 1900s; they have an astounding Art Nouveau madness about them.

• Jazz Mural, *late 1940s, Xavier Gonzalez*

The third floor of this stout building houses the research library of the Louisiana Historical Center, which preserves many manuscript collections and is also the custodian of the state's colonial archives. There is one treasure on public view on the third floor landing: Xavier Gonzalez's late 1940s mural of *Dixie's Bar of Music* depicting many jazz performers active in the 1930s. From the glass doors on this level there is a view out over the green Governor Nicholls Street Wharf toward the funnels of freighters from around the world. Elevators here permit you to exit the Mint from its rear, Barracks Street door. Note the well-designed cast-iron galleries that cover the city-facing side of the building. You are now across the street from the French Market (see page 213).

㉙ GHB Jazz Foundation / Jazzology Records

For a description, see page 64.

Breezy Woldenberg Park, built atop a concrete dock, helped revive the riverfront in 1989. The steamboat Natchez *still plies the great river; in the distance is the Upper Pontalba Building.*

What This Tour Covers
Preliminaries
Introduction: A City Edge Reborn

1. The French Market
2. Washington Artillery Park
3. Jax Brewery Mall
4. Moonwalk on the Mississippi River
5. Steamboat *Natchez*
6. Woldenberg Riverfront Park
7. Aquarium of the Americas
8. Liberty Monument
9. Canal Place Shopping Centre and Westin Hotel

Tour 5

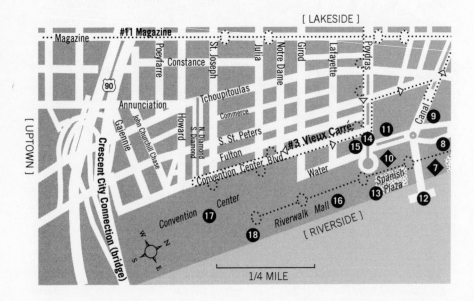

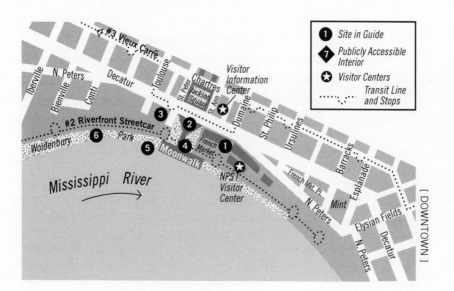

What This Tour Covers

This walk follows the bank of the Mississippi River, at once the oldest and now the newest part of New Orleans. It strings together a variety of new attractions and includes a place where you can touch the river as well as the best observation deck from which you can look out over the city. You will probably not want to do everything on this tour; choose the things that interest you and make your own tour using the Riverfront streetcar. The free ferry ride and the World Trade Center panorama are recommended.

Preliminaries

**BEST TIMES TO
DO THIS TOUR**

Try to go when the **World Trade Center observation deck** is open. Woldenberg Park on the river is a pleasant walk at night, with the twin bridges and the ships on the river all lit up.

Transit

The **Riverfront streetcar** pulls together all the attractions along the river; it starts running about 6 A.M. (7:40 A.M. on weekends) and shuts down at about 11 P.M. (ask the conductor for the exact time). The **#3 Vieux Carré jitney bus** takes riders straight from the Convention Center to the French Quarter from about 5 A.M. (8 A.M. on weekends) until about 7 P.M. (6 P.M. on weekends).

Parking

The **French Market Corporation** operates a paid parking lot behind the market; enter from Decatur Street at St. Peter Street. You can return here easily via the Riverfront streetcar; get off at the Toulouse Street stop.

Restaurants, Food Markets, and Cafés

There are several places to eat in and near the French Market, starting with **Café du Monde** at the uptown end of the market. Café du Monde is open every day around the clock and serves *café noir* or *café au lait* and *beignets* (donuts without holes, with or without powered sugar).

Off Dutch Alley is **Bella Luna,** a predominantly Italian and seafood restaurant with an artistic interior and a sweeping view of the river and the city. **Progress Grocery Company** is an excellent place for take-out mufulettas (cold cut and cheese sandwiches on soft round bread with an olive salad relish) and other Italian delicacies. **Louisiana Pizza Kitchen** is popular with residents and visitors. **Fiorella's Cafe** is a downhome favorite.

Bella Luna
914 N. Peters Street, off Dutch Alley; reservations advised; jackets for gentlemen; open Monday to Saturday 6 P.M. to 10:30 P.M., Sunday 6 P.M. to 9:30 P.M.; expensive; 529-1583

Progress Grocery Company
Just outside the market proper, at 915 Decatur Street, between Dumaine and St. Philip Streets; 525-6627

Louisiana Pizza Kitchen
95 French Market Place, at Barracks facing the Old Mint; open until 11 P.M., later on weekends; 522-9500

Fiorella's Cafe
1136 Decatur Street between Ursulines and Gov. Nicholls; breakfast and lunch only; 528-9566

Introduction:
A City Edge Reborn

A century ago, when New Orleanians and visitors sought waterfront recreation, they took carriages or railroad cars out to the shore of Lake Pontchartrain. There, a series of lakeside resorts, yacht clubs, and an amusement park flourished, leaving the Mississippi River to railroads, industry, docks, and shipping. Today the center of the New Orleans riverfront has undergone a complete transformation, shifting from docks to recreation along this postindustrial city edge. Throughout the eighteenth and nineteenth centuries the riverfront was intensely active. Boats coming downriver—loaded with cotton, grain, lumber, and all the products of the vast interior of North America—met ocean-going vessels here, the ships that carried this wealth out to the world. New Orleans was the point of transfer, sale, finance, and storage. As the new American commercial city grew, shipping, warehousing, wholesaling, banking, insurance, retail, hotels, and entertainment created their own precincts in the bustling port city (see Tour 6 for the Central Business District). As Benjamin Moore Norman wrote in 1845 in the city's first guidebook, *Norman's New Orleans:*

> This is completely a commercial community . . . and money is the universal ambition. . . . During the business season, which continues from the first of November to July, the levee, for an extent of five miles, is crowded with vessels of all sizes, but more especially ships, from every part of the world—with hundreds of immense floating castles and palaces, called steam boats; and barges and flat boats innumerable. No place can present a more busy, bustling scene. The loading and unloading of vessels and steam boats—the transportation, by some three thousand drays, of cotton, sugar, tobacco, and the various and extensive produce of the great west, strikes the stranger with wonder and admiration. The levee and piers that range along the whole length of the city, extending back on average of some two hundred feet, are continually covered with moving merchandise. This was once a pleasant promenade, where the citizen enjoyed his delightful morning and evening walk; but now there is scarcely room, amid hogsheads, bales and boxes, for the business man to crowd along, without a sharp look out for his personal safety.

This activity was strung out along the old street atop the original levee. Its control center was the U.S. Custom House just inside the old French Quarter at Canal and Levee (now Tchoupitoulas) Streets. Because the river kept depositing silt along the batture (riverbank) here, the city was able to expand several blocks riverward in the 1840s. About 1905 the Dock Board began building metal storage sheds along the river's edge, and eventually the city was completely cut off from the Mississippi. Paralleling the docks were eight railroad lines further isolating the city from the river. Moving cargo was labor intensive, and many men made their living along the bustling docks. The docks continued to be active into the 1950s. In the post–World War II period, New

York city planner Robert Moses proposed a riverfront expressway that would have further walled off the city from the river. In a major preservationist victory, citizen protest stopped that destructive proposal in 1969.

French Market
Between Decatur and N. Peters Streets, from St. Ann to Barracks;
522-2621

The shift from railroads to trucks began pulling warehousing out of the city in the 1950s and 1960s. The first convention-oriented development near the river was the Rivergate exhibition hall, with its billowing concrete roof built in 1968 at the foot of Canal Street (and demolished for the new casino in 1995). In 1966 the high-rise World Trade Center had opened across the street. It was partially built over the Belt Line railroad that served the docks.

The first break in the wall of metal sheds that cut the city off from its greatest natural feature was Eads Plaza, between the World Trade Center and the water, which became Spanish Plaza in 1976. In 1977 the first phase of the Hilton Hotel opened at the foot of Poydras Street overlooking the river. Beginning in 1979 Joseph Canizaro's ambitious Canal Place shopping mall, hotel, and high-rise office tower opened at the foot of Canal Street near the Rivergate and World Trade Center.

The 1980s saw accelerated change along the river. A second public access was opened at Moonwalk across from Jackson Square in the French Quarter. The old Jackson Brewery nearby was converted to tourist uses in 1984. The Louisiana World Exposition of 1984 initiated the transformation of the Warehouse District upriver from Poydras Street; the International Pavilion for that fair became the first phase of the city's new convention center. Twenty-six old warehouses were restored and adapted for the exposition. While the fair was not an economic success, it did push out most of the remaining light industrial and warehouse uses in the blocks between Poydras Street and the elevated expressway leading to the bridges. The stimulus given to the rehabilitation of historic structures by the tax act of 1981 helped fuel this shift. This change created the Warehouse/Arts District with its contemporary galleries along Julia Street and nearby condominiums (see Tour 7). In 1986, the Rouse Company's Riverwalk Marketplace opened, replacing the Upper Poydras Street Wharf with a popular three-level shopping mall. In 1988 the city opened the Riverfront streetcar line and equipped it with vintage rolling stock. This tourist-oriented line links the convention center upriver with the French Quarter downriver. In 1989 the old Bienville Wharf was demolished and replaced with pleasant Woldenberg Riverfront Park, and the next year the Audubon Institute opened the adjacent Aquarium of the Americas. This brought a major family attraction to the new riverfront. In the 1990s a series of riverboat casinos tied up to the booming riverfront. Today the riverfront is a solid row of visitor-oriented attractions, all built since 1976. The once-hidden riverfront is now accessible and alive.

❶   The French Market, *1813, Gurlie and Gillot; many subsequent architects; 1936 WPA renovation; 1975 major renovation*
The Café du Monde announces the historic French Market, a seven-building complex with a rich history. Jazz bands are often playing in the market's cafes. The market covers a long, thin triangle of land on the riverside of Decatur Street from St. Ann to

**National Park Service
Visitor Center**
*In the French Market on
Dutch Alley at the foot of
Dumaine Street; open
daily 9 A.M. to 5 P.M.;
589-2636*

Barracks Streets, which is bisected by French Market Place. An intriguing pedestrian alley threads between the historic buildings. Nestled here is the **National Park Service Visitor Center,** with maps and information on the city and on far-flung Jean Lafitte National Historical Park and Preserve (see page 82). The Decatur Street side of the market is thronged with visitors; the interior alley has benches and is usually quiet and peaceful.

There may have been a Native American gathering place near here before the founding of New Orleans, for here was the landing on the riverbank that led to the portage (trail) to Bayou St. John and Lake Pontchartrain (see Tour 3). Until the end of the nineteenth century Choctaw herb and medicinal plant vendors frequented the market. The first enclosed market was erected near here by the Spanish in 1782. After a great fire and hurricane, the Meat Market (the Café du Monde building only) was erected in 1813 to designs by Gurlie and Gillot. The bustling market kept adding buildings over time and sold fruits, vegetables, meat, poultry, fish, and wild game. Audubon bought some of his vivid bird specimens here. In 1835 space was set aside in the market for Native American and African American vendors. Dr. Thomas L. Nichols described the market in 1845 (*Forty Years of American Life,* 1864): "The creoles . . . go to Mass [in the cathedral] and also go to the market, which, on Sunday morning, is more crowded, more noisy, and fuller of negro and creole gaiety than on any weekday." Behind the market, along what is now French Market Street, was Gallatin Street, with lodgings frequented by sailors, market workers, and prostitutes. In this district Mardi Gras was especially ribald. As Perry Young wrote in his *The Mistick Krewe* of 1931, "In Gallitania—the sailor region below Jackson Square—all the females were out in male disguises, and the men were mostly dressed as women." Modern hygiene was introduced to this tropical market by Union General Benjamin F. Butler, who ordered its cleansing in 1862. The notorious Black Hand Gang that extorted money from Sicilian businesses once flourished here as well. As late as 1880 George Augustus Sala could report that, "As for the confusion of tongues in the market, it was simply delicious. French, Italian, Spanish, Portuguese, Dutch [German], and 'Gombo' contended with each other for supremacy; but French predominated" (John Magill, *Preservation in Print,* 1991). The decayed complex was thoroughly renovated in 1937 by the WPA, who also introduced refrigeration. The coffee stands in the market were long a popular stop for New Orleanians after a night on the town. Truman Capote described the market in 1945. After writing all night,

at that dawn hour I would walk through the humid, balconied streets, past St. Louis Cathedral and on to the French Market, a square crammed in murky early morning with the trucks of vegetable farmers, Gulf Coast fishermen, meat vendors and garden growers. It smelled of earth, of herbs and exotic, gingery scents, and it rang, clanged, clogged the ears with the sounds of vivacious trading.

In 1973–75 the city renovated the old market, but this time it replaced most of the wholesalers and food vendors with shops and cafes for visitors. Produce is now limited to the small Farmer's Market between Ursulines Avenue and Governor Nicholls Street at the far end of the complex. A weekend **flea market** is held under the WPA-built metal canopy between Governor Nicholls and Barracks Streets. The outstanding **annual mask fair** held in Dutch Alley just before Mardi Gras draws mask makers from across the country.

2   **Washington Artillery Park**
The strip of land facing Jackson Square is named Washington Artillery Park. The heavy-handed concrete structure with the staircases, built in 1976, offers a good overview of the square with its symmetrical grouping of landmarks. (You can walk around it at St. Peter Street next to Jax's Brewery, if you want to avoid the stairs.) Street performers and pierced punks favor the amphitheaterlike space facing Decatur Street. **Lenny's Newsstand,** which has a good selection of magazines, is tucked under the structure near Café du Monde. An **information booth** here sells tickets to the Audubon Zoo, the aquarium, and other attractions. Up the stairs, down the other side, through the 1953 concrete flood-wall gate, and across the streetcar tracks is another short flight of steps that leads to the top of the levee and down to the batture, the slope on the riverside of the levee.

3   **Jax Brewery Mall,** *1891, Dietrich Einsiedel; conversion, 1984, Stephen Bingler*
Ireland-born David Jackson came to New Orleans in 1854 and with his brother became a dealer in salt. He sold that business to his nephews, and in 1886 bought the famous Gem Saloon at 127 Royal Street, the informal headquarters of the earliest Carnival krewes. In 1891 Jackson formed the Jackson Brewing Company and built this massive brew house catercorner from Jackson Square. His picturesque, castlelike brewery, designed by German-born architect Dietrich Einsiedel, continued in operation until 1974. The 1984 adaptation by architect Stephen Bingler inserted a six-story, twentieth-century building inside the five-story, nineteenth-century brewery to create a vertical mall of shops and restaurants, now including the **Hard Rock Cafe** and **Planet Hollywood.** When the building was converted, a crenelated tower was added to the Decatur Street front and a mansard roof with dormer windows was added to the rear. These additions were deliberately not direct copies of old forms and have recessed, rather than protruding, decorative

Flea Market
Every weekend between Gov. Nicholls and Barracks Streets

Annual Mask Fair
In Dutch Alley, just before Mardi Gras

Washington Artillery Park
Facing Jackson Square, Decatur Street between St. Ann and St. Peter

Lenny's Newsstand
Facing Jackson Square at 702 Decatur Street;
569-8700

Information and Ticket Booth
Facing Decatur Street, at St. Peter; tickets for the Aquarium of the Americas, IMAX theater, Audubon Zoo, RTA bus passes also available; open daily 8:30 A.M. to 5 P.M.;
596-3424

Jax Brewery Mall
Decatur Street, between St. Ann and Toulouse; open Sunday to Thursday 10 A.M. to 9 P.M.; Friday and Saturday 10 A.M. to 10 P.M.;
587-0871

Hard Rock Cafe
529-5617

Planet Hollywood
522-7826

The Marketplace
400 block of N. Peters Street

Tower Records
529-4411

Tower Video
581-2012

Bookstar
523-6411

The Louisiana Music Factory
210 Decatur Street, near Bienville; 586-1094

Beckham's Bookshop
228 Decatur Street, near Bienville; open seven days a week; 522-9875

Moonwalk

details. In 1987 a second phase of the project opened with the conversion of the five-story Millhouse next door. A third phase, the **Marketplace,** farther up Decatur Street at N. Peters Street, houses **Tower Records** and **Video** stores and **Bookstar.** Also nearby is the **Louisiana Music Factory,** a prime source for local music, and **Beckham's Bookshop,** with two floors of old books and classical records.

4   Moonwalk on the Mississippi River, *1981, Cassio Cochran*
At the river's edge is Moonwalk, named after Mayor Maurice "Moon" Landrieu (1970–78) and built in 1981. Timber bleacher-like steps reach right down to the water. You can put your hand in the mighty Mississippi River here, and you should pay homage to this great Presence. From here you can see why New Orleans is called the "Crescent City"; it sits at a great bend in the wide river with views up and down the swift stream. It was, of course, this tawny river that brought the commerce and the peoples of the world to this difficult site. This is a cool and breezy spot on even the sultriest nights. Francis Baily described the old New Orleans levee in the late 1790s: "Here was a handsome raised gravel walk, planted with orange trees and in the summertime served for a mall and in the evening was always a fashionable resort for beaux and belles of the place" (*Journal of a Tour, 1796–97, 1969*). Lovers still favor this quiet spot. But, oh, the harsh "security" nighttime lighting.

The Mississippi was named by the Chippewas, who called it *misi sipi,* "the big water." The Mississippi-Missouri River basin includes all or part of thirty-one states and drains one-third of the United States. This twin river system is 3,986 miles long with total navigable tributaries exceeding 15,000 miles in length. It is the third-longest river system in the world, after the Nile and the Amazon. The mouth of the river is about a hundred miles downstream from New Orleans. The booming Port of New Orleans and the Port of South Louisiana are the busiest ports in terms of tonnage in the nation. It exports grain from the Midwest and oil and petrochemicals from Louisiana, and it imports coffee, steel, and general cargo. The Port of New Orleans' Dock Board has opened up and transformed the riverfront facing the French Quarter and Central Business District while upgrading its facilities uptown at the Nashville and Napoleon Avenue Wharfs. The river is higher than the city, and massive levees and a flood wall have been built to protect New Orleans from her creator. During high water in the spring, when the current is swiftest, you will be amazed at how fast big tankers come barreling down the river. They must move faster than the swollen current or else their rudders can't navigate the many bends in the sinuous river. At night the picturesque steamboat *Natchez* can be seen from here, with the Central Business District high-rises beyond. The twin bridges, the Crescent City Connection, are also festively lit. Disorienting as it may be, the river here is flowing due *north.* Charles Joseph

Latrobe, architect Benjamin Latrobe's son, described the bustling riverfront in 1832 (from *Cities of the Mississippi* by John W. Reps, 1994):

> The lower end of [Jackson] square is open to the levee and the river, whose margin appears lined for upwards of two miles with ships and boats of every size as close as they can float. Highest up the stream lie the flats [flatboats], arks, and barges, and below them are the tier of steam boats, fifty of which may be seen lying here at one time. Then comes the brigs ranged in rows, with their bows against the breast of the levee; these are succeeded by the three-masters, lying in tiers of two and three deep, with their broadside to the shore, and the scene presented by the whole margin of the river as you look down upon it from the levee, or from the roof of Bishop's Hotel in a sunny morning after a night of storm, when the sails of the whole are exposed to the air, and their signals or national flags abroad, is one of the most singularly beautiful you can conceive.

⑤ Steamboat *Natchez*

A multisided pavilion here sells tickets to the sternwheel steamboat *Natchez*, the largest excursion boat plying the river from New Orleans. Two-hour cruises make a circle up and down the river without making any landings. The *Natchez*, with its great white body and red sternwheel, makes a festive and historic sight when seen glittering at about 8 P.M. on the dark river.

⑥ Woldenberg Riverfront Park, *1989, Cassio Cochran*

Built on the site of the old Bienville Wharf and dedicated in 1989, Woldenberg Riverfront Park is a pleasant grassy space with a promenade along the river and a curving path lined with willow trees. The park was a gift to the city from the Woldenberg Foundation in memory of New Orleans businessman Malcolm Woldenberg, who is depicted in a bronze statue talking to a young boy. The stainless-steel sculpture consisting of pylons, rings, and cables at the back of the park is *Ocean Song* by New Orleans sculptor John T. Scott.

⑦ Aquarium of the Americas, *1990, The Bienville Group*

The Audubon Institute's Aquarium of the Americas focuses on the aquatic environments of North and South America. In front of the building, the colorful sculptures of sea life on tall columns are by Ida Kohlmeyer. Behind the white-tile-clad, cut-out screen wall are exhibits alive with more than seven thousand sleek fish, other sea creatures,

Steamboat *Natchez*
Toulouse Street Wharf behind Jax Brewery; departures at 11:30 A.M. and 2:30 P.M.; adults $14.75, children six to twelve $7.25; cruise and lunch $20.25 for adults and $12.75 for children; dinner and jazz cruises depart at 7 P.M., adults $38.75 and children $19.25; the evening cruise without dinner is $18.75 for adults and $10.75 for children

Woldenberg Riverfront Park
Foot of Conti Street

Aquarium of the Americas
Foot of Canal Street at the river; parking in Canal Place Shopping Centre at Iberville and Wells Streets; open daily 9:30 A.M. to 5 P.M., until 8 P.M. on Thursday, 6 P.M. on Friday and Saturday; adults $9.75, seniors $7.50, children twelve and under $5; Entergy Imax Theater, adults $6.50, seniors $5.50, children twelve and under $4.50; combination tickets available; 861-2537

John James Audubon
*Departures from the
aquarium are at 10 A.M.,
noon, 2, and 4 P.M.;
departures from the
Audubon Zoo are at 11
A.M., and 1, 3, and 5 P.M.;
a round-trip costs $12.50
for adults and $6.25 for
children under twelve;
one-way tickets are $9.50
and $4.75; 586-8777*

Liberty Monument
*Foot of Iberville Street,
between the aquarium
and Canal Place Shopping
Centre*

**Canal Place Shopping
Centre**
*333 Canal Street, at
N. Peters; 522-9200*

and exotic birds. Major exhibits include the Mississippi River, the Gulf of Mexico, a Caribbean reef, and the Amazonian rain forest. The green glass cylinder cut at a slant that houses the rain forest exhibit is a landmark in contemporary New Orleans. In 1995 the Entergy Imax Theater opened with a five-and-a-half-story-high screen and state-of-the-art sound system; films shown here feature the life of the sea. A modern boat, the **John James Audubon,** links the Aquarium of the Americas downtown with the Audubon Zoo uptown. You can make a round-trip, or just go one way. An enjoyable itinerary is to take the St. Charles Avenue streetcar uptown to the zoo in the morning, see Audubon Park and Zoo (see Tour 9), and then take the boat back downriver at 5 P.M. to end the day with dinner in the French Quarter. The dock in front of the aquarium is the landing for the *Cajun Queen* (see page 32), which cruises the harbor.

8   Liberty Monument, *1891*
This now-banished, partially dismembered, grafitti-splattered, gray granite obelisk with erased and revised inscriptions has had an extraordinary—and telling—history. For this Victorian monument recapitulates the contentious history of the post–Civil War South from "Redemption" in the late 1870s to the present day. Erected in 1891 on a prominent spot at the foot of Canal Street where the streetcars circled it, it commemorates the Battle of Liberty Place on September 14, 1874, when the White League attacked the biracial Reconstruction-era Metropolitan Police (see page 235). The names on the shaft list the members of the White League who fell in that insurrection. In 1932 an inscription was added stating that "United States troops took over state government and reinstated the usurpers but the national election in November 1876 recognized white supremacy and gave us our state." That plaque was removed in 1989. In 1990 the African American–led city government removed the monument for street work and put it in storage. Supporters of white supremacist David Duke filed a lawsuit and forced the re-erection of the historic monument since federal funds (!) had been used for the street improvement. The city government then banished it to this obscure spot next to the streetcar tracks and under a towering utility pylon. Another plaque was added to the base of the monument listing the members of the Metropolitan Police who were killed along with a baffling inscription stating that the Battle of Liberty Place was "a conflict of the past that should teach us lessons for the future."

9   Canal Place Shopping Centre and Westin Hotel, *1979, John Carl Warnecke & Associates; Perez Ernst Farnet Architects*
This three-level, marble-lined shopping mall, fourplex cinema, **Westin Hotel,** and thirty-two-story office building was built by Joseph Canizaro in 1979. It is New Orleans' most upscale shopping center and features Saks Fifth Avenue, Brooks

Brothers, Gucci, Bally, Laura Ashley, the Forgotten Woman, Williams-Sonoma, and other luxury shops, as well as a shop for fine jewelry designed by New Orleanian **Mignon Faget.** The mall also houses **Canal Place Cinemas,** a first-run movie house, and the **Southern Repertory Theater** on the third level.

      Canal Place provides space to three cutting-edge showcases for Louisiana arts and crafts that are well worth visiting if you are interested in contemporary crafts and art furniture as a souvenir of your visit. **RHINO: Contemporary Craft Company,** a non-profit cooperative, showcases Louisiana artists and artisans and features jewelry, ceramics, metalwork, glass, and other artworks. Prices are reasonable and the quality and selection are among the best in the city; they can ship your purchases. **La. Showcase** is expensive and features innovative contemporary art furniture, lamps, mirrors, and other furnishings, many made by leading New Orleans and Louisiana designers. **Fyberspace by RHINO** offers "wearable art" for women—artistic hand-made or -woven clothing and painted fabrics. These three shops are worth a detour for the sophisticated art lover.

Westin Canal Place
100 Iberville Street, at N. Peters; 566-7006

Mignon Faget
Level 1; 524-2973

Canal Place Cinemas
581-5400

Southern Repertory Theater
Level 3; 861-8163

RHINO: Contemporary Craft Company
Level 1; 523-7945

La. Showcase
Level 1; 558-0054

Fyberspace by RHINO
Level 2; 523-8558

⑩   World Trade Center Enclosed Observation Deck and Panoramic View, *1966, Edward Durrell Stone*

Cross Canal Street and enter the front doors of the World Trade Center. Pay at the desk in the lobby to ascend the exterior, glass-walled elevator to the observation level on the thirty-first floor. Walk the full circuit of the deck for a superb overview of the twisting, turning Mississippi River and the city and region it spawned. Designed by Edward Durrell Stone and completed in 1968, this cross-shaped, thirty-three-story high-rise was built as the International Trade Mart with $17 million in tax-exempt bonds on city property. It houses consulates and trading companies.

World Trade Center Observation Deck / Panoramic View
2 Canal Street; open daily 9 A.M. to 5 P.M.; adults $2, children $1

      Step to the right after exiting the elevator. The sequence of views is as follows: (1) the Warehouse/Arts District (Tour 7) on the near side of the elevated Pontchartrain Expressway, whose use shifted when the Louisiana World Exposition was held along its river edge in 1984; (2) beyond the expressway, the Garden District and Uptown (Tours 8, 9, and 10), the elite residential districts that reach toward the bend in the river; (3) the twin spans of the Crescent City Connection, built in 1935 and 1958, that lead to the West Bank; (4) the great crescent with Algiers Point beyond the ferry landing; (5) beyond Algiers and across the river, the tall brick smokestack of the Kaiser Aluminum Corporation and the oil refineries in Chalmette, the Chalmette Monument and Park (see page 72), the site of the Battle of New Orleans in 1815, and, not visible in this direction, Lake Borgne, which opens into the Gulf of Mexico; (6) the variously colored metal sheds of the docks of the Port of New Orleans; (7) the low-rise French Quarter (Tours 1 and 2) with light gray St. Louis Cathedral; (8) on the far

New Orleans Casino
Under construction

Canal Street–Algiers Point Ferry
At the foot of Canal Street; runs from about 6 A.M. to about 9:30 P.M.; free

Blaine Kern's Mardi Gras World
233 Newton Street in Algiers; open daily 9:30 A.M. to 4:30 P.M.; adults $5.50, seniors $4.50, children twelve and under $3.50; 361-7821

horizon, the flat sheet of Lake Pontchartrain, the city's historic back door and the direction from which French explorers came in 1699; (9) in the foreground, green Woldenberg Riverfront Park; (10) wide Canal Street, flanked by modern high-rise hotels; (11) between the light pink First NBC Center high-rise and the Hibernia Bank with its colonnaded rooftop belvedere, the narrow canyon of Gravier Street, the hidden spine of the historic banking district (Tour 6); and, finally, (12) the post-1970 high-rise spine along Poydras Street, with white, fifty-two-story One Shell Square, the tallest building in New Orleans. The ungainly high-rise to the far left with the protruding, boxy top is forty-five-story Plaza Tower, completed in 1969.

11   New Orleans Casino, *construction suspended 1995, Perez Ernst Farnet / Modus*
This vast, 214,000-square-foot, brick-clad, neo–Beaux Arts casino, with its turquoise-colored metal roof and twin domes, was designed by Perez Ernst Farnet. Construction on the huge building came to a halt just before Thanksgiving in 1995. The unfinished casino stands on the foundations of the modernistic Rivergate exhibition hall with its billowing concrete roof, designed by Curtis & Davis, that opened in 1968 and was demolished in 1995.

12   Canal Street Ferry to Algiers Point
Just beyond the plaza in front of the aquarium at the foot of Canal Street is a poorly signed and uninviting concrete staircase that rises over the streetcar tracks and leads to the pedestrian entrance to the Canal-Algiers Ferry. (Automobiles and bicycles enter from ground level below.) This six-minute, free ferry ride across the river is highly recommended. From the ferry you get a sense of the power of this great river and its relentless current. You will see no small recreational craft sailing here; that would be like bicycling on an interstate. Instead you get a glimpse of the freighters, tankers, and long sausagelike strings of barges that ply this vital artery. Often the steamboat *Natchez* or the sternwheeler *Creole Queen* will pass by, giving just a hint of the long-gone days of the famous Mississippi riverboats. Freighters still moor alongside the long green shed of the Governor Nicholls Street Wharf, site of the ancient Native American and later colonial French portage overland to Bayou St. John and Lake Pontchartrain (and the reason why the city is located here). This is also the deepest spot on the Mississippi, some 191 feet deep.

As the ferry approaches Algiers Point there is a view of the two square towers of the Italianate-style Algiers Courthouse of 1896. Algiers was annexed to the City of New Orleans in 1870 and suffered a great fire in 1895. Its most famous resident was Martin Behrman, the political boss who served as mayor of New Orleans from 1904 to 1920 and from 1924 until his death in office in 1926. There is little reason to disembark at Algiers, although a free shuttle bus can take you three blocks up Brooklyn Avenue to **Blaine Kern's Mardi Gras World**, where many Carnival floats are built. On the trip back across the river there is a fine view of St. Louis Cathedral.

13   Spanish Plaza / *Creole Queen* Landing

When leaving the Canal Street Ferry landing, turn left and descend the stairs into Spanish Plaza. This riverside plaza was dedicated in 1976 and has a large round fountain encircled with tiles representing the provinces of Spain. This was originally Eads Plaza, where the *President* docked and was long the only pedestrian amenity to break the wall of warehouses along the riverfront and give New Orleanians and visitors access to the river. Looking around here you see the skyline of the completely new city built after 1970. The ***Creole Queen*** riverboat docks at the edge of the plaza, and it gives daily two-and-a-half-hour cruises downriver to Chalmette Battlefield.

14   *Poydras Street High-rise Spine*

In the 1960s the city widened Poydras Street to accommodate a new generation of office building development. A spine of glass-clad towers sprang up from the river to the Louisiana Superdome. Nicknamed "Texas on Poydras," many of these high-rises housed the regional offices of Big Oil before the oil bust in 1986.

15   Hilton New Orleans, *1977, Newhouse and Taylor*
    Hilton Riverside, *1983, Perez and Associates*

The Hilton consists of two structures, a tower built in 1977 and a long, low building layered over the Riverwalk mall, added in 1983. Its principal entrance is at the foot of Poydras Street.

16   Riverwalk Marketplace, *1986, R. Allen Eskew*

This popular half-mile-long, three-level, linear shopping mall at the edge of the river was developed by the Rouse Company and opened in 1986. There are more than 140 stores here, including The Gap, The Body Shop, Banana Republic, The Nature Company, and Sharper Image. The Abercrombie and Fitch store near the entrance is good for contemporary casual clothing for young men. Riverwalk attracts the shoppers who a generation ago would have thronged the sidewalks of Canal Street but who today seek the controlled environment of an air-conditioned mall.

17   Ernest N. Morial Convention Center, *Phase III architects: Cimini, Meric, Duplantier; Billes-Manning Architects; Hewitt-Washington & Associates*

Begun as the International Pavilion of the Louisiana World Exposition of 1984, the Ernest N. Morial Convention Center is now one of the leading convention facilities in

***Creole Queen* Cruises**
Spanish Plaza; leaves daily at 10:30 A.M. and 2 P.M.; adults $13, children under twelve $6; evening dinner and jazz cruise departs at 8 P.M., adults $39, children under twelve $18; reservations recommended; 524-0814

Hilton New Orleans–Hilton Riverside
Foot of Poydras Street; 561-0500

Riverwalk Marketplace
Poydras Street to Julia Street, at the river; open Monday to Thursday 10 A.M. to 9 P.M.; Friday and Saturday 10 A.M. to 10 P.M.; Sunday 10 A.M. to 7 P.M.

Ernest N. Morial
Convention Center
900 Convention Center
Boulevard; 582-3000

Julia Street Wharf
1 Julia Street; 558-0817

the nation and is a major economic engine in Louisiana. The convention center is linked to the Riverwalk Marketplace and was built in two phases. A third phase is slated to open in 1998. When completed the building will have 1.1 million square feet of space in ten halls capable of accommodating fifty-nine hundred exhibit booths, all on one floor that seems to stretch from New Orleans to Baton Rouge.

(18) Cruise Ship Dock / Julia Street Wharf

The riverside of the Riverwalk Marketplace along the Julia Street Wharf is where cruise ships calling at New Orleans dock. The colorful, futuristic funnels of cruise ships occasionally terminate the view down Julia Street in what was once the Warehouse District but is now the Arts District (see Tour 7). The Riverfront streetcar can take you back to the Toulouse Street stop near Jackson Square in the French Quarter.

*Tropical color explodes from Paul Ninas's 1949 murals
in the Fairmont Hotel's Moderne Sazarac Bar. The Sazarac cocktail is
a New Orleans specialty.*

What This Tour Covers
Preliminaries
Introduction: An Architectural Archaeology of the
    Old Cotton Capital

Detour: For Aficionados of Cast-Iron Architecture

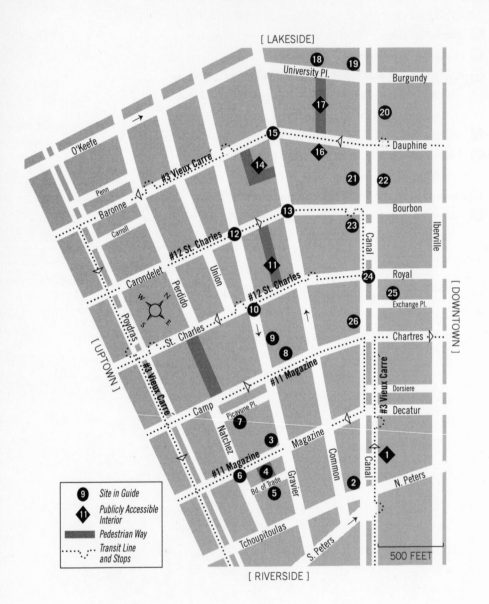

Tour 6

[LAKESIDE]

University Pl.

Burgundy

18
19

17

20

O'Keefe

Dauphine

15

#3 Vieux Carré

16

Penn

14

Baronne

21
22

Carroll

13

Bourbon

#12 St. Charles

12

23

Union

Carondelet

Perdido

11

Canal

Iberville

[DOWNTOWN]

Poydras

#12 St. Charles

24

Royal

10

25

St. Charles

9

Exchange Pl.

8

26

Chartres

[UPTOWN]

#11 Magazine

#3 Vieux Carré

Dorsiere

Camp

Picayune Pl.

Decatur

7

1

Natchez

3

Magazine

#11 Magazine

6

4

2

N. Peters

Bd. of Trade

5

Gravier

Common

Canal

Tchoupitoulas

S. Peters

500 FEET

[RIVERSIDE]

9   Site in Guide

11 Publicly Accessible
    Interior

    Pedestrian Way

    Transit Line
    and Stops

What This Tour Covers

This walk explores a part of New Orleans most visitors rarely pay any attention to as they hurry from the French Quarter to the Garden District: the Central Business District, or CBD, wedged between Canal and Poydras Streets. Yet the CBD *is* the modern city, and it harbors many unacknowledged architectural treasures, from the straightforward brick commercial buildings of the 1840s to the late Victorian and Edwardian bank cluster at the 200 block of Camp Street, to the stately banking halls of the early twentieth century, to the Moorish splendor of the Church of the Immaculate Conception, to the sleek First NBC Center high-rise of 1985. This walk begins on Canal Street at the landmark Custom House, passes up the narrow skyscraper canyon of Gravier Street to the banking core along Carondelet Street, and stops at the Moderne sanctuary of the Sazarac Bar in the Fairmont Hotel. From the hotel you can return to Canal Street to board the St. Charles Avenue streetcar to head to the Garden District uptown; or you can catch a cab for a quick hop to the French Quarter.

Preliminaries

BEST TIMES TO DO THIS TOUR

Business days during banking hours is when the Central Business District is most active.

High-rise Observatory

The only high-rise with a public observatory is the World Trade Center near the foot of Canal Street. It offers a superb overview of the city and its region (see page 219). From there you can look right down Gravier Street, the hidden spine of the old Central Business District.

Parking

This is the heart of the city, and street parking is not easy. A recommended central place to park that is always open is the valet-served garage for the Sheraton Hotel, at the downtown-riverside

Vieux Carré jitney bus
In front of the Custom House, on Canal Street at Decatur

Coleman E. Adler & Sons
722 Canal Street;
523-5292

Pokorny's Shoes
109 St. Charles Street;
525-1261

Meyer the Hatter
120 St. Charles Street;
525-1048

Rubenstein Brothers Men's Wear
102 St. Charles Street, corner of Canal;
523-5292

De Ville Books and Prints
344 Carondelet Street, near One Shell Square;
525-1846

Creole Celebration
1555 Poydras Street;
527-5244

Saenger Theater
See page 199

Orpheum Theater
See below, page 247

corner of Camp and Common Streets. Enter from Canal Street and leave your car at the attendant's booth. You can taxi back here from the Fairmont Hotel at the end of this exploration.

Public Transit

The **#3 Vieux Carré jitney bus** stops on Canal Street at Decatur Street in front of the Custom House; this jitney can take you through the French Quarter to Jackson Square or Esplanade Avenue.

Shopping

Canal Street and the CBD now feature athletic-wear stores, along with a few classy outposts like **Coleman E. Adler & Sons,** which sells jewelry and fine china. **Pokorny's Shoes** is great for water-proof walking shoes; **Meyer the Hatter,** open since 1894, is definitely worth checking out for hats and umbrellas. Other notable shops in the area are **Rubenstein Brothers Men's Wear** and **De Ville Books and Prints.**

For contemporary luxury shopping, see Canal Place and the Riverwalk Marketplace in Tour 5.

Restaurants

The daily special at **Creole Celebration,** an inexpensive Creole diner, is always excellent. The Baquet family also operates the fancier Zachery's Uptown, see page 53.

Theaters

Two theatrical gems survive in New Orleans, and both are in the Central Business District. The **Saenger Theater** was designed by Emile Weil and opened in 1927, and it presents touring Broadway shows. The **Orpheum Theater** of 1918 is the home of the Louisiana Philharmonic Orchestra.

Introduction: An Architectural Archaeology of the Old Cotton Capital

Times are not good here. The city is crumbling into ashes. It has been buried under a lava-flood of taxes and frauds and maladministrations so that it has become only a study for archaeologists. Its condition is so bad that when I write about it, as I intend to do soon, nobody will believe I am telling the truth. But it is better to live here in sackcloth and ashes, than to own the whole State of Ohio.

—Lafcadio Hearn to H. E. Krehbiel in 1880 in
The Life and Letters of Lafcadio Hearn, 1906

Urban geographer Pierce F. Lewis once likened New Orleans to a double-yolked egg. One yolk is the famed French Quarter, the other is the now overlooked, American-developed Central Business District. Separating the two is wide Canal Street, traditionally considered the great cultural divide in the Crescent City. Taking the long historical view we can now see three phases in commercial New Orleans' evolution. First was the dominance of the French Quarter, from the laying out of the city in 1721 to the coming of the Americans in the first decades of the 1800s. Next came the pulsating expansion of the new American city in the old Faubourg Ste. Marie from the 1820s through the long reign of King Cotton to the catastrophic oil bust of 1986. Today we are in a third phase where the French Quarter is bustling again while the CBD languishes. It is a strange, circular fate for the once-vigorous American capital of the opulent Cotton Kingdom.

What is today the Central Business District was originally a plantation granted to the city's founder, Jean-Baptiste Le Moyne, sieur de Bienville, in 1719. In 1726 Bienville sold his land to the Society of Jesus, which built a missionary headquarters and sugar cane plantation near what is now Common and Magazine Streets. When the Jesuits were suppressed in Spanish, Neopolitan, and French territories, the land was auctioned off to private owners in 1763, and it eventually became the property of Bernard and Marie Gravier. Between the city limits and Bienville's plantation were the *Communes de la ville,* a swath of land between what is now Iberville Street in the French Quarter and Common Street in the CBD. This land was reserved by the French Crown for the city's never-completed fortifications. When the United States purchased Louisiana, this buffer zone became federal property. In 1807 Congress relinquished title to the City of New Orleans with the understanding that a canal would be excavated there, linking the Mississippi River with the Carondelet Canal's turning basin near what is today Armstrong Park behind the French Quarter. That canal was never dug; instead, in 1812, the municipality laid out a wide street with a broad median running down its center and sold off the flanking lots. Thus was born Canal Street and its wide "neutral ground."

In 1788, after the catastrophic Good Friday fire in the French Quarter, Bernard and Marie Gravier subdivided their plantation adjoining the town commons to create Ville Gravier, later renamed Faubourg Ste. Marie, the city's first "suburb." One river-to-swamp street that cut through their development is now named Gravier Street and is the hidden spine of the historic business district. The street at the city edge of their subdivision is named Common Street, since it was the margin of the original city commons. Building was slow in the new faubourg since most New Orleanians preferred rebuilding in the compact French Quarter. Only after the American purchase in 1803 and the subsequent population explosion did significant building spill over into this area. By the 1820s what the Americans called the Faubourg St. Mary began to fill up with brick commercial buildings near the busy wharfs and East Coast–style red-brick town houses on the inland blocks behind them (see the "Thirteen Sisters" on Julia Street, page 263). From the 1820s into the 1860s the narrow lots behind the docks were built up with elegantly simple four-to-five-story, brick-and-timber commercial buildings, often with monolithic, New England granite piers along their ground floors. The second floor of these buildings had high ceilings and tall, narrow windows; this was the best floor. A surprising number of them survive in the blocks between Tchoupitoulas and St. Charles Streets. Unfortunately, many of these fine old commercial buildings were demolished for parking lots between 1960 and 1980.

At swampy New Orleans' docks, inland river transports met ocean-going ships. As goods and money were exchanged, fortunes were amassed. Shippers, sailors, chandlers, teamsters, wholesale merchants, lawyers, insurance agents, bankers, writers, and prostitutes were drawn to the thriving port. On the land side of Tchoupitoulas Street were the offices of the factors who handled the trade between the planters of the fertile Mississippi valley and cotton-hungry Europe across the Atlantic. The key economic actors were the factor, the planter, the broker, the wholesaler, and the banker. The factor was the agent for either his own company or one headquartered in England or New York City. The New Orleans factor also usually acted as the purchasing agent for the inland planter. The cotton planter turned his crop over to the factor, who determined the sale price and where the cotton would go. The cotton broker reported sales and prices. The bankers furnished capital on short terms to the factor, who in turn advanced money on longer terms to the planter for seeds and slave purchases. New Orleans became the greatest slave auction center in the United States as surplus slaves from soil-exhausted Virginia and the Carolinas were transported overland to New Orleans or "sold down the river" to be auctioned to planters opening up the virgin lands from Mississippi to East Texas. As A. Oakley Hall noted in his guide *The Manhattaner in New Orleans* in the flush year of 1851:

> Adown the riverward streets flow rapid streams of human heads and legs, whose escape from an entanglement is quite a disappointment; sailors; stevedores; steamboat hands; clerks; planters; wealthy merchants too; running to and from with divers projects in their head, and all the solutions to the end in the *quod erat demonstrandum* of money.

The same writer noted that here was "a little of Boston, there a trifle of New York, and some of Philadelphia." The dominant economic link, however, was always with New York City. For New Orleans did not ship its cotton directly to Liverpool and the great cotton market there; instead it shipped most of the baled and compacted white gold to New York for transshipment to Europe. In return, credit and all manner of goods came from or *via* New York City to New Orleans. Crescent City banks were dependent on those on Wall Street, the key link then as now between Europe and the Americas. Her wholesalers also had strong ties to New York City.

Until the late 1820s the key New Orleans banks were located along Royal Street in the old French Quarter (page 128). In the 1830s banking and insurance moved over into the American sector in the Faubourg St. Mary. Magazine Street became banker's row, with many of the leading financial institutions of the South housed there in elegant buildings. Later the banks shifted to Camp Street, and still later to Carondelet Street, where they cluster today. Luxury retail also skipped out of the French Quarter, shifting from Chartres Street to Canal Street and the edge of the growing American district.

The 1850s were a booming decade and most businesses expanded their niche in the humming city. Carondelet Street became the center for cotton and shipping companies and the location of the Cotton Exchange. St. Charles Street had its famous domed hotel and elite places of amusement. (In this guide, St. Charles Street refers to the stretch from Canal Street to Lee Circle; St. Charles Avenue runs uptown from Lee Circle to S. Carrollton Avenue.) Canal Street now dominated retail and clothing. Magazine Street became the center for wholesale clothing, boots, and shoes. Newspapers and printers clustered along today's sleepy Picayune Place. Poydras Street specialized in bagging and rope. Upriver from Poydras were the large warehouses that served the bustling docks (today's Arts District, see Tour 7). The Civil War and federal occupation set the city back only temporarily, and building resumed quickly during the sharp, if brief, cotton boom of the late 1860s. The 1870s were a politically turbulent decade in the Crescent City, and its momentous clashes, such as the "Battle of Liberty Place," took place along and near Canal Street.

The long era from the 1880s to the Stock Market Crash of 1929 saw the Central Business District change dramatically. In the 1880s business buildings got taller and fancier. The red-brick-and-sandstone New Orleans National Bank (now Whitney Bank) at Camp and Common Streets was the epitome of the city's Victorian castles of commerce. The ten-story, Chicago School, Hennen (now Latter & Blum) Building at Carondelet and Common Streets, completed in 1895, was the city's first modern, steel-frame skyscraper. Carondelet Street solidified its position as the Wall Street of the South, even to the point of erecting correct, Wall Street–like, gray Indiana limestone–clad office buildings. About 1920 the Hibernia Bank commissioned a New York architectural firm to design a twenty-three-story, steel-frame, limestone-clad headquarters at Carondelet and Gravier Streets. Built atop cypress pilings, it rose as high as builders then dared to go on the city's swampy soil. It stood unchallenged for more than forty years as the city's dominant skyscraper. Its rooftop belvedere is a classical gracenote on the city's skyline and is visible in varied seasonal illuminations to the nighttime crowds that throng Bourbon Street.

Canal Street also boomed in the early twentieth century. During the heyday of streetcars, most of the city's major lines met at wide Canal Street, making it the seam in the city between uptown and downtown. The retail shops along the busy boulevard flourished, and eventually large department stores established themselves there as the city's retail anchors. Maison Blanche's superb 1909, white, terra-cotta-clad, steel-frame palace of commerce survives as the epitome of department store design on wide Canal Street. The city's major theaters also clustered along the easily accessible thoroughfare where it crossed the Rampart Street streetcar line. Canal Street became the city's principal public stage and the destination of its grandest Mardi Gras parades, a civic role it retains.

As in nearly all American cities, skyscraper construction came to a halt after the Stock Market Crash of 1929. After 1940 many of the old retail buildings along Canal Steet were given slick, stuck-on, modern facades with billboardlike illuminated signage. The core stayed central to the metropolitan region even as the city lost its dominance in the South to Atlanta, and later to Houston and Miami. But by the 1960s stagnation began to afflict the CBD and Canal Street. The construction of the approaches to the new bridge over the Mississippi that opened in 1958, and of elevated superhighways on the uptown and lakeside edges of the old commercial district, resulted in blight in those parts of the city. Automobile-owning city dwellers and new suburbanites began shopping outside high-sales-tax Orleans Parish. The middle class fled to federally subsidized suburbia, and the relative proportion of black poor in the city increased.

The municipal government engaged in massive public works projects to rescue the declining city. To accommodate a new generation of large, boxlike, glass-clad high-rises the city widened Poydras Street on the uptown edge of the CBD in 1963. In 1966 the thirty-three-story World Trade Center opened at the foot of Canal Street near the river, and the same year the modernistic Rivergate exhibition hall opened across the street (demolished in 1995 for the enormous new Harrah's Casino). Under Ernest N. "Dutch" Morial, the city's first African American mayor, the areas around the old commercial core changed dramatically. In 1972 One Shell Square, a white, travertine-clad, fifty-one-story high-rise, and still the tallest building in the city, was erected at Poydras and St. Charles Streets. It initiated "Texas on Poydras" as developers built and insurance companies backed a string of new office towers leased to national oil companies at high rents. Favorable tax laws stimulated this billion-dollar wave of building that produced ten million square feet of Class A office space and completely transformed the city's skyline with glass-clad towers. At the peak of the oil and gas boom in 1982, the branch offices of some thirty-five major oil companies occupied about a third of the new CBD's office space. Among them were Amoco, Exxon, Mobil, Chevron, Getty, Gulf, Texaco, and Shell. Shell Offshore has stayed and continues to drill deep wells in the Gulf of Mexico off Louisiana.

To anchor the lakeward end of widened Poydras Street, the State of Louisiana erected the gargantuan Louisiana Superdome, the largest column-free room in the world. Design work on the "dome" began in 1967 and construction started in 1971; it opened in 1975. In 1973 the high-rise New Orleans Marriott opened on the site of the old Godchaux department store, initiating the complete transformation of the river end of Canal Street abutting the French Quarter. These and later projects built a loose ring of much larger buildings around the historic banking core. Unfortunately, the huge new buildings brought in their wake a backwash of uncontrolled demolition for parking lots, which riddled the heart of the old office district with invasive parking lots and ugly garages and made a desert of a vast swath of the old city between the CBD and the Superdome.

When the oil bust hit like a category 5 hurricane in 1986, the national oil companies regrouped to Houston and other headquarters cities, leaving New Orleans seriously overbuilt. Rents fell from $25 to $28 a square foot to $12 and $13 a square foot. Today, as a group, the high-rises in New Orleans are worth about half of what they cost to build during the boom. The result of this fall in the value of new office towers and the subsequent lowering of rents was to drain tenants away from the city's pre-1930 office buildings between Canal and Poydras Streets. The steady growth in tourism has led to a wave of conversions of these older office buildings into hotels in the heart of the old CBD. This has steadily shrunk the city's total supply of office space, so that by 1996 occupancy in the newer towers began to approach 85 percent. In the double-yolked egg of New Orleans, the French Quarter has proved the salvation of the once-dominant American business district across Canal Street.

Canal Street, 1812, Jacques Tanesse, surveyor

Canal Street is 171 feet wide from curb to curb and is the traditional dividing line between uptown and downtown. The streets that cross it have different names on either side of it, or are counterintuitively designated North on the downtown French Quarter side and South on the uptown CBD side. On both sides, address numbers begin at Canal and become higher the farther away they are upriver or downriver from the main stem. Canal Street was laid out by City Surveyor Jacques Tanesse in 1812, who also surveyed Esplanade Avenue on the other side of the French Quarter. This spacious boulevard first attracted elegant American town houses and elite Protestant churches, including Christ Episcopal Cathedral. But as happened on Fifth Avenue in New York City, retail eventually invaded the prestigious residential street with its good transportation links, and by the 1850s Canal Street had become the favored location of the city's luxury shops. Ornate, cast-iron-fronted commercial buildings were built on the narrow house lots here. (The most elaborate cast-iron survivor now houses All American Jeans at 622 Canal Street, originally the Merchants Mutual Insurance Building of 1859.) Many Canal Street stores eventually sprouted wide galleries that sheltered the sidewalk in front of them in an almost uninterrupted row, a very practical arrangement in this sunny and then suddenly rainy city. Unfortunately, the city ordered their removal in 1929–30. Department stores emerged along Canal Street as the population

United States Custom House / Great Marble Hall
423 Canal Street, on the block bounded by Canal, Decatur, Iberville, and N. Peters Streets; open to the public Monday to Friday 8 A.M. to 5 P.M.; use Canal Street entrance; free; 670-2082

grew and the streetcar line network thickened; only a downsized Maison Blanche survives today. In 1882 Canal was the first street in New Orleans to be illuminated with electric lights. It became the destination of the city's most elaborate Carnival parades and until 1991 Rex toasted the Queen of the Carnival in front of the Boston Club on Canal. On V.J. night in August 1945, Canal Street was the scene of communal jubilation. This was, perhaps, the street's historic peak, for after the automobile changed shopping patterns, the street began to drift downmarket. The construction of large high-rise hotels at the river end of Canal has kept the street from steeper decline.

1   United States Custom House / Great Marble Hall, *1848–80, Alexander Thompson Wood and others; restoration, 1996, Waggoner & Ball Architects*

This somber, gray granite building is one of the most important landmarks in Louisiana. Before the "temporary" imposition of the income tax to finance World War I, the federal government's principal source of revenue was customs duties. The custom houses Washington erected in the nation's principal ports reflected their economic importance to the central government. This ponderous, fortresslike building is the fourth custom house to occupy this site, and it stands where French Fort St. Louis once stood and later the Spanish Custom House. From 1807 to 1819 a custom house designed by Benjamin Henry Latrobe stood here. The present building was begun in 1848 with Alexander Thompson Wood as architect. Then-Captain P. G. T. Beauregard served as superintendent of what became one of the largest building projects in the nation from 1853 to 1860. The building's construction was interrupted by the Civil War, and it took thirty-three years to complete. Over the years numerous architects held the title of Architect of the Custom House.

Built of Quincy, Massachusetts, granite, its four facades are each marked by four colossal fluted columns with Egyptian-style lotus capitals. Its twenty-four niches have never held any statuary. The massive building sits atop a mat of cypress timbers laid in an excavation that was protected by a timber cofferdam. The cofferdam's seams were caulked with cotton, and this gave rise to the myth that the building is built atop cotton bales. The heavy structure has subsided three feet into the marshy ground. The great Marble Hall within, which measures 125 feet by 95 feet with a height of 54 feet, is surrounded by fourteen white marble Corinthian columns and is one of the finest late Greek Revival rooms in the nation. Bas-reliefs of Bienville, Andrew Jackson, and a pelican with its young, the emblem of the State of Louisiana, grace the room. The ceiling consists of an iron frame with large plates of ground glass. The floor is of white and black marble and inset with heavy glass "portholes" to light the rooms below. The 1938 WPA guide remarked that "as one enters from the comparatively dark and narrow corridors, the sunlight-suffused hall appears to be the glorified counting-room of a king."

After the Union occupation of New Orleans in 1862, General Benjamin Butler established his headquarters in this impregnable structure. The upper part of the building became Federal Prison No. 6 and briefly housed Confederate prisoners of war. During the turbulent decade of social and political Reconstruction in the 1870s, appointments to the custom house became the most important source of Republican (central government) patronage in the once-rebel state. Branded the "Custom House Ring," these men were the backbone of federal power in post-war Louisiana; they supported a brief experiment in biracial government. Then, at about four o'clock on September 14, 1874, the White League skirmished with Union troops in Canal Street in front of the custom house. Dubbed the "Battle of Liberty Place" by the white supremacist Democratic forces, the casualties on both sides numbered more than one hundred wounded and twenty-five dead. The insurrection triggered a crisis in Washington that led President Grant to dispatch troops to prop up the beleagured Republicans in New Orleans. A political deal after the disputed Hayes-Tilden presidential election of 1876 gave the Republicans the White House in return for the withdrawl of federal troops from Louisiana and the South. The Democratic party then took over state and municipal governments in Louisiana and began the imposition of white supremacy and *de juré* racial segregation that lasted until the Civil Rights Movement of the 1950s and 1960s (see page 218).

New Orleans Marriott
Canal Street at Chartres;
581-1000

ITT Sheraton New Orleans Hotel
500 Canal Street at Magazine; 525-2500

Old New Orleans Canal and Banking Company
301 Magazine Street, corner of Gravier

2   **New Orleans Marriott,** *1973, Curtis & Davis*
The rose and beige Brutalist tower of the New Orleans Marriott was erected in 1973 and designed by Curtis & Davis. It occupies the site of the old Godchaux Department Store and heralded the conversion of lower Canal Street into a tourist district. The dull gray slab of the **ITT Sheraton New Orleans Hotel,** with its postmodern penthouse across Canal, was built in 1983 and designed by Farnet Architects. Cross Canal Street and walk up Magazine Street. Near Magazine and Common Streets was the pioneer Jesuit mission and sugar cane plantation established in 1723.

3   **Old New Orleans Canal and Banking Company,** *1844, James Dakin*
This three-story, gray granite Greek Revival bank was designed by the noted James Dakin and built in 1844. The two fluted, granite Doric columns flanking its entrance, and the entablature over them, were retained from a previous Canal Bank on the site designed by Captain Richard Delafield in 1829. Dakin's design is simple in the extreme; the windows have no projecting lintels and are cut cleanly into the smooth surface of the wall. The windows on the second floor are tall and slender, while those on the third floor are shorter by about a third; this gives the building the illusion of greater height. The New Orleans Canal and Banking Company was an "improvement bank" organized to finance the digging of the New Basin Canal that linked the back of the American sector with Lake Pontchartrain. Many Irish laborers died of yellow fever in

Board of Trade Plaza
316 Magazine Street

Board of Trade Building
Board of Trade Place

Banks's Arcade Fragment
*336 Magazine Street,
corner of Natchez*

400–408 Magazine Street

the construction of this canal; they were cheaper than slaves. The Canal Bank is the ancestor of today's First National Bank of Commerce.

4   Board of Trade Plaza, *1968, Koch and Wislon*
In 1968, in an early example of "preservation" in the CBD, Richard Koch and Samuel Wilson, Jr., designed this small gated park on the site of the St. James Hotel of 1859. Cast-iron columns from the old hotel were recycled for the pavilion at one end of the park. Walk through this small oasis with its splendid cast-iron fountain, like a giant fluted cup, to the Board of Trade Building across narrow Board of Trade Place.

5   Board of Trade Building, *1883, James Freret*
Designed by James Freret and built in 1883, this building was known as the Produce Exchange until 1889. For many years its great interior space hummed with activity as traders tracked the prices of Mississippi valley commodities from cotton to grain. Walk to narrow Natchez Street and turn right to the corner building with the double cast-iron galleries.

6   *Natchez and Magazine Streets*

•   **Banks's Arcade Fragment,** *1833, Charles F. Zimple*
The corner building with the granite base and fine, red-brick upper floors was designed in 1833 by Charles F. Zimple for Thomas Banks. (Zimple also created one of the most informative maps of New Orleans ever made.) In the 1830s this was the heart of the business district. Originally the multiuse building stretched across the entire frontage of Magazine Street and had a block-long, three-story-high, glass-roofed arcade where Board of Trade Place is today. In it was a richly appointed salon that could accommodate five hundred people and was a popular place for public meetings. Its third floor had sleeping rooms. In 1835 a committee of New Orleans Friends of Texas met in Banks's Arcade to aid and promote the Texas Revolution. This surviving corner fragment of Banks's Arcade was restored in 1941 by Emilio Levy for J. Aron & Company, coffee importers.

•   **400–408 Magazine Street, corner of Natchez / Poydras Street / Architectural Mural**
To the left, an endless-seeming row of fine cast-iron brackets support a shed roof that shelters the flagstone-paved sidewalk. Granite piers with granite lintels march down the sidewalk. This structure consists of five identical four-story stores built in the 1840s. The florid brackets are a late nineteenth century addition. At the Poydras end of this building is a city-healing mural painted in 1993 by Richard Daffold that

"wraps" the landmark's architecture across the exposed brick wall, where demolition created a neighboring parking lot. Across Poydras Street is the blank white wall of the Hale Boggs U.S. Courthouse & Federal Office Building, built in 1976 and designed by August Perez and Associates and Mathes, Bergman, and Associates.

7 *Natchez Street to Picayune Place*

• **Picayune Place Historic District / Old Newspaper Row,**
1840–50s
Cross Magazine Street and continue up narrow Natchez Street, which makes a subtle jog here. This street was named for Natchez, Mississippi, the next river port north of New Orleans and a place with intimate connections with antebellum New Orleans' cotton trade. The street is lined with old red-brick commercial buildings from the 1840s and 1850s. Turn right into narrow, one-block-long Picayune Place, now a deserted service alley. The buildings here originally had entrances on this narrow alley and also on Camp or Magazine Streets. This was once the center of the nineteenth-century newspaper and printing district. One building here, built in 1850 and with its front entrance at 326–28 Camp Street, housed the *Daily Picayune,* an ancestor of today's *Times-Picayune.* The picayune was a small Spanish American coin worth about a nickel, the price of early newspapers. Continue to Gravier Street and turn left. Right before you turn is a surreal view through the one surviving back wall of an antebellum building unfortunately demolished for a parking lot.

8 *Camp Street Between Gravier and Common:*
Great Commercial Architectural Cluster

• **Old I. L. Lyons Building / Omni Royal Crescent Hotel,** *1888, D. W. Kendall; hotel conversion, 1995*
Built in 1888 of pressed brick with a rusticated granite base, this eight-story building housed I. L. Lyons and Company, an important regional drug distributor. The building is notable for the elaborate cast-iron plates at the ends of the rods that reinforce it. The building echoes the commercial buildings of Chicago of the same period, although it does not have a steel frame. In 1995 the building was converted into the 101-room **Omni Royal Crescent Hotel.** Across Camp Street is one of the greatest architectural groupings in New Orleans.

• **Old Louisiana Bank & Trust Company,** *1906, Ditoll, Owen & Goldstein; 1997, Brooks Graham*
This ten-story, steel-frame building was built for the Louisiana Bank & Trust Company and has a white stone, three-story base and red-brick-clad upper floors. The original

Picayune Place Historic District

Omni Royal Crescent Hotel
224–28 Camp Street;
527-0006

Old Louisiana Bank & Trust Company
611 Gravier Street, corner of Camp

Old Tutonia Insurance Company
217 Camp Street

Norman Mayer Memorial Bulding
211 Camp Street

Old New Orleans National Bank
201 Camp Street, corner of Common

Camp Street entrance with its polished granite columns is now filled in; the building has also unfortunately lost its ornate cornice. From 1945 until 1995 the building's banking hall housed the International House, a luncheon club. Many consulates once had their offices here before the construction of the World Trade Center. In 1998 it is slated to be converted into a hotel.

•   **Old Tutonia Insurance Company,** *1880s*
This diminutive, three-story architectural gem was constructed in the 1880s for the Tutonia Insurance Company, which insured fire and marine risks. It has a rusticated stone base with a great central arch supported by inset polished dark gray granite columns. Two caryatids with women's heads appear between the third-floor windows. A fanciful parapet with a niche and a statue of a suggestively dressed woman holding over her head a lion's skin (emblematic of an insurance policy?) caps the design. A steeply pitched mansard roof originally crowned this forceful design. The building is slated to become part of the new hotel next door.

•   **Norman Mayer Memorial Building,** *1900, Andry and Bendernagel*
The property on which this extravagant building stands was owned by Paul Tulane and was part of the endowment he left in 1882 to create Tulane University. In 1900 this six-story, steel-frame building with its lavish brick and cream-colored terra-cotta exterior was built by Tulane as income property. The arched entrance is exuberantly decorated with cornucopias and garlands. A central bay projects from the third to the fifth floors. The building is reminiscent of pre–World War I luxury office buildings in London. Unfortunately, two of the ground floor arches have been filled in.

Next door is an unnumbered extension of an L-shaped annex built by Whitney National Bank in 1959 that also faces Common Street. It has gray granite walls and gold-framed windows.

•   **Old New Orleans National Bank / Whitney National Bank International Division,** *1884–88, Thomas Sully; 1995, Williams and Associates Architects*
Concluding this remarkable block of architectural stars is this four-story, red-brick-and-stone, late Victorian commercial castle designed by Thomas Sully and built between 1884 and 1888. Originally the New Orleans National Bank, this building's eclectic design has a heavy rusticated red sandstone base with tall, arched openings. The corner entrance has a massive polished red granite column with a white stone capital ornamented with grotesque faces. Elegant red terra-cotta decorations with paired griffins appear in the spandrels between the second and third floors. An elaborate dormer with more decoration caps this exuberant design. As originally built, the building had a high-pitched pyramidal roof. This architectural rarity was meticulously

restored by Whitney National Bank in 1995 to house its international banking division. Backtrack to Gravier Street and turn right.

Whitney National Bank Safety Deposit Vaults
619 Gravier Street

(9) **Whitney National Bank Safety Deposit Vaults,** *1888, Sully and Toledano*

Bank of Louisiana
300–304 St. Charles Street, corner of Gravier

Best seen from across the street, this is one of the most powerful architectural statements in New Orleans. Designed by Sully and Toledano and built of massive rusticated blocks of red granite, this facade is especially notable for its four polished granite columns with simple capitals of a singular design. They give this small build-

Regions Bank
301-311-317 St. Charles Street, corner of Gravier

ing a sense of Egyptian monumentality without copying Egyptian motifs. The lintel over the central opening is extravagantly massive. Bronze grilles like puddled curtains secure the tall first floor windows. The cornice is also highly unusual; it looks like shinglework but is carved out of red granite. It echoes the virile designs of architect Frank Furness of Philadelphia. This building was the headquarters of the Whitney National Bank from 1888 until the construction of the adjoining light pink granite-clad skyscraper in 1911. Thomas Sully also designed many of the commodious houses along St. Charles Avenue uptown (see Tour 9). From this block of Gravier Street there is a fine distant view of the Hibernia National Bank of 1921 with its exclamatory classical belvedere. Walk up Gravier Street and cross St. Charles Street to look back at the important intersection of Gravier and St. Charles.

(10) *St. Charles and Gravier Streets*

• **Bank of Louisiana,** *1855, Gallier, Turpin, and Company*
These twin, four-story, Italianate-style brick-and-stucco commercial buildings originally housed two stores and were built for Charles Mason, an agent of Robert Heath in England. They have cast-iron piers along their ground floor, permitting wide openings with folding panel-like door-windows. A narrow balcony faces St. Charles Street. The upper stories have round-headed cast-iron lintels over their windows. Drawings of the original buildings show them painted pastel colors and with a now-lost, covered cast-iron gallery supported by slender iron columns over the sidewalk.

• **Old Touro Row / Regions Bank,** *1851, Thomas Murray, builder*
This four-story, brick-and-stucco row originally consisted of six stores built by Thomas Murray for investor and philanthropist Judah Touro. The ground floor has decorated cast-iron piers. A cast-iron decorated balcony runs across the second floor with access from its tall, narrow windows. A narrow shed roof shelters this balcony and is trimmed with delicate, lacelike cast iron. This overlay of fanciful iron work considerably lightens this solid, blocklike building. Today, it houses Regions Bank.

Whitney National Bank
228 St. Charles Street,
corner of Gravier

First NBC Center and Atrium
201 St. Charles Street,
between Common and
Gravier; American
Express office in atrium

On this corner stood the First Presbyterian Church, erected in 1819, but which burned in 1851. It became the Reverend Theodore Clapp's Congregationalist Unitarian Church of the Messiah, known in the antebellum city as the "Strangers' Church." This theologically advanced minister questioned the dogmas of original sin and eternal damnation and drew a large congregation. We have in Madaline Edwards's recently discovered diary a record of the sense of liberation that liberal Protestantism introduced to mid-nineteenth-century New Orleans.

• **Whitney National Bank,** *1911, Clinton and Russell with Emile Weil; Common Street Annex, 1920*

The trademark corner clock projecting over the sidewalk at St. Charles and Gravier Streets announces the headquarters of Whitney National Bank. Organized in 1883, this establishment bank moved into this pale pink granite-clad, steel-frame building in 1911. Designed by the New York City firm of Clinton and Russell with Emile Weil of New Orleans, the building projects an image of solidity and understated opulence. The bronze plaques with the emblem of the State of Louisiana and the lamps flanking the St. Charles Street entrance are quite fine. The building consists of a fourteen-story tower on the Gravier Street side and a five-story wing facing St. Charles Street.

⑪   First NBC Center and Atrium / Memories of the St. Charles Hotel, *1985, Moiyama & Teshima Planners Ltd. and The Mathes Group*

Light pink, granite-clad, fifty-three-story First NBC Center is New Orleans' premier business address and is the most New Orleans–responsive high-rise in the city. It is the city's second-tallest structure (One Shell Square is slightly taller). Designed by Moiyama & Teshima Planners Ltd. of Toronto and The Mathes Group of New Orleans, the building is trapezoidal in section and has just over one million square feet of floor space. Its facade has a Y design that is repeated in the dark green spandrels between the bands of windows. A stepped-back top with large dormers crowns the tower. It is notable for being the only tall building to marry traditional New Orleans galleries with the sky-scraper form. The tower is set back and has a three-story section facing St. Charles Street with a double gallery sheltering the sidewalk. The tower was developed by local and European investors and financed by a Canadian and a German bank. When the bottom fell out of the office market after the oil bust, and when real estate limited partnership tax laws changed in 1986, the palatial skyscraper was taken over by the Toronto bank that lent the money to build it. In 1994, First NBC Center, which cost $115 million to build, was bought by a Connecticut investment group for $63 million.

Pass through the front entrance into the tall atrium within. To the right is the Stella Jones Gallery (see page 87). First NBC Center stands on one of the most important sites in American New Orleans. For here stood the elegant St. Charles Exchange Hotel, the grandest hotel in the South. Built in 1835–37 and designed by James Gallier, Sr., and his partner Charles Dakin, the St. Charles Hotel was at the center

of the social, economic, and political life of New Orleans and of the
Old South. Gallier designed the first hotel with a monumental
Corinthian columned portico and capitol-like colonnaded dome,
which loomed over the antebellum city. The St. Charles Hotel—

Hampton Inn
226 Carondelet Street;
529-9990

with its luxury suites, huge dining rooms, elegant salons, fancy shops, baths, and vast
barroom—was the opulent American-patronized rival of the Creole-favored St. Louis
Hotel in the French Quarter (see page 124). Under its 203-foot-high dome, slave
auctions were conducted for the Southern planters who sojourned here during the busy
winter social season. In 1851 a fire gutted the building and it was replaced with a
similar structure, only without the extravagant dome. Here Jefferson Davis met with
secessionist leaders. After the Union occupation of the city in 1862, General Benjamin
Butler had his lodgings here. This second hotel burned in 1894 and was replaced the
next year by a new seven-story, U-shaped, steel-frame Beaux Arts or Italian Renaissance design by Thomas Sully. This third St. Charles Hotel continued to be an elite
gathering place in New Orleans and was where Presidents McKinley, Roosevelt, and
Taft stayed when visiting the Crescent City. It was demolished in 1974.

Walk straight through the First NBC Center atrium into the lobby
of the adjoining Hampton Inn and exit onto Carondelet Street. This interconnection
with its neighbor continues an old American downtown tradition lost when the
International style popularized isolated towers-in-a-plaza after World War II.

• **Old Southern Trust and Banking Company / Hampton Inn,** *1903, Daniel Burnham;*
hotel conversion 1994
This sober, classically detailed, thirteen-story Edwardian office building was built in
1903 for the Southern Trust and Banking Company and designed by Chicago's famed
Daniel Burnham. The Boston Club once occupied an upper floor here. In 1994 it was
converted into the **Hampton Inn,** the latest trend in the CBD. The UNO Downtown
Center is in this building.

⑫ *Carondelet Street Between Gravier and Common Streets: Old Wall*
Street South
Carondelet Street was originally named for the Baron de Carondelet, who was
appointed governor of the French Province of Louisiana in 1791. The two blocks of
Carondelet Street between Union and Common Streets emerged as the heart of the
New Orleans banking district during the first decades of this century. Here elegant,
steel-frame, skyscraper bank buildings with impressive ground-floor banking halls
were built, monuments to the last efflorescence of the cotton-dominated South. A new
cotton exchange stood at the center of this district. This tight grouping has a Wall
Street–like feeling conveyed through the density of the cluster and the use of gray
Indiana limestone cladding. While most corporate offices have shifted to post-1960s
Poydras Street, banking has stayed put here with the Whitney National Bank on St.
Charles, the Hibernia National Bank and Bank One on Carondelet, and First NBC a
block away on Baronne Street.

Dryades Savings Bank
231 Carondelet Street,
corner of Gravier

Hibernia National Bank
and Banking Hall
313 Carondelet Street

• **Old New Orleans Cotton Exchange / Dryades Savings Bank,** *1922, Favrot and Livaudais*

The fine steel-frame, limestone-clad building with the beveled corner on the downtown-lakeside corner of Carondelet and Gravier Streets was completed in 1922 and designed by Favrot and Livaudais. The Marine Bank was housed on the first floor, the cotton exchange itself was located in a double-height space on the second floor, lighted by the great arched windows, and cotton brokers' offices occupied the upper floors. Its fine green copper cornice is a rare survivor in the CBD. This elegant building is the third cotton exchange to be built on this site, and it replaced an exuberant Second Empire–style cotton exchange erected in 1883. In 1875 Edward King described this key corner in his book *The Great South:*

> In the American Quarter during certain hours of the day cotton is the only subject spoken of; the pavements of all the principal avenues in the vicinity of the Exchange are crowded with smartly dressed gentlemen who eagerly discuss crops and values . . . whose mouths are filled with the slang of the Liverpool market; and with the skippers of the steamers from all parts of the West and Southwest. From high noon until dark the planter, the factor, the speculator, flit feverishly to and from the portals of the Exchange, and nothing can be heard above the excited hum of their conversation except the sharp voice of the clerk reading the latest telegram.

The New Orleans Cotton Exchange operated here until 1962 and finally shut down in 1964, ending New Orleans' historic role in cotton trading. Recently the African American–owned Dryades Savings Bank opened its offices in the handsome building.

• **Hibernia National Bank and Banking Hall,** *1921, Favrot and Livaudais*
Built in 1920–21 and designed by Favrot and Livaudais, this elegant twenty-three-story skyscraper was the tallest building in New Orleans for forty-three years and was not surpassed in height until 1962. Its steel frame is clad with light gray Indiana limestone. Classical elements, including monumental Corinthian columns along its base, make this a distinguished design. Like all pre-air-conditioning towers, it was built with narrow wings to maximize natural ventilation. Atop the tower is a landmark, circular, colonnaded, white terra-cotta-clad belvedere that is floodlit at night. Originally it accommodated a public observatory with an unobstructed view over the city and the crescent-shaped river. Later it supported the antenna of WDSU, the city's first television station. Today the belvedere is lit in different colors for special days, including purple, green, and gold for Mardi Gras. The grand polished marble banking hall of the Hibernia Bank is one of the finest in the city and well worth experiencing. Built in basilica form, this temple to finance has fluted travertine Corinthian columns on all four sides of its great space. A deeply coffered gilded ceiling caps the room. The classical detailing disguises the fact that the space is a rhombus, not a rectangle. The Hibernia

Bank & Trust Company was founded by twelve Irishmen in 1870; today it is Louisiana's largest statewide bank.

Latter & Blum Building
203 Carondelet Street, corner of Common

⑬   *Carondelet and Common Streets*

Bank One
200 Carondelet Street, corner of Common

• **Old Hennen Building / Latter & Blum Building,** *1895, Thomas Sully*
The Hennen Building was designed by Thomas Sully and opened in 1895. This eleven-story building is considered New Orleans' first skyscraper and was the first steel-frame building in the Crescent City. John Morris, the investor who commissioned the building, sent architect Sully to Chicago to observe the path-breaking commercial designs in that city. The well-proportioned block reflects the sobriety and strength that was the hallmark of the Chicago School of architecture. Three stacks of bay windows appear on the Carondelet Street facade and five stacks of bays appear on the Common Street side. In 1920 architect Emile Weil remodeled the first and second floors with a limestone facing in the Renaissance style, loosely based on the facade of the Boston Public Library.

• **Old National American Bank and Banking Hall / Bank One,** *1929, Moise H. Goldstein*
Across Carondelet Street from the Latter & Blum Building is this twenty-three-story, Art Deco skyscraper built just before the 1929 Stock Market Crash halted the construction of office buildings for a generation. Designed by Moise H. Goldstein for the National American Bank, this is Louisiana's most important Art Deco commercial tower. Its base is clad in polished black granite, and its upper stories are sheathed in Indiana limestone. Three zigguratlike setbacks make the tower appear taller than it is. The building is topped by a water tower; soon after the building's completion this tower was capped by a great metal, Art Deco finial with lightning bolt designs. Inside is an intricately ornamented lobby and beyond it a banking hall with a red marble floor, bronze and marble tellers' cages, and a coffered ceiling from which Art Deco chandeliers are suspended.

(Aficionados of Art Deco are urged to visit the Louisiana State Capitol in Baton Rouge. Built by Huey Long in 1931–32 and designed by Weiss, Dreyfous & Seiferth, this unusual skyscraper capitol building was inspired by Bertram Grosvenor Goodhue's Nebraska State Capitol. It is lavishly decorated with colored stone, sculpture, murals, and elaborate plaster and bronzework. It is one of the greatest Art Deco designs in the United States. Long's elegant tomb faces the monument he built.)

• **Old Federal Reserve Bank / Security Center,** *1923, Rathbone deBuys*
The Security Center with its monumental columns was constructed in 1923 as the home of the New Orleans branch of the Federal Reserve Bank of Atlanta. The federal

Security Center
147 Carondelet Street,
corner of Common

First National Bank of
Commerce Banking Hall
210 Baronne Street, at
Common

Old Sears Building
201 Baronne Street, at
Common

bank was housed here until the construction of a new building at St. Charles and Poydras Streets in 1966 (see page 261).

14   *Up Common Street to Baronne*

•   **First National Bank of Commerce Banking Hall / Old Canal Bank Building,** *1927, Emile Weil*
Walk up Common Street. Just past the Latter & Blum Building is the inconspicuous glass-doored side entrance to the eighteen-story First National Bank of Commerce (First NBC) Building at the corner of Baronne and Common. It was designed by Emile Weil in a modified Italianate Renaissance style and built in 1927. Enter here and turn right and then right again into the magnificent two-story-high banking hall of First NBC. All the buildings on this block are linked by internal ground-floor corridors, the traditional way that American office cores were developed in the late nineteenth and early twentieth centuries. This is obviously useful in New Orleans' hot and rainy climate. First NBC's banking hall is surrounded by marble pilasters and capped by a fine coffered ceiling. This bank is the descendant of the New Orleans Canal and Banking Company of 1831, whose 1844 granite building we saw at Magazine and Gravier Streets. Pass through the banking hall and exit out to Baronne Street, named for the Baronne de Carondelet, the wife of the Baron de Carondelet.

15   *Baronne and Common Streets*

•   **Old Sears Building,** *1931*
Across Baronne is the old Sears Building with black granite trim and a beveled corner. This mildly Moderne building was built by Feibleman's department store and represents a rare style in New Orleans. As offices left the CBD, so did downtown shopping, which shifted to malls. This building is slated to become a hotel. About eight blocks uptown (left), at Julia and S. Rampart Streets, was the turning basin for the New Basin Canal, financed by the Canal Bank and excavated between 1831 and 1835. It linked the back of the American city with Lake Pontchartrain. The New Basin Canal competed with the earlier Creole-built Carondelet Canal of 1795, which ended at its turning basin near where Armstrong Park stands today, just outside the French Quarter. The New Basin Canal was filled in between the late 1930s and early 1950s.

• **Père Marquette Building,** *1925, Scott Joy and William E. Spink*

Turn right on Baronne and pass the Père Marquette Building, built in 1925 and designed by Scott Joy and William E. Spink; it's a fine steel-frame building with mildly Gothic Revival ornament. The building is named for Jacques Marquette, the seventeenth-century Jesuit explorer and missionary who, with Louis Joliet, came down-river by boat from French Canada and discovered that the Mississippi debouches at the Gulf of Mexico. This block was bought by the Society of Jesus in 1848, which established the College of the Immaculate Conception here in 1849. The school merged with Loyola University of the South when the Jesuits built a new campus uptown in 1911 (see page 310). There are plans to convert this sky-scraper into a hotel.

Père Marquette Building
150 Baronne Street, at Common

Church of the Immaculate Conception
130 Baronne Street; masses daily at 7:30 A.M. and noon; Saturday at noon and 4 P.M.; Sunday at 8, 9:30, 11 A.M., and 7:30 P.M.; Stations of the Cross and Benediction Friday at 12:30 P.M.; 529-1477

⓰   Church of the Immaculate Conception, *1929–30, Wogan, Bernard, and Toledano*

After their expulsion in 1763, the Society of Jesus returned to Louisiana in 1831. This Moorish-style church is one of the architectural surprises in New Orleans and one of the most exotic interiors in the fantasy-loving Crescent City. It is the second Moorish-style church to stand here. The first was built between 1851 and 1857 to the designs of John Cambiaso, S.J., who had lived in Spain and admired Moorish architecture, and architect T. E. Giraud. That early brick church employed more than two hundred tons of cast iron, manufactured in Baltimore, including cast-iron pews. In 1926 that build-ing was demolished and Wogan, Bernard, and Toledano designed a larger modern replacement, also in the Moorish style and reusing the old church's cast-iron columns and pews. The dark red brick church with its white stone trim is worth careful exami-nation. Three Moorish arches frame its entrances, which have bronze doors that slide into the wall. Above them appear delicate Venetian Gothic tracery framing stained-glass windows. The upper part of the facade has an eight-pointed-star rose window flanked by delicately ornamented Moorish arches. Twin octagonal towers with green copper onion domes and crosses complete this intricate facade. The original church was to be capped by two minaretlike towers of open cast-iron work 186 feet—eighteen stories—high!

Enter the church, passing the large smiling marble angels proffering the holy water fonts. The Moorish style is carried over into the tall interior, with pointed arches and elaborate decorations. The spiral columns and elaborate pews are noteworthy uses of the cast iron so identified with antebellum New Orleans. The blaz-ing Moorish-style gilded bronze altar with pointed arches and three fanciful onion domes was designed by architect James Freret of New Orleans for the 1851 church. It was crafted in Lyons, France, and was awarded the first prize at the Paris Exposition of 1867–68. In the niche over the altar is a white marble statue of the Virgin Mary with a starry halo carved by Denis Foyatier and commissioned by Queen Marie Amelie,

Rectory of Immaculate Conception Church
130 Baronne Street

Fairmont Hotel
123 Baronne Street;
529-7111

consort of King Louis Philippe of France. The dogma of the Immaculate Conception, that Jesus was conceived without original sin, was promulgated by Pope Pius IX in 1854. The richly colored stained-glass windows were made in Munich, Germany, and memorialize the early history of the Society of Jesus. In the back of the church, to the right, is a mosaic shrine to Our Lady of Prompt Succor, the patron of Louisiana and New Orleans.

• **Rectory of Immaculate Conception Church,** *1899, perhaps James Freret*
To the left of the church is this unusual, light yellow and red brick rectory; its elaborate white marble entrance has a Moorish arch surrounding the emblem of the Society of Jesus. Over the pointed arch is inscribed: *Fides Quaerens Intellectum* (I believe that I may understand). This narrow building is reminiscent of the style of the lost College of the Immaculate Conception that once stood on this block.

17   Fairmont Hotel / Old Roosevelt Hotel and Grunewald Hotel, *1925, Favrot and Livaudais; 1908, Toledano and Wogan; 1965*
Across Baronne Street from the Jesuit church is the golden metal and glass marquee of the Fairmont Hotel. The Fairmont consists of four linked buildings with an axial corridor-lobby. The Baronne Street building was built in 1925 in a mildly Spanish Renaissance Revival style and designed by Favrot and Livaudais. The University Place building on the other side of the block was built in 1908 as the Hotel Grunewald and designed by Toledano and Wogan in the Beaux Arts style, with stacks of bay windows across its white terra-cotta facade. The Roosevelt Hotel was named for President Theodore Roosevelt in 1923. It was one of the first buildings with air-conditioning in the South. In 1965 it became the Fairmont Hotel.

Enter the grand hotel and walk down the impressive corridor-lobby, which is festively decorated at Christmastime. Halfway down on the left is the entrance to the Sazarac Cocktail Lounge with its cozy Moderne interior and fine murals painted by Paul Ninas in 1949. This is a most New Orleanian spot and the best place to try a Sazarac cocktail, a tasty concoction of rye whiskey, sugar, Peychaud and Angostura bitters, and lemon juice. Seymour Weiss became the manager of the Roosevelt Hotel in 1925 and eventually its owner. Weiss met Huey Long at the 1-2-3 Club on Baronne Street, where both of them went to play the ponies. Weiss became a key backer and confidant of Governor Huey Long and his financial director, controlling the vast sums of "deduct" money (money automatically deducted from the salaries of state employees) that oiled the Long political machine. The "Kingfish" made the Roosevelt Hotel his New Orleans headquarters until his assassination in 1935. Later, when Huey's younger brother, Earl K. Long, became governor, the Roosevelt continued to be the nerve center of Louisiana politics. The hotel was conveniently close to the Sho-Bar, the Bourbon Street strip club where the sixty-three-year-old politician encountered twenty-three-year-old Blaze Starr. Democratic Party election night rallies—and elite Carnival balls including Rex and Comus—continue to favor the historic Fairmont.

Leave the hotel through the University Place entrance. This street takes its name from the fact that the University of Louisiana was located here in the 1840s; that institution became Tulane University after Paul Tulane's generous bequest and moved to a new Richardsonian campus on St. Charles Avenue uptown in 1894 (see page 312).

Orpheum Theater
129 University Place;
Louisiana Philharmonic
Orchestra, 524-3285

Walgreen Drug Store
900 Canal Street, corner
of Baronne; 523-7201

(18)   Orpheum Theater / Louisiana Philharmonic Orchestra, *1919,*
G. Albert Lansburgh and Samuel Stone
The flat, terra-cotta decorated facade of this theater is treated like a subtle theatrical backdrop with a wealth of decoration in shallow relief. It was designed and built by the Orpheum Circuit Company in 1918 and originally staged vaudeville shows. This vintage theater was restored in 1981 and is now the home of the Louisiana Philharmonic Orchestra.

Audubon Building
931 Canal Street, corner
of Burgundy

Old Kress Building
923 Canal Street

(19)   Walgreen Drug Store, *circa 1938; expanded 1997*
This round-cornered, 1930s period piece dates from the days when Canal Street was the commercial center of the entire metropolitan region. A generally neglected, and now increasingly rare, type of commercial design, this building epitomizes the bright lights of the big city. The zappy neon signs were added to the sleek Moderne building about 1950. The Chess, Checkers, and Whist Club was once housed in a turreted late-Victorian building that stood on this corner. Across Canal Street is the 900 block with a trio of important early-twentieth-century commercial landmarks.

(20)   900 *Block of Canal Street*

•   **Audubon Building,** *1910, Favrot and Reed*
The eight-story Audubon Building at the corner of Canal and Burgundy was built in 1910 and designed by Favrot and Reed. Originally promoted as a hotel, it is a fine example of big city mixed-use buildings from the height of the streetcar era.

•   **Old Kress Building,** *1911, Emile Weil*
The former Kress Building was built in 1910 and designed by Emile Weil, with a handsome ornamental terra-cotta frame surrounding a strong central composition of windows. In 1963 the entire facade was covered over with a modernistic metal curtain wall with a honeycomb pattern. The facade was restored in 1983. In 1997 it was announced that the building would become the automobile entrance for the Ritz-Carlton New Orleans.

Maison Blanche Department Store
901 Canal Street, at Dauphine; 566-1000

Boston Club / Mercer House
824 Canal Street

Chateau Sonesta Hotel
800 Iberville Street; 586-0800

• **Maison Blanche Department Store / Ritz-Carlton New Orleans,** *1909, Stone Brothers*

This thirteen-story, white terra-cotta-clad, steel-frame combination department store and office building was built in 1906–9 and designed by the Stone Brothers. It is a superb example of turn-of-the-century, Beaux Arts commercial architecture, a true palace of commerce. The department store continues to operate in the lower floors of the building. In 1997 plans were announced to convert the upper stories into the Ritz-Carlton New Orleans. This corner was once the location of Christ Episcopal Cathedral.

㉑   Boston Club / Mercer House, *1844, James Gallier, Sr.*

Halfway down the uptown (CBD) side of the 800 block of Canal Street is this three-story, white-painted, brick-and-stucco town house built in 1844 for Dr. William Newton Mercer, a physician with extensive cotton plantations near Natchez, Mississippi. Designed by James Gallier, Sr., it is the only surviving originally private residence on lower Canal Street. An elegant wrought-iron gallery wraps around the facade at the second floor. The semi-octagonal wing that projects into the side garden was added in 1882. More additions were made to the back of the building when it became the home of the Boston Club in 1884. This gentleman's club was founded in 1841 and took its named from a once-popular card game. For many years it was traditional to erect a temporary viewing stand over the sidewalk here during Carnival and to drape the facade of the clubhouse with strings of lights. Here Rex, King of Carnival, stopped in front of the gaily decorated building to toast the queen of Carnival on Mardi Gras.

㉒   Chateau Sonesta Hotel / Old D. H. Holmes Department Store, *1880s, various architects; 1913, Favrot and Livaudais; hotel conversion, 1995, Angela Cronin*

Across Canal Street from the Boston Club is the recreated copper marquee and restored facade of the former D. H. Holmes department store. Under the clock in front of Holmes is where Ignatius J. Reilly's misadventures begin in John Kennedy Toole's comedic masterpiece *A Confederacy of Dunces.* The history of this building is quite complex. The first D. H. Holmes store on this site was a Gothic Revival building erected in 1849. As the store grew, it bought adjacent lots and built additions. The Canal Street facade dates from 1913 and is Beaux Arts in style, while the Iberville Street facade to the rear dates from 1905. When Holmes closed in 1989, the city was given the building. The new hotel is a public-private partnership between the city and private investors. The Chateau Sonesta Hotel chose to "turn the building around" and make its principal entrance face the intersection of Iberville and Dauphine Streets, a telling demonstration of the vitality of the French Quarter and the decline of the CBD. This would never have happened in the nineteenth century when Iberville Street was Customhouse Street, a notorious strip of low brothels.

23   Zero Stop for the St. Charles Avenue Streetcar

The "zero" streetcar stop is on the uptown-riverside corner of Canal and Carondelet Streets. This is the best place to catch the cars headed uptown, not crowded stop #1 at St. Charles and Common Streets.

24   *Canal Street and the 100 Block of St. Charles Street: Historic Center*

The median here was the original site of the statue of Henry Clay, which now stands in the center of Lafayette Square (see page 260). This spot was the pivot of the old city, its psychological epicenter, halfway between the French Quarter downtown and the American sector uptown. In the nineteenth century this was where political rallies and mass gatherings assembled. The first block of St. Charles Street from Canal to Common is an important fragment of the old cotton capital. The key phases of the city's history can all be read here. The corner buildings (the Pickwick Club and Rubenstein Brothers Men's Wear) are old landmarks. The former Kolb's Restaurant, two buildings with extraordinary cast-iron galleries, the blank International-style bank on the downtown-lakeside corner of St. Charles and Common, and now the new and city-mending, contextually designed Courtyard by Marriott hotel across the street give a compact summation of the American sector's evolution.

• Pickwick Club / Old Crescent City Billiards, *1826; complete remodeling 1874, Henry Howard*

On the uptown-lakeside corner of St. Charles and Canal Streets is the elegant Italianate home of the Pickwick Club (upstairs), floating over a strip of ordinary shopfronts. This imposing building is the thoroughgoing 1874 remodeling by the important architect Henry Howard of an earlier, 1826 structure. Its two-story-tall, Italianate-style windows are especially handsome. In 1950 this landmark became the home of the Pickwick Club, a gentleman's club organized in 1857. Many Pickwickians have traditionally been members of the Mistick Krewe of Comus, which also first appeared in 1857.

• Old Kolb's Restaurant, *1845*

These two 1840s buildings with two- and three-story cast-iron galleries are a classic pair of Old New Orleans architecture. They are highly visible at this location on the famous street. The building at 125 St. Charles Street was erected in 1845 for the Louisiana Jockey Club. The buildings long housed Kolb's German Restaurant, which closed in 1996. Plans have been announced to convert these gems into the Jockey Club Hotel. The old Kolb's electric and neon sign is a true rarity, as is the 1884 belt-driven ceiling fan system inside the first floor of the closed restaurant.

Zero Stop for the St. Charles Avenue Streetcar
Canal and Carondelet Streets

Crescent City Billiards / Pickwick Club
115 St. Charles Street

Old Kolb's Restaurant
123, 125 St. Charles Street

Courtyard by Marriott
124 St. Charles Street;
800-321-2211

Old Bank of America
115 Exchange Place, off
Canal Street

Old Merchants Mutual
Insurance Building
622 Canal Street

• **Courtyard by Marriott,** *1995, Lyons & Hudson*

This modern hotel is designed to blend in with its setting, and it reinterprets the proportions and appearance of the mid-1850s Verandah Hotel that once stood here. It is a sensitive piece of contemporary city mending and epitomizes the emerging appreciation of the architectural importance and quality of the old Central Business District.

Detour: For Aficionados of Cast-Iron Architecture

There are two buildings that lovers of American cast-iron architecture should not fail to see. One is on Canal and the other in a service alley off it.

25   Old Bank of America, *1865, Gallier and Esterbrook*

Sandwiched between a corner fast-food restaurant and the utilitarian garage of the Holiday Inn on narrow Exchange Place is the neglected cast-iron facade of the old Bank of America. This five-story Italianate-style structure with its round-headed windows was designed by Gallier and Esterbrook and built in 1865; it has an arcade with six Corinthian columns on its ground floor. The landmark's arcade has been blocked-in with roll-down steel doors. Exchange Place was an alteration to the original street plan of the French Quarter and was cut through in 1831. Today it is a service alley, but it was once a prestige business address and linked Canal Street with the back of the Merchants Exchange that faced Royal Street and the elite Creole-favored St. Louis Hotel on St. Louis Street (see page 124).

26   All American Jeans / Old Merchants Mutual Insurance Building, *1859, W. A. Freret, Jr.*

This is New Orleans' other great cast-iron facade; it was built for the Merchants Mutual Insurance Company in 1859 to designs by W. A. Freret, Jr. Its twisted "barley sugar" columns are unusual. This architectural relic floats above a modern glass shopfront in that netherland that most people rarely lift their eyes to see.

*Fine carving enlivens the woodwork of the Richardsonian
Patrick F. Taylor Library of 1889. It is part of the University of New Orleans'
Ogden Museum of Southern Art in the Arts District.*

What This Tour Covers
Preliminaries
Introduction: From Warehouses to Art
    in the Postindustrial City

Continuation
Streetcar Connections

Tour 7

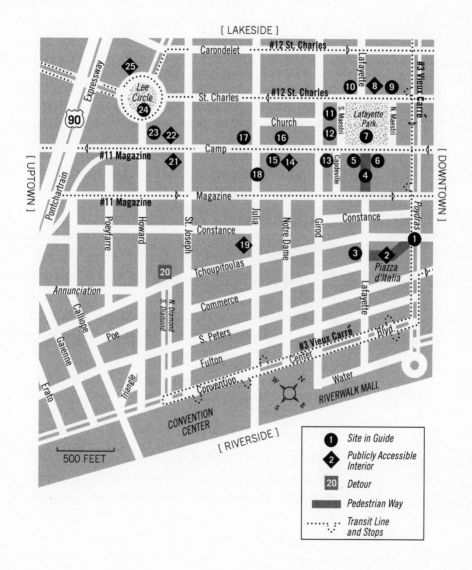

[LAKESIDE]

Carondelet

#12 St. Charles

Lafayette

#3 Vieux Carré

25

Lee Circle

24

St. Charles

#12 St. Charles

10

8

9

11

S. Maestri

N. Maestri

Lafayette Park

90

Expressway

23

22

17

Church

16

12

7

[UPTOWN]

Camp

#11 Magazine

21

15

14

13

Capdeville

5

6

18

4

Pontchartrain

Magazine

#11 Magazine

[DOWNTOWN]

Julia

Constance

St. Joseph

Constance

Notre Dame

Girod

Constance

Poydras

1

Poeyfarre

Howard

19

Tchoupitoulas

20

3

2

Piazza d'Italia

N. Diamond
S. Diamond

Commerce

Lafayette

Annunciation

Calliope

Poe

S. Peters

Galvez

Fulton

#3 Vieux Carré

Blvd

Triangle

Convention

Center

Water

Erato

N
W   E
S

RIVERWALK MALL

CONVENTION CENTER

[RIVERSIDE]

500 FEET

1 Site in Guide

2 Publicly Accessible Interior

20 Detour

     Pedestrian Way

⋯ Transit Line and Stops

Warehouse District Arts Association
Write for map/brochure, P.O. Box 30633, N.O., 70190

Art for Arts' Sake
Tickets and information, 523-1216

What This Tour Covers

This walk covers part of the old American sector—from the instant ruins of the postmodern Piazza d'Italia through the federal courts district to the superb Greek Revival old City Hall facing Lafayette Square, to Julia Street's happening art galleries and the Contemporary Arts Center in the former Warehouse District, to the old-fashioned Confederate Museum. It ends at the new arts institutions on Lee Circle, including the future Ogden Museum of Southern Art and the K&B outdoor sculpture collection.

Preliminaries

Tuesday through Saturday, between about 10 A.M. and 4 P.M., is when most art galleries and the two museums on this tour are all open. Phone specific galleries to be sure they are open. High summer is a slow time here; the art season resumes in the fall. A brochure with a map is available from the **Warehouse District Arts Association.** On Saturday mornings there is an active open-air Green Market at Magazine and Girod Streets from 8 A.M. to noon.

Gallery Openings

Coordinated gallery openings take place the first Saturday of each month from 6 to 9 P.M., summer months excluded. The beginning of the fall season on the first Saturday in October is especially recommended. **Art for Arts' Sake** marks the annual fall opening at the Contemporary Arts Center and the Julia Street galleries. This is the best time to see and meet almost everyone active in New Orleans' burgeoning art scene.

Parking

There is ample street parking here, though you must watch the parking meters. This tour can be done by automobile.

Transportation

The #3 Vieux Carré jitney bus stops at Poydras and Tchoupi-toulas, near the Piazza d'Italia. The St. Charles Avenue streetcar stops in front of the K&B sculpture garden at Lee Circle where this tour ends. The #11 Magazine bus passes through the district, linking it with uptown shopping (see Tour 10).

Restaurants

There are a number of excellent places to eat in this area. **Mother's Restaurant** is across Poydras from the start of this walk and serves good, inexpensive local food; go at off-peak times to avoid the crowds.

Mike's on the Avenue is an expensive but superb restaurant, serving Asian-Southwestern contemporary cuisine in a beautiful room with a comfortable sound level. **Emeril's** is also expensive, and can be uncomfortably loud; it's best at off-peak times. The menu features memorable eclectic regional dishes.

Mother's Restaurant
401 Poydras Street, at Tchoupitoulas; 522-9656

Mike's on the Avenue
628 St. Charles Street; reservations recommended; 523-1709

Emeril's
800 Tchoupitoulas, at Julia; reservations recommended; 528-9393

Introduction: From Warehouses to Art in the Postindustrial City

After the United States purchased Louisiana in 1803, the English-speaking newcomers began to build upriver from the old French Quarter in what they dubbed Faubourg St. Mary (see Tour 6). In 1822 St. Mary's Market was built below Tchoupitoulas Street, between North and South Diamond Streets, in what is now the Arts/Warehouse District, and the blocks around it began to fill up with buildings. In 1825, Place Gravier in the Faubourg St. Marie was renamed Lafayette Square in commemoration of the Marquis de Lafayette's visit. Significant building activity began here in the 1830s as American New Orleans boomed. After the city was divided into three municipalities in 1836, the English-speaking Americans erected their elegant and imposing Greek Revival City Hall (now Gallier Hall) facing Lafayette Square. Elite Protestant congregations erected churches near the square, and the English-speaking Irish Catholics began St. Patrick's Church on nearby Camp Street in the late 1830s. Fine Federal, and later Greek Revival and Italianate-style, red-brick town houses with rear slave dependencies began to fill up the blocks in the American sector. The "Thirteen Sisters" of 1833 on Julia Street are the best surviving examples of this early wave of Anglo-American residential construction.

As commerce expanded along the docks, and after new "suburban" subdivisions such as the Garden District opened, the old town houses near Lafayette Square were converted to business uses or subdivided for rooming houses. The elite Protestant congregations drifted away, following their congregations uptown. Only Gothic Revival St. Patrick's Church stayed in the neighborhood. When New Orleans was reunited as a single municipality in 1852, Gallier Hall became the city hall for the consolidated Anglo-American dominated city. The federal government built a post office across Lafayette Square from the city hall, and eventually other federal offices and the Fifth Circuit Court clustered around the old American square, well away from the Creole French Quarter. Here they remain today, much expanded, with their attendant nearby lawyers' offices, some housed in converted nineteenth-century town houses.

Behind the docks, warehouses were built. In the 1830s and 1840s they were generally narrow two- and three-story brick buildings with wood shutters. By the 1860s warehouses became much larger (a good example is the two-story brick warehouse that now houses the Louisiana Children's Museum, see page 265). After 1900, steel and concrete, and better elevators, allowed warehouses to become even larger and much taller. The five-story, hundred-thousand-square-foot Bemis Building at 329 Julia Street, built in 1902, was the first reinforced concrete building in New Orleans. The expansion of railroad lines in late-nineteenth-century New Orleans resulted in those corporations buying up and rebuilding the large parcels on what is now the riverside of Convention Center Boulevard. Upriver from about Howard Avenue to Erato Street, an industrial district emerged including iron foundries and a few cotton textile mills. The towered, red-brick Maginnis Cotton Mill of 1882—occupying the block bounded by Constance, Poeyfarre, Annunciation, and Calliope Streets and visible from the elevated bridge approach—is a monumental example of American Victorian industrial architecture. But it was an anomaly, for fatefully, New Orleans did not establish a large, high-wage manufacturing sector. Most of her industrial activity was limited to cotton presses (which squeezed cotton bales into smaller sizes for shipping), sugar refineries, tobacco factories, coffee roasteries, and businesses catering to the local market. Although one-third of the nation's cotton crop passed through New Orleans in the 1870s, the city never developed a substantial textile industry. In the twentieth century, New Orleans fell even further behind other American cities in manufacturing. When interstate highways and trucks superceded railroads after World War II, they pulled warehousing out of the old city to cheaper suburban land. Obsolete inner-city factories shut down, and the Warehouse District began a steep decline.

In 1981 the Preservation Resource Center restored and moved into one of the landmark "Thirteen Sisters" row houses on Julia Street. Then, in 1984, the Louisiana World Exposition was held on the old riverfront railroad properties adjacent to the Warehouse District. The fair spilled over into half a dozen old warehouses along Fulton Street. When the fair closed, it left as its permanent contribution to the city a new convention center (since much expanded) to serve the growing visitor industry (see Tour 5 on the new riverfront). Old South Front Street was renamed Convention Center Boulevard. A wave of loft conversions for residential uses began in the sturdy old buildings. They had the advantages of secure parking, relatively large living spaces, and no nearby slums. Young urban professionals in particular favored the emerging area. By 1994 there were some one thousand apartments in the district with about twenty-five hundred residents, making this New Orleans' newest neighborhood, with just a bit less population than the now-depleted French Quarter. The average resident is in his or her mid-thirties, and there are few children in the neighborhood. Almost all have automobiles and drive to other areas to work or shop. Wide Julia Street became New Orleans' Gallery Row; many of the city's best contemporary art galleries and one of its best auction houses cluster here and add immeasurably to the artistic vitality of the city. The opening of the Contemporary Art Center in 1990, in a handsome turn-of-the-century warehouse—and the plans for the University of New Orleans' Lee Circle Center for the Arts, including the Ogden Museum of Southern Art—have given the district an expanding role in the region's cultural life. The name now given to the old Warehouse District—the Arts District—marks its complete transformation in the postindustrial era.

Art in New Orleans Today

New Orleans is experiencing a great burst of creativity in the visual arts. The magic mix of paradoxically unfavorable economics and a favorable attitude toward contemporary art is drawing new artists here and keeping home-grown artists from moving away. The economic paradox is that the building abandonment unfortunately epidemic in contemporary New Orleans is good for artists, especially young artists. Most artists are poor, and rising real estate values in New York City and San Francisco, for

**Poydras Street
High-rise Spine**

example, make it impossible for artists to find cheap studio space there. Here the evacuation of the city by warehousing and industry has freed up acres of old buildings with few competing demands for the space. In many cases, what look like abandoned or boarded-up buildings from the outside are actually low-rent artist's studios. The abandonment of neighborhood corner retail space all over the city (as even the poor now shop by car out on the highways) has freed up more space for impecunious artists.

The second force that drives the flourishing art scene in the Crescent City today is psychological and intangible. However hard it is to define—and impossible as it is to quantify—there is an artistic dimension to New Orleanian culture. Notice the way women, both rich and poor, dress in this city. New Orleans ladies, you quickly discover, love color, bold color, especially *iridescent* color; they like modern designs, be they large-scale florals or abstractions. Carnival and Mardi Gras, no doubt, account for this distinctive taste. Every year New Orleanians look forward to the momentary splendor of bravura displays of fantasy, form, and rich color; call it Art. Everyone here is annually exposed to a riot of fabulous mythologies, elaborately worked-out themes, and wild artistic make-believe—in gorgeous floats that shimmer and shake, in elaborate, fantastic costumes, and in mysterious-yet-communicative masks. It is bred into the bone that beautiful things bring joy to life. New Orleans' identity is bound up with the arts, music especially, then food, and for many others, the visual arts as well.

Contemporary artists gravitate toward this city, drawn by its deep irrational streak and passion for symbolism and color. It mirrors their own vision of the world, a vision that would short-circuit linear thinking with visual knowledge immediately absorbed. Artists want to be appreciated, and New Orleans, unlike many richer cities (and certainly unlike conformist suburbia), offers appreciation in abundance. In general, people here value artists and art not for their "investment value" but for the pleasure of having beautiful things surrounding them everyday. While it is a slender pillar that supports the fine arts and that buys in the pricey Julia Street galleries, the taste of the New Orleanians who *do* buy art is open and adventurous. They are aware that this city has a long tradition of fine painters, so collectors keep looking. A strong Jewish community, and a vibrant gay world, also exist here, and in Western culture both flourish where the arts are moving ahead. Savvy visitors from elsewhere come here to buy art at prices that are comparatively low. Visitors should take the time not just to see our museums of past artists but to venture into the contemporary art galleries to experience what this old-yet-ever-new culture is producing today.

❶   Poydras Street High-rise Spine, *1960s and later*
In the 1960s New Orleans remade itself by widening Poydras Street to create an appropriate setting for modern high-rises. The construction of white, severely rectangular One Shell Square on the corner of Poydras and St. Charles in 1972 brought the city-deadening tower-in-a-plaza concept to New Orleans. At fifty-one stories, it remains the tallest building in the city. Fortunately, the new high-rise spine skirted the

older financial district built before 1930 (see Tour 6). Contemporary Poydras is anchored by the gargantuan Louisiana Superdome, erected in 1975 (see page 68). Most of the new office towers along "Texas on Poydras" were built for oil companies during the great oil and gas boom that peaked in 1982. During the go-go years, some thirty-five major oil companies occupied 30 percent of the downtown's prime space. Among them were Amoco, Exxon, Mobil, Chevron, Getty, Gulf, Texaco, and Shell. When the bust came in 1985 and oil plunged from $28 to $15 a barrel, plans for new buildings stopped. The parking lots and available building sites along unfinished Poydras are a marker of the long recession in the "oil patch."

Piazza d'Italia
Poydras and Tchoupitoulas Streets

American Italian Museum
537 S. Peters Street, between Poydras and Lafayette; open Wednesday, Thursday, and Friday, 10 A.M. to 4 P.M.; free; 522-7294

Martzell, Lamothe & Gay Building
338 Lafayette Mall, at Tchoupitoulas

Shriver-Edisen Building
322–36 Lafayette Mall

Lafayette Mall

2 Piazza d'Italia / Postmodern Fountain, *1978, Charles W. Moore and August Perez and Associates*
This now-derelict work is the most important piece of contemporary design in New Orleans. When it opened in 1979, it was hailed by architecture critic Paul Goldberger as the "most significant new urban plaza any American city has erected in years." The Piazza d'Italia today is a surreal ruin. Built to honor the city's Italian American community, the $1.6 million plaza and its fountain were the path-breaking design of Los Angeles architect Charles W. Moore, and it helped launch postmodern architecture. Moore's smiling face adorns what were once working water spouts. This neon-lit stage set made great photographs, but it didn't last.

You can make a detour around the corner to the **American Italian Museum** on S. Peters Street.

3 *View Up Commerce Street*
Narrow, slightly curving Commerce Street is lined with antebellum warehouses and industrial structures from the 1840s and 1850s. The **Martzell, Lamothe & Gay Building,** from about 1850, and the **Shriver-Edisen Building** of 1844 (built by John Randolph Pikes, builder, and restored in 1981 by Koch and Wilson) are good examples of this wave of building.

4 Lafayette Mall, *1984, Charles Caplinger Planners, landscape architect*
The Lafayette Mall was envisioned as a pedestrian connector from the Superdome, through the courts complex at Lafayette Square, to the riverfront. As things turned out, the lakeside end of the mall ends at the Hyatt Hotel, and the riverside ends at the Hilton Hotel. You will see very few pedestrians here, just tightly wound lawyers jogging at lunchtime.

United States Court of
Appeals
600 Camp Street

United States Courthouse
and Hale Boggs Federal
Building
555 N. Maestri Place

Lafayette Square /
Faubourg St. Mary

⑤   Old Post Office / United States Court of Appeals, Fifth District,
1914, Hale and Rodgers; 1962 conversion into courthouse
roof sculptures*, 1914, Daniel Chester French*

This characteristic Beaux Arts palazzo was erected in 1914 for the main branch of the United States Post Office. Hale and Rodgers took various textbook Italian Renaissance elements and combined them in this very official-looking monument. The building's best features are the hard-to-see twenty-five-foot-high copper **sculptures** on the four corners of the roof. Each consists of an open-work globe supported by four female figures representing history, industry, commerce, and the arts; the four sculptures are attributed to Daniel Chester French.

⑥   United States Courthouse and Hale Boggs Federal Building*, 1976, August Perez and Associates with Mathes, Bergman, and Associates*
Out of There, *1974, Clement Meadmore*

This is a typical example of cold, 1970s institutional architecture set in a sterile, unpeopled "plaza" and garnished with a cryptic, black steel public sculpture.

⑦   Lafayette Square / Faubourg St. Mary*, 1788, Carlos Laveau Trudeau, surveyor*
Benjamin Franklin, *1926, unknown sculptor*
Henry Clay, *1860, Joel Tanner Hart*
John McDonogh, *1898, Attilio Piccirilli*

The homeless frequent leafy Lafayette Square in "Federal Land," the cluster of courts, offices, and banking here that is the epicenter of national power in New Orleans. The square was laid out by Spanish surveyor Carlos Trudeau in 1788 and originally named Place Gravier in honor of the subdividers of this land. The city gained possession of it in 1822. It was renamed for General Lafayette in 1825 on the occasion of his visit to the Crescent City. The streets that frame it to the north and south are named North and South Maestri Place after Robert S. Maestri, who served as mayor from 1936 to 1946. Three bronze statues stand in the square. A statue of **Benjamin Franklin** faces Camp Street. The central statue of **Henry Clay,** hidden in the trees, was erected in 1860 and is the work of Kentucky sculptor Joel Tanner Hart. It originally stood in the Canal Street neutral ground, at St. Charles Street, and was the symbolic center of the old city. Clay was a frequent visitor to New Orleans; his daughter had married a Louisianian. The erection of this statue testifies to the conservative Whig political sentiment of elite New Orleans just before the Civil War. The statue was moved to the park in 1901 to facilitate traffic movement on Canal Street. A graceful 1898 statue of **John McDonogh** faces St. Charles Street and Gallier Hall. It was sculpted in New York by Attilio Piccirilli and consists of a bronze bust on a pedestal with a young girl and boy offering floral tributes. McDonogh came to New Orleans from Baltimore as a young man and made a fortune in business and real estate. Never married, he left his fortune for the erection of free schools in Baltimore and New Orleans. For many years it was the custom for the school children of the city to bring flowers to this monument on the first Friday in

May; white children came in the morning and black children came in the afternoon.

　　　　　　Near the center of the park is the granite block of the U.S. Geological Survey monument that marks latitude 29° 51′ 05″ and longitude 90° 04′ 09″. This places New Orleans at about the same latitude as the Great Pyramids in Egypt.

Gallier Hall
545 St. Charles Avenue

Federal Reserve Bank
525 St. Charles Avenue

Louisiana Bar Center
603 St. Charles Avenue

8　　**Gallier Hall / Old City Hall,** *1845–53, James Gallier, Sr.*
　　　bas-reliefs in pediment, *Robert A. Launitz*
　　　The Parade Paused, 1990, George Dureau

Built as the city hall for the Second Municipality when culturally irreconcilable New Orleans was divided into three municipalities between 1836 and 1852, Gallier Hall is one of the finest Greek Revival buildings in the South. It was designed by James Gallier, Sr., in 1845 and dedicated in 1853. The building became the city hall for the reunited, American-dominated city and served that function until the construction of the new International-style City Hall on Loyola Avenue in 1956. At that time the building was renamed Gallier Hall, and it is now used as a place for civic receptions. The mayor reviews the Mardi Gras parades from temporary grandstands erected on its steps. Gallier Hall is distinguished by a monumental portico supported by ten white marble Ionic columns adapted from the north porch of the Erechtheum on the Acropolis in Athens. The building's basement and steps are of gray Quincy granite. In the pediment is a **bas-relief** group sculpted by Robert A. Launitz showing blindfolded Justice attended by Liberty (holding the Phrygian cap to the left) and Commerce (with a sugar hogshead, cotton bale, box, and trunk to the right). Acroteria top the triangular pediment, and anthemion (honeysuckle) ornament the cornice. Two bronze male and female figures brandishing lamps flank the door; both strike languid, seductive poses. The central door is monumental. Inside Ballroom A, the principal reception room to the right of the central hall, is a mural by George Dureau depicting a Carnival parade and entitled *The Parade Paused.*

9　　**Federal Reserve Bank,** *1966, Toombs, Amisano & Wells*

To the right of Gallier Hall is the modern local branch of the Federal Reserve Bank of Atlanta. Unusual concrete "awnings" project over its windows. Its fence protects a sliver of a public garden with a few stone benches. It is a perfect microcosm of a New Orleans garden shaded by oaks and enlivened by splashy palmettos.

10　　**Louisiana Bar Center / Old Soulé Commercial College,** *1902*

The red brick and white terra-cotta trim building to the left of Gallier Hall was built in 1902 to house the Soulé Commercial College and Literary Institute. It originally boasted a clock tower over its front entrance. Private schools were important institutions in nineteenth-century New Orleans, and they drew students from all over the

607–9 St. Charles Avenue

Lafayette Hotel
600 St. Charles Avenue;
524-4441

**F. Edward Hebert Federal
Building**
600 S. Maestri Place

PJ's Coffee & Tea Cafe
*644 Camp Street, at
Girod; 529-3658*

**#14 St. Patrick's Roman
Catholic Church**
*720 Camp Street; masses
on Sunday at 8:30, 9:30
(Latin mass), 11 A.M., and
12:15 P.M.; weekdays
11:30 A.M. and noon;
Saturday at 3:45 and
5 P.M.; 525-4413*

South and the Caribbean basin. Next door is **607–9 St. Charles Avenue,** an 1853 Greek Revival town house built by Edward Gotthiel.

11   Lafayette Hotel, *1916, S. S. Labouisse*
This buff brick hotel is a sophisticated Edwardian design with subtle New Orleanian touches such as its understated ironwork inspired by French Quarter Spanish iron. It represents a high point in urban design in the United States, when buildings knew how to be modern and bigger and yet mesh with the city of which they are an organic part. It was originally an apartment hotel built for Adam Wirth.

12   F. Edward Hébert Federal Building, *1939, Louis A. Simon, supervising architect, Howard L. Cheney, consulting architect*
     Cutting Sugar Cane, *1941, Armin Scheler*
     Flood Control, *1941, Karl Lang*
This limestone-clad building is a fine piece of underappreciated federal architecture. This modern building with its cleanly cut out windows is the perfect foil for the two fine bas reliefs at the ends of its facade. Armin Scheler's **Cutting Sugar Cane** pays homage to the back-breaking labor of harvesting cane, and Karl Lang's **Flood Control** is a muscular monument to public works and a beneficent government.

13   PJ's Coffee & Tea Cafe, *1890s*
This gay Victorian corner building has recently been restored as a welcome coffeehouse.

14   St. Patrick's Roman Catholic Church, *1838–39, Charles and James Dakin, completed by James Gallier, Sr.*
     murals, *1840, Leon Pomarede*
English-speaking Irish immigrants formed their own parish outside the French Quarter in 1833, the second Roman Catholic parish in the city. Its first home was a simple wooden chapel on this site, but in 1837 the parish commissioned James and Charles Dakin to design a grand church in the "Pointed Style of the Second Period of Ecclesiastical Architecture." Inspired by York Minster Cathedral, the brick church was to have a tower 185 feet high, the tallest in New Orleans. But when the church walls were up two-thirds of the way, a dispute broke out between the architect and the client. The result was the dismissal of the Dakins and the engagement of James Gallier, Sr., to simplify the plans and complete the church. Gallier designed the ornate Gothic Revival altar capped by elaborate vaulting with inset stained-glass panels. The present roughcast stucco weatherproofing on the outside of the church replaced a smooth stucco

finish scored and painted to look like stone. St. Patrick's celebrates a Tridentine Latin mass at 9:30 A.M. each Sunday and has attracted loyal parishioners from other parts of the city. Next door is **St. Patrick's Rectory,** a much-altered Italianate building designed by Henry Howard and built in 1874.

⑮　748 Camp Street, *1840s; 1994 conversion*
This vintage red-brick commercial building, built in the 1840s, became Cosimo Matassa's Recording Studio in the 1960s and 1970s. Among the artists who recorded here were Little Richard, Fats Domino, Irma Thomas, Professor Longhair, and Dr. John. From 1994 through 1997 this was the location of Doug's Place, a restaurant which served New Orleans food and exhibited Southern folk art. Upstairs is the **New Orleans Zen Temple.**

⑯　Lighthouse Glass, *1923*
Built as the Lighthouse for the Blind in 1923, this work of "programmatic" architecture was recently transformed into a glass studio occasionally open to the public. It also showcases art works in fabric, metal, and wood.

⑰　"The Thirteen Sisters" / Preservation Resource Center, *1833, Alexander Thompson Wood*
This unusual, intact row of thirteen red-brick row houses is one of the best examples of Anglo-American architecture of its period in New Orleans. These are the kinds of Federal-style buildings that English-speaking newcomers favored when they began to build outside the Creole French Quarter. Each one of these houses has a slave dependency behind it, one of which can be clearly seen from Camp and Julia Streets. Numbers 600 and 604 have their original doorways with delicate fan light transoms. Architect Henry Hobson Richardson lived in one of these town houses as a child. When a boarding house opened in the house at the St. Charles Avenue end, the row lost its cachet. Eventually rooming houses and brothels filled the déclassé row. An automobile repair shop now occupies the last house in the group.

　　In 1981, the **Preservation Resource Center** restored 604 Julia Street, and art galleries have begun filtering into the other buildings. At the PRC office you can inquire about historic house tours and other local preservation programs. The PRC is active in working to bring back New Orleans neighborhoods through its Operation Comeback and Live in a Landmark programs. It sponsors a line of furniture, fabrics, rugs, wallpaper, et cetera, inspired by historic New Orleans furnishings and decorative arts.

St. Patrick's Rectory
724 Camp Street

748 Camp Street

New Orleans Zen Temple
748 Camp Street, upstairs; 523-1213

Lighthouse Glass
743 Camp Street; 529-4494

"The Thirteen Sisters"
600–648 Julia Street

Preservation Resource Center
604 Julia Street; 581-7032

Gallery of Southern Photographers
608 Julia Street;
529-9811

Marguerite Oestreicher Fine Arts
626 Julia Street;
581-9253

Wyndy Morehead Fine Arts
603 Julia Street;
568-9754

Ariodante Contemporary Craft Gallery
535 Julia Street;
524-3233

Galerie Simonne Stern
518 Julia Street;
529-1118

New Orleans Auction Galleries
801 Magazine Street, at Julia; phone for dates of auctions; 566-1849

New Orleans School of Glassworks
727 Magazine Street;
529-7277

Heriard-Cimino Gallery
440 Julia Street;
525-7300

Arthur Roger Gallery
432 Julia Street;
522-1999

Sylvia Schmidt Gallery
400A Julia Street;
522-2000

Le Mieux Galleries
332 Julia Street;
522-5988

⑱   Julia Street's Gallery Row

Julia Street from about Camp to Commerce Streets is the heart of New Orleans' contemporary art galleries. Changing exhibitions here let you see some of the best new art, both regional and national; exploring these serene spaces is highly recommended. The street also has one of the best auction houses in the region and the Louisiana Children's Museum.

Following is a list of some of the galleries and shops you'll find in this area:

- **Gallery of Southern Photographers** In one of the "Thirteen Sisters"; fine Southern photography.
- **Marguerite Oestreicher Fine Arts** Contemporary paintings, sculpture, and prints.
- **Wyndy Morehead Fine Arts** Contemporary paintings, drawings, prints, sculpture, ceramics, and photographs.
- **Ariodante Contemporary Craft Gallery** Furniture, glass, ceramics, jewelry, and decorative objects.
- **Galerie Simonne Stern** Contemporary paintings, sculpture, and prints.
- **New Orleans Auction Galleries** A great place on Saturday mornings during auctions. Features antique estate property of all kinds: furniture, paintings, silver, porcelains, crystal, and Oriental rugs. Gallery on second floor.
- **New Orleans School of Glassworks** Contemporary works in glass from various artists; glassworking demonstrations in the rear studio.
- **Heriard-Cimino Gallery** Contemporary art.
- **Arthur Roger Gallery** Contemporary paintings, sculpture, photographs, and works on paper. The gallery was designed by Bond & Lambert.
- **Sylvia Schmidt Gallery** Contemporary paintings, sculpture, drawings, watercolors, photographs, and prints.
- **Le Mieux Galleries** Contemporary arts, crafts, and custom framing.
- **Christopher Maier Furniture Design** Working studio and showroom for fine wood furniture of original design with references to classical and ancient art and architecture.
- **Still-Zinsel Contemporary Fine Art** Contemporary paintings, sculpture, photography, and works on paper.

⑲   Louisiana Children's Museum, *1861; 1994, Leonard Salvato, McDonald Architects*
Built for the Loubat family of New York City in 1861 and long known as the Great Western Warehouse, this is now a participatory museum for children and their families. It describes itself as "Energetic learning and electrifying fun for kids of all ages. With more than 45,000 square feet of interactive exhibitry, it is *not* your ordinary playhouse!"

⑳   *Detour*:
Leeds Iron Foundry, *1852, Gallier, Turpin, and Company*
James Gallier, Jr., designed this unusual Gothic Revival commercial building for the Leeds Iron Foundry in 1852. It is built of brick with cast-iron elements probably produced by the foundry. Charles J. Leeds served as mayor of New Orleans from 1874 to 1876. His monumental cast-iron tomb in Cypress Grove Cemetery is notable (see page 345). Across Tchoupitoulas Street is a grassy neutral ground with oak trees flanked by North and South Diamond Streets. This was originally the site of St. Mary's Market, an open-air marketplace that served the uptown American sector.

㉑   Contemporary Arts Center, *1906, Stone Brothers; 1990 conversion by Stephen Bingler and Concordia Architects*
The Contemporary Arts Center (CAC) is a public, nonprofit multidisciplinary institution offering year-round visual arts exhibitions, theatrical productions, concerts, and education programs for all ages. This handsome 1906 red-brick warehouse was converted for the CAC and opened in 1990. While architect Stephen Bingler left the exterior intact, he radically remodeled the interior by removing three levels of floors in the front section of the building to create a four-story atrium.

㉒   Confederate Museum / Louisiana Historical Association, *1891, Sully and Toledano; 1908, Stone Brothers, portico*
The Lee Monument of 1884, this old-fashioned museum, and the grand funerary monuments in Metairie and Greenwood Cemeteries (see Tour 11) commemorate the "lost cause" in New Orleans. Memorial Hall, as this building is properly called, was the gift of Frank T. Howard in memory of his father, Charles T. Howard. It was designed by Thomas Sully and erected of pressed brick in 1891 to harmonize with the red sandstone of the former Howard Library next door. In 1908 the Stone Brothers added the elaborate Richardsonian portico and octagonal tower, which are trimmed with red terra-cotta decoration. The

Christopher Maier Furniture Design
329 Julia Street;
586-9079

Still-Zinsel Contemporary Fine Art
328 Julia Street;
588-9999

Louisiana Children's Museum
420 Julia Street; Thursday to Saturday 9:30 A.M. to 5 P.M., Sunday noon to 5 P.M., Monday in summer 9:30 A.M. to 5 P.M.; closed major holidays; museum store; $5 for adults and children; 523-1357

Leeds Iron Foundry
923 Tchoupitoulas Street

Contemporary Arts Center
900 Camp Street, at St. Joseph; gallery open Monday through Saturday 10 A.M. to 5 P.M.; admission free on Thursday; open Sunday 11 A.M. to 3 P.M.; program information 523-1216; box office 528-3800

Confederate Museum / Louisiana Historical Association
929 Camp Street; open Monday to Saturday 10 A.M. to 4 P.M.; small fee; 523-4522

**Ogden Museum of
Southern Art / University of
New Orleans**
*615 Howard Avenue;
phone for hours;
539-9600*

large iron cannon mounted in front of the building is an eight-inch Columbiad and once defended Mobile, Alabama. Inside is a cypress timber hall with exposed ceiling beams. Jefferson Davis lay in state here in 1893 before his remains were moved to Richmond, Virginia. The building is operated by the Louisiana Historical Association, which publishes the quarterly *Louisiana History*. The exhibits here are mostly the donations of Louisiana veterans or their families and include Confederate uniforms, battle flags, and many swords and guns.

㉓   Ogden Museum of Southern Art / Taylor Library / University of New Orleans, *1889, Shepley, Rutan, and Coolidge to designs by H. H. Richardson; 1998, restoration and new building, Concordia + Errol Barron / Michael Toups Architects*
This landmark Massachusetts red sandstone library was erected in 1889 by Mrs. Annie Howard Parrott as a memorial to her father, Charles T. Howard, the head of the Louisiana Lottery Company. It was designed by Louisiana-born Henry Hobson Richardson. Educated at the Ecole des Beaux Arts in Paris, Richardson established his architectural practice outside Boston. He created a stone architecture inspired by the Romanesque buildings he had seen in the south of France. This is his only work in his native region. Richardson died in 1886 at the age of forty-eight, after the design of this building but before its construction. It was completed by his successor firm, Shepley, Rutan, and Coolidge.

The Howard Street facade is asymmetrical, with a polygonal tower to the left, a semicircular arch at the entrance, and a long horizontal wing to the right with a band of windows separated by engaged, clustered columns. Fortresslike slits pierce the rugged stone walls. The Lee Circle end of the library is rounded and has steep-gabled wall dormers capped by stone finials; the reading room was in this end of the building, and the book stacks were at the Camp Street end. A steeply pitched red tile roof caps this powerful architectural composition. The Howard Library books were moved to Tulane University in 1941 to create the Howard-Tilton Library on the Tulane campus. The old library's richly paneled oak interior was painted over when the building became a radio station, and later, lawyers' offices. This jewel was purchased by oil man Patrick F. Taylor, who restored the great oak-beamed rotunda in the renamed Taylor Library.

New Orleanian Roger H. Ogden donated his outstanding collection of Southern art to the University of New Orleans Foundation in order to create the **UNO Ogden Museum of Southern Art** here. The museum is scheduled to open in 1999 and will include forty-thousand-square-foot Stephen Goldring Hall, a modern gallery facing Camp Street. Through exhibitions from the permanent collection, changing exhibitions, docent tours, lectures, classes, film and video programs, graduate internships, and fellowships in American art history and arts administration, and as a multidisciplinary resource for scholars and students, this teaching museum will explore the evolution of visual arts in the South.

㉔   Lee Circle and Lee Monument, *1884, Alexander Doyle, sculptor; John Roy, architect*

Lee Circle was laid out by city surveyor Barthélémy Lafon in 1806 and originally named Place du Tivoli. Lafon named what is now St. Charles Avenue the Cours du Nayades, the route of the river nymphs. (The name was changed in 1852.) He named nearby streets for the nine muses, three graces, and twenty-four Greek gods and demigods. Throughout the first half of the nineteenth century

the circle was bare. Union troops camped here during the occupation of the city. In the post–Civil War years, traveling circuses performed here. In 1870, the year of Lee's death, the Robert E. Lee Monumental Association was organized in New Orleans. In 1876, young New York sculptor Alexander Doyle was commissioned to create this bronze statue of Lee; architect John Roy designed the column. The sixteen-and-a-half-foot-tall statue of the general with his arms crossed stands atop a fluted Doric column carved from white Tennessee marble. The sixty-foot column stands on a four-step pyramidal base of Georgia granite; the handsome bronze urns with the sago palms were added in 1930.

㉕   K&B Plaza / Virlane Foundation Outdoor Sculpture Collection, *1963, Skidmore, Owings, and Merrill*

   The Mississippi, *1963, Isamu Noguchi*

Built for the John Hancock Mutual Life Insurance Company in 1963 and designed by the Chicago office of Skidmore, Owings, and Merrill, this building at 1055 St. Charles Avenue brought modern architecture to New Orleans. The white, precast concrete building has a Le Corbusier–inspired *brise soleil* facade, which, unusual for this style in America, is actually appropriate in this sunny climate. The architects commissioned Isamu Noguchi to create the fountain, consisting of a fluted granite column supporting a crescent and entitled *The Mississippi.* In 1973 the building became the headquarters of the K&B drugstore chain. Sydney Bestoff has assembled a large collection of contemporary sculpture on the building's elevated plaza. The art inside the building can be seen by appointment. The building occupies the site of the lost Beaux Arts New Orleans Public Library, by Allison Owen, which stood here from 1908 to 1960.

Continuation: Streetcar Connections

The St. Charles Avenue streetcar stops in front of the K&B Plaza and can take you to the Garden District or St. Charles Avenue uptown; or, cross the tracks to take the car headed toward the CBD, Canal Street, and the French Quarter.

The Garden District was laid out in 1833 as an early garden suburb and is distinguished by an outstanding cluster of mansions overshadowed by great live oaks. This garden is on the downtown-lakeside corner of Second and Chestnut Streets.

Tour 8

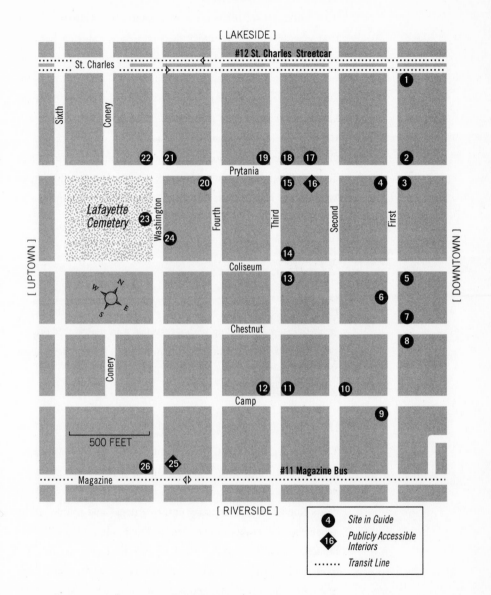

[LAKESIDE]

#12 St. Charles Streetcar

St. Charles

Sixth

Conery

①

②

Prytania

㉒ ㉑ ⑲ ⑱ ⑰

⑳ ⑮ ⑯ ④ ③

First

Second

Third

Fourth

Washington

Lafayette
Cemetery

㉓ ⑭

㉔

[UPTOWN]

Coliseum

⑬

⑤

⑥

⑦

N
W E
S

Chestnut

⑧

Conery

⑫ ⑪ ⑩

Camp

⑨

500 FEET

㉖ ㉕

#11 Magazine Bus

Magazine

[RIVERSIDE]

[DOWNTOWN]

④ Site in Guide

⑯ Publicly Accessible
Interiors

...... Transit Line

What This Tour Covers

This walk surveys the elegant, oak-embowered Garden District that was developed by the city's Anglo-American rich between about 1840 and 1873. This is still an elite residential neighborhood, and there is only one house museum you may visit here, the Davis House, run by the Women's Guild of the New Orleans Opera Association (see page 283). The walk ends at Lafayette Cemetery and then returns up Washington Avenue to the St. Charles Avenue streetcar, where you can continue uptown (see Tour 9). Shoppers may want to walk in the other direction down Washington to catch the Magazine Street bus going uptown to Nashville Avenue (see Tour 10).

Preliminaries

**BEST TIMES TO
DO THIS TOUR**

Early morning is the best time to do this walk, ending with a relaxing, and reasonably priced, fine lunch at Commander's Palace Restaurant or a stop at PJ's Coffee in the Rink.

Mardi Gras Parades on St. Charles Avenue

The lower section of St. Charles Avenue from Napoleon Avenue to Canal Street downtown is the triumphal processional route for many of the city's most famous Carnival parades. The gorgeous floats emerge from their secret uptown "dens" and roll down the avenue to the shouts of the throng. For months afterward the branches of the live oaks overhanging the street are randomly festooned with strings of brightly colored plastic beads. Mardi Gras day is St. Charles Avenue's grandest moment, when fantasy rules and even the twenty-four-hours-a-day streetcars are shut down so that Rex can glory in the annual adulation of his subjects.

Parking

Street parking is not a problem in the Garden District, but be sure to hide all valuables and to lock your car.

Transit

The historic St. Charles Avenue streetcar connects Canal Street with Uptown, passing the Garden District along the way; alight at St. Charles Avenue and First Street to begin the walk. The tour ends at Magazine Street where the #11 Magazine bus can take you farther uptown for shopping (see Tour 10), or back downtown through the Arts District and the CBD to Canal Street.

Restaurants

This walk ends with lunch at **Commander's Palace,** one of the city's best restaurants, and the only one in the Garden District. **PJ's Coffee & Tea Cafe** in the Rink at the end of this walk is good for light refreshments, and **Joey K's Restaurant and Bar** has local fare.

Shopping

After seeing the Garden District and perhaps stopping at the **Garden District Book Shop,** a fine general bookstore with items of local interest, you can walk to Magazine Street and catch the #11 Magazine Street bus up to Nashville Avenue to walk back down that rich cluster of New Orleans shops (see Tour 10).

Guided Tours

If you would like to take a guided tour through the Garden District, there are several that are interesting. The French Quarter Unit of the **Jean Lafitte National Historical Park** offers a free, two-hour, two-mile, ranger-led "Faubourg Promenade" walking tour of the Garden District. The Garden District Association has led annual **spring garden tours** of private gardens in the District since May 1994. If you are in New Orleans during the holidays, the Preservation Resource Center hosts a **holiday house tour** of (often) uptown homes decorated for Christmas. And the novelist **Anne**

Commander's Palace Restaurant
1403 Washington Avenue, at Coliseum; 899-8231

PJ's Coffee & Tea Cafe
In the Rink at 2717 Prytania Street, at Washington; 899-0335

Joey K's Restaurant and Bar
3001 Magazine Street, at Seventh; 891-0997

Garden District Book Shop
In the Rink at 2717 Prytania Street, at Washington; 895-2266

Jean Lafitte National Historical Park Walks
916 N. Peters Street; information and reservations, 589-2636

Spring Garden Tours
For information, write to The Garden District Association, P. O. Box 50836, N.O., 70150-0836; 525-7608

Holiday House Tours
For information, contact the Preservation Resource Center at 604 Julia Street, N.O., 70130; 581-7032

Anne Rice Tours
All tours begin at 2524 St. Charles Avenue; 888-SEE-RICE

Christ Church Episcopal Cathedral
2919 St. Charles Avenue, at Sixth Street; Choral Eucharist Sunday at 11 A.M.; 895-6602

Trinity Episcopal Church
1329 Jackson Avenue, at Coliseum Street; Eucharist Sunday at 8, 10:30 A.M., and 6 P.M.; 522-0276

St. Mary's Assumption Chapel
1516 Jackson Avenue, near Prytania; weekday masses at 7 A.M.; Saturday at 4 P.M.; Sunday at 10 A.M.; on major feast days mass is at St. Mary's Assumption Church, see page 329; 522-6748

Rice offers "A Stroll with the Mayfair Witches" tour daily; bus tours of areas outside the Garden District are also available.

Historic Churches

Two historic Episcopalian churches border the Garden District, **Christ Church Episcopal Cathedral** and **Trinity Episcopal Church**. Both are architecturally noteworthy and also conduct Sunday services and musical programs visitors may wish to attend. Christ Church is the pioneer Protestant congregation in New Orleans and was organized in 1805 as an offshoot of the diocese of New York. Trinity Church was organized in 1847 and does a lot of social outreach. Roman Catholics have recently moved an 1844 frame chapel to Jackson Avenue, near Prytania. The vernacular Gothic building was restored and extended by Barry Fox Associates in 1997 for **St. Mary's Assumption Chapel.**

Introduction: Great Antebellum Houses in an Early Garden Suburb

> There are some very elegant and attractive looking residences in the immediate vicinity of the town. They are surrounded, for the most part, by gardens, rich with the perfume of the magnolia, and shaded with orange groves and a great variety of other trees. These houses are generally inhabited by the permanent residents of the place, either those who have been born in Louisiana or immigrants into the State, who have been long enough within the sedgy limits of the Delta to be thoroughly acclimated.
>
> —Alex Mackay, *The Western World,* 1847

> Their dance cards were filled a hundred years ago.
>
> —A Texan quoted in
> Carol Flake's *New Orleans,* 1994

The Garden District consists of sixty-six blocks bounded by St. Charles Avenue, Magazine Street, and Jackson and Louisiana Avenues. It is memorable for its dark oaks and fine houses painted soft pastel colors with white trim. In an inverse sign of the power, social cohesion, and taste of its residents, the Garden District is *not* a city land-mark district, though it is listed on the National Register of Historic Places. The lush and still socially correct Garden District was created uptown of the business district in the 1840s and 1850s in the palmy days when Anglo-American New Orleans had an elite in flux. The neighborhood has found its social and architectural historian in S. Frederick Starr, whose *Southern Comfort* (1989) remains the best source on the first one hundred years of this enclave. He described the neighborhood as "a metaphor that embraced notions of high economic status, political and social identity, a gracious style of life, and architectural opulence." Established before the Civil War by new money, it passed through painful changes during and right after the war and then crystalized in the late nineteenth and early twentieth centuries as *the* bastion of *comme il faut.*

The Garden District was the third location of Anglo-American elite residence in American New Orleans. Though there were English-speaking house-holders in the old French Quarter above St. Louis Street, it was Faubourg St. Mary (today the Central Business District) that first became the distinctively "American district." There, between Canal Street and Howard Avenue, prosperous merchants built multistory, red-brick row houses. Except for their rear dependencies for the household slaves, they were just like the row houses of Philadelphia and other north-eastern cities. Today, the Thirteen Sisters of 1832–33 on Julia Street (see page 263) are the best surviving monument of that first wave of American building. As business boomed, commerce pushed housing farther uptown. Successful merchants moved to the next area upriver between Howard Avenue and Felicity Street in the 1830s and

1840s. Now dubbed the Lower Garden District, the streets around Coliseum and Annunciation Squares became the second locus of prestigious Anglo-American housing (see page 330). But this area proved to be too small to house the burgeoning Anglo-American elite, and so the next zone upriver, the Garden District, attracted the even wealthier merchantile elite of the booming cotton capital. By 1840 the population of New Orleans had exploded to 102,193, making her the nation's fourth-largest city and the second-most active harbor. It was a polyglot port city that drew immigrants from New England, the upriver border states, and Europe. As the old city became more congested, the wealthy were propelled from the noisy core to the quiet periphery. There they sought to create a healthful retreat—a garden suburb—removed from the jarring social conflict and polluted conditions of the expanding city.

The land that became the Garden District had been bought by New England-born Samuel Jarvis Peters and three Yankee partners in 1832 from Celeste Philippe Marigny Livaudais, the estranged wife of planter Jacques François Esnould de Livaudais. She promptly removed to a French chateau. The partners sank a half million dollars into the former sugar plantation. They engaged surveyor Benjamin Buisson to lay out a simple grid of streets and sold off blocks and lots to other, smaller real estate speculators. Buisson's plan divided each block into only four large, square lots, rather than the twelve narrow rectangular lots of the French Quarter blocks. This invited the construction of large houses. No central squares or important axial streets were reserved in the speculator-designed plan; only quiet Lafayette Cemetery was reserved near the neighborhood's center. Peters gave the suburban subdivision numbered streets from first to ninth (but with no fifth, here Washington Avenue), like those in Philadelphia. The Anglo-American suburb was incorporated as the independent City of Lafayette in 1834, setting it apart from Creole and immigrant New Orleans. The section of the City of Lafayette along Tchoupitoulas Street near the river became the busiest port on the Mississippi for the thousands of flatboats that floated down the Ohio and Mississippi Rivers laden with corn, whiskey, hay, flour, bacon, tobacco, coal, timber, cattle, sheep, and hogs—and Anglo-Americans. Stockyards and slaughterhouses sprang up next to the docks. The nearby blocks were built up with small frame houses for those who worked on the wharfs and in the nearby tallow, soap, and leather industries. Many of these workers were German or Irish immigrants and eventually this area got to be known as the Irish Channel. It was a noisy, tough, working-class neighborhood (see page 320).

The back of the new river-facing City of Lafayette between Magazine Street and what is now St. Charles Avenue, the Garden District, was slower to develop. The economic collapse that followed the banking panic of 1837 ended the flush times in the Mississippi valley, and little building took place on Buisson's large lots. The same economic crisis seriously crippled the old French Creole elite. When good times returned in the 1840s, American merchants dominated the bicultural city. The now-unchallenged English-speaking elite that coalesced in New Orleans in the mid-1840s had a progressive, capitalist mentality. They became the key middlemen between the expanding cotton plantations upriver and the cotton markets in Liverpool, England, and New York City, which fed the "dark satanic mills" of old England and

New England. These English-speaking merchants dominated cotton, credit, whole-saling, shipping, and insurance. While they had important connections inland with the planters, their strongest links were with the money markets in New York City and London. As A. Oakley Hall recorded in his insightful guide *The Manhattaner in New Orleans* (1851):

> "Work, work, work," is the unceasing cry. Every one appears in fear lest day-light should cheat him of a dollar. Except among the Creoles—the aborigines of the place—a man of leisure is a wonder. On [ex]change; on street corner; at the dinner-table; between acts at opera and theater; in the drawing-room; at the ball or soiree; in the sleeping apartments; stocks, cotton, sugar, and money are the liveliest topics.

Most of these go-getters were Northeasterners and border-state men, especially Kentuckians. Other movers and shakers were Englishmen and Irish Protestants with links to the English cotton market. A few Europeans were mixed in with them, but precious few native-born Southerners or Louisiana Creoles. Their strongest ties were not to the city or the region but to Mammon's holy city and its temple-banks. "Yankee" was not a pejorative term in antebellum New Orleans: in fact, Yankees and Brits *were* elite English-speaking New Orleans. Many of these self-made men were upright Presbyterians, not genteel Episcopalians; exceedingly few were Roman Catholics. Politically, they were conservative Whigs in an artisans' Democratic city. They favored a strong national government, protections for private property and banks, and high tariffs. Their national loyalties were to be tested during the Civil War.

The Creole *versus* American tensions in New Orleans resulted in the division of the city into three separate municipalities in 1836 by the Anglo-dominated state legislature. Each municipality had its own board of aldermen and control over district taxes and spending. The Creole French Quarter became the First Municipality, the growing American sector upriver became the Second Municipality (today the Central Business District), and the lightly populated, European immigrant, and truck farming area downriver from Esplanade Avenue became the Third Munici-pality (later called the Creole wards). The improvement-minded Anglo-Americans taxed themselves to modernize their docks, streets, drainage, and policing upriver; the Creoles in the French Quarter downtown did not. Only when English speakers consti-tuted a political majority was the city reunited under a unitary municipal government. To assure a non-Creole majority, the Anglo-dominated state legislature annexed the City of Lafayette (including the Garden District and Irish Channel) to the City of New Orleans in 1852. Though the uptown Whigs were to enjoy only a fleeting moment of political dominance, their municipal consolidation signaled the final shift in power from the tradition-minded Creoles to the progressive Anglo-Americans.

The newly unified city then experienced a building boom in the Garden District that lasted until about 1861. The businessmen who built houses here favored three house types: raised cottages with a central hall, three-bay London plan houses with side halls and double parlors, and five-bay center-hall houses. All enjoyed shady verandas. Their tastes were conservative; they especially favored the Greek Revival style with its dignified columns. As Starr put it: "The self-made Whig oligarchs of the Garden District were more concerned to be of the group than above it." In 1847 the *Daily Delta* noted:

> The rear of Lafayette [the Garden District] is most beautifully situated for dwelling houses. The ground is high and dry and vegetation flourishes in it in amazing luxuriousness. Here are collected many of our wealthy citizens, who have built handsome villas, with gardens and large yards, to be perfect princes of luck and happiness.

By the end of the nineteenth century the Garden District had become a horticultural paradise. Author George Washington Cable, who once lived in the district, noted in *The Amateur Gardener* that there was "sea-green oleander, fifteen feet high and wide." Loquat and orange trees flourished "while high over them towered the date and other palms . . . and the scintillating boughs of the magnolia grandiflora, . . . the giant, winter-bare pecan, and the wide, mossy arms of the vast live-oak." Other trees and plants that flourish here include sweet olive, bananas, boxwood, and azaleas.

The Civil War exposed the split between the national-minded elite and the rest of the New Orleanians. Many Garden District bankers and wholesalers, though they owned household slaves and profited handsomely from the slave-based cotton plantations upriver, were Union men. Some of them removed to the North for the duration of the war. The occupying Federal Army confiscated the houses of some Confederate supporters; they were not that many. Some 94 percent of New Orleans' adult white males took the oath of allegiance to the Union; they had to in order to be able to hold on to their property or to conduct business. After the war, undamaged New Orleans stood as the only intact city in the South. The Union occupiers improved the docks, food markets, and sanitation, and they made an informative map of the city. From 1865 to the panic of 1873 there was a sudden building boom in the Garden District as merchants, reconnected with world markets, erected new dwellings. This wave of building resulted in fancier houses in more diverse architectural styles, including the Italianate and a few French Second Empire piles. In the mid-1870s, elaborate two-story cast-iron galleries were added to existing houses and incorporated in most new ones. This beautiful iron work is one of the memorable features of the district.

The financial crash in 1873 set back New Orleans' economy, and Garden District real estate prices did not recover until about 1890. When business revived, New Orleans had lost her worldwide monopoly of cotton to new cotton producers, including Egypt and Russia. Northern railroads had captured her upper Mississippi valley trade and siphoned it off to booming, building Chicago. The city's port declined dramatically in its relative stature in both exports and imports. Unlike other old port cities, such as Philadelphia and Boston, New Orleans did not shift to manufacturing. Except for a wave of Sicilians, the city stopped attracting fresh

European immigration. Great new manufacturing fortunes were not amassed, and the city's old money clung to the declining, if prestigious, sugar and cotton business. Garden District society now closed its doors to new men except through marriage. Those who prospered in the 1890s and early 1900s built farther uptown along St. Charles Avenue, not in the hermetic Garden District. The Old Guard now elaborated a romantic myth of Southernness, and in 1884 erected a monument to General Robert E. Lee at Lee Circle on St. Charles Avenue as a symbol of a unanimous Confederate sympathy that had never been so simple in fact. Some members of the surviving French Creole elite now married members of high-status Anglo-American families, thereby consolidating New Orleans' thin upper crust. Exclusive men's club life and its offshoot, old-line Carnival organizations, flourished as never before. The period from the 1870s to World War I saw the artistic apogee of Carnival and Mardi Gras. Magnificent public parades with extravagant floats inspired by erudite ancient mythology, and lavish private masked balls with costly gowns, real jewels, and elaborate costumes, flourished as never before or since. Ancestor worship became more and more important.

2344 St. Charles Avenue
At First Street; streetcar stop #14

Like all grand nineteenth-century residential boulevards leading out of old commercial cores, St. Charles Avenue was invaded by commercial uses, especially once the automobile freed the wealthy from public transit and allowed them to remove to suburbs such as Old Metairie. The combination of increased traffic on the avenue as uptown developed, the construction of the elevated highway on the upriver side of Lee Circle, real estate speculation, and then white flight and the dramatic expansion of the Central City ghetto all served to degrade the downtown end of St. Charles Avenue. The post-1973 oil boom caused the demolition of many large old houses on spacious lots facing the avenue for commercial building. The oil bust later emptied some of these buildings and left them derelict. Here and there on lower St. Charles Avenue are large empty lots where historic houses were demolished for speculations that were never financed. Heavy automobile traffic where the principal radial streets cross the avenue has resulted in the destruction of corner mansions and their replacement with intrusive commercial uses. The first apartment house appeared on the avenue about 1908. From the 1950s to the 1970s several large apartments and condominiums were built facing the avenue varying from the marginally acceptable to the unsightly. Upriver of Napoleon Avenue, elegant St. Charles Avenue survives almost intact.

1   **2344 St. Charles Avenue,** *1850s, Greek Revival with additions*
Little is known about the early history of this highly characteristic New Orleans building. It is a fine example of antebellum Greek Revival house design in this city and serves as an appropriate gateway to this walk. Responding directly to the climate, these elegant buildings were built for maximum natural ventilation and protection from the sun and rain. The tall ceilings and floor-to-ceiling windows with their elegantly proportioned panes govern the design. The first- and second-floor galleries provide protected places in which to sit and observe the street. (Porches to the rear and side of many such

Louise S. McGehee School for Girls
2343 Prytania Street, at First

Thomas Toby House
2340 Prytania Street, at First

houses provided private indoor-outdoor areas.) These are the finest flowers of New Orleans house design and were built with either simple Greek Revival or fancier Italianate columns. When built in groups and nestled under ancient oaks, they create memorable, sociable streetscapes. This house has been converted into apartments. Across First Street are two one-story, brick, suburban houses. Built since air-conditioning and television, they are both porchless and inward-looking. Inappropriate in this location, their low height breaks the monumentality of St. Charles Avenue. Harsh night lighting completes the effect.

2 **Louise S. McGehee School for Girls / Bradish Johnson House,** *1872, Lewis E. Reynolds*

This showy pile was New Orleans' first great house in the French Second Empire style. It was built for wealthy, New York–born sugar planter Bradish Johnson during the turbulent Reconstruction era. Paired Corinthian columns support the porch. Its mansard roof is punctuated by a dormer with a round window and trimmed with cast iron cresting along its roofline. The interior of the mansion boasts a glass-domed, curved marble staircase and an early passenger elevator. Architect Lewis E. Reynolds was born in Norwich, New York, and practiced in Cincinnati, Louisville, New York City, and New Orleans. S. Frederick Starr characterized Reynolds as "an American polymath. Only part architect, he was equally a craftsman, pedagogue, philosopher, visionary, Yankee tinkerer, and crank." From 1892 to 1929 this was the home of Walter Denegre. Since 1929 it has housed the Louise S. McGehee School for Girls, which has added a modern classroom building next door. Fine magnolia trees and a mimosa tree flourish in the front garden.

3 **Thomas Toby House,** *circa 1838, Greek Revival plantation-style house; 1855, alterations*

This Greek Revival cottage raised up on brick piers is thought to be the oldest house in the Garden District and dates from about 1838. It recalls upriver Anglo-American plantation houses. Raising the house up off the damp earth protected it from flooding, caught what breezes there might be, and also provided service rooms under the principal floor. Thomas Toby was a Philadelphian and a wheelwright. He lost part of his fortune backing the Texas revolution in the 1830s. In 1855, J. H. Behan, carpenter, and Robert I. Lilly, builder, made extensive improvements to the house. The house still occupies its original quarter-block lot; this minimum lot size guaranteed that only substantial houses would be erected in the Garden District. The dark green plants just inside the fence are commonly called cast-iron plants for their endurance, and they are found in many old Southern gardens.

④ **French Consulate,** *date and architect unknown*
On the uptown-riverside corner of Prytania and First Streets is the orange-brown brick Georgian Revival French Consulate. The architect and date of this fine house are unknown. It became the French Consulate in 1957. Over the Tuscan columns of the entrance portico is the escutcheon of the French Republic.

French Consulate
2406 Prytania Street

Joseph C. Morris House
1331 First Street, at Coliseum

White House
1312 First Street

Joseph Carroll House
1315 First Street

Brevard-Wisdom-Rice House
1239 First Street

⑤ **Joseph C. Morris House,** *1869, Samuel Jamison and James McIntosh*
The *Daily Picayune* commented in 1869 that "the old fashioned, straight up and down box houses are, we are pleased to see, giving way to those more tasteful in design. . . . Among the most beautiful residences which have been lately erected in the Garden District is that of Mr. J. C. Morris, corner of First and Coliseum. It is a two-story and attic brick stucco house with octagonal wings, constructed with such nice regard to the unities that the eye is charmed at once." The Italianate style swept New Orleans in the late 1850s, vanquishing the earlier Greek Revival taste. These spectacular cast-iron galleries were manufactured in New Orleans by Jacob Baumiller's foundry. Owner Joseph C. Morris was a prosperous cordage dealer.

⑥ **White House,** *circa 1849; 1878, turned and remodeled*
Built in 1849 in the Greek Revival style, this two-story frame house was turned and remodeled in 1878, and slant-sided bay windows were added to the right-hand side of the facade. The floor-to-ceiling windows on the left-hand side with their elegant narrow panes are typical of the Greek Revival style, while the larger panes in the bay window are of later Victorian manufacture. The multicolored "painted lady" color scheme is recent and not characteristic of New Orleans.

⑦ **Joseph Carroll House,** *1869, Samuel Jamison*
This substantial Italianate mansion was built after the Civil War by a Virginia-born cotton factor. It is distinguished by fine cast-iron galleries, which form a lacy screen in front of the stern masonry block. Around the corner on Chestnut Street is an elegant and solid-looking carriage house. Mark Twain attended lavish parties here in 1886. Great live oaks, Chinese fan palms, and giant elephant ear plants flourish in the spacious garden.

⑧ **Brevard-Wisdom-Rice House,** *1857, James H. Calrow; 1869, hexagonal bays added*
This magnificent house was built for commission merchant Albert Hamilton Brevard and designed by James H. Calrow. It displays the Greek Revival style blended with the Italianate. Note the two-story front gallery with Ionic columns on the first floor and

Payne-Strachan House
1134 First Street

Warwick Aiken House
2427 Camp Street

1137 Second Street

Archibald Montgomery House
1213 Third Street

General John Bell Hood House
1206 Third Street

Corinthian columns on the second floor. In 1869 the house was expanded for Emory Clapp, who added the library wing on the Chestnut Street side and hexagonal bays. The woven wire fence is a rare survivor and was made by the New York Wire Railing Company. This was the home of Judge John Minor Wisdom; in 1989 it became the home of vampire chronicle novelist Anne Rice. The gardens are superb.

9   Payne-Strachan House, *1849*

The architect of this Greek Revival, five-bay, center-hall, columned house is unknown; first owner Jacob U. Payne may have designed it himself using pattern books. The first-floor gallery columns are Ionic; those on the second floor are modeled on those at the Tower of the Winds in Athens. The house's interior woodwork is Greek Revival in style and follows the designs in Minard Lafever's 1833 pattern book, *The Modern Builder's Guide*. Kentucky-born Jacob Payne was an opulent cotton planter and an antisecession Whig. Jefferson Davis, the first and only president of the Confederate States of America, died here on December 9, 1889, while visiting Judge Charles Erasmus Fenner, Payne's son-in-law. The Ladies' Confederate Memorial Association erected a tasteful granite monument here in 1930 with Davis's *vita* on one side and an exhortation on the "Christian chieftain" on the other.

10   Warwick Aiken House, *1859*

This assured Greek Revival, brick-and-stucco house is painted a mild *café au lait* color. Its portico has box columns and fluted columns; its rectilinear central doorway is quintessentially Greek Revival. The house has been divided into apartments.

Across Camp Street, at **1137 Second Street,** is a profile view of a fine Queen Anne house with stained-glass windows with a palmetto motif. This 1890s house has elaborate wood trim and fine terra-cotta roof ridge tiles characteristic of Old New Orleans.

11   Archibald Montgomery House, *1868, Henry Howard*

This unusual peach-colored house in the Italianate style was built for the Ireland-born railroad promoter and Crescent City Railroad president Archibald Montgomery. It was designed by the prolific Henry Howard and built in 1868, and it has fine wooden porches with paired, thin columns. Characteristic Italianate-style brackets appear under the eaves.

12   General John Bell Hood House, *1852*

This terra-cotta–color corner house in the French Second Empire style has two front bays over its wide first-floor gallery. The emphasized parapet lends the house presence.

This was once the home of the Confederate general John Bell Hood, who moved to the Garden District after the Civil War.

13   **Michel Musson House**, *1850, Italianate; 1884, cast-iron gallery added*
This Italianate house was built for Michel Musson, a French Creole and the Postmaster of New Orleans and president of the New Orleans Cotton Exchange. Musson was Impressionist painter Edgar Degas's uncle, and he is immortalized as the broker examining a sample of cotton in Degas's 1873 painting *The Cotton Factor's Office*. Musson lived here only a few years before moving downtown to the Creole section. Eight household slaves served this house. In 1884 two bay windows were removed from the facade and the cast-iron gallery was erected.

14   **Walter Grinnan Robinson House**, *1859, Henry Howard*
Virginia tobacco merchant Walter Grinnan Robinson built this house in 1859. Designed by Henry Howard, it is reputed to be the first house with indoor plumbing in the city. Inside are elaborate frescos by Domenico Canova, one of the many European artists and craftsmen who came to booming New Orleans before the Civil War. The double gallery with rounded ends is unusual, as is the placement of the service wing to the left of the house rather than behind it. A fine cast-iron gallery appears on the right-hand side of the house. This is one of the largest mansions in the Garden District. The stable is noteworthy.

15   **Thomas Gilmour House**, *1853, Isaac Thayer, civil engineer and builder*
This five-bay, center-hall house was built for English cotton merchant Thomas Gilmour by civil engineer and builder Isaac Thayer. A planned columned portico was never built; instead there is a cast-iron gallery.

16   **Women's Guild of the New Orleans Opera Association / Davis House**, *1858, William Freret, Greek Revival; 1880s, remodeled in the Queen Anne style*
This house was designed as a Greek Revival town house with a side hall and a double gallery. In the 1880s the right-hand side with the octagonal tower was added and the interior was remodeled in the Victorian taste. In 1966 Mrs. Seebold donated the house and its furnishings to the Women's Guild of the New Orleans Opera Association, which opens the house for public tours, the only such house in the Garden District. Inside is a small museum of opera mementos.

Michel Musson House
1331 Third Street, at Coliseum

Walter Grinnan Robinson House
1415 Third Street, at Coliseum

Thomas Gilmour House
2520 Prytania Street

Women's Guild of the New Orleans Opera Association / Davis House
2504 Prytania Street; open Monday to Friday 1 to 4 P.M.; small fee; 899-1945

Joseph H. Maddox House
2507 Prytania Street

Lonsdale-McStea-Rice House
2521 Prytania Street

Charles Briggs House
2605 Prytania Street

Colonel Short's Villa
1448 Fourth Street, at Prytania

⑰   Joseph H. Maddox House, *1852, John Barnett*

This Greek Revival, five-bay, columned house was built for New Hampshire–born Joseph H. Maddox, the editor of the *New Orleans Daily Crescent.* He lost his house in the recession of 1854. In 1867 Alfred Moulton, a subsequent owner, made the double parlor into a ballroom and commissioned a Viennese artist to decorate it.

⑱   Lonsdale-McStea-Rice House, *1856, Henry Howard*

This towering, five-bay, center-hall, Italianate-style house was designed by Henry Howard and built by J. K. Collins & Company, builders. It was commissioned by New York–born Henry T. Lonsdale, who made two fortunes, the first by cornering the market for gunnysacks. Ruined in the panic of 1837, he rebounded and made a second fortune as the city's largest coffee broker. Coffee was, and is, one of the most important commodities imported through New Orleans. Lonsdale lost his second fortune in the post-Civil War turmoil in 1868. The house was long owned by the Redemptorist Fathers, who built a chapel here; in 1996 the property was bought by Anne Rice. (The author also owns 2524 St. Charles Avenue, at Third, a fine raised Greek Revival house built in 1857 for Sophronie Claiborne Marigny.)

⑲   Charles Briggs House, *1849, James Gallier, Sr.*

London-born Charles Briggs made his fortune as an insurance executive. In 1849 he commissioned this, the Garden District's only Gothic Revival house, from architect James Gallier, Sr. Architect T. K. Wharton called this "the most tasteful [house] in the suburb." The house lacks the usual fancy work of such houses and seems the better for it. The porch and window openings are clean and strong. The companion guest cottage echoes the lines of the main house. Briggs's servants, who were free, not slaves, were housed in an originally separate, two-story, Gothic Revival clapboard structure.

⑳   "Cornstalk Fence House" / Colonel Short's Villa, *1859, Henry Howard*

This is probably the best-known house in the Garden District, not because of the fine house but because of its unusual cast-iron fence. This Italianate villa was erected in 1859 for Kentucky-born commission merchant and honorary colonel Robert Henry Short. It was designed by noted New Orleans architect Henry Howard. The interior detailing of the house is in the earlier Greek Revival style. The curved bay window on the Prytania Street side was added in 1906. The remarkable fence with the cornstalk pattern was made in Philadelphia at the Wood & Perot foundry and erected by the local firm of Wood & Miltenberger. The base of the fence posts have pumpkins and are entwined with morning glories. Much of New Orleans' famed cast iron came from Northern foundries. (There is another cornstalk fence in the French Quarter at 915 Royal Street.) This villa was confiscated by Federal authorities during the occupation of New Orleans and returned to Colonel Short after the war.

㉑   Crescent City Skating Rink / The Rink Shopping Center, *circa 1884; 1979, remodeled*
Clara Hagen built the Crescent City Skating Rink in 1884, the same year that the World's Cotton Centennial Exposition opened uptown in Audubon Park. The vernacular frame structure had a variety of subsequent uses; at one point it was a mortuary. In 1920 it became an automobile garage, and in 1979 it was converted into shops. Inside is the Garden District Book Shop and PJ's Coffee & Tea Cafe.

The Rink Shopping Center
2727 Prytania Street, at Washington

Old Southern Athletic Club
1500 Washington Avenue, at Prytania

City of Lafayette Cemetery
See Tour 11

Commander's Palace Restaurant
1403 Washington Avenue, at Coliseum; 899-8231

㉒   1500 Washington Avenue / Old Southern Athletic Club / Behrman Gym, *1880s, Moorish-Victorian gym facade; 1996 house, Piet Kessels*
Built for the Southern Athletic Club, this corner frame structure was built in the late 1880s as private athletic clubs began to be fashionable among the wealthy. It is a delightfully eclectic building with Moorish Victorian details at the entrance and over the second-floor windows. In this gym, "Gentleman Jim" Corbett trained for his twenty-one-round World Championship fight with John L. Sullivan in 1892. The gym eventually became the property of the Orleans Parish School Board. It was sold at auction in 1993 and the rear gymnasium section demolished. The facade and front portion were converted into a single-family house.

㉓   City of Lafayette Cemetery, *1833, Benjamin Buisson, city surveyor*
See page 341 for Lafayette Cemetery.

㉔   Commander's Palace Restaurant, *1880*
This turquoise-and-white, turreted Victorian building was erected in 1880 for Emile Commander, who operated a restaurant on the first floor and lived upstairs. The rambling building combines Queen Anne massing with Eastlake details. During the 1920s a speakeasy operated here. Since 1974 it has been Commander's Palace Restaurant, the Brennan family's flagship restaurant, a culinary and social summit in New Orleans.

Continuations:
Return to the St. Charles Avenue streetcar to head uptown to upper St. Charles Avenue and Audubon Park and Zoo (see Tour 9), or walk down Washington Avenue to Magazine Street to the Magazine Street bus and the shops and restaurants along upper Magazine (see Tour 10). If you walk down Washington Avenue, you will pass:

New Orleans Fire Department Museum and Educational Center
1135 Washington Avenue, near Magazine; open Monday to Friday 9 A.M. to 2 P.M.; free; 896-4756

25   New Orleans Fire Department Museum and Educational Center, *1851, remodeled 1949*

At 1135 Washington Avenue, just above Magazine, is the plain red-brick facade of the Fire Department Museum with its antique equipment and firefighters' memorabilia and photographs.

Bosworth-Hammond House
1126 Washington Avenue

26   Bosworth-Hammond House, *1859, Thomas K. Wharton*

Across the street, at 1126 Washington Avenue, is the bow-front, Greek Revival, double-galleried Hammond Mansion, suffering from demolition by neglect and slowly falling into ruin. Built in 1859 and designed by Thomas K. Wharton, the gentle bow of the double gallery mitigates the rectilinearity of most Greek Revival architecture. Architect Wharton's diary is preserved in the New York Public Library. This is a masterpiece of New Orleans architecture. The slow-motion loss of such an architectural gem is a telling comment on New Orleans today.

*Wide, oak-embowered St. Charles Avenue, the city's grandest
residential boulevard, is the triumphal way for the Rex parade as it rolls downtown
toward Canal Street on Mardi Gras at midday.*

What This Tour Covers
Preliminaries
Introduction: The Greatest Boulevard of
Mansions in the South

26 Vaccaro House

27 Milton H. Latter Memorial Public Library

28 De La Salle High School

29 New Orleans Jewish Community Center

Jefferson Avenue to Nashville Avenue

30 The Octavia

31 Danneel Park

32 Benjamin-Monroe House

33 McCarthy House

34 Coates House

35 "Tara" / Palmer House

36 5718 St. Charles Avenue

37 5726 St. Charles Avenue

Key to Tour 9B appears on page 292.

Tour 9

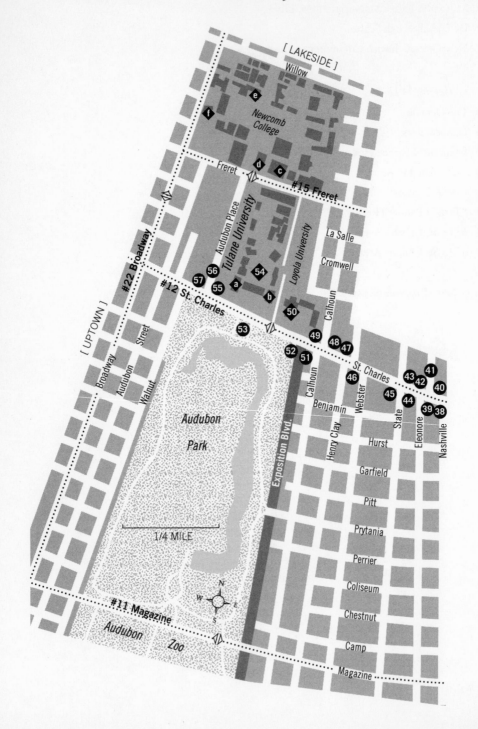

[LAKESIDE]

Willow

e

f

Newcomb College

Freret

d   c

#15 Freret

Audubon Place

Tulane University

La Salle

Cromwell

Loyola University

56

57   55   a   54

b

50

#22 Broadway

#12 St. Charles

[UPTOWN]

Broadway

Audubon

Walnut

Street

53

52   51

Calhoun

Benjamin

Henry Clay

Audubon Park

Exposition Blvd.

49

48 47

St. Charles

46

45   44

Webster

State

Eleonore

43
42
40
41

39 38

Nashville

Calhoun

Hurst

Garfield

Pitt

Prytania

Perrier

Coliseum

Chestnut

1/4 MILE

N
W   E
S

#11 Magazine

Audubon   Zoo

Camp

Magazine

Tulane University has a number of interiors that are publicly accessible, marked with small black diamonds:

- ⓐ Amistad Center
- ⓑ Middle American Galleries
- ⓒ Howard-Tilton Library
- ⓓ Jones Hall
- ⓔ Newcomb Art Gallery
- ⓕ Rogers Chapel

Sites #1 to #13 are on a Streetcar Tour and do not appear on any map

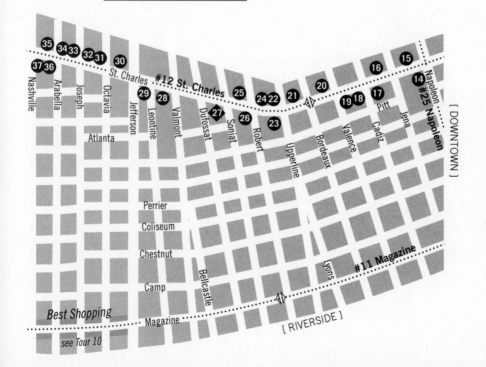

⑭	Site in Guide
◆50	Publicly Accessible Interior
▬	Pedestrian Way
⋯	Transit Line

Continuations

Exposition Boulevard or Audubon Street to Magazine Street
/ Audubon Zoo
Central City: The Other Uptown

What This Tour Covers

This tour travels up gently curving St. Charles Avenue on the 1920s streetcar and traces the spine of New Orleans' elite Uptown District. It is necessarily divided into two parts: a twenty-minute streetcar ride (with one optional stop at the Latter Memorial Public Library housed in a 1907 mansion), and a walk from Nashville Avenue to Audubon Park past some of Uptown's most impressive houses and visiting the park and Tulane and Loyola Universities. Driving, of course, provides you with the most flexibility in touring the avenue, though the streetcar is better because you ride higher up and see more of the houses raised up on berms. After your tour you can walk down either Exposition Boulevard along the edge of Audubon Park or Audubon Street to the Magazine Street bus, which heads back to Canal Street after passing some of the most interesting shops in the city (see Tour 10).

Preliminaries

This tour can be done almost anytime since— except for Carnival parades!—the St. Charles Avenue streetcar never stops running. The best times are when the Newcomb Art Gallery at Tulane is open. There are vespers daily at 5 P.M. at the Most Holy Name of Jesus Church on the Loyola University campus. Audubon Park is alive with uptowners exercising from about 5 to 7 P.M. To ride up and down St. Charles Avenue on the streetcar at twilight is memorable (see page 297).

Parking

It is easy to do this tour by automobile. However, St. Charles Avenue is an important artery, and you should not drive more slowly than the flow of traffic. Curbside parking is available along the avenue and in front of Tulane and Loyola Universities and Audubon Park.

Kung's Dynasty
1912 St. Charles Avenue,
near Felicity; 525-6669

Rigatoni Restaurant
3442 St. Charles Avenue,
at Delachaise; 899-1570

Columns Hotel and Bar
3811 St. Charles Avenue;
899-9308

Your Daily Bread
7457 St. Charles Avenue;
861-4663

La Madeleine French
Bakery and Cafe
601 S. Carrollton Avenue,
at St. Charles at
Riverbend; 861-8661

Cafe Atchafalaya
901 Louisiana Avenue, at
Laurel; 891-5271

Upperline Restaurant
1413 Upperline Street,
between Prytania and
St. Charles; 891-9822

Figaro's Pizzerie
7900 Maple Street, at
Fern; 866-0100

Chicory Farm Cafe
723 Hillary Street, near
Maple; 866-2325

Zachary's Restaurant
8400 Oak Street, at
Cambronne; 865-1559

WTUL 91.5 FM
865-5887

Music Department
Box office 865-5269

Summer Lyric Theater
865-5269

Restaurants, Cafes, and Bars

There are only a few restaurants on the avenue itself. **Kung's Dynasty** serves Chinese food in a classic 1840s, double-galleried house; sit in the front room if you can. The front tables at **Rigatoni Restaurant** look out at St. Charles Avenue; the restaurant serves good Italian food.

The terrace bar at **Columns Hotel and Bar**, overlooking the avenue, is popular with locals, as is the Sunday champagne brunch. **Your Daily Bread,** a bakery, is good for snacks and refreshment, and it offers excellent Carnival king cakes. The seven-grain bread is recommended at **La Madeleine French Bakery and Cafe,** a popular place for lunch and midday snacks.

There are several good restaurants tucked away on the side streets of Uptown, including **Cafe Atchafalaya** and **Upperline Restaurant. Figaro's Pizzerie** offers indoor and outdoor seating and serves good Italian cuisine. **Chicory Farm Cafe,** an excellent vegetarian restaurant in an old house, has its own farm for mushrooms and makes its own cheese. **Zachary's Restaurant,** in a cozy Victorian cottage, features authentic New Orleans cooking.

Tulane University

In addition to the chapel, galleries, and archives described in this tour (#54), Tulane University has a hip college radio station, **WTUL 91.5 FM;** you can also call the **Music Department** or the **Summer Lyric Theater** to find out performance schedules. The **Tulane University Bookstore** is in University Center.

Shopping

The upriver end of Magazine Street is Uptown's longest and best shopping street (see Tour 10). Maple Street is the University District's small, nontourist shopping enclave, with a sprinkling of local shops and restaurants. Farther up the streetcar line, off Carrollton Avenue along Oak Street, are a couple of good music venues and restaurants. See Music listings on page 61.

The Live Oaks

The tunnel of ancient-seeming live oaks that make St. Charles Avenue so distinctive was planted about 1890–1910. **Save The Oaks, Inc.** was founded in order to collect donations for their sorely needed fertilization and pruning.

Tulane University Bookstore
University Center; open Monday to Thursday 8 A.M. to 6 P.M., Friday 8 A.M. to 5 P.M., Saturday 11 A.M. to 4 P.M.;
865-5913

Save The Oaks, Inc.
P.O. Box 15833, N.O., 70175-5833

Introduction: The Greatest Boulevard of Mansions in the South

Oak-lined St. Charles Avenue is the most impressive linear landmark in New Orleans. The avenue's gentle curvature as it follows the high ground of the natural levee creates a memorable experience of continual anticipation and surprise. The traveler moves uptown on the streetcar past an ever more impressive array of grand houses and power-house institutions. As late as 1885, St. Charles Avenue was still an alternately dusty or muddy unpaved morass, depending on the rains. All that changed at the end of the nineteenth century when a burst of prosperity and civic pride transformed the avenue into a showcase street with a parade of large houses and key religious and educational institutions. Those who made money in the "New South" from the 1880s into the 1920s built not in the secluded, off-the-beaten-track grid of the Garden District but along the eminently visible ribbon of upper St. Charles Avenue. Elite leadership and public subscription erected the fine Robert E. Lee Monument in 1884–85 as the gateway to the avenue on what was renamed Lee Circle. A group of mostly new arrivals organized the World's Industrial and Cotton Centennial Exposition way uptown in undeveloped Audubon Park; it operated during the winter social seasons of 1884 and 1885. In 1882 St. Charles Avenue was paved with asphalt, the first such modern street in New Orleans. In 1893 the St. Charles Avenue streetcar line was electrified, replacing the old-fashioned mules with modern motive power. In the same decade, sewer and water pipes were finally laid under the showplace street. Most important for the aesthetics of the avenue, live oaks (*Quercus virginiana*) were planted along both sides, which have today matured into a tunnel of ancient-looking trees with wonderfully writhing surface roots. A froth of magenta azaleas blooms along the neutral ground in March; a precious few Rex flags fly from the homes of former kings during the Carnival season; at Christmastime tasteful white lights twinkle in the evergreen gardens.

The men who built these spacious houses on large, visible lots were generally not the scions of the antebellum elite. They made their fortunes after the war in such urban endeavors as cotton brokerage, cigar manufacturing, wholesaling, Canal Street department stores, and banana importation. The city's more open economy after the Civil War created opportunities for some of New Orleans' Jewish merchants to succeed and rival the established wealthy. They, in particular, favored upper St. Charles Avenue. The large, turreted Jewish Widows and Orphans Home, designed by Thomas Sully and erected in 1886, became *the* architectural statement on the avenue and a symbol of Jewish philanthropy (today the site of the Jewish Community Center, #29). Touro Synagogue moved uptown to St. Charles Avenue in 1909, and Temple Sinai, the first Reform congregation in New Orleans, was built farther uptown in 1927 next to the universities. Other key religious and educational institutions relocated uptown as well. In 1884 St. Mary's Dominican College built an imposing new building on their plot at St. Charles Avenue and Broadway Street, which they had occupied since 1865. In 1886 the Society of the Sacred Heart moved to the avenue and, in 1900, began its embracing, symmetrical landmark school for girls. In 1894 secular Tulane University opened its first impressive Romanesque Revival stone college building, Gibson Hall, facing the avenue. (Tulane's Uptown campus now covers 110 acres and has become the city's single largest private employer.) In 1904 the Society of Jesus built a preparatory school next to Tulane University, which in 1912 became Loyola University (now Loyola University of the South), housed in red brick Tudor Revival splendor. The Jesuit Gothic Revival Church of the Most Holy Name of Jesus was built next to Loyola in 1914. Many elite Protestant congregations also migrated to the avenue, joining Episcopal Christ Church Cathedral, which had built its fourth cathedral on the avenue facing the Garden District in 1887.

The commodious houses built along St. Charles Avenue were designed by the best New Orleans architects, many by the prolific Thomas Sully of the firm of Sully and Toledano. Other architectural firms active here were Andry and Bendernagle; deBuys, Churchill, and Labouisse; Favrot and Livaudais; and B. M. Harrod. Many of these houses are in the Queen Anne style and are built of pine and cypress, painted the traditional white. The exteriors of these large houses are usually distinguished by generous porches, gable roofs, irregular shapes, and occasionally, by elaborate shingle work. Their interiors were planned for large-scale entertaining, with very large roomlike central halls opening onto even larger rooms to create flowing spaces for lavish receptions. A distinguishing exterior characteristic of St. Charles Avenue houses are the many cut-plate-glass front doors and sidelights which sparkle in rainbow colors at night as you pass by on the streetcar. Other styles on the avenue include strong Richardsonian Romanesque and exuberant Colonial Revival piles and stately Renaissance Revival palazzos. Some of these houses are built of Bedford, Indiana, limestone with tile roofs; a few are monumental. A few large Craftsmen houses from the early twentieth century with horizontal lines and overhanging eaves also sit restfully along the upper reaches of this fashionable boulevard.

Today St. Charles Avenue can be divided into three sections: the unfortunately ragged and principally commercial strip from Lee Circle to Jackson Avenue, the mixed residential and apartment house corridor from Jackson Avenue to Napoleon Avenue bordering the Garden District, and the splendid residential and institutional zone from Napoleon Avenue to Broadway Street. Like many of the nation's best late-nineteenth-century boulevards, lower St. Charles Avenue beyond Lee Circle began to shift to commerce in the 1920s. Upscale automobile showrooms, hotels, and other businesses invaded the residential avenue and demolished many of the houses from the 1840–80 period that once lined the downtown end of the street. Many of the oak trees here were eventually cut down to make these businesses more visible to drivers. When New Orleans was hit by the oil bust, some of these businesses folded, making the gateway end of the avenue a problem zone today. The Central City ghetto has also expanded on the lakeside, coming to within a block of the avenue. The middle section of the avenue, from Jackson Avenue to Louisiana Avenue, was the scene of speculative demolition and the construction of large, often undistinguished apartment buildings during the oil boom of the 1970s. In the summer of 1972, "improvement" accelerated and ten houses were demolished along the avenue. New Orleanians woke up to the fact that the coherence of their grand avenue was in danger. Mobilized residents formed the St. Charles Avenue Committee and pressured the city to pass a moratorium on demolition while the future of the street was studied. In 1975, responding to citizen concerns, the city council created a Historic District Commission. The first two areas the new commission gave landmark protection to were St. Charles Avenue from Jackson Avenue to Jena Street (the middle part of the avenue slated for more apartment buildings) and the endangered lower Garden District. The upper end of the avenue has always been zoned for one- and two-family residences, and it retains almost all of its fine architecture, spacious gardens, imposing temples, and schools. Since 1985, Uptown's ten thousand buildings have been listed on the National Register of Historic Places.

While white flight has afflicted so much of New Orleans, Uptown, and especially the University Section, continues to be *the* place to live. There are several reasons for this. First, Uptown remains the focus of the social life of the city. Also, while these houses are large, they are generally not overly large and can accommodate today's smaller families and reduced levels of domestic service. New Orleans' too-low property taxes do not drive families out of big houses. A cluster of excellent private schools—Episcopal, Roman Catholic, and secular—allow the wealthy to stay in Uptown and raise families independent of the decayed public schools. An important part of the Jewish population of metropolitan New Orleans has stayed in the city and supports several synagogues and an active community center. Tulane and Loyola Universities are also strong anchors and bring a rich, international cultural life to the section. Last, Audubon Park is a community anchor and is enjoyed by residents of all ages; it is Uptown's liveliest public space. In underparked New Orleans it is a model of what well-maintained parks can do for neighborhoods. For all these reasons, upper St. Charles Avenue and the major Uptown streets that radiate from it have retained their livability and prestige. There are also many pleasant rows of modest frame houses on the sidestreets in Uptown, and they have seen the most restoration in recent years.

Tour 9a:
A Streetcar Ride to Nashville Avenue

It takes about fifteen minutes to travel by streetcar from Canal Street to Christ Church Episcopal Cathedral, across the street from the Garden District, where this listing begins. If you like, you can stop at the Latter Memorial Public Library (#27), the only grand house on St. Charles Avenue that's open to the public. A bit more than ten minutes more on the streetcar takes you to Nashville Avenue, the starting point for this short walk along the avenue from Nashville Avenue to Audubon Park and Tulane and Loyola Universities. Only the sites on the walk appear on the map.

Washington Avenue to Louisiana Avenue

①   Christ Church Episcopal Cathedral, *1886–87, Lawrence B. Valk, Gothic Revival*

This congregation was organized in 1805 and held its first service at the Cabildo. Originally connected to the diocese of New York, its first three cathedrals were on Canal Street on the edge of the French Quarter. In 1886 this Gothic Revival church was designed by New York City architect Lawrence B. Valk and the congregation moved uptown. In the south choir aisle is the tomb of the Right Reverend Leonidas Polk, the first Episcopal bishop of Louisiana and the "fighting bishop" who was commissioned a general, fought for the Confederacy, and died in battle in 1864. Adjoining the cathedral is the Harris Memorial Chapel, built in 1889 and designed by Sully and Toledano. The cathedral lost its steeple in the hurricane of September 30, 1915.

②   Van Benthuysen House, *1868–69; remodeled in 1883 and 1896*

This elegant corner house with the large side garden and columned pavilion was built in 1868–69 and then extensively remodeled in 1883 and again in 1896. It served as the German Consulate before World War II.

③   The Patios, *1950s, architect unknown*

This jail-like eyesore was inflicted on the grand avenue in the 1950s and shows just how frightfully low speculative building sank before the imposition of design controls and the St. Charles Avenue Historic District in 1975. It is, alas, a very "Sun Belt" design and all too typical of recent building.

④   House of Bultman Funeral Home

This very large white funeral home with Alice in Wonderland Parcheesi-token-like fence finials and corner clock was confected in the 1940s by Fred Bultman, who connected three existing nineteenth-century houses behind a new box-columned facade.

Louisiana Avenue to Napoleon Avenue

⑤   Faubourg Bouligny

The stretch of Uptown from Louisiana Avenue to Napoleon Avenue was once known as Faubourg Bouligny. It was all originally part of the large plantation granted to Jean-Baptiste Le Moyne, sieur de Bienville, by the Superior Council of Louisiana in 1719.

Christ Church Episcopal Cathedral
2919 St. Charles Avenue, at Sixth (right); Sunday eucharist at 7:30 and 9 A.M.; choral eucharist 11 A.M.; 895-6602

Van Benthuysen House
3029 St. Charles Avenue, at Eighth (right)

The Patios
3101 St. Charles Avenue, at Eighth (right)

House of Bultman Funeral Home
3338 St. Charles Avenue, at Louisiana (left)

Faubourg Bouligny

Unity Temple
*3722 St. Charles Avenue,
at Peniston (left); Sunday
healing forum at 9:30
A.M.; devotional service at
11 A.M.; Wednesday
prayer and healing service
at 11 A.M.; 899-0715*

Isidore Newman House
*3804 St. Charles Avenue,
at Peniston (left)*

Columns Hotel
*3811 St. Charles Avenue
(right); 899-9308*

Over time the land was subdivided first into pie-wedge-shap
sugar cane plantations, and then later into blocks and lots f
faubourgs, or suburbs. In 1807, a section became Faubourg Pl.
sance; in 1834, Faubourg East Bouligny was laid out; in 1847, pz
became Faubourg St. Joseph; and in 1855, another section becan
Faubourg Delachaise. All were later incorporated into the City
New Orleans.

Underneath the wide, landscaped medians of the principal radi
boulevards that cross St. Charles Avenue—Jackson, Louisian
Napoleon, Upperline, Nashville, and Carrollton Avenues—a
wide collector sewers that drain each neighborhood. These stor
sewers were excavated between 1899 and 1904, improving existi
drainage canals. At the head of this system are giant screw pumf
designed by A. Baldwin Wood, that can pump up to twenty-fo
billion gallons of rainwater a day out of the low-lying city and in
Lake Pontchartrain. New Orleans is as human-made and continually sustained an en
ronment as Holland.

6   Unity Temple, *1961, Leonard R. Spangenberg*
The unusual circular forms of this 1961 church announce too clearly that it w
designed by a student of Frank Lloyd Wright. Architect Leonard R. Spangenberg u
lized the circle to symbolize unity. This is the home of the New Orleans Unity Socie
of Practical Christianity, a nondenominational religious organization.

7   Isidore Newman House, *1905*
This substantial corner house was built in 1905 of Bedford, Indiana, limestone f
Isidore Newman, who began life as a peddler and grew wealthy extending credit to cc
ton planters after the Civil War. Several members of the Newman family built lar;
stone houses on the avenue. The independent, nondenominational Isidore Newma
School farther uptown on Jefferson Avenue was founded in 1903 by this civic-mind
New Orleanian.

8   Columns Hotel / Hernsheim House, *1883, Thomas Sully*
This eye-catching building began life as the home of Simon Hernsheim, a wealthy cig
manufacturer, and was originally designed in 1883 by Thomas Sully as an Italianat
style house. It later became a genteel boarding house, and in 1953, a hotel. Its tow
was removed and the giant order Doric columns were pasted onto the front of tl
building to make it look more "Southern." Inside, the main staircase and much of tl
original woodwork and stained-glass survive. Louis Malle filmed *Pretty Baby* here,
Hollywood version of the life of New Orleans photographer Ernest J. Bellocq.

9   **Rayne Memorial Methodist Church,** *1876, Charles Lewis Hillger*

This red-brick Gothic Revival church with its slender steeple was built in 1876 and designed by Charles Lewis Hillger. It is a fine example of the elaborate brickwork of New Orleans' best master masons. The church was built as a memorial to William Rayne, who was fatally wounded at Chancellorsville. His father, Robert Walker Rayne, a wholesale shoe merchant before the war and a manufacturer of cotton ties afterward, gave the land and a large donation for the erection of this church. A Sunday school building was added behind it in 1925. This is the oldest Methodist church building in New Orleans.

10   **Sully House,** *1887, Thomas Sully*

This Queen Anne/Shingle–style house with a side porte cochere was built in 1887 by architect Thomas Sully of the firm of Sully and Toledano as his own residence. The house is unusual for its slightly battered (sloping) lower walls, and it has an unusually fine texture in its shingle work and window mullions. Sully is known to have designed at least two dozen large houses on St. Charles Avenue, more than any other architect.

11   **4110 St. Charles Avenue,** *1963, Victor Bruno*

This double house, made to look like a single residence, was designed in 1963 by New Orleans architect Victor Bruno, a disciple of Frank Lloyd Wright. Palm Terrace is a small street laid out in the early 1920s and is lined with small, low-budget, Hollywood-Hills Spanish stucco houses. Very strange.

12   **Wallis House,** *1890s, Thomas Sully*

This large Shingle-style house with its generous front gallery is notable for its assured massing, textured shingle work, and the blue ceramic tiles that decorate the upper part of its second story. It was designed by the prolific Thomas Sully in the 1890s. John S. Wallis was the president of the Louisiana Sugar Refining Company, an important enterprise in late-nineteenth-century New Orleans. Today the large house is divided into apartments.

13   **Touro Synagogue,** *1909, Emile Weil*

Touro Synagogue is the oldest Jewish congregation in the Mississippi valley; it has its roots in the 1881 amalgamation of the German-Jewish congregation Shagari Hesed (Gates of Mercy), which was organized in 1828, and the Spanish-Portuguese congregation Nefuzoth Yehudah (Dispersed of Judah), founded in 1846. The consolidated

Rayne Memorial Methodist Church
3900 St. Charles Avenue, at General Taylor (left); Sunday services at 8:45 and 11 A.M.; 899-3431

Sully House
4010 St. Charles Avenue (left)

4110 St. Charles Avenue
At Palm Terrace (right)

Wallis House
4114 St. Charles Avenue (left)

Touro Synagogue
4238 St. Charles Avenue, at General Pershing (left); services at 8 P.M. Friday and 10:30 A.M. Saturday; 895-4843

Napoleon Avenue

Hiller House
4417 St. Charles Avenue
(right)

congregation named itself in honor of Judah Touro, a New Orleans merchant who was born the son of a rabbi in Newport, Rhode Island, in 1775. A merchant, patriot, and philanthropist, Touro is said to have never left New Orleans except to visit the battlefield at Chalmette. He liberally supported Jewish, Protestant, Catholic, and nonsectarian charities and founded the Touro Infirmary, the Shakespeare-Touro Home for the Aged, and a free public library. At his death in 1854, the old bachelor made gifts to many charities and to Jewish congregations and benevolent societies across the country. He was buried in Newport under a granite obelisk with the Hebrew inscription: "The last of his name / He inscribed it in the Book of Philanthropy / To be remembered forever."

Touro Synagogue is in the Byzantine Revival style and was designed by architect Emile Weil and dedicated in 1909. It is built of grayish-yellow brick and has handsome terra-cotta ornamentation. Inside, in the center of the shallow dome, is a blue stained-glass window representing heaven. The pulpit and the ark were donations of Judah Touro and are made of Lebanon cedar. In 1989, Lyons & Hudson designed the contemporary, yet compatible, Norman Synagogue House next door with a gated courtyard. Its beautiful abstract stained-glass window facing St. Charles Avenue was designed by Ida Kohlmeyer. This new chapel is one of the most sympathetic additions to an old building in contemporary New Orleans.

Napoleon Avenue to Jefferson Avenue

14 Napoleon Avenue

This wide radial boulevard was the widest street in Faubourg Bouligny. Charles F. Zimple, the chief engineer of the New Orleans and Carrollton Rail Road Company, laid out this subdivision on the former Avart plantation in 1834. The surveyor, Pierre-Benjamin Buisson, a chauvinist and a former captain of artillery in Napoleon's army, is credited with choosing the names of the streets here. He named the widest street for his hero and the flanking streets after Napoleonic victories. There are streets named Constantinople, Marengo, Milan, Jena, Cadiz, Valence, and Bordeaux; off the avenue are Austerlitz and Lyons Streets. Berlin Street was renamed General Pershing during World War I by history-challenged New Orleanians. An enormous drainage canal is buried under the Napoleon Avenue neutral ground and carries rainwater to the pumps and Lake Pontchartrain.

15 Hiller House, *1896, Thomas Sully*

This Renaissance Revival mansion was built in 1896 and designed by Thomas Sully. Alfred Hiller was born in Massachusetts and owned the largest cement dealership in the South.

16   **Academy of the Sacred Heart,** *1900, Diboll and Owen*

Set back from the avenue behind tall iron gates with an entrance arch, the Academy of the Sacred Heart is a social and architectural landmark in uptown New Orleans. Les Mesdames des Sacré Coeur are an elite teaching order of Roman Catholic nuns founded by St. Madeline Sophie Barat in France in 1800. The order came to New Orleans in 1818 and opened a convent and girls' school at Dumaine and Dauphine Streets in the French Quarter. As fashion moved uptown, so did the Mesdames. In 1887 the order purchased the Calhoun-Peters Greek Revival mansion of 1847 together with two squares of land planted in orange trees fronting on St. Charles Avenue. After thirteen years in the old house, the Mesdames decided to build a new school. They engaged the architectural firm of Diboll and Owen, who designed an H-shaped brick convent and school with a handsome colonnaded gallery in 1900. Originally two stories, the school was expanded in 1906 and 1913 into the impressive three-story building that graces the avenue today. The bell in its cupola came from the Aurora plantation in Algiers across the river. A white-painted, cast-iron statue of the Sacred Heart of Jesus was placed in the central niche from which it raises its arms to embrace all who pass by. The fine black cast-iron fountain with its swan and pelican motif is a superb New Orleanian Victorian embellishment. Today the Academy of the Sacred Heart has 760 students in grades K through twelve. Roman Catholic schools have long been important in New Orleans. In 1993, the city had thirty-five Roman Catholic parochial schools. In the greater metropolitan area in that year there were 52,252 Catholic grammar and high school students.

Academy of the Sacred Heart
4521 St. Charles Avenue, between Jena and Cadiz (right)

Smith-Coplin House
4534 St. Charles Avenue, at Cadiz (left)

St. George's Episcopal Church
4600 St. Charles Avenue, at Cadiz (left); Sunday services at 8 and 10:30 A.M.; Thursday Eucharist at 9:30 A.M.; 899-2811

17   **Smith-Coplin House,** *1906, F. P. Gravely*

The impressive limestone mansion with the spacious grounds and great oak trees on the corner of St. Charles Avenue and Cadiz Street was built in 1906 and designed by the F. P. Gravely Company for William Mason-Smith, the president of the New Orleans Cotton Exchange. The restful lines and red tile roof make this a Mediterranean-style building. In 1994, a thorough restoration of the house brought it back to its original appearance. The compatible building behind it was built in 1994 and houses garages and servants' quarters.

18   **St. George's Episcopal Church,** *1900*

This austere brick church was begun in 1899 and completed in 1900 in the Romanesque style then popular in New Orleans. St. George's Episcopal School, with three hundred students, is at General Pershing and Camp Streets and is a neighborhood anchor.

Ernst House
4631 St. Charles Avenue,
at Valence (left)

Brown Mansion
4717 St. Charles Avenue,
at Valence (right)

Hernandez House
4803 St. Charles Avenue,
above Bordeaux (right)

Genella Houses
4901 and 4905 St.
Charles Avenue, at
Upperline (right)

Casa Grande
4900 St. Charles Avenue,
at Upperline (left)

Flaspoller House
4941 St. Charles Avenue,
at Robert (right)

19   Ernst House, *circa 1900, F. P. Gravely*

This very fine Georgian Revival house was constructed about 1900 and built by F. P. Gravely. The large wooden house is distinguished by a round porch to the left, fine ornamental railings, bay windows, and pronounced dormers.

20   Brown Mansion, *1905, Favrot and Livaudais*

The monumental, limestone Brown Mansion is the largest house on St. Charles Avenue. It was designed in the Richardsonian Romanesque style by the local firm of Favrot and Livaudais for William Perry Brown, an opulent cotton broker. The house was begun in 1902 and completed in 1905 and is one of the great landmark houses in New Orleans. Local lore has it that when Brown married Margueritte Braughn he promised her the finest residence on the avenue.

21   Hernandez House, *circa 1866*

The Hernandez House is an unusual Italianate, mansard-roofed house with double galleries and a three-story, square tower. It was built about 1866 and remodeled in the 1870s. It was once the home of Joseph Hernandez, the president of the New Orleans and Carrollton Rail Road in the 1870s; he made the line profitable. The house later became the Rugby Academy, a private boys' school, and was eventually moved closer to the avenue. It was recently restored.

22   Genella Houses, *1885–89*

Behind large old magnolia trees is this pair of double-galleried houses built between 1885 and 1889 by Mrs. Louisa Genella, who subdivided the large corner lot. The two buildings are basically the same but have slight differentiations in their fancy wood trim. They are excellent examples of New Orleans 1880s Victorian houses, which preserved the basic form of the 1840–50s Greek Revival double-gallery house but overlaid it with more elaborate machine-sawn gingerbread.

23   Casa Grande

This early-twentieth-century, corner apartment house displays the vogue for Spanish and Mediterranean styles that Hollywood made so popular all over the country. The building was converted into condominiums in 1985.

24   Flaspoller House, *1905, Francis J. MacDonnell*

A semicircular portico with fluted Doric columns distinguishes this fine corner house. Designed by Francis J. MacDonnell and built in 1905, this Colonial Revival house was built for Henry Flaspoller. A later change inserted the second-story room under the portico. The front garden sets off the building perfectly; a conservatory appears on the Robert Street side of the house.

Orléans Club, *1868; remodeled 1907, Emile Weil*
Built in 1868 for Colonel William Lewis Wynne, this elegant house, with its delicate cast-iron gallery, was built as a wedding gift for Colonel Wynne's daughter, Mrs. George C. Garner. The house was remodeled in 1907 by Emile Weil in the French Second Empire style with a mansard roof. In 1925 it became the home of the Orléans Club, a woman's social and cultural club. The club holds meetings and lectures each Tuesday. In the 1950s, the club built the small auditorium to the left of the old house. It is a favored Uptown venue for debutante teas and wedding receptions.

Vaccaro House, *1910, Edward Sporl*
This half-timbered, Tudor-style corner house with a deep porch was designed in 1910 by architect Edward Sporl. Joseph Vaccaro and his brother founded the Standard Fruit and Steamship Company and made a fortune importing bananas from Central America.

Milton H. Latter Memorial Public Library, *1907, Favrot and Livaudais*
This is the only grand house on St. Charles Avenue that the public can visit. Since 1948 it has served as the Uptown branch of the New Orleans Public Library; visitors can see its interior during library hours. The library has produced an interesting brochure on the mansion and the families who have lived here. This baronial Indiana limestone mansion occupying a full block front was built in 1907 for Mark Isaacs, the owner of a Canal Street department store. It was designed by Favrot and Livaudais and set up high on a man-made earthen berm. It is a fusion of the Mediterranean and Prairie styles with restful horizontal massing under a steeply pitched red tile roof. A Chicago firm decorated the interiors. The ceilings in the front rooms came from France and were once in a French Quarter mansion. Local artist John Geiser painted the Dutch murals and the German mottoes in the Blue Room. Originally there was a ballroom on the third floor. Behind the house is an early free-standing automobile garage. The mansion was originally staffed by twelve servants. After passing through other hands, it was bought by real estate magnate Harry Latter and his wife in 1948 and given to the city as a memorial to their only son, Milton H. Latter, who died at Okinawa during World War II. The city has preserved the formal rooms on the first floor as reading rooms and converted the second-floor bedrooms into book stacks. In 1983–85, with a gift from Shirley Latter Kaufman and a city bond issue, the mansion was restored by architect Samuel Wilson, Jr., with interiors restored by Allen House. Reboard the streetcar and alight at Nashville Avenue, seven blocks farther uptown.

Orléans Club
5005 St. Charles Avenue, at Robert (right)

Vaccaro House
5010 St. Charles Avenue, at Robert (left)

Milton H. Latter Memorial Public Library
5120 St. Charles Avenue, between Soniat and Dufossat (left); open Monday to Thursday 11 A.M. to 6 P.M.; Saturday 11 A.M. to 5 P.M.; closed Friday and Sunday; 596-2625

De La Salle High School
5300 St. Charles Avenue,
between Valmont and
Leontine (left); 895-5717

New Orleans Jewish Community Center
5342 St. Charles Avenue,
between Leontine and
Jefferson (left); 897-0143
for programs

The Octavia
5421 St. Charles Avenue,
at Octavia (right)

Danneel Park
St. Charles Avenue, at
Octavia (right)

㉘   De La Salle High School, *1952, Burk, Lebreton, and Lamantia*

This low-rise, yellow-brick, Roman Catholic boys' high school is conducted by the Christian Brothers. It was designed by Burk, Lebreton, and Lamantia and opened in 1952. This modern school occupies the site of New Orleans University, founded in 1869 as the Union Normal School on land donated by the Freedmen's Bureau. It was the first institution of higher learning for recently emancipated African American men, and in 1884 it purchased a former sugar cane plantation here for the construction of an imposing red brick school building. In 1935, New Orleans University and Straight College merged to form Dillard University, which built a handsome new neo-Greek Revival campus on Gentilly Road (see page 87).

㉙   New Orleans Jewish Community Center, *1966, Curtis and Davis*

This simple, white-painted, brick-clad building was designed by Curtis and Davis and opened in 1966. The kinetic sculpture mounted on its plain facade is by Lin Emery. This active community center stands on the site of the Jewish Widows and Orphans Home, begun in 1886 and designed by Thomas Sully. That three-story, turreted, red-brick building was long a landmark on upper St. Charles Avenue. The orphanage closed in 1946, and two years later the land was transferred to the New Orleans Jewish Community Center. The center traces its roots to the founding of the Young Men's Hebrew Association in 1891.

Jefferson Avenue to Nashville Avenue

㉚   The Octavia, *1907, Favrot and Livaudais*

This early, luxury, twenty-unit apartment house was built in 1907 and designed by Favrot and Livaudais. The Edwardian building was converted into condominiums in the 1970s.

㉛   Danneel Park

This small corner park is a favorite of toddlers as well as their nannies or young parents. It was donated to the city by the reclusive Rudolph Danneel and his brother, Henry. Bachelor Rudolph was a wealthy cotton merchant in the firm of Danneel and Francke and left this park as a memorial to his parents.

32   **Benjamin-Monroe House,** *1916, Emile Weil*
This suave Italian Renaissance Revival limestone mansion was designed by Emile Weil and constructed in 1916. It was built for E. V. Benjamin, who came from Cincinnati and built a large chemical company. The restrained house has paired Ionic columns, a wrought-iron railing at the second floor, and a stone balustrade across its top.

33   **McCarthy House,** *1903, Soule & MacDonnell*
This large red brick house with its imposing white Ionic portico was built in 1903 for T. H. McCarthy, a wealthy lumber man who made his fortune in cypress. The contemporary marble statues that stand on its lawn are by Robert Schoen.

34   **Coates House,** *1913, Favrot & Livandais*
This large red-brick house with its green tile roof is built up on a high earthen berm to keep the building dry during flooding. The generous front porch has handsome proportions; its square pillars are decorated with escutcheons, as are those of the porte cochere on the Arabella Street side. There is more than a hint of Chicago's Prairie style in the general feeling of this design, which dates from 1913.

35   **"Tara" / Palmer House,** *1941, Andrew M. Lockett*
Popular with the public, if not with architectural critics, this large, white-painted brick house was built in 1941. It was designed by Andrew M. Lockett in imitation of the fictional plantation house Tara in Margaret Mitchell's *Gone with the Wind* of 1936. The house was built for George Palmer, who in 1955 added a bomb shelter in the garden reputed to be able to support his family for seventy-two hours.

36   **5718 St. Charles Avenue,** *1889, Louis Lambert*
This exuberant Queen Anne–style house with a corner turret was built in 1889 to designs by Louis Lambert for William Girault.

37   **5726 St. Charles Avenue,** *1889, Louis Lambert*
Next door is another Queen Anne–style house designed in 1889 by Louis Lambert. It was remodeled and "classicized" by Lambert about 1900, with a Doric-columned porch added when Victoriana went out of fashion.

Benjamin-Monroe House
5531 St. Charles Avenue, at Joseph (right)

McCarthy House
5603 St. Charles Avenue, at Joseph (right)

Coates House
5631 St. Charles Avenue, at Arabella (right)

"Tara" / Palmer House
5705 St. Charles Avenue, at Arabella (right)

5718 St. Charles Avenue
(left)

5726 St. Charles Avenue
(left)

Hillman House
5800 St. Charles Avenue,
at Nashville (left)

Palacio House
5824 St. Charles Avenue
(left)

1 Rosa Park
(right)

Rosa Park
(right)

Tour 9b:

A Walk from Nashville Avenue
to Audubon Place

38 **Hillman House,** *circa 1870*

This prototypical Louisiana raised cottage set in deep gardens was built about 1870 for John W. Hillman, a cashier with the Land and Pledge Association. The elegant house is a combination of the Greek Revival and Italianate styles; Corinthian columns support its gallery. It is most probably built of native cypress painted the traditional white. These early houses responded intelligently to the Louisiana climate. They were raised up off the ground to survive floods and to catch any occasional breezes. They have steeply pitched roofs to shed tropical downpours. Their floor-to-ceiling windows maximize ventilation, as do their louvered jalousies (shutters). The deep overhang of their porches permits the windows to be kept open during rainstorms. The Werlein family, who owned a music store on Canal Street, lived here from 1880 to 1943.

39 **Palacio House,** *1867–68, Henry Howard*

This superb raised cottage hidden behind lush gardens was designed by the noted architect Henry Howard in 1867–68 for Antonio Palacio, a native of Bilbao, Spain. The dormer windows were added to improve ventilation in the early 1920s.

40 **1 Rosa Park,** *1900, Favrot & Livaudais*

This white-painted, frame, 1900 Colonial Revival house has vigorous massing and is a compilation of many architectural shapes and elements. Note the curving, double-columned porch, the fan-lighted doorway opening onto the second-floor porch, and the assertive, overhanging gable that caps the composition. These fusions of the Queen Anne and Colonial Revival styles are among the most inventive of American house designs.

41 **Rosa Park,** *1891*

This planned private street, the first in New Orleans, was laid out in 1891 to capitalize on the boom in uptown real estate. As avenue frontage became dearer, developers created private perpendicular streets that took the prestige of the avenue and extended it back into the block. This still-private street was named for Rosa Solomon DaPointe, a society beauty who lived at St. Charles and Foucher in a no longer extant Moorish-style mansion. Mrs. DaPointe was famous for her fanciful parlors, which she occasionally decorated as ice caverns or Middle Eastern bazaars. She also wrote, acted in, and staged her own theatricals in a small theater behind her mansion. The fine iron finial-capped gateway of Rosa Park dates from 1895.

42 **"Wedding Cake House" / de la Houssaye House,** *1896,*
Toledano and Wogan
This spectacular Georgian Revival mansion was built in 1896 and designed by Toledano and Wogan. Few houses are as extravagant as this one is, with its opulent decoration, unusual column capitals, carved swags, brackets, balustrades punctuated with posts capped by urns, Palladian windows, flaring brick chimneys, and dormers with broken pediments. It is a tour de force of nineteenth-century domestic architecture and craftsmanship—an "over the top" exercise in opulence and luxurious comfort. Note the size of its generous windows and its many porches, balconies, and bay windows. The house has recently undergone a superb restoration, including the installation of appropriate gardens with an ornamental pool. Note the handsome, cubical carriage house to its rear with its rooftop balustrade.

43 **Wilson House,** *1971, John Frazer*
Set behind a brick-paved, semicircular entrance drive is this contemporary French Second Empire mansion designed by Houston architect John Frazer in 1971. It is one of the best modern buildings on the avenue.

44 **St. Charles Avenue Presbyterian Church,** *1924–30, W. W. Van Meter*
This church had its beginnings in 1905 when the First Presbyterian Church on Lafayette Square (since demolished) opened an Uptown evening Sunday school on this site in the home of former Governor McEnery. The church was chartered in 1920, and in 1930 the present, appropriately sober, Gothic Revival church designed by W. W. Van Meter was dedicated.

45 **6000 St. Charles Avenue,** *1895, Thomas Sully*
This stately, symmetrical, white, corner Georgian Revival house was designed in 1895 by the prolific Thomas Sully. The house is distinguished by a semicircular entrance portico with an elaborate, swag-decorated entablature and a balustrade with urn-capped newel posts. Broken pediments crown the large first-floor windows and the rooftop dormers. The State Street side has large bow windows; the other side of the house has large, screened-in porches. This is one of the most festively decorated houses on the avenue at Halloween, Christmas, and Mardi Gras.

46 **6110 St. Charles Avenue,** *1904, Favrot and Livaudais*
This large white stucco house is strikingly designed in the Swiss Chalet style, and it has dark green wood half-timbering and a sheltering green tile roof. It was long the home of philanthropist Stella Hirsch Lemann, who gave Madame John's Legacy to the Louisiana State Museum (see page 144).

"Wedding Cake House" / de la Houssaye House
5809 St. Charles Avenue, at Rosa Park (right)

Wilson House
5931 St. Charles Avenue, at State (right)

St. Charles Avenue Presbyterian Church
5954 St. Charles Avenue, at State (left); Sunday communion at 8:30 A.M., worship at 10:30 A.M.; 897-0101

6000 St. Charles Avenue
(left)

6110 St. Charles Avenue
(left)

Schlieder House
6145 St. Charles Avenue
(right)

Temple Sinai Reform Congregation
6227 St. Charles Avenue, at Calhoun (right); services at 6:15 P.M. on the first Friday of each month, 8:15 P.M. all other Fridays; 10:15 A.M. on Saturday; 861-3693

Loyola University of the South
6363 St. Charles Avenue, at Calhoun (right); 865-2011; events 865-3428; Marquette Theater box office 865-3824

The Most Holy Name of Jesus Roman Catholic Church
6367 St. Charles Avenue; weekday masses at 6:30 A.M.; Sunday masses at 7:30, 9, 10:30 A.M. (sung) and 6 P.M.; Saturday at 7:30 A.M.; vespers daily at 5 P.M.; open only for services

47   Schlieder House, *1923, Favrot & Livaudais*

This princely limestone house, set behind a semicircular driveway, was built in 1923 in the Italian Renaissance villa style. It has an elegant, arched entrance portico and restful lines. The mansion is set in spacious grounds with a tennis court to the right-hand side. It has been recently restored and is often festively decorated.

48   Temple Sinai Reform Congregation, *1927, Emile Weil, Moise Goldstein, and the firm Weiss, Dreyfous, and Seiferth*

Organized in 1870 as the first Reform congregation in New Orleans, Temple Sinai's first location was near Lee Circle. This suave Byzantine-Moderne, yellow brick building was built in 1927 to designs by Emile Weil, Moise Goldstein, and the firm of Weiss, Dreyfous, and Seiferth. The modern addition with the Tablets of the Law was constructed in 1970. This congregation has always been in the vanguard of religious and community reform. In 1949, when Dr. Ralph Bunche came to New Orleans to speak, the auditorium at Temple Sinai was the only hall that would host a racially integrated audience.

49   Loyola University of the South

This imposing horseshoe of red brick buildings with white terracotta trim is the St. Charles Avenue face of the nineteen-acre Loyola campus. The central building is Marquette Hall and was built in 1910–16. To its right is Thomas Hall, also built in 1910; to the left is the Most Holy Name of Jesus Roman Catholic Church. All were designed by deBuys, Churchill, and Labouisse. The two university buildings are Tudor Revival; the large church is Gothic Revival. On the lawn in front of Marquette Hall is a gleaming white statue of the Sacred Heart of Jesus. Statues of St. Ignatius Loyola (left) and Father Marquette, S.J. (right), appear in the niches of Marquette Hall. Loyola University began in 1904 as Loyola Academy, a Society of Jesus preparatory school. In 1912 it became Loyola University. Today it is a coeducational university with some fifty-six hundred students. Tuition was about $12,500 in 1996. The first Jesuit college in New Orleans was the College of the Immaculate Conception, which opened in 1849 in what is today the Central Business District next to the Church of the Immaculate Conception (see page 245).

50   The Most Holy Name of Jesus Roman Catholic Church, *1918, deBuys, Churchill, and Labouisse*

Begun in 1914, dedicated in 1918, and designed by deBuys, Churchill, and Labouisse in the English perpendicular Gothic Revival style, this Jesuit church is a memorial to sugar broker Thomas McDermott and was given by his sister, Kate McDermott. It has a steel frame and a red-brick-and-limestone-trimmed exterior. Sculptured marble angels proffer holy water inside the entrance. There is a magnificent high altar with a marble crucifix, and also side altars dedicated to the Blessed Mother, St. Joseph, and St. Ignatius of Loyola. Holy Name of Jesus is the wealthiest Catholic parish in New Orleans.

Round Table Club
6330 St. Charles Avenue, at Exposition Boulevard (left)

Exposition Boulevard (left)

Audubon Park
St. Charles Avenue, between Exposition Boulevard and Walnut (left)

51 Round Table Club, *1896, Toledano and Wogan*
The Round Table Club, a men's club, was organized in 1898 to pursue "literature, science and art." It moved uptown in 1919 and is housed in this large Georgian Revival house designed by Toledano and Wogan and erected in 1896. The house faces Exposition Boulevard and Audubon Park.

52 Exposition Boulevard
A hooded stone gateway announces Exposition "Boulevard," actually a sidewalk bordered by the vast park on one side and fine late Victorian houses on the other. There are restrooms in the pavilion visible just inside the corner of the park here. Exposition Boulevard was planned during the 1884–85 World Industrial and Cotton Centennial Exposition staged in Audubon Park. These houses back onto Calhoun Street. Exposition Boulevard makes a unique walk to Magazine Street and the #11 Magazine bus that can take you back to Canal Street down the best Uptown shopping street.

53 Audubon Park, *1871; 1898, John Charles Olmsted, park plan*
Facing Loyola and Tulane Universities is 340-acre Audubon Park, part of the late-eighteenth-century sugar cane plantation of Jean Étienne Boré, the first planter to develop a commercially successful method for granulating sugar in 1795. It later became part of his son-in-law Pierre Foucher's plantation. (Some old Foucher plantation oaks grace the zoo.) Union troops camped here between 1862 and 1867. The wedge-shaped tract was purchased by the Board of Commissioners of City Park, a Louisiana state agency, in 1871, and was first called "New City Park." It was later renamed in honor of naturalist and artist John James Audubon, who briefly worked in New Orleans in 1821 and 1837. The undeveloped tract became the site of the World's Industrial and Cotton Exposition in 1884–85. The park was transferred to the Audubon Park Commission in 1914; they began landscaping it in 1916 to plans by John Charles Olmsted. Today it is a handsome oak-dotted retreat with large lawns, artificial lagoons, winding paths, and a golf course. The urn-capped, Beaux Arts gateway pylons were designed by Moise Goldstein as a memorial to Maurice Stern. The graceful Gumbel memorial fountain just inside the main entrance is the work of Austrian-born Isidore Konti and was dedicated in 1919. The partially nude bronze female figure with a bird resting on her hand represents the *Meeting of the Air and Water,* an appropriate theme in New Orleans. It was the gift of Beulah Joseph and Cora

Tulane University
6823 St. Charles Avenue;
865-5000

Amistad Research Center
Tilton Hall; open Monday
to Friday 8:30 A.M. to 5
P.M., Saturday 1 to 5 P.M.;
free; 865-5535

Middle American Research
Institute
Dinwiddie Hall, fourth
floor; open Monday to
Friday 8 A.M. to 5 P.M.,
Saturday 8 A.M. to 1 P.M.;
free; 865-5110

Howard-Tilton Library
Special Collections
Howard-Tilton Library,
top floor; glass cases just
outside Special
Collections; 865-5685;
library hours 865-5604

Hogan Jazz Archive
Howard-Tilton Library;
by appointment,
865-5688

Southeast Architectural
Archive
Jones Hall; 865-5391
for hours

Newcomb Art Gallery
Woldenberg Art Center;
next to the Art Building
on Newcomb Place on the
Tulane-Newcomb
Campus; open Monday to
Friday, 10 A.M. to 5 P.M.,
Saturday noon to 5 P.M.;
free; 865-5327

Myra Clare Rogers
Memorial Chapel
Facing Broadway Street;
Roman Catholic mass
Saturday at 5 P.M. and
Sunday at 9 and
11:30 A.M.; 866-0984

Moses in memory of their parents, Simon and Sophie Gumbel. A free shuttle bus operates from near the entrance gate to the zoo at the river end of the park (see page 84).

54   Tulane University

The trio of Bedford limestone, Richardsonian Romanesque buildings that face St. Charles Avenue in a wide U are the oldest buildings on the Tulane University campus. The central building, Randall Lee Gibson Hall, was built in 1894 and designed by the New Orleans firm of Harrod and Andry. The building to the left is Tilton Hall, a richly decorated 1901 design by Andry and Bendernagle, with windows by Louis Comfort Tiffany. It houses the **Amistad Research Center,** an archives and gallery dedicated to African American history and the Civil Rights Movement (including gay rights) founded by the interdenominational American Missionary Association. The art collection here includes works by African American artists and also examples of African art. The building to the right is Dinwiddie Hall, built in 1936 and designed by Moise Goldstein. On the fourth floor here is the gallery of the **Middle American Research Institute,** with pre-Columbian archaeological treasures from Mexico and Central America. Through the main quadrangle and across Freret Street is the modernistic **Howard-Tilton Library.** On its top floor, just outside Special Collections, are glass cases with changing exhibits of rare archival materials. The **Hogan Jazz Archive** (by appointment) is also here. In Jones Hall next door is the **Southeast Architectural Archive,** a treasure trove of materials on Southern architecture that mounts small changing exhibitions. On the adjoining Newcomb College campus is the recently opened **Newcomb Art Gallery;** one room here is dedicated to early-twentieth-century Newcomb College pottery and crafts. On the other side of the Newcomb campus, facing Broadway Street, is the modern **Myra Clare Rogers Memorial Chapel** with three superb windows by Louis Comfort Tiffany from the old Newcomb chapel in the Garden District.

Tulane University had its beginnings in 1834 as the Medical College of Louisiana and became the University of Louisiana in 1847. In 1881 the then-public institution received a munificent gift from merchant Paul Tulane and became a private university with its own board of administrators. Paul Tulane was born in Princeton, New Jersey, in 1801 and came to New Orleans in 1822. Here he became a successful dry goods merchant selling clothes, hats, and shoes; he also invested in real estate. In 1873 he retired to Princeton. A bachelor, he decided to endow a college in Louisiana. In 1881 he asked Randall Lee Gibson to confer with him

in New Jersey and sketched his plans for higher education in his former home. With the Tulane gift, the university moved from Common Street and University Place (on the same block as today's
Fairmont Hotel) to this ninety-three-acre, wedged-shaped tract of
land facing Audubon Park. Tulane was founded as a whites-only
men's college; it was racially integrated in 1963. Its sister institution, Sophie H. Newcomb College, is today an integral part of
Tulane University. It was founded in the Garden District in 1886 by
Mrs. Josephine Louise LeMonnier Newcomb in memory of her
only child. In 1918 that woman's college moved to Broadway Street to a tract of land
adjoining Tulane and began the construction of a series of red brick Georgian Revival
buildings, the earliest of which were designed by James Gamble Rodgers. The newly
expanded Newcomb Art Gallery in the Woldenberg Art Center is worth seeing. In the
modern Newcomb Chapel facing Broadway Street are three extraordinarily fine
Tiffany windows made in 1905 for the college's Garden District chapel. They depict
King David with his harp, the Good Samaritan, and St. Cecelia. In 1996 Tulane
University had 10,667 students and almost 2,500 full-time employees. It is the largest
private employer in New Orleans. Tuition was a little under $20,000 in 1996.

1 Audubon Place
(right)

Audubon Place
(right)

**Tulane University
President's House**
2 Audubon Place (right)

55   1 Audubon Place, *1911, Favrot & Livaudais*
This spacious limestone house with the small playhouse in its front yard was built in
1911 for William S. Penick, a partner in a molasses company. With its restful horizontal lines, generous porches, and red tile roof, it owes a stylistic debt to the Prairie School
of turn-of-the-century Chicago.

56   Audubon Place, *1894, H. Grandjean, surveyor*
Just beyond the Tulane-Newcomb campus is the Romanesque Revival stone and iron
gate to Audubon Place, a private enclave laid out in 1894. It was developed by George
Blackwelder of Fort Worth, Texas, who created a millionaires' street owned by the
twenty-eight property owners who front on it. The private Audubon Place Commission
owns and maintains the street and its lushly landscaped median and pays for the guards
at the gate. Visitors may not enter without an invitation from one of the residents.

57   Tulane University President's House / Jay-Zemurray Mansion, *1908, Toledano
and Wogan*
Two stately, white-columned porticos grace the Jay House of 1908; one portico faces
St. Charles Avenue and the other exclusive Audubon Place. This Colonial Revival mansion is one of the most commanding in New Orleans and was long the home of Samuel
Zemurray, the founder of the United Fruit Company and a wealthy importer of
bananas. *La frutera,* as it was known in Latin America, was a transnational economic
and political power in Central America early in this century. Zemurray became a noted

John James Audubon
cruise
586-8777

philanthropist and gave his house to Tulane to serve as the official residence of the university's president.

Continuations:

Exposition Boulevard or Audubon Street to Magazine Street

There are two recommended continuations of this tour that connect you with Magazine Street and its fascinating shops. The first is a twenty-minute walk down Exposition Boulevard (a sidewalk, not a boulevard) along the downtown edge of Audubon Park. The second, more rewarding path is a thirty-minute walk down Audubon Street (not Boulevard, Court, Place, or Terrace, but *Street*), one block from the uptown edge of the park. This beautiful, embracing, oak-embowered street harbors fine stucco villas from the palmy 1920s among its many styles, all set in verdant gardens. As you reach the river end of Audubon Street at Magazine, you leave the (relatively) high ground for the flood-prone low ground; two-story houses become one-story cottages.

This neighborhood is where Mahalia Jackson, Uptown's celestial voice, was born on October 26, 1912. Though Mahalia later moved to Chicago, she never lost her bond with New Orleans' Baptist and Spiritualist churches, and she returned to be buried outside her hometown in 1972.

At Audubon and Magazine Streets there is a view of the still well-maintained levee. Turn left (downtown) to the vintage bus shelter at Magazine and Broadway (the zoo is here). Take the #11 Magazine bus from here to Nashville Street to shop, or continue on to Canal Street and the edge of the French Quarter.

Audubon Zoo

At the main entrance to Audubon Park on St. Charles Avenue, at stop #37, there is a free shuttle bus to the Audubon Zoo. The **John James Audubon** cruises from the zoo back down to the foot of Canal Street.

Central City: The Other Uptown / #15 Freret Bus

Behind the screen of grand houses along St. Charles Avenue lies another Uptown, the devastated African American Central City ghetto. A safe way for visitors to glimpse this unvisited side of the city is to ride the #15 Freret bus from its beginning at Carondelet and Canal (the same stop as the zero stop of the St. Charles Avenue streetcar) to Tulane University. On the uptown side of the elevated Pontchartrain Expressway you pass semiabandoned Dryades Street /Orthea Castle Boulevard (see page 196), blocks of once-fine antebellum houses that are now dilapidated, trash-strewn lots and the 1,403-unit, yellowish brick C. J. Peete public housing project, built in 1939–41, with boarded-up windows and bleak "courtyards." Freret Street itself was once a lively neighborhood shopping street. Past Napoleon Avenue there are modest houses with tended yards, and past Jefferson Avenue are the larger houses of the fashionable University Section all the way to Tulane University. You can walk from Freret Street to St. Charles Avenue through the leafy quadrangles of the Tulane campus to board the streetcar for a scenic return trip.

Tour Ten
Magazine Street

*The vintage shopfronts of Uptown's narrow, curving Magazine Street
have blossomed with used furniture stores, antique shops, bookshops, a good newsstand,
cafés and restaurants, galleries, and elegant boutiques.*

What This Tour Covers

Preliminaries

Introduction: Six Miles of Eclectic Shops

Continuation

Coliseum Square and the Arts District

Tour 10

Segment 1
Exposition Blvd. to Nashville Ave.

Segment 2
Nashville Ave. to Jefferson Ave.
recommended shopping strip

Segment 3
Jefferson Ave. to Napoleon Ave.

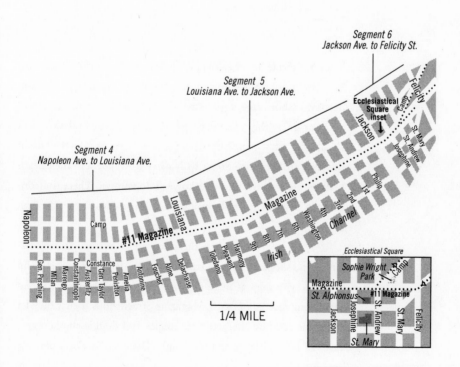

Segment 6
Jackson Ave. to Felicity St.

Segment 5
Louisiana Ave. to Jackson Ave.

Segment 4
Napoleon Ave. to Louisiana Ave.

Ecclesiastical
Square
inset
↓

Felicity

Camp

St. Mary

St. Andrew

Josephine

Jackson

Philip

1st

2nd

3rd

4th

Washington

Channel

Napoleon

Camp

Magazine

#11 Magazine

Louisiana

Irish

Delachase

Foucher

Aline

Toledano

Pleasant

Harmony

9th

8th

7th

6th

Constance

Antonine

Amelia

Peniston

Gen. Taylor

Austerlitz

Constantinople

Marengo

Milan

Gen. Pershing

1/4 MILE

Ecclesiastical Square

Sophie Wright
Park

Camp

Magazine

St. Alphonsus

#11 Magazine

Jackson

Josephine

St. Andrew

St. Mary

Felicity

St. Mary

What This Tour Covers

This tour lists many of the individual small shops that make Uptown *the* contemporary shopping mecca. It breaks the six-mile-long street into six segments, and it also includes the landmark churches at Ecclesiastical Square just off Magazine Street that are too often overlooked by natives as well as visitors.

Preliminaries

BEST TIMES TO DO THIS TOUR

Saturday from 10 A.M. to 6 P.M. is a good time to explore narrow, curving Magazine Street for the first time. Parking is easiest on weekdays. On the evening of the first Saturday of each month (summer excepted), the galleries along Magazine and Julia Streets open exhibits and host receptions that draw interesting crowds.

How to Explore Magazine Street

Since Magazine Street is long, it's best to focus your explorations. First decide whether you want to concentrate on art galleries and decorator shops (the upper stretch of the street) or old furniture and antiques (the lower part of Magazine). General shoppers should probably choose the upper sector. Drive or take the bus all the way up Magazine Street to Nashville Avenue and then begin walking back down the street toward downtown. There is a continuous row of great shopping all the way down to Jefferson Avenue.

Although there are many antique stores, galleries, and shops in the long stretch between Jefferson and Jackson Avenues, you may want to dig deeper on a subsequent visit. An interesting feature of many Magazine Street shops is that they let you penetrate the characteristic single- and double-shotgun cottages of New Orleans and the South. These agreeable, if narrow, frame buildings were the bulk of the city's nineteenth-century working-class housing and are still key in the city's housing stock. (Apartment buildings were not popular in pre-1960 New Orleans.)

The shotgun house is a one-story frame cottage consisting of a long row of rooms in single file perpendicular to the sidewalk. They got their name from the apocryphal story that a shot fired through the front door would go right through the building and out the back door without hitting anything. As a matter of fact, the doors inside a shotgun house do not usually line up in an uninterrupted row. Their rooms are generally high-ceilinged and of a good size, perhaps fourteen feet square. Double shotguns were even more economical to build with their party wall, and they abound in old New Orleans neighborhoods. In New Orleans parlance, a camelback is a shotgun house with a two-story section in the back. (This second rear floor often had its own side entrance off an alley alongside the house.)

Skip down Magazine Street by bus from Jefferson Avenue and alight at Jackson Avenue to explore the shorter, funkier cluster of used furniture and antique shops between Jackson and Felicity. At Magazine and Josephine you can probe just one block into the Irish Channel to Josephine and Constance Streets and Ecclesiastical Square to glimpse the Baroque bell tower of St. Mary's Assumption Roman Catholic Church of 1858–60 and the impressive Renaissance Revival facade of St. Alphonsus Roman Catholic Church of 1855–57 across the street.

Parking

Street parking is generally available along Magazine Street. There is a parking lot behind Feet First Ladies Discount Designer Shoes at 5500 Magazine Street, at Octavia Street. The meter maids are relentless on the residential side streets.

Cafes, Bakeries, and Restaurants

There are several cozy cafes and bakeries sprinkled through the uptown part of Magazine Street. A recommended restaurant here is Casamento's Oyster Bar (see page 50).

Introduction:
Six Miles of Eclectic Shops

The street where New Orleanians shop for old furniture, books, antiques, rugs, contemporary art furniture, new art, and decorative arts is six-mile long, curving, narrow Magazine Street. It stretches from Canal Street to **Audubon Park** (see Tour 9, page 311) and is served by the #11 Magazine bus. The most concentrated shopping is from Jefferson to Nashville Avenues. The street takes its name from the state tobacco warehouses, *magazins,* that the French colonial authorities operated at Magazine and Common Streets on the edge of today's CBD. (Pungent perique tobacco was the first sought-after Louisiana export.) Here run-down and there lively, the long string of Victorian houses and small shops that line Magazine parallels mansion-lined St. Charles Avenue. It was, and still is, the seam between two worlds, the Garden District and Uptown to its lakeside, and the Victorian working-class neighborhoods between it and the riverside wharfs.

Today the Irish Channel, the best-known historic working-class district here, consists of the blocks bounded by Magazine and Tchoupitoulas, and from Jackson to Louisiana Avenues. This crescent-shaped area is built up with inexpensive, one-story frame houses. Practical, two-family double-shotgun houses are plentiful here. Many have Victorian gingerbread brackets decorating their facades, not more costly cast iron. This was originally an immigrant neighborhood with many Irish and German families who settled here from the mid-1830s to about 1860. By the early twentieth century, the Irish Channel was a tough, insular, white ethnic Roman Catholic neighborhood. On the river edge of the neighborhood were the animal pens and slaughterhouses, lumber and brick yards, and light industry and warehousing that backed up on the busy nineteenth-century wharfs and that employed the neighborhood's many unskilled laborers. In Anne Rice's Mayfair novels, Michael Curry, an Irish Channel kid whose family had lived in the same double-shotgun house on Annunciation Street for three generations, escapes his cramped world by crossing the great social divide of Magazine Street and wandering around in the plush Garden District. Irish Channel life also appears memorably in John Kennedy Toole's comedic masterpiece *A Confederacy of Dunces.* Success and encircling suburbia drew away its sons and daughters. The Irish Channel was designated a National Historic Architectural District in 1976 and has seen recent investment and improvement. In the early 1970s the far downriver end of the old Irish Channel was rechristened the Lower Garden District in an effort by its restoration-minded new residents to burnish its image.

In 1938–41, the multiblock, 1,450-unit St. Thomas housing project was begun in the downriver part of the Irish Channel below Jackson Avenue. Originally rented only to white working-class families, it became predominately black by the mid-1970s. Only 812 units were occupied in 1995. There is a high incidence of illiteracy and unemployment in "the bricks" today, and life is hard here and all too often violent. Ecclesiastical Square, with its two landmark 1850s Roman Catholic churches and spectacular bell tower, abuts the St. Thomas housing project, and caution is advised there.

Above Louisiana Avenue and all the way to Audubon Park, the blocks flanking Magazine are part of the Uptown District. The houses here are also modest one- and two-story, single- and double-shotgun houses. Some are camelbacks, houses that are one story in front and two stories in the rear. Originally an area populated by mechanics and lower-middle-class families, these blocks have experienced considerable recent gentrification. Today the blocks closest to Audubon Park are professional and middle-class, young-family oriented areas. New residents have restored their Victorian cottages and enhanced their enfolding gardens. The blocks near the foot of State Street typify revived Uptown.

St. Clare's Monastery
720 Henry Clay Avenue, at Magazine; 895-2019

New Orleans Adolescent Hospital
Three blocks bounded by Henry Clay Avenue, State and Tchoupitoulas Streets and the Mississippi River; main entrance on State Street; not generally open to the public; 897-3400

Magazine Street was a low-key shopping strip serving mostly local needs until the early 1970s. As tourism boomed, rents escalated in the French Quarter, and this, coupled with low rents in old shopfronts and small converted frame houses here, drew second-hand shops, the decorator trade, auction houses, and dealers in beautiful objects both antique and contemporary to Magazine Street. Magazine Street has the sense of discovery that French Quarter shops once had but rarely do today. New Orleanians who patronize the many shops, restaurants, and services on this long street tend to drive from spot to spot. Visitors should either drive, take a taxi, or use the bus to hopscotch down the street and not attempt to walk all of it.

1 *Magazine Street, Exposition Boulevard to Nashville Avenue*
The following sections proceed *from uptown to downtown* along Magazine Street. This first section is six blocks long.

• *Exposition Boulevard*
For a description of this sidewalk bordering Audubon Park, see Tour 9, page 311.

• **St. Clare's Monastery,** *1912, William R. Burk*
This brick monastery stands behind a high brick wall at the corner of Henry Clay Avenue and Magazine Street. The chapel near the corner has an exterior statue of St. Clare contemplating a monstrance exhibiting the host. The Franciscan emblem of crossed arms, here before the Sacred Heart, surmounts the entrance. The *retardataire* building looks Victorian but was built in 1912.

Detour:
New Orleans Adolescent Hospital / Old United States Public Health Service Hospital
This complex of twenty-one buildings built between 1831 and 1959 is best glimpsed through the wire mesh fence along Leake Avenue. Successively the location of a sugar

Blade Action Sports
6108 Magazine Street;
891-7055

Nina Sloss Antiques and Interiors
6008 Magazine Street;
895-8088

Perlis
6070 Magazine Street;
895-8661

Enoch's Framing & Gallery
6063 Magazine Street;
899-6686

Taqueria Corona
5932 Magazine Street;
lunch and dinner daily;
897-3974

Martinique Bistro
5908 Magazine Street;
dinner only, Tuesday to
Sunday; 891-8495

National Art & Hobby
5835 Magazine Street;
899-4491

The Tulip Tree
5831 Magazine Street;
895-3748

Cafe Luna
802 Nashville Avenue, at
Magazine; 899-3723

Quilt Cottage
801 Nashville Avenue, at
Magazine; 895-3791

Wirthmore
5723 Magazine Street;
897-9727

cane plantation, a sawmill, and a brick factory, the United States Marine Hospital Service bought this extensive property in 1883 to serve merchant seamen and navy men. The original frame complex faced Tchoupitoulas Street and the river and was set in a large grove of fragrant orange trees. The tall brick wall surrounding the property was built in 1895. In 1931 the complex was handsomely rebuilt in brick in the Classic Revival style. Inside the wall at the corner of Henry Clay Avenue and Tchoupitoulas Street is the Polycarpe Fortier house, a Creole cottage built about 1831–34, with wings and a front gallery added about 1858–62. It is probably the oldest building in Uptown. The director's house on the grounds is a fine Italianate Victorian house with a complex architectural history. The federal government closed all eight Public Health Hospitals in 1981; the handsome complex then became the State of Louisiana's New Orleans Adolescent Hospital.

From Henry Clay Avenue to Nashville Avenue

- **Blade Action Sports** Sells and rents in-line skates; Audubon Park is nearby.
- **Nina Sloss Antiques and Interiors** Antique French and English furniture and accessories.
- **Perlis** Men's, ladies', and boys' Uptown preppy clothing; sports shirts with a Perlis Louisiana crayfish make good souvenirs.
- **Enoch's Framing & Gallery** A typical shotgun cottage filled with prints, including Walter Anderson hand-colored prints; specializes in Carnival memorabilia.
- **Taqueria Corona** Inexpensive.
- **Martinique Bistro** Moderate.
- **National Art & Hobby** Art and craft supplies and beads.
- **The Tulip Tree** Refinished golden oak furniture and accessories.

2 ## Magazine Street, Nashville Avenue to Jefferson Avenue

This section of Magazine Street covers four blocks.

From Nashville Avenue to Arabella Street

- **Cafe Luna** A small cozy coffeehouse in a corner Victorian cottage with a front porch.
- **Quilt Cottage** Quilts and fabric for quilts.
- **Wirthmore** French and Chinese antiques.

- **Art Smart, Inc.** A gallery with the fresh spirit of contemporary New Orleans design; gifts, painted furniture, chandeliers and lamps, flatwear, linens, glass, and accessories.

- **Chez Nous Charcuterie** An outstanding place for gourmet take-out food, including Creole and Cajun dishes packed for travel; fine selection of cheeses, pâtés, soups, salads, entrees, and desserts. One of the places where Uptown does its catering.

- **Dos Jeffes Uptown Cigars** Large selection of imported hand-rolled cigars; humidors.

- **Former Arabella Bus Barn** This large utilitarian structure was built after the 1884 Cotton Exposition and has successively housed mule-drawn streeetcars, electric streetcars, and diesel buses. Its roof is made of eight-inch-by-twenty-inch cypress beams sheathed in old-growth cypress boards. The nasty buses moved to a new Canal Street facility in 1995, and the future of this historic structure has not yet been decided. Many neighbors want small retail and residential uses for this utilitarian landmark.

From Arabella Street to Jefferson Avenue

- **Vizard's** Chef Kevin Vizard's restaurant featuring contemporary New Orleans cuisine.

- **Uptown Costume & Dance Company** Tights and shoes for dancers; costumes, rubber masks, make-up, wigs, hats, marjorette boots.

- **The Persian Cat Needlecrafts** Canvases, yarns, needles, supplies, and books.

- **Pied Nu** Sophisticated chairs and sofas, linens, accessories and ladies' clothing.

- **All Natural Foods & Deli** Organic produce, bulk foods, vitamins, and a vegetarian deli with a couple of tables on the sidewalk; take-out.

- **Artifacts** Furnishings and accessories, many by local and national artists; art, lamps, ceramics, jewelry, and gifts.

- **MiGa Women's Apparel** Fine contemporary women's clothing.

- **RATB Designs by Ruby Ann Tobar-Blanco** Jewelry, accessories, and clothing designed by this local artist.

- **Feet First Ladies Discount Designer Shoes** The name describes the goods; there is a parking lot with its entrance on Octavia Street behind this 1931 former market building.

Art Smart, Inc.
5707 Magazine Street;
891-0110

Chez Nous Charcuterie
5701 Magazine Street, at Arabella; 899-7303

Dos Jeffes Uptown Cigars
5700 Magazine Street;
899-3030

Former Arabella Bus Barn
5600 Magazine Street

Vizard's
5538 Magazine Street;
895-5000

Uptown Costume & Dance Company
5533 Magazine Street;
895-7969

The Persian Cat Needlecrafts
5525 Magazine Street;
899-6050

Pied Nu
5521 Magazine Street;
899-4118

All Natural Foods & Deli
5517 Magazine Street;
open daily; 891-2651

Artifacts
5515 Magazine Street;
899-5505

MiGa Women's Apparel
5513 Magazine Street;
895-2552

RATB Designs
5509 Magazine Street;
899-3189

Feet First Ladies Discount Designer Shoes
5500 Magazine Street;
899-6800

Magazine Flowers and Greenery
5434 Magazine Street, at Octavia; 891-4356; 897-6682

PJ's Coffee & Tea Cafe
5432 Magazine Street; open daily 8 A.M. to 11 P.M.; 895-0273

Scriptura
5423 Magazine Street; 897-1555

Lenny's News
5420 Magazine Street; 897-1183

Angele Parlange Design
5419 Magazine Street; 897-6511

Retroactive
5418 Magazine Street; 895-5054

Melange Sterling–Madeleine Guice Nicoladis
5419 Magazine Street; 899-4796; 800-513-3991

British Antiques
5415 Magazine Street; 895-3716

Beaucoup Books
5414 Magazine Street; 895-2663; 800-543-4114

UTOPIA
5408 Magazine Street; 899-8488

CC's Coffee House
900 Jefferson Avenue, at Magazine; 891-4969

First National Bank of Commerce
830 Jefferson Avenue, at Magazine; 552-2610

- **Magazine Flowers and Greenery** A superb flower and plant shop.
- **PJ's Coffee & Tea Cafe** Fresh roasted coffees; the cafe is a local gathering spot.
- **Scriptura** Fine writing papers and related gifts.
- **Lenny's News** Uptown's best newspaper and magazine newsstand.
- **Angele Parlange Design** Hand-painted fabrics, designer cushions and pillows; furniture by this gifted local artist.
- **Retroactive** A great place for vintage clothing and 1940s memorabilia.
- **Melange Sterling–Madeleine Guice Nicoladis** A sterling flatwear pattern matching service; estate and antique holloware.
- **British Antiques** English, French, and Asian antiques.
- **Beaucoup Books** An excellent bookstore for local and Southern literature, cookbooks, travel, children's and foreign language books; artistic postcards.
- **UTOPIA** Painted furniture, jewelry, and hand-block-printed clothing.
- **CC's Coffee House** Community Coffee's "New Orleans Blend" of coffee and chicory is the favorite local coffee; this new coffeehouse in a corner Queen Anne building has become a popular hangout.
- **First National Bank of Commerce** There is a walk-up ATM here.

3 *Magazine Street, Jefferson Avenue to Napoleon Avenue*

After this point the shops are much less concentrated; Victorian houses both large and small predominate. The following selected sites are widely spaced out over thirteen blocks.

• **Poydras Home for Elderly Ladies**
Set deep within an entire block of lawns is this pavilionlike building, which has housed elderly ladies since 1959. This institution has its roots in a girls orphanage founded by merchant Julien Poydras in 1817. It moved to this site, the former Rickerville plantation, in 1857.

From Leontine Street to Napoleon Avenue

• **New Orleans Academy of Fine Arts / The Academy Gallery** New Orleans' best private art school offers courses in drawing, painting, watercolor, sculpture, and art history; the gallery sells works by noted local and other artists.
• **The Westgate** Art, literature, and esoterica about Eros and Thanatos (Death), all in a purple-painted house; strangely New Orleanian.
• **Upperline Restaurant** A locally favored Creole restaurant in a comfortable domestic setting with changing art; dinner only; reservations advised.
• **The Bead Shop** Jewelry, pottery, books on jewelry making, and beads.
• **Carol Robinson Gallery** Painting, sculpture, and ceramics by regional and national artists.
• **Uptown Music** Musical instruments; tambourines.
• **Casamento's Oyster Bar** A New Orleans classic; raw and fried oysters and gumbo served in an immaculate 1940s tiled interior; recommended.
• **Gizmo's** Collectibles, old tools, kitchen items, and more.

Poydras Home for Elderly Ladies
5354 Magazine Street

New Orleans Academy of Fine Arts / The Academy Gallery
5256 Magazine Street;
899-8111

The Westgate
5219 Magazine Street;
899-3077

Upperline Restaurant
1413 Upperline Street,
near 4800 block of
Magazine; open daily;
891-9822

The Bead Shop
4612 Magazine Street;
895-6161

Carol Robinson Gallery
4537 Magazine Street;
895-6130

Uptown Music
4514 Magazine Street;
891-6515, 800-277-6515

Casamento's Oyster Bar
4330 Magazine Street;
closed from May to
August; 895-9761

Gizmo's
4118 Magazine Street;
897-6868

Neal Auction Company
4038 Magazine Street;
Saturday auctions, call for
times; 899-5329

Five Centuries Antiques
4023 Magazine Street;
891-2600

Davis Gallery
3964 Magazine Street;
897-0780

Jacqueline Vance Oriental Rugs
3944 Magazine Street;
891-3304

Bremermann Designs
3943 Magazine Street;
891-7763

Anne Pratt Imports
3937 Magazine Street;
891-6532

Casey Willems Pottery
3919 Magazine Street;
899-1174

Mario Villa Gallery
3908 Magazine Street;
895-8731

Jean Bragg Antiques
3901 Magazine Street;
895-7375

Shadyside Pottery Shop & Art Gallery
3823 Magazine Street;
897-1710

Futonia
3811 Magazine Street;
899-4356

Little Miss Muffin
3806 Magazine Street;
895-8622

❹ Magazine Street, Napoleon Avenue to Louisiana Avenue

This section also stretches for thirteen blocks.

Continuing toward Louisiana Avenue

- **Neal Auction Company** One of the best auction houses in New Orleans; excellent for antique furniture, paintings, silver, porcelain, Oriental rugs, bric-a-brac. Auctions are conducted on occasional Saturdays and are frequented by Uptowners. Phone for viewing days and dates of Saturday auctions.
- **Five Centuries Antiques** Classic furniture from many periods.
- **Davis Gallery** African tribal art; jewelry; basketry; ceramics; recommended.
- **Jacqueline Vance Oriental Rugs** Good selection of new and antique Oriental rugs.
- **Bremermann Designs** French antique furniture and reproductions; objets d'art.
- **Anne Pratt Imports** Mexican glazed ceramics, hand-blown glass, painted and iron furniture.
- **Casey Willems Pottery** Usable pottery; facebowls; potter at work Monday to Saturday, 10 A.M. to 5 P.M.; recommended.
- **Mario Villa Gallery** Bronze, brass, steel, and copper furniture and lamps designed by this acclaimed local artist; recommended.
- **Jean Bragg Antiques** Paintings, Newcomb and other art pottery, vintage linens.
- **Shadyside Pottery Shop & Art Gallery** Potter Charles Bohn's shop; also antique Japanese pottery and raku.
- **Futonia** Futons and bedding.
- **Little Miss Muffin** Some children's things, gifts.

- **J. Schneider's** Has antique and vintage modern furniture.
- **Cole Pratt Gallery** Contemporary fine arts.
- **Jacadi** European children's clothes, furniture, and prams.
- **Bon Montage** Children's clothes and gifts.
- **Evans Gallery** Contemporary art.
- **Custom Linens** Fine European linens and accessories.
- **Harry's Ace Hardware** Uptown's best hardware store.
- **Didier, Inc.** Antique American furniture.
- **Blackamoor** Antique furniture; Chinese and English porcelain; American art pottery; estate jewelry; best to phone first.

5 *Magazine Street, Louisiana Avenue to Jackson Avenue*

Magazine Street starts to get funkier along this fourteen-block stretch.

- **Cafe Atchafalaya** Southern cuisine, seafood, chicken and dumplings; moderate.
- **New Orleans Music Exchange** Electric guitars, sound systems, et cetera.
- **Underground Sounds** Modern music and rad noize.

J. Schneider's
3806 Magazine Street;
891-7751

Cole Pratt Gallery
3800 Magazine Street;
891-6789

Jacadi
3727 Magazine Street;
895-2100

Bon Montage
3719 Magazine Street;
897-6295

Evans Gallery
3701 A Magazine Street;
897-2688

Custom Linens
3638 Magazine Street;
899-0604

Harry's Ace Hardware
3535 Magazine Street;
896-1500

Didier, Inc.
3439 Magazine Street;
899-7749

Blackamoor
3433 Magazine Street;
897-2711

Cafe Atchafalaya
901 Louisiana Avenue, at Magazine; open Saturday and Sunday all day; open Tuesday to Friday lunch and dinner only; closed Monday; 891-5271

New Orleans Music Exchange
3342 Magazine Street;
891-7670

Underground Sounds
3336 Magazine Street;
897-9030

**Morgan-West
Studio/Gallery**
3326 Magazine Street;
895-7976

Divine Light
3316 Magazine Street;
899-6617

**Children's Hour Book
Emporium**
3308 Magazine Street;
899-2378

Semolina
3242 Magazine Street;
open Monday to Saturday
for lunch and dinner;
895-4260

The Bulldog
3236 Magazine Street;
891-1516

Mystic Cafe
3226 Magazine Street;
891-1992

Wilkerson Row
3137 Magazine Street;
899-3311

Useless Antiques
3127 Magazine Street;
891-4341

George Herget Books
3109 Magazine Street;
891-5595

**Rue de la course Coffee
House**
3128 Magazine Street;
899-0242

Magazine Arcade Antiques
3017 Magazine Street;
895-5451

As You Like It
3025 Magazine Street;
897-6915, 800-828-2311

- **Morgan-West Studio/Gallery** Painted furnishings and accessories; crafts in all media.
- **Divine Light** Herbs, oils, spiritual candles, including the St. Expedite candle.
- **Children's Hour Book Emporium** Large selection of books, videos, and CDs for children.
- **Semolina** Generous portions of pastas including seafood and chicken pasta dishes; young crowd; inexpensive.
- **The Bulldog** Describes itself as "Uptown's international beer tavern."
- **Mystic Cafe** Turkish and Italian foods blend here.
- **Wilkerson Row** Custom wood furniture.
- **Useless Antiques** Antiques, glass lighting globes.
- **George Herget Books** A New Orleans institution; great selection of used books; fiction, music, art, Louisiana, New Orleans, Civil War, cookbooks, postcards.
- **Rue de la course Coffee House** An airy cafe popular with college students; tea is a good bet here.
- **Magazine Arcade Antiques** A large selection of antique furniture and furnishings; quirky gadgets.
- **As You Like It** Sterling silver flatware, active, inactive, and obsolete patterns; silver holloware and jewelry; recommended.

- **Joan Vass, New Orleans** Joan Vass cotton knits, ladies' clothing and accessories.

6 *Magazine Street, Jackson Avenue to Felicity Street*

This final four-block section includes a short detour to Ecclesiastical Square.

From Jackson Avenue to St. Andrew

- **Jim Smiley Vintage Clothing** Vintage clothing from many periods.
- **Positive Space** New art, readings, and performances.
- **Bush Antiques & Beds Au Beau Reve** Antique furniture; large selection of antique beds, mirrors, iron furniture, china, and religious art.
- **Mona Mia's Antiques** Paper ephemera and jewelry.

Detour:
Ecclesiastical Square's Landmark Churches

- **St. Mary's Assumption Roman Catholic Church**, *1858–60, architect unknown*

From Magazine and Josephine walk one block toward the river to Josephine and Constance. Exercise caution here; you are a block from the St. Thomas Housing Project. From this corner there is a view of the facade and bell tower of St. Mary's Assumption Roman Catholic Church, the finest example of Italianate/German Baroque architecture in New Orleans. Built between 1858 and 1860, great decorative brick arches dominate its imposing facade. Its architect is unknown. The superb tower is 142 feet tall and contains bells cast in France. The exuberant Baroque design is carried into the interior where great pendentives support the vaulted roof. The elaborate high altar and stained-glass windows were crafted in Munich. This impressive church was built by the Redemptorist Fathers to serve the large German-speaking Catholic population of the old Irish Channel. Badly damaged by Hurricane Betsy in 1965, the landmark was restored in 1975.

- **St. Alphonsus Art and Culture Center / Old St. Alphonsus Roman Catholic Church**, *1855, Louis L. Long*

Across Constance Street is the brick facade of St. Alphonsus Roman Catholic Church with its twin square towers. Also once served by the Redemptorist Fathers, this large Renaissance-style church served the Irish of the Irish Channel. This Italianate-style church was designed by Louis L. Long of Baltimore and built in 1855. Planned spires

---

Joan Vass, New Orleans
1100 Sixth Street, at Magazine; 891-4502

Jim Smiley Vintage Clothing
2001 Magazine Street; 528-9449

Positive Space
2023 Magazine Street; 522-9344

Bush Antiques & Beds Au Beau Reve
2109–11 Magazine Street; 581-3518

Mona Mia's Antiques
2105 Magazine Street; 525-8686

St. Mary's Assumption Roman Catholic Church
Sunday masses at 8:30, 10 (Spanish), and 11:30 A.M.; 522-6748

St. Alphonsus Art and Culture Center
Friends of St. Alphonsus; P.O. Box 57143, N.O., 70157; 524-8116 for tours and events

O. J. Hooter's Furniture Company
1938 Magazine Street; 522-5167

Gallery I/O & I/O+
1812 & 1804 Magazine Street; 581-2113

The Cat Practice
1808 Magazine Street; 525-6369

St. Vincent Guest House
1507 Magazine Street; guest house, 523-3411; tea room, 523-2318

Rue de la course Coffee House
1500 Magazine Street; 529-1455

Sophie Wright Park
Magazine and Camp Streets

were never built atop the square towers. Its interior has frescoes painted by Domenico Canova and fine stained glass. The hard-fired brick of the mid-nineteenth century withstood the elements better than the soft "lake brick" available earlier; these buildings did not have to be covered with stucco to protect them. New Orleans brick masons achieved the highest development of their craft in the mid-1850s, and these two churches are enduring monuments to their skill. In 1856 the Redemptorists built Notre Dame de Bon Secours a block away on Jackson Avenue for French-speaking Catholics (its altar was moved to St. Mary's when the French-language church was demolished in the 1920s). Impressive brick schools, a rectory, a convent, and service buildings were clustered around these three great churches, making this an important center for worship and education. These national parishes dwindled as Catholics moved up and out of the Irish Channel. Today, only St. Mary's is an active church, and it has a small congregation. The Friends of St. Alphonsus presents occasional concerts and other events in the deconsecrated church, and these are the best times to see the usually locked interior. St. Alphonsus also has a Sacristy Museum.

St. Andrew Street to Felicity Street

- **O. J. Hooter's Furniture Company** Behind this faded facade is a great selection of used and antique furniture.
- **Gallery I/O & I/O+** Top-notch local and national artists; jewelry, lighting, furniture, and contemporary sculpture.
- **The Cat Practice** Art and jewelry about, yes, cats.
- **St. Vincent Guest House / Old St. Vincent Infant and Maternity Home** This substantial three-story red-brick building with its distinguished cast-iron galleries was erected in 1864. It was designed by Thomas Mulligan for the Sisters of Charity of St. Paul, who long operated a maternity home and orphan asylum here. The fine cast-iron galleries were added in 1884. The Tea Room here serves afternoon tea.
- **Rue de la course Coffee House** A gathering spot for the Lower Garden District.
- **Sophie Wright Park** Where Magazine and Camp Streets form a Y is Sophie Wright Park, with its statue of the educator sculpted by Enrique Alferez in 1988.

Continuation:
Coliseum Square and the Arts District

From Magazine and St. Andrew you can catch the Magazine Street bus back to Canal Street and the French Quarter. The downtown bus branches off Magazine and runs down Camp Street, passing the triangular park of historic Coliseum Square, which is framed by old oaks shading landmark houses. The bus crosses Julia Street in the Arts District, which has contemporary art galleries and the New Orleans Auction House (see page 264).

*Flaming urns carved from red Maine granite and a bronze statue of Mourning
grace the J. A. Morales tomb in Metairie Cemetery. It was designed after a mausoleum in
Munich and built in 1911 for Storyville madame Josie Arlington, née Mamie Diebler.*

What These Tours Cover
Preliminaries
Introduction: The Elegant Abodes of the Dead:
  Death and Culture in New Orleans

Tour 11

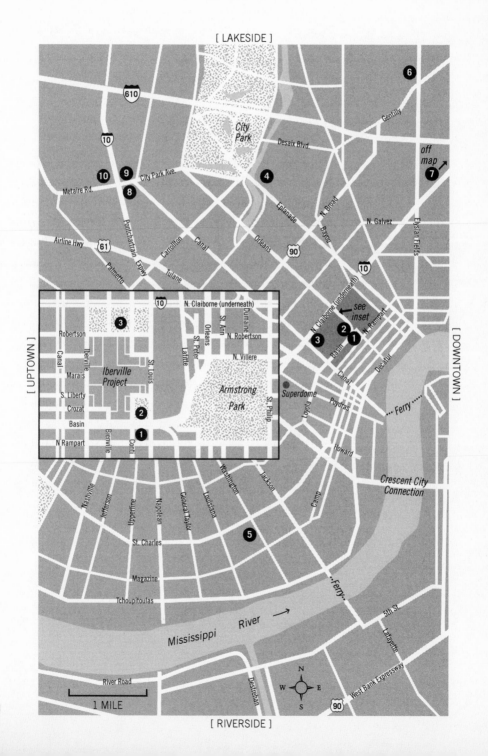

[LAKESIDE]

City Park

610

10

Desaix Blvd.

10 9 City Park Ave.

Metaire Rd. 8 4

Pontchartrain Espwy Esplanade

N. Broad

N. Galvez

Airline Hwy 61 Carrollton Canal Orleans 90 N. Rampart

Palmetto Tulane

N. Claiborne (underneath)

Elysian Fields

off map 7

10

[UPTOWN]

10 N. Claiborne (underneath) see inset

Robertson

Canal

Iberville

Marais

S. Liberty

Crozat

Basin

N Rampart

Bienville

Conti

St. Louis

Lafitte

St. Peter

Orleans

St. Ann

Dumaine

N. Robertson

N. Villere

Iberville Project

Armstrong Park

St. Philip

3

2 1

3

Basin

N Rampart

Superdome

Canal

Decatur

[DOWNTOWN]

Poydras

Loyola

Ferry

Howard

Crescent City Connection

Washington

Jackson

Nashville

Jefferson

Upperline

Napolean

General Taylor

Louisiana

Camp

St. Charles

5

Magazine

Ferry

Tchoupitoulas

5th St.

Mississippi River

Lafayette

West Bank Expressway

River Road

1 MILE

N
W E
S

90

Destrehan

[RIVERSIDE]

Jazz funerals
WWOZ events line,
840-4040

All Saints' Day
November 1

What These Tours Cover

There are more than thirty historic cemeteries in New Orleans. Here are tips on ten of the most interesting, scattered across various parts of the city. Choose carefully; few visitors will be able to see them all.

Preliminaries

BEST TIMES TO SEE THE CEMETERIES / SAFETY IN THE CEMETERIES Elite late Victorian/Edwardian Metairie Cemetery makes a fine car excursion any day and is one of the best maintained and most secure places in New Orleans. It, along with nearby Cypress Grove Cemetery, City Park, and the Bayou St. John neighborhood, makes a good drive on a rainy or hot day (see Tour 3). Most of the cemeteries listed here are relatively safe, although you should always be aware of your surroundings in these often unpeopled necropolises. Unfortunately, fascinating St. Louis Cemetery No. 1 and St. Louis Cemetery No. 2 are the least safe. Many cemeteries close at 3 P.M.; a good time to explore them is usually about 10:30 or 11 A.M. It is best to go in groups and to carry no valuables. Guided tours are another safe way to see city cemeteries, although exploring them with a couple of friends and a copy of the Friends of the Cabildo's *New Orleans Architecture, Vol. III: The Cemeteries* is still best. Metairie Cemetery has its own fine book, as does the St. Roch Cemetery and Old Mortuary Chapel.

Jazz funerals are rare events in New Orleans, but they do still occur; call WWOZ's events line to find out if one is scheduled during your visit.

All Saints' Day, November 1

On one day of the year, **All Saints' Day** (the day after Halloween), mounted police guard all the cemeteries in New Orleans. This is the day New Orleanians should explore usually off-limits St. Louis Cemetery No. 2. All Saints' Day is celebrated on November 1 and

All Souls' Day on November 2, the day of the dead in the Catholic liturgy. In forgiving southern Louisiana, All Saints' Day has long been celebrated as the day of the dead.

Save Our Cemeteries Walking Tours

Save Our Cemeteries is a nonprofit, volunteer organization founded in 1974 to help rescue the city's decaying historical cemeteries. They conduct paid walking tours. Numbers are limited and reservations are advised. Donations to Save Our Cemeteries are used to help preserve the city's historic cemeteries.

Two other organizations working to help preserve these cemeteries are the **New Orleans Archdiocesan Cemeteries Preservation Fund** and the **Hebrew Rest Cemetery Association.**

Save Our Cemeteries Walking Tours
2045 Magazine Street, N.O., 70130; paid Sunday walking tours of St. Louis Cemetery No. 1 start at 10 A.M. at a cafe in the French Quarter; another walk on Monday, Wednesday, and Friday at 10:30 A.M. features Lafayette Cemetery in the Garden District; 588-9357

New Orleans Archdiocesan Cemeteries Preservation Fund
1000 Howard Avenue, Suite 500, N.O., 70113-1921; 596-3050

Hebrew Rest Cemetery Association, Inc.
6227 St. Charles Avenue, N.O., 70118; Temple Sinai 861-3693

Introduction:
The Elegant Abodes of the Dead: Death and Culture in New Orleans

Sudden death was long a too-frequent visitor, and a perpetually menacing presence, in Old New Orleans. So unhealthy was Louisiana that the early missionaries branded it "the wet grave." This swampy setting was a perfect breeding ground for the clouds of mosquitoes that carried yellow fever. Pools of stagnant water in the muddy streets, and the open wooden cisterns that collected rainwater from the roofs, were also efficient mosquito hatcheries. Smallpox was another rampant killer in the early city. In addition, poor sanitation and impure drinking water spread waterborne diseases such as Asiatic cholera, typhoid, and diphtheria. Finally, the diseased crews of ships entering from the Caribbean often introduced ghastly, unidentified plagues. The city's commercial interests resisted imposing quarantines since they hurt the port's reputation and stopped its business. If yellow fever was known to be loose in the city, other ports would refuse to receive ships from New Orleans. In desperate but futile attempts to ward off the pestilence, barrels of pitch were set afire in the narrow muddy streets of the French Quarter to fumigate the city. The billowing clouds of black smoke covered the city in a thick, acrid pall that made life even gloomier for the city's terrified inhabitants. Summer and fall was the fever season, and all those who could afford to do so left the city for spas or cities in the North or to sojourn in Europe. Not until 1900 did army surgeon Walter Reed and his associates on the Havana Yellow Fever Commission, drawing on the work of Cuban physician Carlos Finlay, determine that the ubiquitous *Aedes aegypti* mosquito spread the lethal "Yellow Jack." The long-term solution was improved drainage throughout the city, the screening and eventual outlawing of open cisterns, and mosquito abatement. The last yellow fever epidemic to strike New Orleans hit in 1905.

New Orleanians divided themselves into the "acclimated" and the "unacclimated": the seasoned Creoles and Africans who seemed to resist the recurrent fevers and the unseasoned newcomers, especially the Anglo-Americans, who quickly succumbed to them. In 1804, Governor Claiborne, who lost his wife and daughter to yellow fever, wrote: "The Number of Deaths have been very great; —I verily believe, more than a third of the Americans who emigrated thither in the course of the last 12 months have perished, and nearly every Person from Europe who arrived in the City during the Summer Months" (from *The Past as Prelude: New Orleans 1718–1968,* 1968). Black-bordered death notices were a common sight on the lampposts of the beseiged community. Funerals and processions to the cemeteries were all too frequent and were constant reminders of how tenuous life was and how indiscriminate death is. At times during especially severe epidemics, putrifying corpses were stacked like cordwood in front of the city's mortuary chapel on Rampart Street. In one very bad summer, that of 1853, nearly eleven thousand persons were buried between June 1 and October 1. And that only counts those with burial certificates; many more died unrecorded or perished in flight as they carried the pestilence away with them. Many were found dead in their beds, in their shops, or in the streets. No one, not even the acclimated Creoles and African slaves, knew for certain if they would survive the fever season. Entire households could disappear in a single fever-ravaged summer month. Panics and crime waves often accompanied these scourges of nature. In 1897, when the mayor set aside a school building as a temporary yellow fever hospital, a panicked mob set fire to it.

Living in such a death-haunted place fostered a taste for funerary pomp and a need for many ever-expanding cemeteries. The pervasive fear of death also probably had much to do with the peculiar psychology that developed in this city—its famous energy for parties, for gay, almost manic celebration. Life, New Orleanians knew from tragic experience, could be cut off at almost any moment. So enjoy it to the full! Share your momentary good fortune with family and friends today, for you may lose them next summer. And in the winter, before the hot weather brings random death in its train, throw yourself wholeheartedly into the whirl of the social season. Present your daughters to society, cement your relationships and secure your property through marriage, and dance till dawn. The perpetual shadow of death is one reason why New Orleans so elaborated the Carnival season. The tradition of jazz funerals among the black poor also has its roots in the need to make something joyous out of grim death. White Creole culture developed a morbid fascination with death. As Creole journalist J. Roger Baudier, Sr., remembered in the 1930s (from *Creole Collage,* edited by Leonard V. Huber, 1980):

> *Cousine* Rosalie, another old relative, was always on the verge of having some-thing happen to her. A gloomy soul, she was deeply devoted to *Notre Dame des Douleurs, Notre Dame des Delivrance,* and *la Sainte Face* of the Carmelites. She never missed a wake or a funeral. Her brother-in-law called her a *saule pleureur* [weeping willow]. . . . Her brother called her the president of *Les Dames de Condoleances.* She knew all the family tombs in the St. Louis cemeteries and every Sunday went to her mother's tomb with a bouquet. On All Saints' Day she knew which tomb had flowers and which had none. Another member of the family called her *le chein necrologique* [the necrologi-cal dog] since she stopped at every corner lamp post to read the black bordered death notices customarily tacked on them.

Today the *Times-Picayune* continues the tradition of publishing relatively lengthy obit-uaries and brief memorials, and many New Orleanians open to them first each day.

All this death made cemeteries for the dead more necessary than parks for the living. The sudden loss of healthy young people to epidemics also resulted in the desire to commemorate them. Not only should the passing funeral rites be grand and solemn, so too should be the enduring tomb that the lover or family could visit and then decorate on All Saints' Day. The water-logged soil here makes it impossible to dig graves in most parts of the city. Coffins buried during the dry months had the

Our Lady of Guadalupe Chapel
Just outside the French Quarter at 411 N. Rampart Street, at Conti; daily masses at 7 A.M. and noon and Sunday at 7:30, 9:30, 11:30 A.M., and 6 P.M.; perpetual novena to St. Jude at 4:40 P.M. Saturday and at various times on Sunday; parking on N. Rampart near the church is best; 525-1551

disconcerting tendency to pop out of the ground when it rained. The solution was to build above-ground tombs of stucco-covered brick, a custom that the Creoles seem to have adopted from the Spanish, not the French. The two main types of above-ground tombs are described under "St. Louis Cemetery No. 1" (page 339). Some French-trained architects such as J. N. B. de Pouilly refined these tombs in elegant and well-proportioned forms that are chastely decorated with Neoclassical (not Christian) emblems of death such as inverted torches and flaming urns.

New Orleanians traditionally decorated family tombs on All Saints' Day, long the best business day of the year for New Orleans florists. Brick-and-stucco tombs were then repaired from the past year's ravages and brilliantly whitewashed for this special day. Flowers, especially yellow chrysanthemums and red coxcombs, were placed before the refreshed tombs. Young children attended their parents on these annual forays and ran around in the labyrinth of tombs and narrow allées playing hide-and-seek; the cemeteries were familiar to them from an early age. At St. Louis Cemetery No. 3, the custom of setting out *immortelles* (once wreaths made of black glass beads strung on wire, but now, unfortunately, memorials of plastic flowers) continues. At the oldest cemeteries, such as St. Louis No. 1 and No. 2, many of the families have died out or moved away. Some of the brick-and-stucco tombs there are just piles of rubble slowly returning to the earth. Out in the Louisiana countryside, however, some Creole of color clan burial grounds continue to be freshly whitewashed, spread with clean sand, and decked with flowers on All Saints' Day. Countless candles are lit atop the refreshed tombs as dusk falls. Matriarchs then receive adults and older children amid the tended graves as the countless flames honoring all the still-remembered souls glow yellow in the twilight.

❶   Our Lady of Guadalupe Chapel / Shrine of St. Jude / Old Mortuary Chapel, *1827, Gurlie and Guillot*
Completed in 1827, this is the oldest existing church building in New Orleans. It was sited just outside the old city limits across the street from St. Louis Cemetery No. 1, since it was thought that corpses inside the city spread uncontrollable diseases. It served as a mortuary chapel in the yellow-fever-plagued community and kept funerals from monopolizing St. Louis Cathedral. It was designed and built by Gurlie and Guillot and was originally known as the chapel of St. Anthony. Its sober facade has pleasing proportions and is marked by a practical triple-arched entrance loggia. The brick-and-stucco chapel is capped by a simple belfry and steeple. In *The South-West. By A Yankee,* Joseph Holt Ingraham wrote a description of a funeral here in 1835:

> I gained the portico, where I had a full view of the interior, in which was neither pew nor seat, elevated upon a high frame or altar, over which was thrown a black velvet pall, was placed a coffin, covered also with black velvet. A dozen

huge candles, nearly as long and as large as a ship's royal-mast, standing in candlesticks five feet high, burned around the corpse mingled with innumerable candles of the ordinary size, which were thickly sprinkled among them, like lesser stars, amid the twilight gloom of the chapel. The mourners formed a lane from the altar to the door, each holding a long, unlighted wax taper, tipped at the larger end with red, and ornamented with fanciful paper cuttings.

St. Louis Cemetery No. 1
Just outside the French Quarter at Basin Street, between St. Louis and Conti; open 10 A.M. to 3 P.M.; park on Basin Street near the gated entrance, or on N. Rampart Street near Our Lady of Guadalupe Chapel

Modernizations have made the interior somewhat sterile except for the antique furniture used around the altar and the extraordinary chapel of St. Jude to the front left. St. Jude is the saint of desperate cases; he has many devotees in the Crescent City, especially among her many poor. With respect and some trepidation you may walk around his statue, with a flame dancing atop its head, and enter the back of his shrine. Here you sense the hopes that sparked all these flickering candles and the fervor of all the prayers that continually saturate this holy place. Many of the devout leave offerings of flowers and petitions written on scraps of paper. The mosaic at the back of the shrine depicts Pentecost and shows the Holy Spirit descending as a dove amid beautiful supplicating angels. To the right of the main altar is the chapel of city firefighters and police. A statue of New Orleans' own invented St. Expidite stands on an unnoticed shelf on the wall to the left of the front doors as you exit the church. Outside the church and to the right is another large statue of St. Jude and an unfortunately unaesthetic concrete grotto dedicated to Our Lady of Lourdes paved with ex-votos. The gift shop inside the rectory next door has the best assortment of holy cards in New Orleans.

2   **St. Louis Cemetery No. 1 / Protestant Cemetery Remnant,** *1789*

Historic St. Louis Cemetery No. 1 was established under the Spanish in 1789 and replaced a now-built-over burial ground on St. Peter Street just inside the French Quarter. (Nearby St. Louis Cemetery No. 2 was opened in 1823 and the more distant St. Louis Cemetery No. 3 near Bayou St. John in 1856.) This roughly square plot is surrounded by brick walls with three tiers of vaults known as "ovens" because of their shapes. These vaults are rented by the year and reused over time; a body must be interred for a year and a day before it can be moved. The cemetery is an intensely urban mosaic of above-ground tombs and irregular narrow aisles. Above-ground tombs are necessary in most of New Orleans because the high water table here means that graves cannot be dug in the soggy soil.

The free-standing tombs are principally of two types: family tombs with from one to three vaults stacked one over the other, and much larger mutual benefit society tombs with many vaults. Both family and society tombs can be continually reused. When space is needed for a new burial, the previous occupant's remains are placed in the *caveau,* an ash pit under the tomb, and the old casket is taken away and burned. In this way space is conserved, costly tombs are reused, and family ashes are

St. Louis Cemetery No. 2

Three blocks between N. Claiborne Avenue and N. Robertson Street, from Iberville to St. Louis; open 10 A.M. to 3 P.M.; do not park outside cemetery, but drive through the gate on Bienville Street, between N. Robertson and N. Claiborne

commingled for eternity; both practicality and sentiment are served. Sometimes the name of the new occupant is carved on the marble slab that seals the vault, but often it is not. Thus there is no way of knowing just how many internments each vault has received. Since there is no natural stone near New Orleans, most tombs are built of soft red brick covered with whitewashed stucco, which will decay if not maintained. Imported marble was only used for the tablets that seal the vaults.

This cemetery has tombs in all conditions, from spanking new restorations to melancholy piles of rubble. Near the principal entrance is the pyramid-shaped tomb of the Varney family. Recently, metal plaques have been attached to some tombs identifying their famous occupants. Many pioneer New Orleanians are among them. The most visited tomb here is the Glapion family tomb, popularly thought to be the resting place of Marie Laveau. Probably the daughter of Charles Laveaux, a free man of color, Marie was born in 1783 and became both a hairdresser and New Orleans' most famous voodoo priestess. Marie Laveau herself always claimed to be a good Catholic, and she died in 1881. Known as the "wishing tomb," many visitors make small red Xs on this whitewashed tomb with bits of red brick. Curious offerings are often found here as well. Also buried in St. Louis Cemetery No. 1 toward the Canal Street side is Homer Plessy *"décédé le 1 Mai 1925 age de 63 ans."* His name is forever memorialized as the unsuccessful plaintiff in the momentous court case of Plessy v. Ferguson, whereby, in 1896, the U.S. Supreme Court sanctioned more than half a century of racial segregation. Chess genius Paul Morphy, who died in 1884, is another famous New Orleanian Creole entombed here. The most imposing tomb in St. Louis Cemetery No. 1 is the white marble society tomb erected in 1857 by the Italian Mutual Benevolent Society. Designed by Pietro Gualdi, it is capped by a statue of a woman holding a cross. Two niches in the elaborate twenty-four-vault tomb shelter statues of Italia and of Charity. The other society tombs nearby are also worth examining. Among them is the tall tomb of the Society of St. Anne. Throughout the cemetery there are fine wrought- and cast-iron crosses, railings, and gates. At the back of the consecrated Catholic ground was a space reserved for the burial of non-Catholics. Most of these remains were removed when Protestant Girod Street Cemetery opened after 1822. (Deconsecrated and demolished in 1957, today it is the site of New Orleans Centre near the Superdome.) The most notable tomb that survives in the emptied Protestant section was designed by Benjamin Latrobe in memory of Elise Lewis, the first wife of American Governor William C. C. Claiborne. Behind the non-Catholic section was the graveyard for African Americans, since lost to street widenings.

③   St. Louis Cemetery No. 2, *1823, Antoine Phillip Le Riche*

This is one of the most important, and most abused, places in all of New Orleans. May the future be kinder to it than the uncaring present. St. Louis Cemetery No. 2 consists of three separate walled-in blocks sandwiched between the Iberville Public Housing

Project and I-10 along N. Claiborne Avenue. Countless drivers stream by it daily on the elevated interstate with little sense of how important a place this is in New Orleans history and architecture. This walled cemetery was also once the lakeside border of Storyville, the notorious but tolerated turn-of-the-century red light district. Because it is cut off by the highway, backs up on a desperately poor housing project, and is not policed, this is considered the most dangerous cemetery in the city. As such, do not park outside the cemetery; drive through the Bienville Street gate and stay on the axial road, and don't walk out of sight of your car. NOPD mounted patrols on November 1 make that the best day to see this rewarding, if decayed, cemetery.

St. Louis Cemetery No. 2 was sited a bit farther away from the city than St. Louis Cemetery No. 1 because of the then-prevalent theory that "miasmas" emanating from cemeteries spread diseases. Designed by Paris-born architect and engineer Antoine Phillip Le Riche and dedicated in 1823, it has a simple plan with an axial *Grande Allée* that cuts through the middle of its three separate blocks from Iberville to St. Louis Streets. Of the three blocks, Square 2, the central one between Conti and Bienville Streets, is the richest architecturally. The center of the central block has a cross axis named Priest's Aisle, and many important tombs are clustered here. Square 3, the block between Bienville and Iberville Streets toward the Canal Street end, has many tombs erected by African American burial societies. In this block is the tomb of Mother Henriette Delille, who founded the Sisters of the Holy Family in 1842, a religious order composed of free women of color who ministered to orphans and the elderly and continue to conduct St. Mary's Academy in eastern New Orleans. Another tomb here is the resting place of the Societe Dames et Damoiselles du Silence. The sale in 1845 of the part of Square 3 nearest Canal Street financed the purchase of the land for St. Louis Cemetery No. 3, way out near Bayou St. John (see page 175).

St. Louis Cemetery No. 3
3421 Esplanade Avenue, just before Bayou St. John and City Park; open 10 A.M. to 3 P.M.

City of Lafayette Cemetery No. 1
In Garden District between Washington Avenue, Prytania, Sixth, and Coliseum Streets; open 10 A.M. to 3 P.M.; park on Washington Avenue near the gated entrance

Commander's Palace Restaurant
1403 Washington Avenue, at Coliseum; 899-8231

4 St. Louis Cemetery No. 3, *1856*
Only the front section of this 1856 cemetery (nearest Esplanade Avenue) with all its angel-topped tombs is noteworthy. In fact, this is the largest gathering of carved stone angels in New Orleans. The modern section in the back of the cemetery is cookie-cutter sterile, and the tombs look like filing cabinets; it is a lesson in the decline of funerary art in the modern period.

5 City of Lafayette Cemetery No. 1, *1833, Benjamin Buisson*
This is a relatively safe cemetery with characteristic New Orleans above-ground tombs, though it is not as interesting as St. Louis No. 1, or as architecturally distinguished as the central square of St. Louis No. 2, Cypress Grove, or Metairie Cemeteries. This land

was originally part of the Livaudais sugar plantation, which was subdivided in 1832. This plot was dedicated as a cemetery in 1833 within the then-separate Anglo-American–dominated City of Lafayette (today the Garden District). It is indicative of the centrality of death in New Orleanian culture that the new American city placed a cemetery, not a public park, at its heart. Its simple plan, consisting of two axial avenues and four square sections, was laid out by city surveyor Benjamin Buisson; its relatively wide avenues were designed for large funeral processions. This was only the second cemetery for Protestants, and many Protestant Irish and German residents of the City of Lafayette are entombed here. The melange of last names and foreign birthplaces carved on many tombs testifies to the flood of migrants from New England, the Tidewater South, Northern Ireland, England, France, and the West Indies to this booming, polyglot, nineteenth-century port. The multicultural combinations of surnames on the same tomb record the intermarriage of Anglo-Americans, Germans, Irish, and French Creoles in uptown New Orleans. Among the interesting tombs here is the society tomb of the elite Jefferson Fire Company No. 22, erected in 1852, with a prominent carving of a fire engine. There are also some fascinating Victorian epitaphs on a few of the tombs here. The Alfred Millard tomb of 1853 proclaims with Christian certitude: "There is no death! What seems so is transition." The Samuel Jerome Bennett tomb of 1859, erected by his mother after he died at twenty-six, mourns:

> The light of other days have faded,
> And all their glories past;
> For grief with heavy wing hath shaded,
> The hope too bright to last.

In 1852 the City of New Orleans annexed Lafayette and this cemetery became the property of the newly consolidated municipality. In 1858, wall vaults were built enclosing the freestanding tombs. A century later Lafayette Cemetery No. 1 was a virtually abandoned ruin with trees growing from the roofs of many tombs. In 1969 the city proposed tearing down the decayed encircling wall vaults, paving the avenues, and enclosing the cemetery with a chain-link fence. Garden District residents, led by Mrs. John B. Manard, protested this desecration; in the 1970s the vaults were restored and new magnolia trees were planted along the principal avenue.

If you're visiting City of Lafayette Cemetery No. 1 at lunch or dinnertime, try **Commander's Palace Restaurant,** across Washington Avenue (see page 285).

6   Hebrew Rest Cemetery, *1860*

The first Jewish cemetery in New Orleans was established by the German Jewish Congregation Shanari Chasset (Gates of Mercy) in 1828 and was located in the then-suburban City of Lafayette at Jackson Avenue and Saratoga Street. It was replaced by a playground and its remains transferred to Hebrew Rest Cemetery. Spanish Portuguese Jews, Polish Jews, and other national congregations opened their own cemeteries as the city's Jewish population grew and became more diverse. In the late nineteenth century, mergers of congregations resulted in the consolidation of their separate burial grounds. Of the several Jewish cemeteries that survive, Hebrew Rest Cemetery on Gentilly Ridge, facing Elysian Fields Avenue, is the most interesting architecturally. The original plot on this relatively high ground was purchased in 1860 and was added to in 1894. The natural ridge here permits below-ground burial, which is more in keeping with Jewish burial customs than above-ground tombs. All the graves here face east toward the rising sun. A fine cast-iron gate on Elysian Fields Avenue announces the entrance to this reverently cared-for burial ground.

A less architecturally interesting but more centrally located Jewish cemetery, **Sha'aray Tefilev,** or Gates of Prayer, is uptown at Joseph Street, between Pitt and Garfield Streets. Founded in 1850, this cemetery was once enclosed by a brick wall. Its founding congregation now meets in suburban Metairie. If you're looking to take out a picnic lunch, **Langenstein's** gourmet supermarket is across the street.

Sha'aray Tefilev
Joseph Street, between Pitt and Garfield Streets; open 10 A.M. to 3 P.M.; park along Joseph Street near main gate

Langenstein's
1330 Arabella; 899-9283

St. Roch Cemeteries No. 1 and No. 2
1725 St. Roch Avenue, just lakeside of N. Claiborne Avenue; open 8 A.M. to 4 P.M.; park as close as possible to the main entrance on St. Roch Avenue; a clean restroom is immediately to the left of the gate; an informative booklet on St. Roch Chapel and the Campo Santo is for sale at the caretaker's office to the right of the entrance

7   **St. Roch Cemeteries No. 1 and No. 2 / Shrine of St. Roch,** *1874, Father Peter Leonard Thevis*

The St. Roch (pronounced Saint Rock) cemeteries and chapel are dear places to Catholic New Orleanians of a traditional bent. They were the center of fervent pilgrimage inside the city for the sick and afflicted into the late 1940s and still carry a trace of pre–Vatican Council II Catholicism. This cemetery and its Gothic Revival chapel were begun in 1874 by Father Peter Leonard Thevis, a German-born priest who served the old downtown "Faubourg des Allemands," the centers of German settlement such as Faubourg Marigny. When the yellow fever epidemic of 1868 struck the city, he urged his parishioners to pray to St. Roch and vowed to build the saint a shrine if his congregation was spared. His flock at Holy Trinity German National Church in Bywater was spared, and Father Thevis began the building of this shrine to St. Roch, the intercessor for the sick and the victims of plagues. At the heart of the cemetery is a Gothic Revival chapel whose altar features a statue of St. Roch, who was born in 1295 in Montpellier, France. He is shown as a plague-stricken pilgrim displaying his sores and carrying a staff and water gourd and accompanied by the faithful dog that brought him food when he was sick and alone. Four altar panels tell of St. Roch's travels, travails, and his heroic service to plague victims. August 16 is the feast of St. Roch; high mass is celebrated then in this small chapel.

The St. Roch cemeteries are side by side: the front cemetery (No. 1) with the Shrine of St. Roch at its center, and the second cemetery (No. 2), added in

Cypress Grove Cemetery
On Metairie Ridge, near the terminus of Canal Street at City Park Avenue; open 8 A.M. to 4 P.M. daily; accessible via the 40, 41, 42, 43, and 44 bus lines that run on Canal Street; there is a convenient United Cabs taxi stand on City Park Avenue at the entrance to the St. Patrick Cemeteries about a block from the entrance to Cypress Grove Cemetery; you can drive into this cemetery and linger where you like

1895, with St. Michael's Chapel at its heart. It is the front cemetery, its chapel, and the small room off to the side of the chapel's altar filled with ex-votos that is of most interest to visitors. The front section is enclosed by wall tombs punctuated by small shrines for the fourteen Stations of the Cross, marble statuary groups depicting stages on Jesus' way to Calvary. It was long the custom for pious Catholics to visit nine churches on Good Friday and to conclude their pilgrimage at St. Roch's, where the service of the Way of the Cross was conducted. It was also customary to pray at this shrine for the sick and disabled. As Roger Baudier, Sr. wrote in his booklet *St. Roch Chapel and the Campo Santo* (1975):

> In the little room to the side of the miniature sanctuary of St. Roch's Chapel the visitor sees one of the strangest collections of objects that he has probably ever laid eyes on, except if he has visited ancient European shrines. Here hang crutches of all sizes, leg braces for children and for adults, some with shoes attached; false teeth, perfect replicas of legs, arms, feet, hands, heads, ears, a liver, a lung, pairs of eyes—a wide array of almost weirdly realistic objects. The floor is paved with small marble slabs, bearing the words "Merci" or "Thanks" engraved on them. These are ex-votoes—objects that vividly and graphically express the thanks of clients of St. Roch for favors obtained.

❽   Cypress Grove Cemetery, *1840*

Colossal and severe Egyptian Revival pylons and caretaker's lodges flank the entrance to the beautifully named Cypress Grove Cemetery, which was founded in 1840 by the Firemen's Charitable and Benevolent Association. Cypress Grove is relatively safe and is close to Metairie Cemetery; the two make a good pair to visit and demonstrate the shift from exuberant Victorian taste to the more sober Edwardian styles. Before the creation of the municipal Fire Department in 1891, voluntary firemen's associations often functioned as elite private men's clubs; they were also political powerhouses at election time. Cypress Grove's entrance gate was designed by West Point–trained civil engineer Frederick Wilkinson and is the most imposing gateway in New Orleans. In the early nineteenth century the Egyptian style, with its overtones of solidity, death, and eternity, was thought especially appropriate for cemetery gates and ambitious tombs. New Orleans' cemeteries have a few superb 1840s Egyptian Revival mausoleums constructed of massive blocks of hard, gray granite. They were most likely designed and cut in the great stone quarries at Quincy, Massachusetts, and then shipped south for assembly. Though Cypress Grove Cemetery is neglected and has a few tombs in ruins, it has at least been spared the unsympathetic modernizations of so many recently "restored" cemeteries. Traces of the glittering white clam shell roads traditional in the

Gulf Coast South have here fortunately escaped being paved over with soulless asphalt. A sprinkling of magnificent cypresses, magnolias, and live oaks also distinguish this sadly, if romantically, neglected stone world of solemn commemoration. There is an interesting absence of crosses and other Christian symbols in this powerful mid-Victorian memorial landscape.

Cypress Grove is laid out as a long, flat oval with three major drives running down its length and many shorter transverse drives like the rungs in a ladder. The most interesting tombs are the oldest ones in the front third of the grounds, and they need to be examined on foot. The Ferry monument of 1841, to your immediate right as you enter, was designed by J. N. B de Pouilly and is surmounted by a broken marble column symbolizing the untimely death of a young man who lost his life fighting a fire. De Pouilly emigrated from France in 1833 and worked in New Orleans for forty-two years, leaving his mark on the fabric of the booming city. Though he designed churches, houses, and commercial buldings, his most influential contributions may have been his elegant funerary monuments, such as this one. While the broken column is unusual, the tomb itself is characteristic of de Pouilly's sense of proportion and good taste. From here look back toward the entrance gate to experience a remarkable classical skyline of urns and monuments against an open sky. Nearby is a large, white marble society tomb with a colonnaded cupola erected in 1840 by the members of the Perseverence Fire Company No. 13. Farther down the central drive on the left-hand side is the fine Greek Revival–style Maunsell White tomb of 1863, with two sober Doric columns also designed by de Pouilly. Maunsell White made his most New Orleanian fortune manufacturing peppersauce. Visible behind the Maunsell White tomb on the parallel drive to the left are the grand Slark and Letchford tombs. Robert Slark's domed tomb, erected in 1868, is in the Gothic Revival style and looks like a miniature church. The Letchford tomb next to it is a memorable, if somewhat disconcerting, design consisting of a giant Gothic Revival crockett (finial) pressing down heavily on four stubby columns. It is a remarkably expressionist design and was erected in 1868 for Letchford's wife, Sarah Augusta Slark, who predeceased him. Visible in the far distance is the strange rear wall of a neo-Victorian/Venetian folly with several round windows and two steeples erected in the 1960s on Bottinelli Place, a cul de sac off Canal Street. The sadly ruined Katie C. McIlhenny tomb of 1889 stands under old cypress trees, whose roots have virtually destroyed it. Its memorably Victorian inscription for "Katie and Her Little Bud" recalls her death in childbirth:

> How beautiful the yesterday
> That stood over me like a rainbow,
> I am alone.
> Soon as she found the key of life
> It opened the gates of death.

Another tragically vandalized tomb is the rusted cast-iron Leeds tomb of 1844 on the right-hand side of the cemetery toward the front. This superbly proportioned Greek Revival tomb stands in its own gated enclosure, is elegantly

Greenwood Cemetery
Across City Park Avenue from Cypress Grove Cemetery is Greenwood Cemetery; open daily from 8 A.M. to 3 P.M.; 482-3232

Metairie Cemetery
On Metairie Ridge near I-10 and Metairie Road; the cemetery office is located in a modern building at 5100 Pontchartrain Boulevard, N.O., 70179; open daily from 8 A.M. to 3 P.M.; two one-hour tape tours with cassette players are available for free loan at the office, along with good maps; 486-6331

decorated with Greek motifs, and is capped by a flaming urn. Its fantastic downspouts are fashioned like grotesque sea monsters. Leeds owned the Leeds Iron Foundry (see page 265), and it is probable that this outstanding tomb was cast in New Orleans. It may have been designed or inspired by de Pouilly and is an extremely important piece of American cast-iron architecture. Cypress Grove Cemetery deserves *sensitive* restoration, for we are losing all too many important works of American design here. Photographers will find this a rewarding place to compose melancholy pictures.

9   Greenwood Cemetery, *1852*

Across City Park Avenue from Cypress Grove Cemetery is Greenwood Cemetery, founded in 1852. Like Cypress Grove, it is owned by the Firemen's Charitable and Benevolent Association. Its most conspicuous monuments can be enjoyed from City Park Avenue without entering it. The first, going from downtown to uptown, is the tomb of Lodge No. 30, Benevolent and Protective Order of Elks, surmounted by a bronze elk, which was erected in 1912 and designed by Albert Weiblen. It is sinking into the ground unevenly because it sits on the site of buried Bayou Metairie. Next is the large, Gothic Revival Firemen's Monument of 1887, sheltering a statue carved by Alexander Doyle of a volunteer fireman holding a hose. Next is the cemetery entrance and a modern bell tower. At the far corner of Greenwood Cemetery, standing in splendid isolation facing City Park Avenue just before elevated I-10, is the large, terraced Confederate Monument capped by a white marble soldier. Mounted on the four sides of its square plinth are busts of Generals Robert E. Lee, Stonewall Jackson, Albert Sidney Johnston, and New Orleans' own "fighting bishop" Leonidas Polk. Its inscription reads: "In commemoration of the heroic virtues of the Confederate Soldier this monument is erected by the Ladies' Benevolent Association of Louisiana, 1874." This was the same year as the "Battle of Liberty Place." Three years later the conquered South was "redeemed" and the long, harsh reign of the "Bourbon" Democrats began. Serene Metairie Cemetery is just beyond the underpass and to the right up Pontchartrain Boulevard.

10   Metairie Cemetery, *1872, Benjamin Morgan Harrod*

Two one-hour tape tours with cassette players are available for free loan at the cemetery office, along with good maps. One tour highlights "Soldiers, Statesmen, Patriots and Rebels" and the other "Great Families and Captains of Commerce." Visitors from outside New Orleans should probably take the first tour, which is a virtual Valhalla of the lost Confederacy and locates the memorials of the Army of Northern Virginia, the Army of Tennessee, and Generals P. G. T. Beauregard and Albert Sidney Johnston. New Orleanians will probably be interested in the second tour, which highlights the tombs of locally prominent families, including quite a few captains of Rex and Carnival royalty.

New Orleans' long and deep tradition of funer-
ary pomp and art has its contemporary continuation in serene,
artistic, immaculate, and immense Metairie Cemetery. Its extravagant above-ground granite tombs represent the zenith of New

Semolina's
*5080 Pontchartrain
Boulevard; 486-5581*

Orleans funerary architecture. Sited on the high ground of Metairie Ridge, this cemetery was founded in 1872 when the Metairie Cemetery Association bought the old
Metairie Race Course and engaged engineer Benjamin Morgan Harrod to design a
spacious, landscaped, American-style cemetery. A moving force in the association was
Charles T. Howard, a native of Baltimore, who ran the Louisiana State Lottery Company, a political and economic powerhouse in the post–Civil War state. A frequently
recounted New Orleans story has it that the elite Metairie Race Course blackballed him
for his association with the Radical Republicans and that he vowed, "I'll make a
cemetery out of your racetrack!" Benjamin Morgan Harrod used the old oval of the
racetrack as the heart of his plan when he designed Metairie Avenue. Inside this
spacious oval he set three smaller oval avenues with circular plots at the ends of the
innermost oval. Axial passages crisscross the grand plan. As originally developed,
lagoons encircled the cemetery. Trees and landscaping created a spacious Anglo-
American park-cemetery very different from the tightly packed, treeless, urban
cemeteries built by the Spanish and the Creoles. Before the development of Aubudon
and City Parks, landscaped Metairie Cemetery was a favored destination for leisurely
carriage drives and meditative strolls. Since 1969 the landmark cemetery has been
owned by Stewart Enterprises, Inc., which continues the long tradition of generous
public access and careful maintenance of this New Orleans showplace.

Metairie Cemetery has more than two thousand above-ground
tombs that, while designed in many different architectural styles, were unified by
design controls that mandated the use of gray granite and forbade the use of brick-and-
stucco and cast iron. Nor were cast-iron fences permitted around individual tombs.
Instead, low granite curbs define the plots, creating a seemingly open landscape in
which the individual granite mausoleums stand. The great tombs here were built in the
late nineteenth and early twentieth centuries and include superb examples in the Egyptian, Greek, Roman, Gothic, Moorish, Romanesque, Neoclassical, and other revival
styles. Many of the finest tombs were designed and built by the Albert Weiblen Marble & Granite Company, who had their own granite quarry at Stone Mountain in
Georgia. There is an impressive row of large Italian American society tombs along
Avenue B, including the Minerva Benevolent Association, Cristoforo Colombo Society,
San Bartolomeo Society, Contessa Entellina Association, Santa Maria del Socorso
Sciacca, Trente, and Trieste tombs. There is also a section of Jewish family tombs. Since
the two tape tours and maps are so useful, and Henri A. Gandolfo's book *Metairie
Cemetery: An Historical Memoir* is so complete, visitors should use them as their
guides. The book is for sale in the cemetery office.

If you're visiting Metairie Cemetery near lunch or dinnertime, try
Semolina's pasta restaurant on Pontchartrain Boulevard at Metairie Road.

TOUR TWELVE
Up the River Road

Destrehan on the historic River Road upriver from New Orleans is a French colonial sugar estate of the late 1780s that was remodeled in the Greek Revival style during the booming 1830s.

What This Tour Covers
Preliminaries
Introduction: Some Great Antebellum Plantations
  Open to the Public

Continuations
  Laura and Madewood Plantations

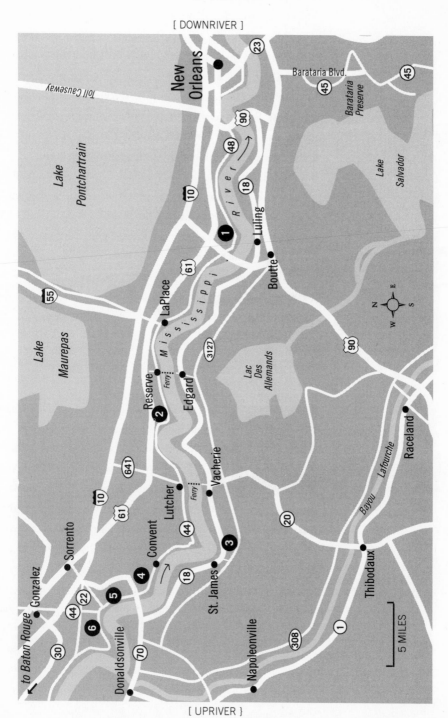

Tour 12

New Orleans

Toll Causeway

Barataria Blvd.

23

45

45

90

Barataria
Preserve

48

Lake
Pontchartrain

18

Lake
Salvador

10

1

Luling

Boutte

61

Mississippi River

LaPlace

55

3127

90

N
E
S
W

Reserve

Ferry

Edgard

Lac
Des
Allemands

2

641

Vacherie

Lutcher

Ferry

Raceland

Bayou Lafourche

10

3

20

61

44

Sorrento

Convent

18

308

4

St. James

Thibodaux

Gonzalez

22

5

Napoleonville

1

44

6

Donaldsonville

30

70

5 MILES

to Baton Rouge

What This Tour Covers

The name "River Road" refers to the variously named and numbered two-lane blacktop roads that follow the levee on both sides of the Mississippi River. There are many important plantation houses along the road on both the east and west bank of the river between New Orleans and Baton Rouge, the state capital to the northwest. Several ferries and two bridges make it possible to go up the east bank (the New Orleans side) and to return via the west bank. Destrehan and Houmas House, on the east bank, are recommended. Oak Alley, on the west bank, is the icon of Louisiana plantation houses. Laura (see page 360) has an acclaimed interpretive program. This string of great antebellum sugar estates (the locally preferred term) is now interspersed with giant petrochemical refineries, which are otherworldly when all lit up at night. You can make memorable two- or three-day excursions up and down the River Road, staying at historic bed-and-breakfast inns and then returning to New Orleans.

Preliminaries

BEST TIMES TO DO THIS TOUR / DRIVING TIPS

On Thanksgiving, Christmas, and New Year's Day many of these museum houses are closed. Almost any other time of the year is good, though the summer is hot. April and May are when spring flowers are at their peak. A special time here is mid-October to January 1, during grinding season, when the cane fields are first set afire and then mechanically harvested. While many visitors see the city first and then its surroundings, Destrahan is only minutes from New Orleans Airport via Highways 310 and 48, and it makes historical sense to see first the rich delta country for which New Orleans has always been the center. It is best to be off the road here between 3:30 P.M. and 5 P.M., when the petrochemical plant workers change shifts and speed down this narrow, twisting road in their shiny pick-up trucks.

Maps and Information

The best guide to the River Road is Mary Ann Sternberg's *Along the River Road: Past and Present on Louisiana's Historic Byway* (1996). Another useful tool is photographer David King Gleason's fold-out map and guide **Plantation Homes Along the River Road.** It is especially useful if you are planning a multiday excursion in sugar country. The Greater New Orleans Tourist & Convention Commission publishes a free *New Orleans Plantation Country Map* (see page 14).

Bus Tours

Gray Line Tours offers three different plantation tours. The Destrehan Plantation Tour, lasting two-plus hours, leaves New Orleans at 10 A.M. and visits Destrehan, a superb Louisiana Colonial-style plantation house that was remodeled in the Greek Revival style. The Oak Alley Plantation Tour, lasting three and a half hours, leaves New Orleans at 1 P.M. and visits Oak Alley on the west bank. The River Road Plantations Tour, a full day's tour, leaves New Orleans at 9 A.M. and includes visits to Nottoway and Houmas House plantations. Lunch at Nottoway is extra.

　　　　Tours by Isabelle offers two different plantation tours, both via thirteen-passenger vans. One five-hour tour leaves New Orleans at 1 P.M. and travels up the east bank to tour Tezcuco and Houmas House. Another tour leaves at 9 A.M. and returns at 5 P.M., traveling to the west bank and Bayou Lafourche to see Oak Alley, Madewood, and Nottoway plantations, with lunch in Madewood's formal dining room.

　　　　New Orleans Tours, Inc., also offers plantation tours; call or write for information.

Bed-and-Breakfast Inns

For information about bed-and-breakfast inns in this area, consult the **Louisiana Bed and Breakfast Directory,** which lists bed-and-breakfasts by region.

Plantation Homes Along the River Road
Available at some historic house shops and by mail from 1766 Nicholson Drive, Baton Rouge, LA 70802; 383-8989

Gray Line Tours
1300 World Trade Center, N.O., 70130; 587-0861, 800-535-7786, fax 587-0708

Tours by Isabelle
P.O. Box 740972, N.O., LA 70174; 391-3544, fax 391-3564

New Orleans Tours, Inc.
4220 Howard Avenue, N.O. 70125; 592-1991, 800-543-6332

Louisiana Bed and Breakfast Directory
Available from the Louisiana Office of Tourism, P.O. Box 94291, Baton Rouge, LA 70804-9291; free

Lafitte's Landing Restaurant
Off the River Road at the Sunshine Bridge, near Donaldsonville on the West Bank; 473-1232

The Cabin Restaurant
At the intersection of Hwy 44 and Hwy 22, in Burnside on the East Bank near Houmas House; 473-3007

Southern Tangent Gallery
At Cajun Village at the intersection of Hwy 22 and Hwy 70, not far from the Cabin Restaurant in Burnside on the East Bank; open daily 10 A.M. to 5 P.M.; 675-6815

Restaurants and Shops

If you're traveling by car, it is best to pack a gourmet picnic in the city and to stop and eat when you find a quiet spot. There are no outstanding restaurants along the River Road, but there are two fairly well-frequented places. **Lafitte's Landing Restaurant,** off the River Road at the Sunshine Bridge, serves good Cajun and Creole food in a converted house built in 1791 and moved to this spot. On the east bank, near Houmas House, you'll find Al Robert's folksy collage of old cabins housing a collection of agricultural implements; **The Cabin Restaurant,** serving Cajun fare, is among them. Near the Cabin Restaurant is **Southern Tangent Gallery,** which sells the works of self-taught Louisiana painters, potters, quilt-makers, and other craftspeople.

Introduction:
Some Great Antebellum Plantations
Open to the Public

Two great human creations line the Mississippi River between New Orleans and Baton Rouge: the great antebellum plantation houses tourists come to see and the giant petrochemical refineries that surprise and disconcert them. These two industries, sugar and petrochemicals, make visually jarring but actually most Louisianian neighbors. Different centuries collide here. Along both banks of the river are waving green seas of sugar cane fields stetching back from the River Road to the cypress swamps on the horizon. During their opulent heyday, the Louisiana sugar barons built imposing houses here, each of which faced the great river, the region's first transportation artery. After the U.S. Army Corps of Engineers deepened the channel, permitting ocean-going tankers to penetrate as far north as Baton Rouge, oil and other giant chemical corporations erected colossal petrochemical refineries along the river, making this one of the world's most important sources for industrial raw materials and fertilizers. This is no pastoral landscape; it is, rather, the industrial loading dock for the heart of North America. Emission control is the great challenge along the lower Mississippi. The plants are spectacular when all lit up by countless lights; the nighttime view from the Sunshine Bridge is especially impressive. From this elevated vantage point in this flat delta world the vast constructions of white lights of the encircling refineries create a space-age landscape of fantastic "cities" floating in a vast black void.

Growing sugar cane has been a mainstay of Louisiana agriculture since the French colonial period, when it supplanted tobacco and indigo. A rapid series of technological breakthroughs in the extracting and refining of sugar made Louisiana an important sugar producer. Expanding sugar estates also created a great demand for West African slaves to dig the drainage ditches and to work these huge holdings. With their immense wealth, French Creole, and later Anglo-American, sugar barons built expensive grinding mills filled with imported machinery and opulent plantation houses. Sugar has always been an intensely political crop, for it has long been dependent on protective tariffs that keep out cheaper Cuban and Caribbean sugar. The slave-owning Louisiana sugar barons were not ardent secessionists like many inland cotton planters. Instead they were nationalistic Whigs keenly aware of their dependence on laws made in Washington. The great plantation houses built by sugar declined when domestic sugar declined. Mosaic disease attacked the cane fields in the 1920s, and the owners of great mansions did not have the money to keep them up. Other houses were inherited by many heirs who could not agree on who would pay for their upkeep. Many families eventually lost their lands, and important houses were left vacant and then were lost to fire and neglect. By the 1940s their melancholy condition led surrealist photographer Clarence Laughlin to call them "ghosts along the Mississippi."

Note: *There is an entrance fee at these privately owned but publicly accessible historic properties that contributes toward their preservation. Most are closed on important holidays; phone ahead to confirm fees and hours.*

Destrehan Plantation
9999 River Road, Destrehan, LA 70047; open Monday to Sunday 9:30 A.M. to 4 P.M.; $7 adults, $4 teenagers, $2 children; Fall Festival the second week of November; twenty-two miles from New Orleans; eight miles from the airport; 764-9315 or 764-9345

Fortunately, a wave of restoration began in the prosperous late 1940s as Houmas House, Bocage, Ormond, and Evergreen, among others, were brought back to life by new owners whose wealth came from sources other than these waving cane fields. The growth of automobile tourism since the 1950s has made the River Road's antebellum houses second only to New Orleans' French Quarter as a destination for visitors to Louisiana; admission fees, gift shops, and bed-and-breakfast inns now help keep up these big houses. The grand houses that survive were only the showy centerpieces of much larger utilitarian complexes, almost all of which have vanished. Almost all of the sugar estates have lost their elaborate set of outbuildings, including the slave quarters and grinding mills that once made them small villages. Today there are some 750 sugar cane farms in Louisiana averaging about seven hundred acres each. They provide about 15 percent of the nation's sugar and generate some thirty-two thousand jobs in the state. (Both Florida and Hawaii now far outrank Louisiana in cane sugar production.) Sugar continues to be an especially political crop; only the existence of quotas on imports protects American sugar producers from cheaper foreign competition. Even in this time of cries for "less government," deregulation, and "free markets," cane sugar producers have forged effective alliances with northwestern beet sugar growers and managed to preserve a system of price supports and import controls in Washington that keeps these fields under cultivation, many rural Louisianians employed, and domestic sugar prices almost twice as high as they would otherwise be in a "free" market.

❶   Destrehan Plantation, *1787–90, Charles Pacquet; 1830s*
Destrehan was built in 1787–90 in the West Indies style and remodeled in the 1830s in the Greek Revival style. It is the oldest documented intact plantation house in the lower Mississippi valley and an important and beautiful example of early Louisiana architecture. It was built of *bousillage-entre-poteau* construction for Robert de Longny by Charles Pacquet, a free man of color. In 1792 it was acquired by Jean Noël Destrehan de Beaupré, who added twin wings to the house in 1810. (Destrehan and his brother-in-law Etienne Boré perfected the process for the granulation of sugar.) The principal rooms are raised a full story off the flood-prone ground and catch the lightest breeze. Double galleries surround and shade the rectangular house. The whole is surmounted by a great roof with two slopes like a great parasol. The Greek Revival remodeling of the 1830s transformed the thin wooden columns of the French period into imposing Doric columns built of brick and covered in stucco; the interior woodwork was also made more elaborate at that time. In 1914 the plantation was bought by the Mexican Petroleum Company, which built a refinery on the property. The landmark eventually passed to the American Oil Company, and in 1972 Amoco donated the deteriorated house and four acres of land to the nonprofit River Road Historical Society, which has

restored this treasure. The tour here explains the changes in architectural styles from the French colonial period to the Greek Revival and also the process of the landmark's restoration and historically correct refurnishing. A large 1830s mule barn was moved to the property in 1997.

- **Bonnet Carré Spillway**

Between the refinery town of Norco and LaPlace upriver, the highway passes over the Bonnet Carré Spillway (pronounced Bonny Carry), a huge diversion project completed in 1935 that protects New Orleans from Mississippi River floodwaters by diverting excess waters from the river into Lake Pontchartrain and the Gulf of Mexico.

2   **San Francisco Plantation,** *1853–56*

Built in 1853–56 for Edmond Bozonier Marmillion, this unusual Victorian-style raised house is noted for its ornate exterior ornament and interior ceiling frescoes by Milan-born Domenico Canova. So much of the family's wealth went into its construction and decoration that the builder's son, Valsin Marmillion, who himself redecorated the house, christened it *Sans Frusquin,* French Creole slang for "without a penny." In 1879 Achille D. Bourgere bought the plantation and changed its name to San Francisco. This galleried house has its principal floor raised a full story off the ground, as was typical in Louisiana. Its exterior is encrusted with Italianate and Gothic Revival details; the popular description for it is "Steamboat Gothic." Its interior is in the opulent Victorian taste. An unusual feature here are the two great free-standing cisterns with elaborate caps that flank the house. Today the house is surrounded on three sides by the tank farm of Marathon Oil Company, which set up the nonprofit San Francisco Plantation Foundation and underwrote the landmark's meticulous restoration in the mid-1970s.

3   **Oak Alley Plantation,** *1837–39*

Oak Alley is *the* iconic image of the antebellum plantation house. Between the white columned house and the levee is a magnificent allée of twenty-eight ancient oaks some 250 years old. They were probably planted a hundred years before the construction of the present house for a previous house on this site. This Greek Revival plantation house was built in 1837–39 for Jacques Telesphore Roman III and originally named Beau Séjour, which means "good rest." It is seventy feet square and is distinguished by twenty-eight, two-story Doric columns that completely encircle it. This was the first great River Road landmark to be rescued. In 1925 it was purchased by Andrew and Josephine Stewart, who undertook its decade-long restoration. The facade of this great

Bonnet Carré Spillway

San Francisco Plantation
Hwy 44, P.O. Drawer AX, Reserve, LA 70884; open daily 10 A.M. to 4 P.M. except major holidays; $6.50 adults, $3.75 teenagers; $2.50 children six to eleven; forty-five miles from New Orleans; 535-2341, fax 535-3213

Oak Alley Plantation
3645 Highway 18, Vacherie, LA 70090; there is a restaurant and bed-and-breakfast cottages on the grounds; open daily 9 A.M. to 5:30 P.M. from March to October; 9 A.M. to 5 P.M. November to February; $6.50 adults, $3.50 children; sixty miles from New Orleans; 523-4351 in New Orleans; 265-2151 in Vacherie

Manresa Retreat House
Not open to the public but visible from the road just downriver from Convent, Louisiana; mailing address: P.O. Box 89, Convent, LA 70723; 562-3596 for information on men's retreats conducted here by the Society of Jesus

St. Michael's Roman Catholic Church
6476 Hwy 44 in Convent, LA, 562-3211

Tezcuco Plantation House
3138 Hwy 44, Darrow, LA 70725; open daily 10 A.M. to 5 P.M. March to October; 10 A.M. to 4 P.M. November to February; closed major holidays; $5 adults, $3.50 seniors and those thirteen to seventeen, $2.50 children under twelve; bed-and-breakfast accommodations; sixty miles from New Orleans; phone for restaurant hours; 562-3929

house inspired the design of the Governor's Mansion built in Baton Rouge in 1963.

④ Convent, Louisiana:

• **Manresa Retreat House / Old College of Jefferson,** *1833 and later*

Just outside Convent, Louisiana, visible from the River Road, is this extraordinary complex of seven colonnaded Greek Revival buildings begun in 1833 to house the College of Jefferson. A pair of Greek Revival gatehouses built in 1836 announce the entrance to the campus. This college was organized by French Creole planters allied with French-born immigrants who wished to preserve Francophone culture in the face of the tidal wave of Anglo-American immigration to Louisiana. The young Creole gentlemen were expected to speak French one day and English the next. The large main building was erected in 1842. But in 1847 the College of Jefferson closed and the property was sold. In 1859 it was bought by the wealthy sugar planter Valcour Aime, who organized a new school he named Jefferson College. Between 1862 and 1864, the Union army used it as a barracks. From 1864 until it closed in 1927, it was a boarding school staffed by the Marist order. Since 1931 it has been a retreat house for Catholic laymen conducted by the Society of Jesus, who renamed it Manresa Retreat House. Extensive Greek Revival complexes such as this one are very rare. Although Manresa is only open to retreat participants, the complex can be seen from the road.

• **St. Michael's Roman Catholic Church,** *circa 1840*

Unlike planters in most of the South, many Louisiana planters were Roman Catholics, and they built substantial churches for their families and their rural dependents. St. Michael the Archangel was built about 1840 and is a fusion of Gothic and Romanesque elements. Its elaborate altar was exhibited at the Paris Exposition of 1868. The most unusual feature of this sugar country church is the folk art Lourdes grotto built behind the main altar by two parishioners in 1876. The grotto's "boulders" are made from bagasse, the fiber left over in sugar-cane extraction. Its altar is covered in white clam shells.

⑤ Tezcuco Plantation House / River Road African American Museum and Gallery, *1855*

Tezcuco is a modest, Greek Revival, raised cottage plantation house built in 1855 for Benjamin Tureaud, a member of the extensive Bringier clan of sugar planters. It is announced by an impressive allée of live oaks. The estate was named for the Aztec village on the shores of Lake Tezcuco that was Montezuma's last place of refuge when Cortez invaded Mexico. The house was restored in 1950 by Dr. and Mrs. Robert H. Potts, Jr., and was purchased in 1981 by Major General and Mrs. O. J. Daigle. There are various other buildings on the oak-shaded grounds, including a small chapel, a blacksmith's shop, a dollhouse, a gazebo, a carriage house, and a cluster of cabins converted into bed-and-breakfast accommodations.

    Tezcuco is also the site of the **River Road African American Museum and Gallery,** a new nonprofit museum attached to the antique store and dedicated to "positive information about the history and culture of African-Americans." It features a collection of historical documents and memorabilia impressionistically covering much more than slavery. (Those interested in African American history up to the late 1870s should visit the Louisiana State Museum's Cabildo; see page 116.)

River Road African American Museum and Gallery
Mailing address: 40149 Coontrap Road, Gonzales, LA 70737; open 1 to 5 P.M. Wednesday to Sunday, closed Monday and Tuesday; donations accepted; 644-7955

Houmas House Plantation
40136 Hwy 942, Darrow, LA 70725; open daily 10 A.M. to 5 P.M. February to October; 10 A.M. to 4 P.M. November to January; $6.50 adults, $4.50 youths thirteen to nineteen, $3.25 children twelve and under; sixty miles from New Orleans; 522-2262 in New Orleans; 473-7841 in Darrow

6   **Houmas House Plantation,** *late 1700s, Alexandre Latil; 1840, John Smith Preston*
Houmas House is a splendid example of white-columned, Greek Revival plantation house architecture, and it is now filled with antique Louisiana furnishings and graced by ancient moss-draped oaks. In fact, it consists of *two* interesting houses, a four-room, two-story, Creole-style plantation house built in the late 1700s by Alexandre Latil, who with a partner bought this tract from the Houmas tribe, and a much larger Greek Revival mansion built immediately in front of it in 1840 by John Smith Preston. The two buildings are joined by an enclosed carriageway. Together they epitomize the French and Anglo-American periods in southern Louisiana's complex history. The main 1840s house has Doric columns on three sides. Two hexagonal, brick *garçonnieres* flank the house. The property was bought by South Carolinian Revolutionary War hero General Wade Hampton in 1812, and it was his daughter Caroline and her husband who built the Greek Revival house in 1840. The house and its lands were purchased by Irish-born John Burnside in 1858 and became the center of the largest sugar estate in Louisiana. Burnside had been a merchant in New Orleans and had lived in the Garden District before acquiring this huge property, which he expanded to twenty thousand acres with four grinding mills by the time of his death in 1881. During the Civil War, William Howard Russell of the London *Times* described the estate:

> The view from the belvedere on the roof was one of the most striking of its kind in the world. . . . If an English agriculturalist could see 6,000 acres of the finest land in one field, unbroken by hedge or boundary, and covered with the most magnificent crops of tasseling Indian corn and sprouting sugarcane, as level as

Laura Plantation
2247 Hwy 18, Vacherie,
LA 70090; guided tours
daily between 9 A.M. and
5 P.M.; on the West Bank
three miles downriver
from Oak Alley
plantation, fifty-seven
miles from New Orleans;
265-7690; in New
Orleans 488-8709

Madewood Plantation
4250 Hwy 308,
Napoleonville, LA 70390;
open for tours Monday to
Sunday 10 A.M. to 4:30
P.M.; in Bayou Lafourche
on the West Bank
seventy-two miles from
New Orleans and two
miles beyond
Napoleonville; 369-7151,
800-375-7151

a billiard table, he would surely doubt his senses. But here is literally such a sight. . . . [It is] as easy to persuade the owner of such wealth that slavery is indefensible as to have convinced the Norman baron that the Saxon churl who tilled his lands ought to be his equal.

The house was spared the torch during the Civil War when Burnside claimed immunity as a British subject. By the 1890s the plantation was the property of Colonel William Porcher Miles and was producing twenty million pounds of sugar a year. In the early twentieth century, as sugar declined, so did the house. In 1940, Dr. George B. Crozat, a dentist from New Orleans who had made a fortune inventing new techniques, restored the house. He filled it with a fine collection of pre-1840 Louisiana furniture; the upstairs central hall is lined with an outstanding collection of large armoires. Crozat also added rear gardens utilizing many native plants, fragrant sweet olive, and azaleas. This garden is at its peak in the spring.

Continuations:

Laura and Madewood Plantations

The house at Laura Plantation is a raised cottage built in 1805 and Victorianized in 1905; there are twelve historic buildings on the property. A rare slave cabin fills out the story of plantation life at Laura. Madewood Plantation is a magnificent Greek Revival house completed in 1846, with elegantly proportioned rooms designed by the noted architect Henry Howard. You can stay overnight at Madewood; the accommodations are in the main house, in a raised Creole cottage, and in a small cabin on the grounds.

Further Resources

No American city has an illustrated architectural survey superior to the Friends of the Cabildo's **New Orleans Architecture** series. There are now eight volumes in the series, and each is an architecture lover's bible. There is a separate volume on the cemeteries. The books are in many bookstores and also available at the shop of the Louisiana State Museum's 1850 House in the Lower Pontalba Building facing Jackson Square. **The Southeast Architectural Archive** at Tulane University is rich in local drawings and architectural records and presents interesting exhibitions. The French Quarter is best documented in the block-by-block, building-by-building French Quarter Survey at the **Williams Research Center** of the Historic New Orleans Collection. Architect Malcolm Heard's book **French Quarter Manual** is the best book on French Quarter buildings, including plans and cutaway views, and on the Quarter as a total environment.

New Orleans Architecture
Eight volumes, Friends of the Cabildo

Southeast Architectural Archive
Tulane University, Jones Hall; 865-5699 for hours

Williams Research Center
The Historic New Orleans Collection, 410 Chartres Street; open Tuesday through Saturday, 10:30 A.M. to 4:30 P.M.; 598-7171

French Quarter Manual: An Architectural Guide to New Orleans' Vieux Carré
Malcolm Heard, 1997

Key Periods and Landmarks in New Orleans History

This chart outlines the principal periods in New Orleans' complex history. Key landmarks associated with each period that appear in this guide are referenced.

1718–1763: French Colonial Period

A Caribbean three-caste society forms composed of European whites, West African slaves, and, after 1722, some free men and women of color. Native tribes are outside colonial society and almost disappear, blending into the black population.

• French Quarter street plan (see page 107)
• Old Ursuline Convent (see page 145)

1763–1803: Spanish Colonial Period

Continuation of a three-caste legal order of European-descended whites (Creoles), West African–descended slaves, and mixed-race free people of color (Afro-Creoles). Generous Spanish manumission policies create a large group of French-speaking, Roman Catholic free people of color.

• Cabildo and Presbytere (see pages 116 and 142)
• Lanzos House / Madame John's Legacy (see page 144)
• Pitot House (see page 174)
• Waldhorn and Adler (see page 128)
• St. Louis Cemetery No. 1 (see page 339)

1803–1835: Early United States Period

A three-caste society is absorbed into a two-caste nation-state, since the United States recognizes only freemen or slaves.

• Manheim's Galleries / Louisiana State Bank (see page 128)
• The Thirteen Sisters (see page 263)
• St. Louis Cemetery No. 2 (see page 340)

1835–1860: Antebellum Period

The slave-owning South realizes it will soon be dominated politically by the abolitionist North and attempts to secede in 1860, resulting in the four-year Civil War.

• Garden District street plan and Lafayette Cemetery (see page 341)
• Gallier Hall / Old City Hall (see page 261)
• Gallier House (see page 147)
• Royal Café / LaBranche Building (see page 121)

1861–1862: Confederate Episode

On January 26 Louisiana secedes from the Union; on April 30, 1862 New Orleans surrenders undamaged to Admiral David E. Farragut.

1863–1877: Reconstruction Period

After the war, the United States is legally a single-caste (free) society, but there is no redistribution of nonhuman property after the Civil War between whites and freedmen. After 1877, when home rule ("redemption") returns to the South, laws subjugate all African Americans.

• McGehee School for Girls / Bradish Johnson House (see page 280)
• Audubon Park (see page 311)
• Metairie Cemetery (see page 346)

1877–1963: Era of *de juré* Racial Segregation

A two-caste society is created through laws and customs separating and subjugating people of color, who are restricted to "separate but equal" facilities.

• Patrick F. Taylor Library / Howard Memorial Library (see page 266)
• St. Charles Avenue mansion row (see pages 299–313)
• Maison Blanche / Ritz-Carleton Hotel (see page 248)
• Hibernia National Bank (see page 242)

1964–present: Era of Racial Equality

A single-caste society is created by the Civil Rights Act of 1964 and the Voting Rights Act of 1965. While political power passes to blacks, economic power remains predominantly white.

• Louisiana Superdome (see page 68)
• First NBC Center High-rise (see page 240)

Thanks and Acknowledgments

New Orleanians have a gift for friendship, a gift they openly enjoy and love to share. My deepest thanks go to my ever-widening circle of friends in New Orleans, both uptown and downtown, who have made me feel so welcome in my new home. From each of them I have learned something important about this singular society. First among them is Henri Schindler—a true "Mardi Graw"—who has a sixth sense about the mysterious nature of this culture. Others who have shared their knowledge and answered my questions (even when they weren't aware of it!) include Errol Barron, Shelley N. C. Holl, Jon Kukla, John Magill, Katherine Magnuson, Rick Normond, Roger H. Ogden, Peter Patout, Mary Price Robinson, Richard Sexton, Moise S. Steeg, Jr., Chris Waddington, Elizabeth Williams, and Dalt Wonk. For reading my entire manuscript I wish to thank especially John Magill.

The archives I found most useful included the Williams Research Center at The Historic New Orleans Collection, the Southeastern Architectural Archive at the Howard-Tilton Library at Tulane University, the Amistad Research Center at Tulane University, the Earl K. Long Library at the University of New Orleans, and the Louisiana Division of the New Orleans Public Library. The Regional Planning Commission for Jefferson, Orleans, St. Bernard, and St. Tammany Parishes generously supplied base maps for research purposes. The Preservation Resource Center of New Orleans and the Louisiana State Historic Preservation Office's monthly *Preservation In Print* is a gold mine of fresh scholarship on New Orleans architecture. Its continuing series on "Literary Habitats" by Edwin Blair was an especially rich source; quotations from *Preservation In Print* are from that continuing series. The books I mined are too numerous to list, but three must be singled out. First is Pennsylvania State University's Pierce F. Lewis, *New Orleans: The Making of an Urban Landscape* (1976), still the best overview of how New Orleans developed. The Friends of the Cabildo's multivolume *New Orleans Architecture* is monumental and indispensible. Architect Malcolm Heard's *French Quarter Manual* (1997) is the best book on the Vieux Carré. The best social and political history is *Creole New Orleans: Race and Americanization* (1992), edited by Arnold R. Hirsch and Joseph Logsdon of the University of New Orleans. The key source on the French Quarter is the massive, unpublished Vieux Carré Survey on deposit at The Historic New Orleans Collection. The changing exhibits at THNOC also taught me much. Though I have tried my best to include representative African American contributions to the distinctive culture of this northernmost Caribbean city, there is still no good overview of black New Orleans.

At Chronicle Books I wish to thank Jack Jensen, William LeBlond, Karen Silver, and Joni Owen, who showed patience with me when my professional life took a dramatic turn for the better. My meticulous copy editor, Jeff Campbell, merits special thanks. I wish to thank typesetter Neal Elkin and map designer Ellen McElhinny for their fine work.

Last but not least I wish to thank Simon Gunning, an important artist in this artistically alive city, for both his drawings and his friendship.

Index

About the Author

Randolph Delehanty, Ph.D., is a university art museum director, historian, author, and convention speaker. He was born in Memphis, Tennessee, in 1944, and reared in Englewood and Tenafly, New Jersey, in a bilingual English- and Spanish-speaking family. He holds degrees in history from Georgetown University, the University of Chicago (where he was a University Fellow), and Harvard University (where he was a University Prize Fellow and where he earned his doctorate). From 1973 to 1978 he was the first historian for the Foundation for San Francisco's Architectural Heritage. He taught for many years in the Humanities Department at San Francisco State University. He has written nine books, including *California: A Guidebook* and, with photographer E. Andrew McKinney, *Preserving the West,* a survey of the state of landscape and architectural preservation in the seven far western states for the National Trust for Historic Preservation. He and photographer Richard Sexton coauthored *In the Victorian Style,* on San Francisco's domestic architecture and urban development, and *New Orleans: Elegance and Decadence,* an interpretation of the Crescent City's distinctive culture (both Chronicle Books). His most recent books are a revised edition of *San Francisco: The Ultimate Guide* (Chronicle Books), *Classic Natchez,* and *Art in the American South,* an exploration of the visual arts in the region. His next book will be a timeline of New Orleans with special attention to cultural and racial changes. He lives in the Faubourg Marigny in New Orleans and is the director of the University of New Orleans' Ogden Museum of Southern Art at 615 Howard Avenue, New Orleans, LA 70130.

About the Artist

Simon Gunning is a noted New Orleans painter. Born in Sydney, Australia, in 1956, he studied drawing and painting at the Victorian College of Art in Melbourne from 1976 to 1978. Among his teachers was Fred Williams, Australia's greatest landscape painter. In 1979, on his way from Sydney to London to study at the Royal Academy of Art, Gunning passed through New Orleans. The old port city seduced him, and he decided to stay. Today he paints the people and the places around him and the cypress swamps of southern Louisiana. In what is almost a separate body of work, he also draws the female form in red chalk. Gunning's paintings are in many private, corporate, and public collections. He and his wife, Shelly, live in a Creole cottage in New Orleans' Bywater neighborhood, where he works in an attic studio. Together they have filled their house with art and made their back garden a semitropical oasis. Gunning is represented in New Orleans by Galerie Simonne Stern.